ƒP

MESSAGE

in a

BOTTLE

*Stories of Men
and Addiction*

JEFFERSON A. SINGER

The Free Press
New York London Toronto Sydney Singapore

The author gratefully acknowledges the following permissions:

The excerpt of 6 lines from "Dream Song #74" from *The Dream Songs* by John Berryman (Copyright © 1969 by John Berryman) is reprinted with permission of Ferrar, Straus, & Giroux, Inc. Permission to use these lines as published in 77 *Dream Songs* was also granted by Faber and Faber Ltd., London.

The poem, "As the poor end of each day drew near" by Malcolm Lowry is reprinted with permission of the publisher from *The Collected Poetry of Malcolm Lowry* edited by Kathleen Scherf © University of British Columbia Press, 1992. All rights reserved by the publisher. Reprinted by permission of Sterling Lord Literistics, Inc.; Copyright © 1995 by Malcolm Lowry.

The excerpt of 4 lines from "Sailing to Byzantium" by W. B. Yeats is reprinted with the permission of Simon & Schuster from *The Collected Works of W. B. Yeats, Volume 1: The Poems*, Revised and edited by Richard J. Finneran. Copyright 1926 by Macmillan Publishing Company; copyright renewed © 1956 by Georgia Yeats. Permission is also granted by A. P. Watt Ltd. on behalf of Michael Yeats.

*f*P

THE FREE PRESS
A Division of Simon & Schuster Inc.
1230 Avenue of the Americas
New York, NY 10020

THE FREE PRESS and colophon are trademarks of Simon & Schuster Inc.

Manufactured in the United States of America

10 9 8 7 6 5 4 3 2 1

Library of Congress Cataloging-in-Publication Data
Singer, Jefferson A.
    Message in a bottle : stories of men and addiction /
Jefferson A. Singer.
        p.   cm.
    ISBN 0-684-82720-4
    1. Men—Alcohol use—United States.   2. Men—Drug Use—United States.
3. Alcoholism—United States—Psychological Aspects.   4. Drug abuse—United States—Psychological Aspects.
I. Title.
HV5105.S55   1997
362.29'081'0973—dc21   97-35601
                                                                          CIP

for Anne

Contents

Foreword

Only months before he died, the physician and novelist Walker Percy spoke with a friend about one of his books in relation to the others: "Well, you know, *The Message in the Bottle* is in the storehouse, where I've pulled together my ideas; it's from there that I sent out to others—all the novels can be found there, the thoughts in my mind that I put into the form of stories. People always ask me what my experience in medical school had to do with my writing. The answer is, a lot: if you learn to do clinical work, you learn to listen to people talking about themselves; you notice what they say, and how they say it, and you begin to get a sense of what they mean—and that's a big start for a novelist, to have had that kind of [clinical] experience."

I thought of those words as I read this remarkably thoughtful, instructive, sensitively, and lucidly written book—its title so reminiscent of Dr. Percy's collection of philosophical essays, and its subject matter, its manner of presentation, its overall tone, so worthy, too, of comparison with his efforts to understand our nature, our fate as the creature of language who is in search of meaning, and so constantly capable (even when drunk, or high on drugs) of sending messages to others. Jefferson Singer, like Percy, is a clinician with a keen eye and ear for the aspirations and yearnings, the fears and worries of the patients he sees, the individuals he interviews in the course of his research. Like Percy, too, he has had a long-standing interest in the narrative capabilities of us human beings, the different ways we tell people what ails us, or prompts us to behave as we do. In this book he brings to bear with great success his interests and experiences—we learn so very much about certain men who otherwise go unnoticed, or, as the expression goes, get "rebuked and scorned" by the rest of us, who have little interest in extending ourselves in the direction of those who have stumbled, fallen down. The result, then, will be a connection of sorts between a gifted researcher, writer, and us readers, who otherwise, most likely might be uninformed about these fellow citizens, not to mention the many thousands like them across the nation.

To be sure, psychological inquiry is no rare endeavor these days. We live in an age of social science—so very much of our lives has been scrutinized by those who want to tell us about our minds, or our neighborhoods, or our values and expectations. Yet what follows is no mere research project become a book; this is a wide-ranging effort on the part of a writer of broad sensibility (as the Victorians would put it)—an attempt to bring to life a distinct aspect of our human frailty, and also to learn from those in trouble not only about their lives but about our own situation as people who may not be "addicts" but who surely have struggles with frustrations and disappointments, and so doing, have been moved to find one or another kind of escape, refuge, place of seeming peace and quiet. Here is one of Professor Singer's important "messages" in his book: that these exceedingly vulnerable men not only have their "problems," their not inconsiderable "psychopathology" (who of us is without some of that?), but also important and revealing observations and reflections to offer—which, in their sum, become a substantial kind of knowledge, even at times wisdom, for us readers to attend, make our own.

Especially noteworthy and valuable in the pages ahead are the breadth and depth of the author's learning as he reflects upon the lives he presents to us. He is careful to give us strong portraits of these men, so various in their backgrounds, yet in certain respects, so similar in the struggles they have waged; but he is also constantly willing to draw upon his own life as he tries to render and do justice to theirs. The result is a book that tells us not only about a collective "them" (their disorders and early sorrows and later encounters with tragedy) but about an American psychologist who has obviously and unselfconsciously and devotedly immersed himself in literature and philosophy, so that Stendhal and Kierkegaard and others of their kind figure in this book in a natural and edifying way—fellow participants, it can be said, in a young researcher's moral and social inquiry as well as his psychological investigations.

This exemplary kind of writing belongs, really, to a tradition more influential in Europe than America—phenomenological psychology: intellectual work characterized by an abiding respect for human particularity, an insistence on tethering the abstract, the conceptual, to the details of individual lives as they are related by those who, as it were, "own" them, inhabit them—in this book's instance, some men who are, yes, "addicts," but who are also, as we get to understand, very much *themselves*, each with his memories to share, his hopes to express, his anxieties and apprehensions to reveal. We are offered a book valuable for its wealth of psychological and social information, for its first-rate clinical histories and its suggestive discussions of them, but valuable also as a singular and most welcome presence of sorts among us: a psychologist "with a human face," and a most cultivated and discerning mind, has helped link us to certain others through resort to well-shaped clinical narratives accompanied by wonderfully illuminating interpretive essays, an achievement all its own.

—Robert Coles, M.D.

Acknowledgments

I would like to acknowledge the clients and staff of the Southeastern Connecticut Council on Alcoholism and Drug Dependence (SCADD) and in particular the residents and staff of Lebanon Pines in Gilman, Connecticut. The men who agreed to be interviewed for this book did so with a deep conviction that by telling their stories they might help other individuals in their own battles with alcoholism and drug addiction. In all cases, I have changed the men's names and identifying details from their lives in order to protect their anonymity. I owe a great debt of gratitude to Bill Walsh, the executive director of SCADD, and Bill Sugden, the director of Lebanon Pines, for giving me their approval to conduct interviews and for providing support throughout the process. Since the focus of this book is on the reasons men often struggle to achieve sobriety, I know that they will worry that the remarkable work of SCADD and Lebanon Pines might be overlooked. Without the safe haven, careful treatment, and climate of hope that SCADD provides, the prospects for the men I interviewed would be considerably more grim. Debby Mirsky and Joseph Gagliardo, counselors at Lebanon Pines, took an active role in helping me identify men to interview and they are also owed a special thanks.

Connecticut College has supported me in numerous ways that remind me of how privileged I am to work at this fine institution. As always, my colleagues in the Department of Psychology were sources of encouragement and advice. Nancy MacLeod of the Psychology Department office contributed inestimable technical and emotional support. Claire Gaudiani, president of Connecticut College, was particularly helpful in reinforcing my goal to write a book that would reach a readership beyond the academy. The college also provided me with a sabbatical year that allowed me to conduct the majority of interviews for this book and to begin writing the first chapters. I owe gratitude to the University of the Americas–Puebla in Cholula, Mexico, where I served as a visiting professor in the spring of 1996. The Department of Psychology there provided me with the time and resources to do the majority of my writing for this book. I am also grateful to Dean Alex Hybel of Connecticut College who arranged for my position in Mexico through the college's Study Away/Teach Away program.

Before any writing could take place, I relied upon the energy and perseverance of my "Narratives of Addiction" student research group at Connecticut College to transcribe the hundreds of hours of audiotaped interviews. Students who participated in this group were: Amy Canfield, Danielle de Brier, Emily Fisher, Patricia Fitzgerald, Rachel Howell, Shannon Jackson, Matt Loper, Sandra Quiles, Cindi Samor, Gia Syracuse, Andrew Wagner, and Kim Wallace.

Two students worked with me as summer research assistants, Ann Keating and Lauren Half. In addition to her library research, Ann provided valuable early readings and comments on many of the chapter drafts.

Steven Marks, an editor and reviewer, read two chapters and offered very helpful input on the focus and voice of the book. Jeff Kurz, a newspaper editor and reviewer, played a similar positive role.

Peter Salovey, a professor of psychology at Yale University and my frequent collaborator, Gary Greenberg, a clinical psychologist and visiting professor at Connecticut College, and Rand Cooper, a fiction writer, have provided guidance and friendship over many years in helping this book take form. Larry Vogel, another good friend and a philosophy professor at Connecticut College, also helped me in clarifying the existential themes of the men's struggle with sobriety.

I owe an eighteen-year-old debt to Robert Coles, who has graciously written the foreword for this book. As an undergraduate, I took a course with him that inspired me to listen to and learn from the stories of people very different from myself. In my work as a psychologist, teacher, and writer, I have tried to follow his example.

The editorial staff of the Free Press, Susan Arellano, Norah Vincent, Carol de Onís, Caryn-Amy King, and Marang Setshwaelo, have literally brought this book into being. Norah provided some extraordinarily helpful guidance that helped me achieve a clearer articulation of this book's themes. Susan was the editor on my first book, but nothing could have prepared me for the dedication and wisdom she has shown in shepherding this book to publication.

My parents, who are psychologists and authors of numerous books, filled me with a passion both for helping others and for the written word. This book is an effort to blend those two loves. Finally, my wife, Anne, has sustained me through all my years of work with the men of the Pines and through every page of this book. With her, I have found a well of meaning in our life, and our children's lives, that never runs dry.

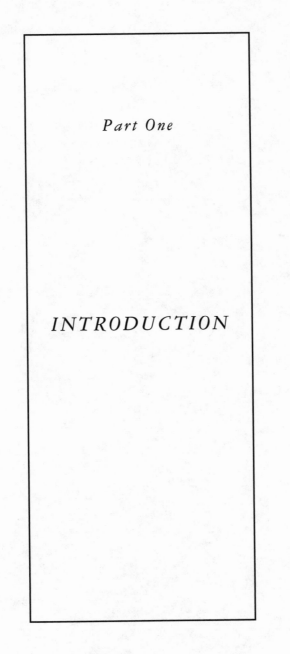

Part One

INTRODUCTION

1. BATTLING SOBRIETY
The Lives of Men Suffering Chronic Addiction

In 1989, through one of those offhand moments that in retrospect turns out to be a life-changing event, I was asked to work as a staff psychologist at a drug and alcohol agency that served a mostly indigent population. The agency was called SCADD (Southeastern Council on Alcoholism and Drug Dependence), located in New London, Connecticut. The associate director who hired me had received grant money that would soon be returned if he did not find a licensed psychologist to join his staff. At the time, I had just begun my work as a professor of psychology at Connecticut College and was meeting with him to discuss student placements. I decided that some community work a couple of days a week away from the ivory tower of my liberal arts college would be worthwhile, as well as enhance my knowledge of the problem of substance abuse. Nothing in my prior work as a therapist or researcher prepared me for the world of chronic addiction I soon encountered.

Over the subsequent seven years, I conducted psychotherapy with a man who in tandem with his wife had murdered his father-in-law with an ax in order to obtain more money for drugs. I helped a counselor tell his client that his father had just shot himself to death. I visited one of our own agency nurses in the ICU shortly before she died of an apparent overdose in response to gambling debts. A Vietnam vet lived out a flashback before me, describing how he lay trapped by gunfire upon a hill next to the lifeless body of his best friend. I listened to a priest weep over his love for another man. I tried to understand how a lonely drunken man could sleep with the young daughter of his second wife. A mother told me how she awoke from a black-out to find her older child trying to revive her younger child, who had choked to death from swallowing a bottle cap. In addition to these moments, I learned each week of the daily defeats that addiction extracts—broken promises, lies, lost relationships and jobs, accumulating debts, chronic health problems, and the perpetual erosion of self-respect and hope.

My role at the agency, according to the terms of the grant through which I was hired, was not primarily to offer treatment for the problems of addiction, but instead to help the staff make sense of how psychiatric conditions and/or psychological conflicts might be contributing to the clients' addiction or pattern of relapse. As the years progressed, I came to realize that this responsibility offered me a unique vantage point in working with the clients. Since the counseling staff and the Alcoholics Anonymous (AA) fellowship were responsible for the heroic day-to-day struggle of sobriety with the clients, I could take the time to fill out the larger picture of a client's life. I helped individuals with whom we worked to explore aspects of their past and their personality that raised recurrent impediments to achieving sobriety. Because I was not asked to provide them with the mechanics of their recovery, I focused more on what recovery would mean for them—what they would gain *and* lose from stopping their use of alcohol or drugs? In asking these questions, I slowly began to understand why many of them feared sobriety and saw their addiction as possessing certain aspects of safety and comfort.

In the course of my work with clients at all different stages of addiction, I became particularly fascinated with men who resided at a long-term facility called Lebanon Pines, run by SCADD. Twenty miles from New London, in a New England setting of pine groves and maples, Lebanon Pines had once been a summer camp for boys, and later a residential facility for troubled adolescents. A resident once told me that he had lived there as a boy, and now thirty years later, had returned as an adult. By the time William Walsh, the founder and executive director of SCADD, took over the property to fulfill his dream of creating a safe haven for "street drunks," the camp facilities had fallen into disrepair. Over the years, the men of Lebanon Pines, "skilled tradesmen long separated from their chosen craft"[1] had done the masonry, carpentry, painting, and landscaping to create a comfortable and attractive setting able to accommodate one hundred men. Lebanon Pines was an innovative and safe alternative to the cycle of emergency rooms, shelters, and brief jail stays that characterized the lives of chronically addicted men; it was also a lot more cost effective.[2]

In meeting these men, I gained entrance into the real meaning of chronic addiction. Though the admission criteria have loosened in recent years, when I first started to see men they were required to have had at least six failed twenty-eight-day treatment programs and a minimum of fifty detoxes before they would be eligible to go up to "the Pines" (extensive prison time was also an alternative criterion).[3] Most of the men had faced extended periods of homelessness and lived in the streets, sleeping in cardboard boxes, abandoned cars, or mission shelters. They worked sporadically or not at all; they had little contact with their families and often had not seen their own children in years.

By living at the Pines, many of them had had their first opportunity in a decade or more to sleep and eat in a regular routine. They would see a dentist and get a pair of eyeglasses, and slowly regain a sense of normality and self-respect. Lebanon Pines provided them with a healthy physical environment and work therapy (each man performed a job to keep the facility running with impressive efficiency). They also attended individual counseling, group meetings, and evening AA.

As they regained their physical health and participated in the recovery program, they would begin, and often not before ninety days had passed, to grapple with the fact of their addictive lives. In the company of peers, with a chance to stay in one place for the first time in a long time, many of the men would step back from their lives and ask why. To ask why necessarily meant rereading their lives and attempting to locate critical events in the development of their addiction. Once this psychological process had started, often stories of loss, trauma, or shame would emerge.

At this point of ninety days or so, some men would get the urge to leave, to go back to the old way of coping. I would often be asked to see the men at this time to consider what might be done therapeutically to help them maintain their focus on recovery. As a result, I would often hear the most private and troubling stories the men had to tell.

Men suffering from chronic addiction are as various as the wide mix of American society—millionaires, hustlers, immigrants, and old-time yankees; chefs, musicians, salesmen, soldiers; ballplayers, fishermen, thieves, engi-

neers, and teachers. They are heterosexual, bisexual, and gay. There is no
one alcoholic or drug-addicted type—no rigid pattern of personality to
which each man conforms.[4] Each has a unique history of family relationships, of successes or failures in school and work, of marriages and friendships. Their history of alcohol and drug use can vary widely as well. Some
have managed years of sobriety and then relapsed (in fact, there have been a
number of relapsed substance abuse counselors who have ended up at the
Pines over the years). Some have never put together more than a week of
abstinence since they were twelve years old. Some have never touched anything other than beer. Some use whatever they can get their hands on,
including glue, gasoline, and sterno fluid. The hard-core alcoholics see themselves as very different from the heroin addicts, and the cocaine addicts as
different from these other two. As one of the men said to me once, "Each
man's life here is like a candle. We all started fresh and even, but our addictions have melted us down at different speeds and into different shapes. By
the end though, we all reach the same point, burned out and at the bottom
of the candlestick."

In working with these men, in trying to find further counseling for them
or additional treatment programs that would increase their chances for
sobriety, I needed to look for their individuality and their particular difficulties and needs. It is true though, that as the "candle burns down" closer to
the bottom, as their addiction reached later stages, many of the men's lives
grew more similar. When they could no longer work, when they had lost
families, and as they grew more dependent on institutional intervention,
the uniqueness of their past lives could be overwhelmed by the similarity of
their addiction's routines. Many men received their disability checks on the
same day. They had only a certain number of rooming houses and motels
that would tolerate their alcohol and drug lifestyles. Their health complications from alcoholism or chronic drug use brought them to the same treatment rooms and created similar limitations on their physical vitality, eating
habits, and sexual lives. The ravages of homelessness and poverty destroyed
their self-esteem and magnified their sense of shame and rejection in
markedly similar ways.[5]

The mutual disappointment experienced by them and their substance
abuse workers after another relapse led to their backing off from feelings, a
subtle graying of hope that might be the beginning of a defense against their
eventual death from their addiction. This protective blunting of empathy can
strip the individuality from the chronically addicted to those who work with
them. Out of both self-protection and a sense of exhausted effort, care

providers can stop seeing these men as different, stop listening to each unique voice and the nuances of its story. An important goal of the stay at Lebanon Pines was to halt this blurring process and to allow the men to speak distinctly again. Their coming down to see me to tell their stories and seek further help was a step toward reclaiming their individuality.

I began to look forward to these referrals from Lebanon Pines. Though most of the men had talked to hundreds of drug and alcohol counselors over the years, a surprising number had never spoken to a psychologist before. Wary of opening up to me at first, most of them would eventually recognize my genuine interest in their stories and would end up telling me a great deal about their lives. As the men from the Pines began to visit with me, I started to write down some of their stories in a journal. I tried to put the narratives down in their own words as closely as possible. I found myself affected not only by the painful content of the stories, but by the clarity and directness of their language. Here is one of the first stories I wrote down, told to me by a man in his early fifties.

I lost my third child, eight years old, high strung. That kid was all wired and ready for anything. He fell through the ice with a buddy. There's a pond not more than a couple of hundred yards from our house. There's a culvert that's got a backwash of sea water running into the pond. Always told the kids don't go near it. Never go there without your Dad.

They went there when they were supposed to be playing in the yard. Slipped off while his mother was in the house. His older brother saw them on the ice, but it was too late. They went through. He had sense enough to call 911, fire trucks and police came, but it was too late. Both of them swept in. I saw them gaff them up later. I saw that gaff and my boy in my dreams for many nights to come.

I went to two wakes in one night, my son's and his friend's. I couldn't stop seeing his face. Get tanked and then pass out, only way to sleep. I blamed his mother for not minding him. Broke us up. Stupid on my part. Wasn't her fault, but I was bull-headed. I wouldn't let go. I lost a fine woman and two other beautiful children because I wouldn't let go. That's the way I've always been—a bull-headed sonofabitch.

Confronted by stories like this from the men of the Pines, I began to ask myself, "How can I make sense of their lives?" Given all the loss and pain that their addictions bring them on top of what they have already suffered, why don't they stop? As someone who had never experienced an addiction, I knew I could not expect to understand the overwhelming physical compulsion addicted individuals feel. Yet I was surrounded by counselors and staff members in recovery who had managed to overcome this physical demand and bring their addiction under control. Similarly, I watched with great admiration as clients who went through our agency joined the AA or NA (Narcotics Anonymous) fellowship and managed to accumulate first months and then years of sobriety. What was it that held back these other chronically addicted men from engaging with AA and reducing the despair in their lives?

The Limitations of the "Disease Concept" and AA in Treating Men with Chronic Addiction

As I studied the addiction literature and talked with a variety of researchers and clinicians in the field of recovery, I became even more perplexed by the men of the Pines. The most pervasive model of addiction in the field remains the "disease concept of addiction."[6] Despite widespread experimental and philosophical critiques of this disease concept model,[7] it has continued to play the dominant role in how many practitioners and the general public think about alcoholism and addiction. The disease concept defines alcoholism as a genetically based progressive disease that results in the inability to control one's consumption of alcohol. If left untreated, the individual will drink self-destructively, ultimately resulting in physical debilitation and death. As the alcoholism progresses, the individual's body grows more and more under the sway of alcohol, building up both tolerance and life-threatening withdrawal symptoms. Once the disease reaches its advanced or "crucial" stage,[8] the alcoholic no longer has any ability to drink in a modulated fashion. As an AA adage puts it, "one drink is too many and too many is never enough." Since this loss of control is seen as a physiological response, the only possible solution is life-long abstinence and the best vehicle for obtaining this abstinence is to enter the "rooms" of AA.

The disease concept model is particularly attractive to individuals in recovery because it offers them a biological and deterministic explanation for their behavior, thereby reducing their heightened sense of shame and self-disgust over their relapses and broken promises on the road to sobriety. Psychiatry is partial to this model because it holds out the possibility that addictions may eventually be eradicated through biochemical intervention and genetic screening.

Though disease concept proponents continue to emphasize alcoholism as a genetically based disease manifested by a loss of control over drinking, the social philosopher Herbert Fingarette has argued quite convincingly that the question of control is much more complicated.[9] For example, if the loss of control is a genetically based feature of the disease, we would need to understand the famous adoption studies conducted by Goodwin. Goodwin did indeed find a genetic component to alcoholism—adopted sons who had a biological father with alcoholism were 3.6 times more likely to become alcoholic than adopted sons who did not have a biological father with alcoholism. Even more persuasively, these differences emerged even if the adopted sons without biological alcoholism were raised by alcoholic parents.

Yet, as Fingarette points out, only 18 percent of the sons with biological fathers who were alcoholics went on to become alcoholics themselves. This means that 82 percent of the sons with a direct paternal link to alcoholism did not become alcoholics. When considered in this light, we clearly must acknowledge the influence of psychological and social factors on the development of the disease.[10]

Regarding the issue of a total loss of control spurred by the ingestion of alcohol, a classic study by Marlatt has suggested this issue is more complicated.[11] Hospitalized alcoholics, who were misled into believing they were drinking alcohol, drank as much of their alcohol-less beverage as alcoholics who actually received alcohol in their drink. Alcoholics who mistakenly believed they were drinking only tonic water, but were actually drinking tonic and alcohol, drank no more than the alcoholics who accurately knew their drink contained only tonic. These findings suggest that psychological beliefs play a mediating role in alcohol consumption and that the degree of control is not solely a physiological mechanism.

Aside from these genetic and experimental findings, we are also faced with the clear fact that individuals with alcoholism do indeed recover and gain control over their drinking through abstinence. Whether or not they could control their intake if they drank again is a separate issue from their ability, with great courage and willpower, to avoid taking that first drink. By demonstrating the strength not to take a drink, they are also demonstrating that the loss of control is not so absolute that it cannot be checked by one's decisions and actions.

Though the disease concept approach resulted in much greater attention and resources devoted by the medical and psychiatric community to addiction treatment,[12] most severely addicted individuals who go through an inpatient rehabilitation program will relapse within the first year out.[13] Even worse, the more chronic and advanced individuals' alcoholism or drug addiction may be, the more likely they are to return to their prior alcohol or drug use after discharge. Cognitive-behavioral psychologists, such as Alan G. Marlatt, have developed innovative relapse prevention programs that apply a series of behavioral and community-based interventions with clients to aid them in minimizing and short-circuiting relapses.[14] Unfortunately, these programs are not yet widespread and require a certain amount of supervision to run effectively. They also require a degree of self-management and organizational effort that many chronically addicted individuals are unable to marshal. For the most part, the best predictors of recovery are the level of social functioning and resources in place prior to the entrance into treatment (i.e., intact family structure, employment, an earlier stage in the disease process).[15]

We tend to read and hear the inspiring recovery stories of celebrities like Betty Ford or Kitty Dukakis, but few people who have remained addicted after efforts at recovery are likely to come forward to tell their stories of disappointment and relapse. We know much less about the individuals who enter the Betty Ford Clinic, attend AA meetings, and then return to their addictions.[16] As these individuals continue to progress in their addiction, using up financial resources, burning bridges with employers and finally family members, they may begin a cycle of detoxes, treatment programs, halfway houses, shelters, jails, and the street that becomes their way of life.[17] They no longer step out of the society to seek treatment; they periodically leave treatment to make brief aborted efforts at living in the "normal" world.

Linked to the disease concept of addiction is the AA model of recovery. Here again this model poses significant problems for men suffering from chronic addiction. Though AA has expanded its literature to cover a wide array of experience (including African-American, Hispanic, and gay/lesbian populations, as well as the dually diagnosed and inmates in correctional facilities), its most familiar narrative can be traced back to AA founder Bill Wilson's original story of recovery, recounted in the AA "Big Book," the founding document of the organization.[18] His and the other confessional stories reflected a simpler era in American society in which alcoholism entailed a fall from middle class respectability.

Bill W., a successful stockbroker, married and at one point fairly prosperous, gradually drank himself into endless job changes, debts, and repeated hospitalizations and rest cures. Through it all his wife stuck with him, extracting yet another promise from Bill, scribbled in the family bible, that he would never touch "the stuff" again. After involvement with a spiritual fellowship called the Oxford group, he had managed longer periods of sobriety, but was still uncertain in his recovery. Finally, when on the road for business and tempted by a hotel bar, he made a desperate call to a local pastor and asked to speak with someone who would understand the cravings he was experiencing. The pastor gave him a list of names that eventually led him to a local doctor, Bob Smith, notorious for his alcoholism. Dr. Bob (as he became known among the AA circle) was reluctant to speak to yet another person who would try to convince him of the merits of sobriety. What Bill Wilson asked him was exactly the opposite—he needed to talk to Dr. Bob in order to maintain his own sobriety. From this historic meeting, the essence of AA and of the self-help movement in general was born, a fellowship of individuals suffering from the same affliction who through shared understanding could bring each other back to health.[19]

Over the next nearly sixty years, a kind of generic cultural script of addiction/recovery did indeed develop.[20] It begins with an individual from a relatively good background (though there may have been prior alcoholism). This individual shows talent and promise, but also is aware of some social fears and self-doubt. He discovers alcohol or drugs as both an escape from stress and a remarkable form of false courage and social ease. Over time, he increases his consumption and dependence on the drug. Simultaneously, he commences a losing battle of denial in the face of his addiction. As he rationalizes and disguises his increasing dependence, he begins to suffer problems at home, at work, and in his community relationships.

Putting off any serious effort at stopping his addictive habit, he makes continual bargains with loved ones and with himself that allow him to avoid the simple fact that he has a disease that is slowly killing him. He does not want to accept the idea that the taking of a drink or drug is akin to unlocking a door to self-destruction.

After suffering a series of devastating losses in his life, that might include his job, marriage, custody of children, standing in the community, and self-respect, he finally reaches a bottom and seeks help. Through recovering individuals, counselors, clergy, hospitals, law enforcement officials, or loyal family members, he finds his way to AA.

In AA, he learns to accept his powerlessness over his addiction and the impossibility of controlling his use of alcohol. He shares his story and listens to others' stories of how alcohol or drugs have devastated their lives. He turns his life over to a higher power (as he personally defines that spiritual presence) and relies upon prayer and the fellowship of AA to guide his life's decisions. He pursues the Twelve Step program, including confession of his transgressions caused by his addiction, a genuine effort to make amends, and the giving back of his recovery through the offering of assistance to other alcoholics seeking sobriety. As he accumulates time in the program, he slowly regains his sense of self-respect and the trust of loved ones in his life. With the strength of sobriety, he returns to work and builds up economic security.

Though the road from this point on continues to have its rocky moments, he is now on his way to a transformation of his life that includes finding a spiritual meaning that may have been lacking in his active alcoholic or drug-using days. With sobriety renewed one day at a time, AA and its message of spiritual fellowship have literally redeemed his life.

No one should underestimate the power and effectiveness of this message. I have traveled and lived all around the world—Australia, Sweden, Thailand, England, Costa Rica, Mexico—and I have noted signs or announcements for AA meetings in every location. Its millions of loyal and sober members are the best testament to the value it can hold for people's lives. However, this script of addiction/recovery holds within it certain assumptions that may apply to some groups more than others. When I considered these assumptions in light of what I was learning about men with chronic addiction, I began to realize why its life-saving message was difficult for many men at the Pines to accept.

First, the script follows a "V"-like pattern. The individual starts at a relatively high level of middle class acceptability and then plunges downward, only to rise up to new heights after recovering. Many of the men I came to know began their lives in poverty, or, even if they had money, their circumstances were violent or destructive.

Second, the script assumes that the individual is a rational and autonomous agent, as opposed to someone who may be suffering from a psychiatric condition, mild mental retardation, or extreme emotional immaturity.

Third, it portrays addiction as caused by a physical disease process in an individual, as opposed to a combination of biochemical and psychological vulnerabilities exacerbated by hostile social conditions such as poverty, racism, homophobia, war, or the empty materialism and consumerism of our culture.

Fourth, it assumes that after the consequences of addiction become glaringly apparent, the individual maintains a strong desire to battle the addiction, as opposed to accepting the addiction and engaging actively in using the drug.

Fifth, it assumes that once the individual hits bottom, the capacity to reach out to a higher power and to other people exists, as opposed to the realization of a profound sense of meaninglessness and isolation.

Sixth, it assumes that individuals will eventually be willing to organize the events of their lives into stories to be shared in the meetings, as opposed to possessing a determined opposition to connecting the events of their lives into coherent narratives.

Seventh, it assumes that family or friends remain available and might indeed accept the individual back into their lives, as opposed to the individual returning to a life bereft of even one intimate relationship.

Eighth, it assumes that the individual will be able to find work and regain a sense of respectability in the community, as opposed to acknowledging the individual's immense difficulties with finding or sustaining employment.

Ninth, above all, it assumes that despite all setbacks, life will be better in sobriety, as opposed to addressing the overwhelming fear of sobriety and the relative ignorance of what a sober life entails.

As I thought about these assumptions and how the men I knew from the Pines often fell short of them, I realized that the AA model assumed a certain level of adjustment and identity formation that many of these men had never attained. It presumes a capacity for trusting relationships and meaningful contribution to the society that are by no means givens for the many men of the Pines. In the AA framework, professionals, homemakers, skilled tradespeople, and businessmen can win sobriety and resume positions of status in the society. Since AA is based on shared stories and conversations, it is perfect for individuals who have familiarity with group meetings—the club members and churchgoers of small town and suburban communities. Many of the men at the Pines did not fit comfortably into this profile and could not avail themselves of its virtues. Similar to all treatment strategies, AA has its limitations; contemporary society is now asking it to respond to levels of social dysfunction and psychopathology that were not previously a part of the AA dialogue.

The Changing Population of Chronic Addiction

Dating to the late seventies and early eighties, Lebanon Pines began to notice a shift in its population from the traditional white male middle class clientele.[21] With the massive deinstitutionalization of the mentally ill that Ronald Reagan initiated during his terms as governor of California and that spread to the rest of the country by the mid seventies, substance abuse agencies began to admit more and more clients who suffered from both problems of addiction and chronic mental illnesses, such as schizophrenia, bipolar illness, or severe anxiety or personality disorders. These individuals were more likely to be single, unemployed, and uncomfortable in group situations such as AA that placed interpersonal demands on them, such as personal revelation or physical closeness (e.g., hugs or holding hands).

Simultaneous with the rising demand for dual diagnosis treatment was the proliferation of clients with dual- or polysubstance addictions. The widespread experimentation with drugs of all kinds in the sixties and the seventies cocaine binge had created a whole new breed of clients who were cross-addicted to mix-and-match combinations of alcohol, cocaine, heroin, amphetamines, barbiturates, and marijuana. Many of the old-timers with years of sobriety had trouble empathizing or connecting with this new form of addict. By the late eighties, crack joined the scene, as well as the renewed popularity of "speedballs," a combination of intravenous cocaine and heroin. Multiply addicted individuals and crack users tended to enter an advanced level of chronic addiction at a much younger age than the classic alcoholic and were much less embedded in the middle-class, respectable world. Individuals who had joined the drug and alcohol scene as youngsters or who had come from economically disadvantaged circumstances had little in common with the quaint midwestern folks depicted in the big books, filled with lofty sentiments about helping others to help themselves.

These younger individuals often lacked the emotional development to sit through long meetings that asked them to step out of themselves and connect with the concerns of others in the group. Having gone from street and gang life to jails, prisons, and rehabs, they did not resonate to old-timers' stories about losing experienced positions in companies or destroying a twenty-five year marriage. Similarly, men and women raised in conditions of poverty and deprivation, and often the recipients of neglect and abuse, did not easily accept the concept of surrender to a benign spiritual force. They had managed to survive thus far on their own wits and self-protection; the idea that they should surrender their will (when their will had kept them alive) seemed simultaneously suspect and ironic.

Even the younger chronic addicts who were willing to take the First Step of AA (accepting one's powerlessness over addiction) displayed great difficulty taking up responsibility for work and relationships. Getting up in the morning, making it to work on time, going to work each day, week in and week out—this level of routine was novel and extremely taxing for many of these younger chronic addicts in recovery. Similarly, the demands of an upfront and reciprocal relationship—honesty, monogamy, patience, and trust—required an emotional security and stability they had never before experienced. Out of fear, frustration, and boredom, many of these younger men and women would find their way back to the street world in which they could feel more familiar and less threatened. Once back among their drug-using peers, it would not be long before they would relapse and resume their prior roles.

In addition to chronically mentally ill addicts and cross-addicted younger abusers, individuals with long-standing psychological conflicts often found that AA alone was not sufficient to achieve a sustained recovery. AA offers a foundation and scaffolding for recovery. It allows people to build an external structure that helps them manage their day-to-day life better and gives them mechanisms to maintain sobriety (e.g., a sponsor, daily meetings, anniversary days, inspirational readings). However, some individuals in recovery also face interior work of such complexity that it cannot be reached by the slogans and daily guidance of AA. Chronic drinking or drugging, problems that must be treated in their own right, may have begun as efforts to repress and escape recurrent memories of trauma or abuse. Sexual and physical abuse of both females and males was a common feature of clients' backgrounds.[22] Individuals with firsthand exposure to sudden unexpected death—combat veterans, parents who had lost a child, survivors of accidents or street violence—presented treatment demands that went beyond mere referral to AA. Similarly, individuals struggling to make sense of their sexuality—gay men and women who wrestled with acceptance of their sexual orientation and with societal homophobia, men with sexual desires for children, men and women with sexual compulsions or fetishes—found that the AA format was not always the most appropriate forum to discuss and work out these conflicts and confusions.

In some cases, individuals' psychological problems worked directly against their ability to attend AA group meetings. For individuals with chronic depression or severe anxiety disorders, both their mood and self-esteem made attendance at meetings excruciatingly difficult. Going to a meeting might lead to conditions of nausea, hyperventilation, or a paranoid self-consciousness bordering on psychosis. In such situations, a simple recommendation of "don't drink and go to meetings" was clearly insufficient. For other individuals, with severe personality disorders—borderline personality or narcissistic personality disorders—the reciprocity and emotional openness of AA meetings could clash with their symptomatology. The borderline individual might yo-yo between idealization and demonization of group members, alternately manipulating and raging against individuals or the group as a whole. Emotionally shallow narcissistic individuals might dominate the group with tales of their personal triumphs and tragic failures, but find little interest or benefit in listening to others' disclosures.

Finally, some individuals entered treatment holding on to secrets—they had engaged in an extramarital affair, committed an act of sexual abuse, stolen money, injured or even killed another person—and they were unable to let go of this secret and face the consequences of other individuals knowing it. AA with its emphasis on public confession offered no solace to these terrified and guilt-wracked individuals. They might first require extensive exploration of their acts in therapy before reaching a point of coming forward to any member of the "outside world" with their private knowledge.

These three categories that I have just outlined tend to characterize the men of the Pines who suffered repeated relapses—(1) the dually diagnosed with chronic mental illness, (2) cross-addicted younger addicts, and (3) individuals with long-standing psychological conflicts. These were the groups who were the least responsive to AA or any other form of treatment. They struggled with a basic sense of identity, interpersonal trust, belief in a higher power, and abiding hope in the possibility of recovery. Though AA contained much wisdom in its writings and its fellowship, there were messages these men needed to uncover before they could make the Twelve Step program work for them.

Looking for the Message in the Bottle

This book is an effort to understand what the messages might be that prevent chronically addicted men from embracing recovery and sobriety. My hope is to offer a portrait of and perspective on these men's lives that will be useful not only to practitioners, but to family members, lovers, friends, and the more general public who are affected by their chronic addiction.

In my efforts to achieve this understanding, I stepped back from the widespread emphasis on the physical aspect of their addiction. Having watched men seizure, wretch with vomit, scream out for drugs, and leave the detox at the risk of arrest or physical collapse, I had no doubt of the physical hold of addiction. What I still could not grasp was why the men did not place more value on building sobriety than continuing to move through these cycles of physical and psychological hell. In pondering this question, I thought back to one of my favorite dictums in psychotherapy. You can't ask someone to give something up unless you give something back in return. What would the men lose in giving up their addictions and what would they gain in sobriety?

Once I framed the question in this light, I experienced a kind of mini-revelation. The disease concept and AA directed my attention to addiction and how addiction posed a problem in addicts' lives. Now suddenly I was looking at things from the other direction. The problem for men in chronic addiction was sobriety, not addiction.

The flipside of any decision not to drink can be found in the men of the Pines' admission to me that often they consciously chose to drink. They were well aware of the mechanisms and steps they could use to gain sobriety. At various points, they put together several months and even years of substance-free time.[23] However, in each case, there came a moment when the desire to reenter their addictive life overwhelmed their desire for sobriety. They explained to me that they had suffered enough relapses to know that picking up a drink or drug did not mean a momentary lapse or brief sojourn from sobriety. In their minds, their choice to drink signaled a rejection of the sober world and a return to the destructive life of addiction.

I now began to focus on the idea that men suffering from chronic addiction either had never found sufficient meaning in a sober life or through years of addiction had squandered any meaning they had once possessed. Chronic addiction was then as much a problem of how these men fit into the sober world as it was of their physical dependency. As I reviewed the lives of the hundreds of men I had known, I saw over and over a profound disruption in their ability to belong to a world in which the ability to love and work were the shared pillars of sober identity.

And suddenly I found myself looking at the men from a very different vantage point than the disease concept perspective or the AA model. As helpful as these two approaches might be in giving men a sensible conceptualization of their addiction and a set of steps to guide their recovery, they were not adequate to the task of explaining the lives or choices of men suffering from chronic addiction. Neither of these approaches could explain why the men battled against sobriety.

To make sense of their battle against sobriety, I could not reduce their struggle to the common denominator of a genetic defect or a physiological problem of control. Similarly, I could not find a way to fit the complexity of their psychosocial difficulties into the simplicity of the Twelve Steps of the AA fellowship (even though such a simplification might benefit them). Instead, to make sense of why they did not want sobriety sufficiently, I needed to expand rather than reduce my understanding of them. The goal I set for myself was to take in the full dimensions of their lives—to see them as whole individuals struggling to achieve a sense of identity, often under the most harsh and destructive conditions.

Accordingly, my focus turned away from the nature of addiction as a disease and toward the question of the meaning of sobriety in their lives. In listening to the men, it had become clear to me that the idea of finding meaning in life, both before their addiction and since its onset, confronted them with certain existential realities that filled them with terror and despair. Put in the barest terms, sobriety demanded that they answer a simple but overwhelming question—Who are you, without the cover of a drug or drink?

The question, "Who are you?" is the fundamental question of identity. Our identity is formed out of the attachments and accomplishments we create in our lives. Identity is based in creating a continuity of self across past, present, and future. Identity allow us to differentiate ourselves from others, at the same time that we define our cultural niches. A man at the Pines is an alcoholic, but he is also a member of an ethnic or religious group. He is someone who goes to AA, but he is also gay, straight, or bisexual. He is someone from a rich, poor, caring or abusive background. How do all of these factors play a role in the men's ability to achieve sobriety?

In each area of identity I have just delineated—definition of the self through *love and work,* definition of the self through *continuity over time,* and differentiation of the self through *distinctiveness and membership*—men suffering from chronic addiction are severely impaired. This impairment leads to a crisis of meaning that confronts them with the imminence of death, the overwhelming burden of freedom, the isolative nature of their lives, and a sweeping sense of purposelessness about their future.[24] Their response to this crisis of meaning is a flight into three defenses against despair—surrender, blind habit, and destruction. The men's efforts to reconcile these three domains of their lives—identity, meaning, and despair—with sobriety form the heart of this book.

A focus on identity and meaning highlights another limitation of the disease concept approach in helping me to understand chronic addiction. When I thought about their addiction as a physical difficulty, I located the problem inside them, making it a personal and biological concern. When I thought about their problem as one of meaning and a capacity to belong in the sober world, I expanded my understanding of them to include the social realm. In his probing book on how individuals assign meaning to life, Baumeister points out,

> Individuals do not, of course, have to create meaning all by themselves. They acquire language, knowledge, attitudes, guidelines for emotion and rational thinking, and value judgments from society. In

short, meaning is owned by the culture and society and passed along to each new member.[25]

The meanings of life available to the chronically addicted were necessarily a function of the lessons they had learned from the subcultures in which they had been raised and to which they had been exposed since beginning their addicted lives. If they could not find meaning in sobriety, was it solely because of their addictive disease or had social conditions contributed to their distrust and discomfort in sobriety? As I thought about the forces in their lives that had interacted with their addiction—childhood abuse, poverty, racism, homophobia, war, our materialist culture—I then had to consider more pointedly and critically not only their limitations, but the limitations of the world we were encouraging them to reenter.

As a participant in the sober society, I then recognized my potential relationship to the conditions that make meaningful sobriety a threatening prospect for many men at the Pines. To the degree that I colluded with or did nothing to change the destructive social conditions that had contributed to and perpetuated their addictions, I could consider myself as playing a role in their addictive cycle. This acknowledgment of my possible complicity in their addiction by no means freed the men from the responsibility they face to gain control over their self-destructive behavior. It only reminded me of my own responsibilities as a citizen and putative healer in the society. No wonder so many of us, myself included, have found a comfort and simplicity in the disease concept of addiction.[26]

There is another level of security that the disease concept brings to the non-addicted individual. Whenever we say someone has a disease, we are also implicitly raising the question of whether we have the same ailment or not. If we answer no, then we have placed the other person into a category—they are diseased and we are not. Their problem becomes a medical concern relevant to their personal health that will be treated by the appropriate professional and/or self-help group. A concern with meaning, as opposed to disease, requires an examination of addiction in a social context that emphasizes the connectedness of addicted and non-addicted individuals rather than their disjunction. Once I acknowledged that the men and I were both in the same existential boat, wrestling with meaning in an often chaotic and destructive society, I could no longer place them into the "other" or "not me" category. This sense of mutuality encouraged me to experience more empathy and patience in my efforts to make sense of their worlds, but it also reminded me that their defenses and despair were identifiable in my own life as well.

I now felt as though I had a daunting task in front of me, but one that, given my training as a personality researcher and clinical psychologist, interested me immensely. My goal was to describe the problem of identity and meaning in chronic addiction in the hopes of gaining insight into why these men could not embrace sobriety.

Understandably, AA-oriented practitioners, pharmacologically inclined psychiatrists, and cognitive-behavioral therapists have other treatment agendas that take precedence over explorations of identity and meaning. And yet, the more I worked with the men of the Pines, the more I felt that these existential problems seemed to play a central role in their lives. What I could offer, then, was not another recovery guide or programmatic treatment, but a way of seeing the men as whole human beings, caught in a struggle to negotiate society's expectations that they establish meaningful relationships and gainful employment. How both social forces and their addictive lives have led them to falter at these two fundamental tasks might be a central reason why they often fail to recover.

A Study of the Men of the Pines

I have already mentioned that I began to record parts of the men's stories in a journal that I kept. I continued to write down their narratives and insights, but I felt I needed to embark on a more formal study of their life histories to achieve my goal of a thorough understanding of their lives. I proceeded to conduct a series of intensive, tape-recorded life history interviews with men from Lebanon Pines who represented a cross section of backgrounds and life problems.[27]

I interviewed the first man for this project in 1991, but did not begin a systematic attempt to interview a number of men until the fall of 1994, during a sabbatical year from Connecticut College. The sabbatical allowed me to change my schedule and spend a full day a week up at Lebanon Pines. Even though I had worked with the men for the previous five years down in New London and often visited the Pines, I found that locating myself up there gave me an additional level of understanding and connection with them. During that four-month period, I attended staff meetings and met with the men for evaluations there instead of at my office in the New London detox facility. I was also able to have many more impromptu conversations and opportunities to spend informal time with them. Most of the men had seen me for evaluations or referrals before I interviewed them, but a few were recommended for the interview by the head counselor at the Pines and were only meeting me for the first time. In all cases, unless a man was discharged within a few days after the interview, I was able to see the men again, either share a lunch with them or see them privately in my office if they requested a session. From that fall and sporadically after until 1996, I managed to conduct thirty-one life history interviews with residents and former residents of the Pines.[28]

Though each of the thirty-one men's stories contained valuable information and emotional episodes, it is impossible to tell all of them in a single book. The stories I have selected highlight the problems of identity, meaning, and despair that I have come to feel are critical to the lives of men suffering from chronic addiction. Some chapters tell only one man's story, others two or more, but every chapter reflects the stories of other men I interviewed and hundreds of other men I have known from the Pines and SCADD.

These men's roads to Lebanon Pines could not have been traveled by female addicts. Over and over I heard an emphasis on the absence of fathers, both physically and emotionally, from the lives of the men. I heard a confusion about how to express love, pain, anger, and even happiness. I heard the relentless burden of expectation for competence, for control, for prowess in business and in bed. I heard a poignant ambivalence about the presence of children in their lives, a desperate pride and love, but an inevitable acknowledgment of impotence and failure in the face of obligation to their offspring. And through all the narratives, running like a black and malevolent stream, was the presence of violence, against them and by them—beatings and sexual abuse in childhood, the brutality of street fights and youth gangs, officially sanctioned rumbles on the football field, the full horror of war, drug-provoked crimes, pay backs and turf wars, pecking order fist fights and knife fights of prison, physical eruptions of rage in the bedrooms and the kitchens of spouses and lovers, and, finally at the end, the naked fear of being rolled, beaten, and left on the curb by the younger addicts, who are shadow versions of their previous incarnations as men who couldn't be "fucked" with.

I am well aware that this is a half story; it tells of the places and roles men must inhabit in contemporary society, but it does not speak to where women live, and how a different set of expectations for them interacts with their addictions. The other half of the story needs to be told in its own right through the voices of chronically addicted women. And when it has been written, it will allow us to make even more sense of the men of the Pines and their struggles to achieve meaningful relationships and a sense of self-respect.

Before I present the stories of the men, it is necessary to provide a basic background in my theoretical perspective on identity and meaning. To accomplish the project of describing the lives of the men of the Pines and their impediments to sobriety, I chose to employ the life-story theory of identity developed by the personality psychologist Dan P. McAdams.[29] I have also drawn upon my own work in the study of autobiographical memory and personality.[30] To explore the question of meaning in the men's lives, I have relied primarily upon the existential perspective of Irvin Yalom.[31] I do not want to bog the reader down in a technical discussion of psychological theory or research; the endnotes to the next chapter contain many references for the reader who shares my professional and personal passion about the topics of personality and identity. For the more general reader or the reader more focused on issues of addiction, this chapter should provide a helpful overview to how I have approached my analysis of identity and meaning in the men's lives. I also introduce my categorization of the three defenses against despair that play such a central role in the men's decision to forfeit sobriety and pick up a drink or drug once again.

Applying this framework to the men's stories in the chapters that follow, we gain clearer insight into why they battle sobriety. Along the way, we uncover some tentative, but hopeful, messages about how the men might relinquish their resistance to sobriety and find a path to recovery. Contained as well in these messages are recommendations for what we can do to help them in this transformation.

When I first proposed to write a book about the lives of men with chronic addiction, one of the potential editors asked, "Who wants to read a book about a bunch of drunks who don't get better?" She was absolutely right, of course.

When we walk down a city block and catch sight of a man with hat in hand at the corner ahead, our instinct is to wish we had chosen a different route or that his eyes will not meet ours. At the site of the 1996 Atlanta Olympics the homeless were rounded up and moved out of the downtown blocks. In a festival devoted to human potential and physical grace, city officials hoped to minimize the presence of men who reminded us of the opposite—wasted lives and physical decline.

Aside from the questionable motives of the Atlanta Olympic planners, I have to agree with them in this one respect—it would be a lot easier if we never had to encounter men reduced to the street by alcoholism and drug addiction. Nevertheless, they are there on the corner and we can't avoid them indefinitely. Yet we have to cross streets; we don't have to read books.

So why read this book, if you are not a helping professional who works with the chronically addicted or someone whose life has been directly affected by severe addiction? The best answer I can give comes from a comment a counselor (who herself was in recovery) made when I presented the ideas from this book to a staff meeting at SCADD. She said, "What you're talking about is not just my addiction, but me. And I don't just mean the addicted me, but all of me. And not just me, but all of us, people with an addiction and people without one."

Ultimately, an investigation of identity in men's chronic addiction leads us to the problem of how these men are linked to our own sense of identity.[32] Their addiction and their recovery, as much as we would like to believe otherwise, are profoundly social questions that implicate us in their resolution. The recurring theme of the chapters ahead is that the men's route to recovery does not depend simply on biology or psychology, but it also demands a social intervention that requires the mutual engagement of both addicted and non-addicted members of society. This kind of mutual engagement can only take place once a sense of shared identity between non-addicted and addicted individuals is recovered. The elucidation of this common identity is a major goal of this book.

2. IDENTITY, MEANING, AND DESPAIR

Midway in our life's journey, I went astray
from the straight road and woke to find myself
alone in a dark wood. How shall I say
what wood that was! I never saw so drear,
so rank, so arduous a wilderness!
Its very memory gives a shape to fear.
(CANTO I, VERSES I–6, *The Inferno*)[1]

At the beginning of a seminar that I teach on addiction, I show my students a picture of a man sleeping on a sidewalk of a city street. His body is curled up next to a steam vent and his hands are tucked between his thighs for warmth. He has pulled up his shirt to cover one ear and buried his chin into his chest. His hair, long and wavy across his forehead, almost blond in the street light, supplies his only pillow. I ask my students, "Who is he?" They waste no time with their replies, "He's an alcoholic," "He's a drug addict who is homeless." "He is a wino sleeping it off on a street corner." At this point, I ask another question, "O.K., he's an alcoholic or a drug addict, what exactly do you mean?" Here again, my students show no hesitation. "He can't stop drinking or using a drug even when he knows it's hurting him." "He has a physical disease of addiction and can't stop himself from drinking."

We go a step more with the exercise. So, I tell the class, we are looking at a homeless man, sleeping on a sidewalk, and he probably suffers from an addiction. Now, how many of you have heard of Alcoholics Anonymous? Every hand in the room goes up. I ask, Does it work? Heads nod and sometimes one or two students with a mixture of pride and self-consciousness mention a relative who is a recovering alcoholic and attends AA.

If every one of you in the room has heard of AA, it's a pretty good bet that this man, who you believe is an alcoholic, has heard of it and perhaps even gone to some meetings. Why hasn't AA worked for him?

Now the quick responses stop and I see the group working out some possible replies. After a brief silence, one student suggests tentatively, "Maybe he tried, but it was too hard to resist the urge to drink and he gave up." Another adds, "Maybe he's lost so much and sunk so low that he doesn't think he can do any better—maybe he's lost his wife and his job and he doesn't think he can ever get them back." Then, one of the somnolent male students who usually sit in the back of the room (this course attracts a certain number of students who have a personal interest in altered states of consciousness) remarks with a sardonic grin, "Maybe he just likes to drink."

At this point I ask the class to think about the chain of inferences we have woven. A man lies sleeping on the sidewalk because of a physical disease. He lies there, despite the fact that a method to arrest this disease is widely known, easily accessible, and helps millions of people around the world every day. When we ask why he has not taken advantage of a very practical solution, we find that our understanding of his addiction as a physical problem becomes more complicated. If, as one student says, the physical urge was too strong for him, then why do others with the same physical problem find a capacity to resist it? Is there something different about this man's biochemistry that makes him even more vulnerable to relapse? Or is it possible that there are circumstances of his life or aspects of his personality that have made it more difficult for him to maintain his sobriety?

Even more, when the students raise the possibility that he has lost any conviction about the possibility of recovery ("he doesn't think he can do any better") or that he prefers a drinking life over a sober one ("He likes to drink"), they have left the realm of physical disease and entered into the arena of meaning. They are asking critical questions about how this man makes sense of his current life and what value a sober life would hold for him. Once they turn to these questions, we can now begin the entire exercise again. Who is this man? He is more than an alcoholic, a sufferer of a physical disease. He is a human being, like any one of us, who is struggling with a sense of identity and purpose in his life. He has a past, present, and future that are linked through his ongoing sense of selfhood, of being the person that he is and no other. How he ended up on the street corner and whether he will remain there or recover are questions that can be answered not simply through the vocabulary of health and disease, but through an exploration of identity and meaning.

Identity, Meaning, and the Life Story

How might we begin to study the identity of a man like the one I have just described, a man suffering from chronic addiction? To begin, we need to define exactly what we mean by identity. Identity in its most fundamental sense is the answer human beings offer to the question, "Who am I?"[2] As Baumeister has chronicled, for most of history and even in contemporary traditional societies, this question could be answered by reference to a set of clear social categories.[3] I am my father's son. I am a member of particular kinship group. I am a serf who belongs to a particular noble's property. I am a member of a religious society. By the nineteenth century, with the demise of feudalism and the ascent of democracy in many western societies, the question of identity became more complicated (at least for men; women were in most cases still rigidly restricted in their efforts at self-definition). As the mobility created by capitalist and imperialist economies spurred men to move from their homes, rise to a higher social class, and experiment with new social and religious ideals, the prospect of constructing rather than inheriting one's identity became a driving romantic vision of the century. Julien Sorel of Stendhal's *The Red and the Black* is an archetypal example of the man of common background who through talent and intelligence (and not a small bit of manipulation) climbs into aristocratic social circles.[4]

As modern science and philosophy of the second half of the nineteenth century called into question dualist conceptions of a spiritual and material world, human beings grew even less anchored to a fixed truth about their role in the world or in the larger universe. The twentieth century, as captured most eloquently in the writings of existential philosophers, became a period of intense questioning about the meaning of existence and the purpose of one's life.[5] More than ever before, each individual faced a personal struggle with the question of "Who am I?" The quest to determine one's identity had become a heroic struggle to locate a sense of ethical purpose, meaningful occupation, and lasting relationship in an unstable, technologically impersonal, and spiritually troubled world.

In the field of psychology, the pioneering work of Erik Erikson[6] is most associated with the study of how human beings forge a sense of identity in the face of the demands of modern society. Though Erikson's ideas emerged out of a psychoanalytic background, he placed much less emphasis on biological drives and psychosexual determinism than a traditional Freudian perspective would have. Erikson concerned himself with the psychosocial adaptation of the individual's personality across the entire lifespan. For him, the eight stages of life from infancy to old age require adjustment and accommodation by individuals at each juncture to the exigencies of the interpersonal and social environment. As individuals progress through the stages, they carry with them evolving configurations of trust and competency that define their capacity for intimacy and achievement. The question of "Who am I?" is answered by how the individual handles the challenges of forging a separate existence from one's parents during late adolescence, finding a life partner during young adulthood, determining ways to contribute to the society through both vocation and parenthood in middle adulthood, and, finally, making sense of one's life course in old age. Erikson wrote that the negotiation of this life journey depends on a kind of triple bookkeeping. The person must simultaneously address (1) the limits and possibilities of their particular body and biological constitution, (2) the limits and possibilities of their own psychological make-up—the manner in which they respond to conflict and anxiety and construct meaning out of personal experience, (3) the limits and possibilities of their particular familial, cultural, and social contexts—the traditions, expectations, and contingencies of their particular family, society, and historical period. Who I am will depend upon the interplay of body, psychology, and society at each developmental challenge of my life.[7]

Considering this model, we can begin to speculate about the implications of this theory of identity for a man suffering from chronic addiction. Trapped in a body constitutionally prone to addiction, he suffers both the destructive physical and psychological consequences of an addictive existence. His capacity to extract meaning from his troubled life or ward off anxiety without reliance on a substance are profoundly compromised. Finally, both familial and social forces may have contributed to the development of his addiction and now actively aggravate his condition through social ostracism and alienation. In Erikson's terms, on the three accounts of identity, the chronically addicted man is in arrears. How then does he answer the question, "Who am I?" To consider his reply, let us turn to a contemporary theory of identity.

McAdams's Life Story Theory of Identity

Dan P. McAdams builds upon the work of Erikson, but puts an individual's self-constructed life story at the heart of the search for identity. McAdams's fundamental proposition about identity is that we answer the question of "Who am I?" by fashioning our own autobiographical narrative. Identity is no more or less than the story we tell of our lives. He writes,

> Identity is an internalized and evolving life story, or personal myth, that binds together the reconstructed past, perceived present, and anticipated future into a narrative configuration so as to confer upon the person's life what Erikson calls a sense of "inner sameness and continuity."[8]

McAdams's life story model suggests that from birth to death, individuals are engaged in the constructive work of self-definition. Their primary tool in the forging of an identity is a narrative, the tale of their own lives. This narrative, which commences in adolescence and is repeatedly refined as individuals move through Eriksonian developmental stages, is guided by two *thematic lines.* Thematic lines are the motivational currents that run through a given narrative, organizing and directing the flow of the story to a desired endpoint. Though there are many thematic possibilities, McAdams has chosen to emphasize two in particular, *agency* and *communion.*[9] These terms are borrowed from Bakan[10] and may also be traced to Freud's dictum about "love and work" as the primary motivators of the healthy individual.[11]

AGENCY
Agency at its most basic level refers to the impulse toward autonomy and separation of the individual in the interest of "self-expansion" and "mastery of the environment."[12] Agency as a motivating influence in human identity is connected to "concepts of strength, power . . . control, dominance, achievement . . . and independence.[13] There are four overarching themes that are consistently associated with agency across individuals' memories, goals, and fantasies—

1. *Self-mastery:* a striving to strengthen the self through the development of skills, self-discipline, control over the environment around oneself, control over one's emotions, and control over others.
2. *Status:* a striving to achieve increased standing or esteem in society, especially in competitive situations. It involves an

active concern with assuming positions of leadership and winning the highest status possible.

3. *Achievement/Responsibility:* a striving to be effective and com-
   petent in life, to overcome challenges and be successful.
4. *Empowerment:* a striving to associate with the power of others
   who hold greater status than oneself. This motive draws upon
   power through linkage to God, an inspirational leader, or a
   powerful organization.[14]

COMMUNION

In contrast, communion is a desire for a connection to an entity larger than
oneself that is achieved through intimacy, interdependence, and nurturance.
It encompasses "love, friendship . . . sharing, belonging, affiliation, merger,
union, care. . . ."[15] The four pervasive themes of communion are:

1. *Love/friendship:* a striving for erotic love relationships and intimate, deeply mutual, friendships.
2. *Dialogue:* a striving to share mutually with another person
   through self-disclosure or, less dramatically, simply to engage
   in pleasant reciprocal conversation with another person in an
   open and noncontractual manner.
3. *Care/help:* a striving to provide or receive care, to nurture or
   support, resulting in the enhancement of physical, social, or
   psychological well-being.
4. *Community:* a striving to merge with a group of people, a
   community, or all of humankind in the interest of unity and
   harmony.[16]

As individuals construct their life stories, these themes of agency and
communion take on different degrees of prominence; their relative prominence helps reflect the particular configuration of an individual's identity.
Most individuals are striving for a balance between these two overarching
motives. Lives that are markedly skewed toward one or the other of the two
themes may be more prone to interpersonal difficulty. Similarly, lives in
which neither theme is successfully realized are likely to be troubled.

For men suffering from chronic addiction, any understanding of their
identity will necessarily examine the respective roles of agency and communion in their lives. As we shall see, the meanings of agency (and its most
obvious manifestation, work) and communion (as it is expressed in love and
friendship) are often warped in unexpected ways by lives lived in addiction.

The men find ways to commune with others that have the trappings of intimacy but remain markedly isolative. They also have the capacity for remarkable achievements in the legitimate and illegitimate spheres of work, but all of their enterprise ultimately becomes distorted by their addictions and eventually exacts more costs than benefits.

Aside from the thematic lines of agency and communion, another key component of McAdams's model is the *ideological setting* of the life story. Every life story can be assessed in terms of the background values or belief systems individuals employ in their moral choices and actions. As individuals construct narratives of the specific incidents in their lives, they do so believing that the world is just or unjust, that people tend to be good or bad, that either loneliness or love is inevitable. These background convictions about "the way the world is" constitute individuals' ideological settings. The ideological stance of individuals' lives tends to develop in adolescence, as individuals move into more abstract modes of thought. In this period, adolescents employ reason and imagination to conceive of societies different from the one they are about to inherit from their parents. The idealism and strong concern with injustice felt by many adolescents can be traced to their developing capacity to imagine, at least in abstract terms, a world better than the one they see around them.

Ironically, for many men the path to chronic addiction begins during this same adolescent period. As we shall see, many of these men enter adolescence already bearing strong scars or difficulties from childhood. As other adolescents begin to weave an ideological background of optimism and hope about the possibilities of the world ahead, these men have begun to craft a world view that harbors a profound fatalism or nihilism about their lives and life in general.

In each story of identity, there are recurring characters who symbolize important features of each individual's self-representation. These *imagoes* are personal archetypes that combine different blends of agency and communion—for example, the successful but distant father (high agency, low communion), or the bumbling, but generous boss (low agency, high communion). We draw upon these imagoes as a way of understanding who we are and who we might become. Initially, we form these archetypes from exposure to family, peers, and cultural influences. Later, we tend to impose our imagoes on new individuals in our lives, incorporating them into our own ongoing life story. In the often violent and disrupted childhoods of men suffering from chronic addiction, the imagoes of neglectful, brutal, and/or addicted parents loom larger than life and cast their shadows over the men's self-image and their subsequent relations with other persons.

The next important component of McAdams's model is the *nuclear episode.* Nuclear episodes are the specific memories from our lives to which we refer in telling the narrative of our life stories. As I have demonstrated in my own work on *self-defining memories,* individuals are prone to connect the major concerns or themes of their lives to particularly vivid, repetitive, and emotionally charged memories.[17] They often rely on these memories to provide both emotional and historical information about what they would be likely to achieve or avoid in the future. Self-defining memories are touchstones of the personality that help individuals to see in clear mental images what matters and does not matter in their lives. In McAdams's model, nuclear episodes are the most significant and life-changing of these memories—they represent critical turning points or moments of affirmation in an individual's life story.

The role of memory and the flight from memory are among the most important ingredients in making sense of the lives of men with chronic addiction. In the chapters ahead, we see how certain men are haunted by memories that seem to rise up within them, replaying scenes of loss or destruction endlessly across their minds' screen. In contrast, other men have learned how to block memory through their addiction. They have created great gulfs of blank space in their personal histories, disjunctions of identity caused by the destruction of the past.

Finally, McAdams proposes that the culmination of each individual's life story is a struggle with *generativity.*[18] In agreement with Erikson, McAdams feels that the construction of identity ultimately leads to the questions: What I have contributed to society and how will I leave a legacy that will live on beyond my own death? This legacy may take a variety of forms, from the knowledge that one has done one's best as a parent to pride in the material achievements of one's work, or satisfaction in the service one has offered to a community group or religious institution. In McAdams's life story framework, generativity refers to the ending of the story, whether one's life narrative resolves gracefully or in a haunting sense of regret.

For chronically addicted men, the question of generativity raises the often buried prospect of the future. If I continue in this life of self-destruction, how will I answer for my life? What account will I be able to give for the time I spent on earth? It is no wonder that many men suffering from chronic addiction die by their own hand or from accidental deaths (exposure, car accident, drowning, etc.); they have looked into the future and found nothing but despair.[19]

Constructed from these various components, a life story offers the individual a way of explaining one's place in the world and the purpose or meaning of one's life. In this sense, a life story of identity functions as a *personal myth*. Our personal myth is more than just the stories we tell about incidents in our lives; it distills these stories into our deepest and most elemental self-knowledge. McAdams writes,

> A personal myth delineates an identity, illuminating the values of an individual life. The personal myth is not a legend or fairy tale, but a sacred story that embodies personal truth.[20]

In addition to delineating the content of identity, the life story assists in the ongoing process of identity formation. McAdams argues that stories allow the individual to feel a unity of self over time. Citing the work of the philosopher Paul Ricoeur, he argues that the creation of a narrative from life's events allows us to order existence in a meaningful way, to make sense of the temporal dimension of life. Just as we call the period of sunlight "day" and the period of darkness "night," we need a way to organize human transactions that occur in time. Stories locate these events in a temporal sequence and allow us to feel a sense of order and familiarity in what would otherwise seem a random flow of human moments.

> When we comprehend our actions over time, we see what we do in terms of a story. We see obstacles confronted, and intentions realized and frustrated over time. As we move forward from yesterday to today to tomorrow, we move through tensions building to climaxes, climaxes giving way to denouements, and tensions building again as we continue to move and change. Human time is a storied affair.[21]

The life story then is necessary to the formation of identity because it addresses the problem of *continuity over time.*[22] There can be no identity without a sense of connection among one's past, present, and future. To know who I am, I must be able to see a linkage to who I was five years ago and who I will be in twenty years. In fact, to make the point that someone has made a radical change in their life (e.g., a divorce, coming out, a change in careers), we will often say, "she has taken on a new identity." The notion of a new identity highlights the concept of how the present or future has become disjunctive or no longer continuous with the past.

The life story also assists the formation of identity through the process of *differentiation.*[23] By forming a unique story of the self, individuals carve out a unique psychological territory. One can say, "I am like no other person because no one else can have exactly the same story as I do. Though the structure of my narrative, its themes and major characters may be found in other individuals'

life stories, these similarities are only an external scaffolding. Inside those ex-
terior similarities exists a world of unique memories and emotional responses that could only belong to me and no one else." This uniqueness is a
structured uniqueness; if our story were too different or our memories too idio-
syncratic, we would feel too profoundly different or alienated from our society.
Our differentiation is always in the context of our given culture. We select from
an existing set of cultural narratives and then add our personal nuances to
these overarching structures. In this way, our life story links us to a shared culture, even as its subtleties distinguish us, one from the other.[24]

Taken as a whole, McAdams's life-story model of identity presents an
inspiring picture of the contemporary individual heroically extracting meaning from the challenges and conflicts of modern life. Individuals in technologically advanced western societies are modern myth makers. In the pursuit
of love and work, they construct ongoing life epics, manufactured out of the
self-defining memories and important personages of their lives. They give an
ethical or ideological tone to their story and direct it toward a meaningful
ending that will generate a legacy beyond their own life. In the fashioning of
a life narrative, they impose order on their actions and locate them in time,
achieving a continuity of self. Finally, by bringing to mind their unique story
and sharing it in dialogue with others, they both locate themselves in a cultural tradition and differentiate themselves as distinctive individuals unlike
anyone else. Interestingly, the process of creating continuity and differentiation is really none other than the repetition of communion and agency. By
linking identity to the past and future, we are locating ourselves in worlds of
ancestors and progeny—we are connecting ourselves to a community across
time. Similarly, by finding aspects of distinctiveness in our identity, we are
declaring our unique agency—the sense of our solitary "I-ness" that exists
within us and will never be repeated again in the history of existence.

McAdams's extensive research on his model has been conducted on a
wide range of normal individuals of all ages and social classes. For the most
part, they have tended to be individuals functioning in the healthy range of
society with no obvious psychiatric conditions or problems of chronic addictions.[25] My own research on self-defining memories has also tended toward a
college-student and middle-class adult population. In this book, I explore
how these models are stretched and shifted when applied to men whose
lives fall outside the mainstream of society. How does one fashion a life story
based in agency and communion when these two themes have become profoundly thwarted or distorted in one's life? How does one achieve a sense of
continuity and differentiation in identity when drugs and alcohol attack

one's sense of time and blur personality with the homogenizing and reductive influence of addiction?

A Problem of Meaning

The crisis of identity implied by these questions leads to a parallel problem of meaning. If a man suffering from chronic addiction cannot answer the question, "Who am I?" by saying "I am a dutiful son, a loving partner, a responsible father, a skilled worker, a citizen of my community, a loyal friend, a member of my religious group," then a pervasive sense of meaninglessness threatens to set in. For a time, the men might have relied upon a negative or outlaw identity that secures status or achievement through destructive acts—"I am the meanest S.O.B. on the street," "I am the heaviest hitter at the bar"—or a sense of self-mastery through negotiation of the hazards of addiction—"I am a survivor of the streets and the detoxes," or empowerment through membership in a street or prison gang (e.g., "The Latin Kings" or "Aryan Nation"), but these efforts provide only brief glimpses of agency for men overwhelmed by addiction. Eventually, they experience defeat in these attempts at identity and arrive at a place like Lebanon Pines with a pervasive sense of having suffered setbacks in all dimensions of life.

In fact, by the time a man makes it to the Pines, he has been stripped of most of the defenses, positive and negative, that we use to protect ourselves from a confrontation with naked existence and the ever-present prospect of death. Irvin Yalom, a proponent of existential psychotherapy, suggests that there are four "ultimate concerns" that confront every human being—death, isolation, freedom, and meaninglessness.[26] Awareness of these ultimate concerns leads to anxiety and the use of defense mechanisms (including substance abuse) to subdue this awareness and reduce our anxiety.

The fashioning of an identity, such as the one depicted in McAdams's theory, is any individual's greatest buffer against the overwhelming anxiety of existence. Ernest Becker argued that the way individuals protect against awareness of mortality and meaninglessness is to merge their personal identity with the values, goals, and daily routines offered by a particular culture or society. He also warned that there may be times in which our "heroic" investment in a particular society causes us to work for and admire false gods,

> . . . just as there are useless self-sacrifices in unjust wars, so too is
> there an ignoble heroics of whole societies: it can be the viciously

destructive heroics of Hitler's Germany or the plain debasing and silly heroics of the acquisition and display of consumer goods, the piling up of money and privileges that now characterizes whole ways of life, capitalist or Soviet.[27]

These words make clear that both the absence of an adequate identity, or a false identity built out of immoral or empty ideals, are equally dangerous to a sense of meaning. Once individuals confront the inadequacy of their identity in face of life's demands, the emotional power of anxiety sets in.

To grasp what Yalom means, think just for a moment of what it feels like to come home alone to an apartment or house at the end of a day. Imagine you have no messages on your answering machine, no plans for the evening. There is no radio, no television, no books or magazines. You cannot see another house's light from any window in your home. You simply sit in stillness for hours and feel the depth and interminable slowness of time. Though an occasional self-actualized soul with a background in eastern mysticism might find such an evening blissful, most of us socialized to a western rhythm would begin to feel a nerve-wracking sense of anxiety. Now if we magnify this sense of nervous isolation a hundred times, we might begin to sense what the sober chronically addicted man stripped of any meaningful identity or of any protective diversions from that knowledge (e.g., drugs or alcohol) experiences day in and day out.

Once the men have reached a period of repetitive relapse in their lives, the continual confrontation with these anxiety-provoking ultimate concerns may be a critical factor in their inability to maintain sobriety. Unable to tolerate the anxiety generated by facing these existential concerns, they revert to the only dependable defense they have learned to block their terror—the use of alcohol and/or drugs.

All of the chronic addicts face *death* repeatedly in their lives, either through early deaths of parents and siblings or through the loss of fellow addicts in their adult lives. Additionally, as they experience the physical demise of their own bodies caused by alcoholism or the near-death experiences of drug overdoses, the immediacy of their own mortality is always evident. The overwhelming presence of death for these chronic alcoholics and addicts often leads to expressions of hopelessness and despair ("It is too late," "There is nothing I can do," "I have destroyed my life").

Freedom is defined by Yalom as the "absence of external structure."[28] In the contemporary western world, devoid of an overarching religious or class-based authority, individuals are responsible for creating their own life structure and purpose through the choices they make and actions they perform. The men suffering from chronic addiction feel alienated from this sense of freedom and personal responsibility. They experience their addiction as an alien force that took control over them; some literally talk about a demon or evil spirit that compelled them to embark on a destructive path. Even as they acknowledge their choice to pick up a drug or drink, they often cannot tell you why they have made that choice ("I knew I shouldn't, but somehow I just decided to do it anyway"). After so many failed rehabilitations and efforts at recovery, they have come to accept the first step of AA, that they are powerless over their addiction, but they have lost all confidence that this acceptance leads to better choices and increased personal responsibility in sobriety.

Both their repeated escape through substances and their constant institutionalization caused by the effects of this substance abuse have resulted in an overwhelming passivity and impulsiveness in the face of life's demands.[29] Rather than take constructive action when faced with stressors or problems, these men have learned the habit of reaching for a drink or drug. In an altered state, they cease to look at the larger picture of their lives, suffering from a kind of myopia that blocks examination of the destructive meaning of their behaviors.[30] Relying on substances to block meaning in their lives, they are also prone to take impulsive actions that lack planning or forethought.[31] Since these behaviors are attributable to whim or impulse, chronically addictive individuals can abdicate responsibility for taking this course of action ("I don't know how it happened. I was walking along and the next thing I know I was in the package store").

Ironically, given a pervasive sense of passivity and lost autonomy, one of the few ways they can exert personal freedom is to pick up a drink in defiance of all the forces encouraging them to stop. Lacking external structures of gainful employment or nurturing relationships that could reinforce their choice to stop drinking, they can at least make the decision to take a drink and feel a brief sense of purposeful action and a completed goal. These momentary acts of freedom inevitably result in a sense of shame and acknowledgment that the addiction and its controlling influence have triumphed again.

Isolation is the constant state of the chronic relapser; they feel at home neither with their drinking companions nor with the successful recovering circle in AA. In Yalom's terms, their isolation transcends loneliness (though their lack of intimacy is a vital concern) and reaches a sense of separation from all humanity. As one of the men we will hear from later in this book describes it, his continual drinking made him feel that he was an alien and all other human beings were "earth people."

Finally, individuals suffering from chronic addiction have lost the guiding purpose of life. Frightened to engage in the activities of sober living, they find sobriety empty and struggle with a sense of *meaninglessness.* In a strange way, the pursuit of their addiction, the hustling up of the next drink or the scoring of the next fix, provides a structure and mission to their lives that is otherwise entirely absent. A phrase that I learned early on in my work with chronic addicts was "I was on a mission," referring to the individual's determined pursuit of drug-taking and consequent self-destruction. In the terms of existentialism, the chasing of a drug or drink is a kind of "engagement," however false that sense of purpose and meaning may be.[32]

Another kind of problem of meaning I witnessed in the men of the Pines is a struggle with how to live lives based in truth, authenticity, and morality, given how far away their addictive worlds have taken them from these values. Both the nature of addiction itself (in its denial-promoting characteristics) and the dire financial circumstances created by addictions encourage a wide continuum of morally compromising behaviors ranging from mild misrepresentations to lying and blatant denial, or from shoplifting and check forging to robbery, assault, and even murder. Sobriety through recovery groups and psychotherapy demands an honesty and authentic relationship with others that may be altogether foreign and anxiety-provoking to many chronic addicts. Chapter 10, "The Torture," examines how the very process of creating an authentic self that can be trusted not only by others, but by oneself, can be compromised by the destructive factors involved in an addicted life.

In light of the men's confrontations with these existential forces, they were highly prone to extreme bouts of despair that often resulted in severe depression and thoughts of suicide. Though the cultural script of recovery described in the previous chapter associates despair with a "hitting bottom" that precipitates a "letting go" and the beginning of a spiritual renewal, the men of the Pines experienced a contrary feeling. Despair served as the continual catalyst for relapse and an ever deepening self-loathing.

The word *despair* is derived from the Latin word *sperare,* which means to hope. The prefix *de* negates the verb, leaving the literal meaning of hopelessness. Despair is a term often used in the existential philosophy of Kierkegaard, Camus, Sartre, and Marcel.[33] The anxiety engendered by contemplation of life's ultimate concerns will mature into deep despair if the individual cannot find ways to address these concerns in productive and meaningful ways.

In brief, the antidote to despair, according to the existential perspective, lies in acceptance of these concerns rather than evasion and defensive maneuvers. We must acknowledge the reality of death and live life with awareness and even celebration of mortality. In accepting freedom, we must accept our own responsibility for our lives and our life choices; we cannot blame others or rely upon external structures that cannot provide meaning (whether traditional religious authority or the material ethos of our contemporary society). In acknowledging isolation, we admit our aloneness, but use it as a starting point to make attachments and forge communities. In combating meaninglessness, we engage with life; in work, in relationships, in art and nature, in politics and social action. Rather than standing back and contemplating our insignificance in the universe, we plunge into the world and finding meaning in the moment-to-moment doings of our daily life. As Yalom writes, "The question of meaning in life is, as the Buddha taught, not edifying. One must immerse oneself in the river of life and let the question drift away."[34]

These affirming and purpose-providing steps associated with sobriety seem to be the hardest ones for the men of the Pines to take. In contrast, they employ certain defensive responses that characteristically block engagement in the daily world of love and work. These defenses only serve to reinforce the disconnection from the sober world that their past history and addiction have engendered. I should add, that though I see these particular evasive responses as especially prominent in addicted lives, it is not difficult to detect their potential influence in non-addicted lives.

In the next section of this chapter, I describe the three most prominent defenses employed by the men of the Pines to protect them from overwhelming anxiety in the face of confrontations with death, freedom, isolation, and meaninglessness. Each of these defenses emerges repeatedly throughout the life stories of the men.

The Surrender of Agency ("Fuck It")

The cry of "Fuck it" is an agonizing and at the same time perplexing crisis in any recovery work. The words signal a severing of all ties to attempts at effective agency and competence in life, yet their blade is sheathed in the lighthearted banter of adolescents partying in the school parking lot: "5th period bell—ahh—fuck it." "Fuck it" really means "Fuck me." A cry of the surrender of agency, it signifies that I don't matter enough to refrain from actions that will destroy my life and precipitate my death. I will lose my wife and children, my home and possessions, my job, my self-respect, my physical health—fuck it. I might as well live in the street, in the shelters, in the jails, because deep down I am a fucking loser and I don't deserve anything else, so fuck me—fuck it.

"Fuck it" is ultimately a giving in to one's terrifying anxiety about finding any meaningful role in life. Convinced that failure, relapse, and death are his inevitable fate, the chronically addicted man chooses to say, "I might as well do the damage to myself before life does it to me." At such moments, the individual turns his capacity for self-mastery against himself. His only sense of control is the harm he can do to his body and to those people who still love him in his life.

Once a man expresses "Fuck it," despair quickly grows to dominate any thoughts of recovery. The only escape from this despair is the momentary relief offered by the drug or drink. The use of the substance is no longer to get high, to have fun. Instead the only endpoint is to separate the self from the self, to be out of thought, out of time, to be in as death-like a state as possible—to black out, to nod out, to be obliterated, to get off, as if stepping off the earth into space, away from any sense of self or other in the world.

Many of us have known at times the impulse to throw in the towel, reach for a drink, and block out the world.[35] The men of the Pines exemplify what it would mean to live on a steady diet of "Fuck its;" the magnitude of their despair underlined for me how quickly and pervasively hopelessness can take control of one's thoughts and actions. The cry of "Fuck it" surfaces through all of the men's stories that follow in this book. It reminds us that there are two avenues to a sense of agency that any individual can travel—one is the independence gained by success, the other the freedom of total loss.[36]

Blind Habit (There Used to Be a Bench)

A friend of mine told me about a visit he made to his old neighborhood. As he turned the corner to his street, there was a group of men passing a bottle. Despite the span of twenty-five years, it was the same crowd he had known from high school and they were still drinking at the same corner. The only thing that was different was that the old bench was no longer there. He suddenly realized that what had attracted them in the first place to that corner of the block was the bench, and now, even though it was gone, they still remained in the same place. I could think of no better metaphor for the distorted fellowship that bonds a group of drinking buddies.

Even as their habit leads to loss or sickness, they return to each other, not necessarily because they continue to share pleasure with each other, but because their association summons an image of pleasure, which, like the bench, may have long ago vanished. The men continue to stand where they do and share their corner (or indirectly, their sense of being cornered), and the possibility of moving, of locating themselves in a new place is out of awareness, or if contemplated, presents a level of difficulty that seems unreachable, risky, and subversive. They cling to each other and the memory of comfortable purpose, provided by the invisible bench (those early days of drinking) that once made this particular corner of the world an attractive and reasonable place to be.

Herbert Fingarette, in his analysis of heavy drinking, calls the organizing of our lives around such benches a *central activity*.[37] Most of our lives, rather than consisting of motivated choices, may function around the relatively unreflective habits based in the central activities of our vocations or relationships. Imagine, waking up tomorrow and no longer having your job or your marriage, how many large and small aspects of your daily life would change. For the men in the stories that follow, sobriety asks exactly this question of them—to start a new day with the central activity, the organizing structure of their lives, removed.

Fingarette feels the concept of a central activity holds a critical key to debates about the nature of addiction. He first asks "But why . . . would someone make decisions that lead to a way of life so self-destructive and so injurious to others?"[38] His response transcends the problem of addiction and speaks to how human beings in general come to experience their lives.

> The general truth is this: Human beings do not always respond
> wisely and with foresight; we often drift, unwitting, into a tangled
> web of decisions, expectations, habits, tastes, fears, and dreams.[39]

The drift that Fingarette identifies is often the momentum of habit, of doing simply what we have done before; we build such habits into a way of living, of getting through the day.

> When we speak of the momentum of a way of life, we are using a
> convenient label to refer to the cumulative impact of many long-cul-
> tivated and interrelated habits of mind, heart, soul, and body. For
> most of us, it is only when we are contemplating a serious change in
> some central activity that we come to consciously realize the
> momentum the activity has acquired.[40]

Blind habit contains a multilayered structure that organizes and defines the activities of our daily life. For the chronic alcoholic, change does not mean simply to stop drinking, but to experience changes in all the other activities and relationships that have become connected to the central act of drinking over the years. Despite all the hardships and losses that accrue with addiction, the chronic addict at least knows who he is, where he will be, and who his friends are. By continuing to drink, he is pulled along by the habitual forces that are associated with that activity and that continue to structure his existence. Without the central act of drinking, not only does the chief focus of his identity cease, but all the linked peripheral ways of his being in the world vanish as well.

For this reason, we might think about the familiar AA concept of hitting bottom in a new light with regard to the chronic addict. Traditionally, to hit bottom has meant to lose everything that mattered—work, loving relationships, self-respect, spiritual faith. In this sense, hitting bottom is a stripping away by alcohol of all the positive central organizing activities of one's life until one is left only with an alcoholic or drugged despair. For the chronic addict whose life is organized around the consumption of alcohol and the world of rehabs and fellow alcoholics, hitting bottom may actually occur when he glimpses the terrifying prospect of sobriety. At such moments, the chronic addict must envision a life devoid of all of the central and linked activities that now shape his daily life. At such sober moments, he is forced to contemplate giving up his life's purpose (to obtain his drug or drink), his primary relationships (with other active chronic users), his weekly activities and routines (visiting liquor stores, soup kitchens, detoxes, street corner alleyways, motel rooms, crack houses or houses of prostitution), and his core identity as a hard-drinking man who is beating the odds for still another day. Ironically, as Fingarette points out, the more seriously a chronic addict contemplates recovery, the more real the possibility of losing all these self-defining aspects becomes.[41] To non-addicts these activities may not seem like reasons to avoid change, but to a chronic addict the loss of this familiar world feels like a true bottom.

As long as a man remains at the Pines or even in a half-way house, he can go without drink and still maintain a sense of identity and meaning as part of a group of chronic addicts working on recovery. Once on his own, despite all the support of AA, he may often feel that he no longer knows who he is or what he can possibly do with the large stretches of time between AA meetings. Slowly he gravitates to his old friends, his old haunts, and perhaps eventually to his old habits. Before long he has found himself, the self that is most familiar and that offers him the "momentum of a way of life," a means to get through each day. In another ironic inversion of the AA mottoes, the chronic addict has learned to see no further than one day at a time. He allows the central activity of his drinking to take him through the day, structuring his daily goals, activities, and associations. When he wakes in the morning, he need only say to himself, "I will drink today," and the rest of the day's events and rituals will carry him through to his nighttime rest, which will be, of course, an alcohol-induced slumber.[42]

Destructive Agency (I'd Rather Drink)

The third, and perhaps most devastating, response chronically addicted men make when confronted with sober lives of love and work is the simple statement, "I'd rather drink." These words reject the very process of engaging with others either through shared labor or love; they represent a solipsistic dedication to stepping out of life and living in a haze of intoxication. If the "Fuck its" are an acknowledgment of defeat and a commitment to self-destruction, as if one has been spurned by life and is now choosing a route to death, loving one's drink or drug to the exclusion of all else is like a love affair with death in which life is the jilted suitor. One man I interviewed, an admirer of Eugene O'Neill[43] and Jack Kerouac, put it in poetic terms.

It was always my ambition to be a drunk. Before that, I wanted to be a priest. Then around fourteen, I tasted the booze. Once I felt the rush, I told myself there's a life. No ties, no obligations. The road and a bottle. Women when I was lucky. I knew with my dark looks (I'd always known) I'd be lucky in that way.

Hopping freights to Denver and the coast. Getting my whiskey under the open sky. Why would I want anything else?

People always tell me I'm a quitter, that I ran away from responsibility and relationships. And I'd agree, but I always told myself, bullshit. I'm not running away. I'm running to something—to feeling free the way most stiffs couldn't. . . .

I tell myself that's the final romance, to die in a single room with a bottle by my head. Now that's a black Irish death—poured out empty in the night like the last pint of the bottle. That's a way to go—a final "fuck you" to the Gods. But I don't know if I have the courage or the strength for it. I may be one of those people who gets sober but feels defeated.

A man addicted to heroin stated these sentiments more succinctly when he told me that his ideal life would be a needle in his arm until he passed out and another waiting on his pillow when he awoke. There is a seductive truth contained here—living life and bearing witness to the inevitability of age and death are no easy matters. As W. B. Yeats once begged the sages, "Consume my heart away; sick with desire/And fastened to a dying animal/It knows not what it is; and gather me/Into the artifice of eternity."[44]

Though Yeats's confrontation with this particular aspect of the human condition drove him to lyric self-expression; some men turn only to the solace of "the booze." In the 1996 film *Trainspotting*, about a group of Scottish heroin addicts, one character weighs sobriety against getting high, "You have to worry about bills, about food, about some football team that never . . . wins, about human relationships and all the things that really don't matter when you've got a sincere and truthful junk habit."[45] This sentiment of the superiority of staying high, as well as the acute pleasure attainable from it, resurfaces repeatedly in some of the men's stories.

In discussing the ways in which individuals use alcohol to escape from the demands and responsibilities of the self, Baumeister points out that individuals are not always escaping from something, but also escaping to something.[46] In the case of "I'd Rather Drink," it is possible that the addicted men began their alcohol and drug careers with the discovery of a kind of ecstasy that an altered state can bring. Baumeister point outs that the Greek roots of the word correspond approximately to a "standing outside of oneself."[47] We are all familiar with the joy of stepping out of ourselves, whether in the throes of music, physical activity, or falling in love.[48] Creative writers and artists have often looked to drugs and alcohol (with mixed results) to assist them in the process of losing self-consciousness and expanding their imaginative visions.[49] For the chronically addicted, that initial impulse toward ecstasy, toward a stance outside the self, now dominates their lives. To be inside their own sober heads feels intolerable. They would rather drink (even if drinking means dying, and perhaps because drinking means dying) than be themselves. What may have begun as an occasional foray into an ecstatic state has ended up a rejection of all life that cannot promise this perpetual release from self.

One might conceive of this stance as a kind of thumbing one's nose at the terms of life, a bitter rebuke to what the sober world has to offer. Ernest Becker cites Kierkegaard's description of this attitude as a "'demoniac rage,' an attack on all of life for what it has dared to do to one, a revolt against existence itself."[50]

Destructive agency is expressed in the addicted individual's open rejection of society's accepted standards of status, achievement/responsibility, or positive empowerment. It is a pact with the underworld.

Identity, Meaning, and Despair—Putting the Framework Together

We can now step back and look at the framework we have constructed to describe the men of the Pines, as exemplified by the chronically addicted man sleeping on the sidewalk whose image began this chapter. Similar to all of us, he begins his life aspiring to answer the question "Who am I?" Perhaps in childhood and certainly by adolescence and young adulthood, traumatic experiences in his life brought on both by inherently destructive conditions of the society and by his own family background (negative imagoes) derail his efforts to craft a personal myth based in positive strivings toward agency and communion. By adolescence, the introduction of alcohol and/or drugs escalates his difficulties and begins to separate him from other young people struggling with questions of identity. Rather than develop an ideological setting based in trust and optimism, he begins to doubt the world and his own place in it. In the two significant arenas of life, love and work, he experiences significant setbacks that are compounded by his developing addiction.

Continually thwarted in efforts to establish a positive identity in conventional society, he may invest himself in the construction of a negative identity linked to his addiction. Over time, the consequences of his negative identity (prison, constant need for money, abusive relationships, physical hardship, and disease) make this approach an equally untenable story through which to find meaning or purpose in his life. Ultimately, his addiction comes to dominate his world and propels him into a revolving cycle of detoxes, rehabs, shelters, hospitals, jails, and alleyways. At this point he feels alienated and disconnected from both the sober and the recovering world. Dragging himself through his marginal world, he finds sobriety associated with an overwhelming anxiety. In response, he retreats into familiar patterns of despair that justify his return to drink or drug. Finally, reaching a long-term residential facility like Lebanon Pines, he gains enough sober time to explore the most basic questions of identity and meaning. His own willingness to find hope and our ability to respond to his multiple needs will determine whether he can break this addictive cycle and maintain sobriety when he leaves the Pines.

Overview of the Chapters Ahead

In the life stories that follow, the passages set in bold type represent direct quotes from the men. My only changes were to remove repetitions and winnow out some of the verbal tics and pause fillers (e.g., "you know," "I mean," "you know what I am saying," "like," etc.). Since most of my questions were simply to clarify a meaning or to ask what happened next, I have avoided, except when necessary, quoting my own words in the verbatim passages I selected.

In the chapter entitled "The Boys of Skipper's Deck," in order to bring the reader more deeply into the daily world of the men of the Pines when they are out on their own and drinking, I took the artistic liberty of dramatizing a poker game at the Skipper's Deck motel. This game was described to me by one of the participants, Tommy Reilly, and I have allowed myself to imagine the thought processes and dialogue of the men. Unlike the verbatim quotations in the rest of the book, which are presented in bold print, the men's words spoken at the end of the chapter are demarcated only by quotation marks to distinguish them as imagined, not actual, dialogue.

In Part II of this book, I look at Problems with Communion for men suffering from chronic addiction. We examine in turn a gay man's ultimately fatal struggle to reconcile his sexual identity with the repression of a homophobic society (Chapter 3, "The Jewel of Prison"), and the ambivalent intimacy men find in the friendship of their drinking circles (Chapter 4, "The Boys of Skipper's Deck").

In Part III, Problems with Agency, I turn to an exploration of how the striving for a sense of autonomy and competence can become corrupted in addicted lives. In Chapter 5, "When the Devil Grabs Your Ankle," I look at how poverty and racism interact with addiction to cripple the development of positive identity in African-American men. In Chapter 6, "Lust and Greed," Doug Richards takes us to the other extreme of society. A self-made multimillionaire insurance broker, he demonstrates how the single-minded pursuit of success and money in this society can be as equally corrupting of meaningful identity as the most abject poverty. In Chapter 7, "Who Was Inside Mickey Mantle?" we look at another form of false agency that often combines with addiction—the athlete as celebrity. Billy Zeitel, a former major league baseball player, shows us how the escapist world we create around our sports idols shares unnerving similarities with the hollow world of addiction.

Having examined disruptions in the content of chronically addicted men's identities, we turn in Part IV to Problems with Identity Formation. In Chapter 8, "War on Memory," we look at what happens in an addicted life when the continuity of identity over time is disrupted. Ever since Tyler Casey experienced combat trauma in Vietnam, he has avoided a united sense of self by using drugs and alcohol to block out the past and extinguish thoughts of the future. Now, with treatment, he has slowly begun to reconnect himself to time, but we see how difficult and frightening this process is for him. In Chapter 9, "The Torture," Michael Cochran, a police informant and the survivor of horrific childhood abuse, challenges the reader to find within his larger-than-life story an authentic and identifiable self. Michael's capacity to survive by merging with the identities of those around him offers a vivid example of the critical role differentiation plays in identity formation. Chapter 10, "Invisible Men," explores the most common type of chronic alcoholic and yet the most elusive. These quiet men moved through childhood and adolescence on the margin of society until they discovered alcohol in adolescence. Quickly addicted, they never initiated the process of forming an identity. Now approaching middle age, they are still in the earliest stages of defining who they are through any consistent efforts at agency or communion.

In Part V, Conclusion, Chapter 11, "Recovering Identity and Meaning," I explore how the men's stories have caused me to reconsider the basic tenets of identity. Their persisting theme of disconnection from both sober and recovering worlds clarified for me that, without a sense of inherent embeddedness in the lives of others and in the world in general, any efforts toward agency or communion are bound to fail or to lack meaning. Drawing on this insight, I argue that the task of recovering identity and meaning includes a recognition of the mutual embeddedness of both addicted and non-addicted in each others' lives. This recognition leads to an awakening of obligation and empathy that affects the kinds of treatment strategies and services we might employ in working with chronically addicted men.

One final caution—as you enter the world of the men from the street corners, be aware that the stories you will hear contain both loss and tragedy. The men are confused and troubled by their lives. They have not reached a point where, like the phoenix, they can rise from the ashes, reborn, new, and full of promise. Yet simply telling their story is a step toward sanity and sense-making. To shape their past into a narrative and to convey it to another person is a tentative move toward ownership of a life often chaotic and out of control. The act of telling conveys an act of caring—it is an antidote to the meaninglessness and nihilism that often accompany addiction. So enter their world, but do not abandon all hope. Even if in the end some of these men cannot make it back from the dark wood they have entered, their words illuminate the struggle for identity and meaning that exists in all our lives.

Part Two

PROBLEMS

WITH COMMUNION

3. THE JEWEL OF PRISON
A Gay Addict's Forbidden Intimacy

John Brown died of complications of AIDS in 1993 at the age of fifty-six. The very first man I interviewed for this book, he told me his life story in the spring of 1991. John's story recounts a struggle for identity complicated not only by addiction, but by the injurious influences of homophobia and racism. Though his addiction became the central problem of his life, his words depict how all three of these forces undermined his efforts to achieve communion both in his personal relationships and in the larger society.[1] Parts of John Brown's life exemplified the acting out of demoniac rage, a willful foray into destruction and rejection of life ("I'd Rather Drink"). At other points, he was more rejecting of himself, hating the body and gender he was given by birth, and deeply shamed by his own impulses ("Fuck it"). Trapped by society's rejection of his desired intimacy, he struggled with a constant sense of isolation, finding comfort only behind prison walls and in a subculture considered deviant by the dominant society.

The two most lasting impressions I have of John are his voice and his long elegant form. Each sentence he spoke flowed in a deliberate measured pace. His voice had a slight theatrical inflection—an actor's voice, or a professor's, or a faded southern belle's. His scholarly presence was heightened by his glasses and the delicacy of his arched eyebrows above their rims. As he spoke, his fingers moved in the air, resting for a moment on my desk, and then taking flight again—long brown fingers with polished and tapered nails. Sometimes he would hold a cigarette between his index and middle fingers, and the cigarette would also travel with the currents of his words, its orange ash a bouncing ball to punctuate his phrases. He would lean back in his chair, letting his long thin legs stretch out before him, striking almost a reclining pose. He would tilt his head back and his buttery drawl or a plume of smoke would float out into the room. Though he spoke with great candor and detail about the most significant incidents and conflicts of his life, his voice and demeanor remained even, conveying a certain philosophical stance toward all that he had experienced and lived. I feel that John knew that he would not live for a long time beyond that day and that this interview could be a way of stating without undue fuss the circumstances of his life.

John's ability to discuss the more painful aspects of his life with a certain detachment and even, at times, a wry bit of humor or irony, also suggested to me an effective defense. He seemed well-trained in protecting himself from revelations of vulnerability. After a lifetime of slurs, attacks, and denigration for both his sexuality and his race, John knew how to keep his distance from his pain. Yet this "clinical" distance, his occasional tendency to refer to himself in the third person, and perhaps his knowledge of his condition, all contributed to a degree of honesty I found unusual in most life stories. The "Johnny" whom he described was not always likable or admirable in his behavior. Yet John helped me to understand the reasons behind "Johnny"'s selfish or destructive behavior.

Growing Up

John was raised in a lower middle class housing project in the northern part of Hartford. He described his neighborhood as family oriented, "where everybody was concerned about everybody else's children." Both his mother and father were in the home, but had marital difficulties and eventually separated by the time he reached high school. Still, he felt his home life had a great deal of structure and discipline.

There was one boss in my house and that was my mother and if you didn't like it, you had the right to move out, run away from home, whatever, but she was the boss and her law was the law.

John was never close with his father and felt that his homosexuality may have contributed to their distant relationship. He wondered too if his feelings of rejection from his father may have led him to seek acceptance from others too ardently. There were times when, in order to find communion, to feel appreciated or loved by another person, he would demean himself or act in ways that undercut his own self-image. In grade school, though he was highly intelligent and always at the top of his class, he would play the class clown. He preferred the attention and the approval of the other students to efforts at serious scholarship. By the time he reached high school, his father had decided it would be more practical for him to attend a trade school rather than to attend the public high.

I was totally against going to trade school. I had desires to go to college, but being he had the last word, that old saying, "you can't fight city hall" prevailed. It was at this time I lost all interest in school; in fact I went from an "A" student to an "F" student in a matter of about two weeks. I deliberately did this sometimes—I used to punish myself, thinking I was getting back at other people, but at the time I didn't recognize that I would be the one who would pay and absorb the cost of doing what I did.

Already in these school years, John had begun a pattern of taking out his frustrations and losses on himself.

John took his first drinks when he was in high school, but there was no immediate attraction for him to alcohol. Unlike many of the men of the Pines, he had not grown up in a family in which alcohol was already a problem for one of the parents. Returning to the theme of avoiding isolation from others, he drank to avoid seeming different or uncool to his peers.

I drank because I wanted to be accepted, but it didn't make me any more accepted than I was already. You know, I didn't feel a great big difference from the people I was with, but I felt this made me all right with the fellas. And being I was in that time where I wanted to be loved by the fellas, as well as accepted, I tried not to do anything that would anger them or cause them to single me out as different. That was that. I went to the service shortly afterward, where once again, for sake of acceptance, I picked up the bottle in Lake Charles, Louisiana.

John had grown fed up with his enforced schooling and quit at age sixteen. His mother, always firmly in control, told him he needed to find work or join the service, but he better not expect to sit home and hang out. He enlisted within three weeks and was in the Air Force at age seventeen. Stationed down in Louisiana, he had his first taste of overt and society-sanctioned racism.

I sat down at the counter of a Walgreen's drug store and ordered a strawberry milkshake with a scoop of marshmallow and a cheeseburger. I sat at the counter and I'm waiting and waiting and waiting. All the waitresses were black, but none had the gall to tell me that I was doing something wrong. And finally, the manager came over and in his southern drawl, he explained that I couldn't sit at the counter and eat, that I would have to take my order to the back door if I wanted it. . . . I refused to eat, left out of there, and went across the street. They were doing the Jimmy Piersall movie, "Fear Strikes Out" and I've always been an avid Boston Red Sox fan and I wanted to see the movie, but they didn't allow blacks at that time into their movie house. About two weeks later, I saw a gorgeous white linen suit in the window of a shop and I went in, priced it, and found it was in my budget, and decided to try it on. They told me niggers didn't try on clothes; they couldn't put clothes back on the racks that had touched a nigger's body.

After these incidents, John stayed on the base and left only for an occasional church service at the black church in town. This was one of the loneliest times in his life. The structured and secure neighborhood of his childhood was no longer available to him because of his unacceptable sexual desires and his reluctance to take up "men's work." Though he went to church, he felt like an impostor and a sinner in the eyes of the minister and the congregants. White society off the base had defined him as a "filthy nigger" whose contact with a garment left it polluted and unfit to be worn. Though he sought solace from acceptance by the other men on the base, he knew that any revelation of his desires would lead to ostracism and possible physical threat. In these four critical arenas, his occupational, racial, spiritual, and sexual identities, he felt a profound sense of isolation and rejection.

His idleness and long hours alone only heightened his desire to express his sexual urges. He continued to battle against his feelings and condemn himself.

It was against the law as far as Uncle Sam was concerned and it was against everything society had taught me I was supposed to do. The only thing society didn't explain to me were that those were honest feelings and there should have been something I could have done with them other than feeling shame and guilt for being me. I didn't give into them at that time.

I asked him if he had had any sexual experiences up to that point. He explained there had been an incident of sexual abuse by some older neighborhood boys when he was seven or eight, but that was an isolated time and there had been no contact of any kind in the subsequent years up to this stint in the military.

I guess I'm as guilty as Jimmy Carter because I would lust in my heart after my friends, but being afraid to express myself at that time, my homosexuality was lived in a state of limbo. Mentally, though, I was gay. I didn't know why. I did a lot of things with girls. However, when someone came along with a baseball bat or a football, I wasn't the best of players, but nevertheless I did what I could. But when the girls came to double dutch, I was there too. I was never an outcast, so to speak. I spread myself so I was accepted, plus I had a very vile tongue in my youth and I could defend myself verbally better than some people could defend themselves physically. So it was always the situation whereas you didn't want to confront Johnny because he will say something that will hurt your feelings and this in a sense kept a lot of weight off of me. . . . I was guilty of sometimes deliberately breaking someone's spirit down, which only added to my stature as being someone with a mean tongue. And even to this day, not as much as I often did, I will resort to that as my ultimate weapon and I will say things that really cut to the quick.

When John's unit was transferred to Casablanca in Africa, he finally had a chance to go out and sample some night life once again. With an older soldier from Detroit, he went into the Medina and tried hashish for the first time. After smoking the drug and downing a few drinks at the bar, he was dragged by a friend to a hotel and thrown into a room with a prostitute.

I wasn't enthralled or thrilled by it; it was a hurry-up G.I. situation. It was different than what I had read. I had always read about Prince Charming and all that bullshit about love and whatnot and I thought this is the way it's supposed to be. But in reality, it's get what you can. I know it wasn't really the meaning I paid for, I can understand her plight, but at the same time I didn't enjoy it. . . . I did manage to bust a nut and go back down with my face saved. I wasn't a failure, but at the same time Johnny didn't enjoy it. You know I did this for Arty from Detroit, who was like a big brother, because he felt this is what I needed.

Soon after, he met another serviceman from New York and had his first gay experience. In 1956 he was given an honorable discharge because of a surplus of men in the service at the time. He lived in New Jersey for a couple of years and even befriended a gay gospel singer, but could not return his confidences and reveal his own sexual identity. After a job offer brought him back to Hartford, he made up his mind not to suppress his own desires any longer. He started by hanging out in the south end of Hartford where he would be unlikely to be seen by people he knew. He discovered a gay club and became a frequent patron.

According to writings at the time,[2] the gay bar was literally the only available social structure for gay individuals to congregate and feel a sense of connection. Though gay bars, not unlike heterosexual singles bars, have traditionally served as vehicles for cruising and hooking up, research based on participant observation and questionnaires makes clear the community and social functions these bars serve.[3] They provide a socialization experience for men who are recently "out," and have no knowledge of what codes of conduct or behaviors might fit with their identity as homosexual.[4] They offer a clearinghouse for information about social events, health hazards, drug connections, and police activities. In our more liberated period and with the specter of AIDS omnipresent, other gay social organizations (political clubs, choruses, theater groups, health networks, therapy and AA groups, among many others) have emerged and reduced the centrality of the bar as the community touchstone. Yet in John's time of the late fifties, prior to the Stonewall revolution and the liberation movements of the late sixties, there was the bar or the alleyway and little else. I asked him about this period and what the world was like for a gay man.

Angry! Anger within the family, anger from the community at large, just a great deal of anger. We were looked upon as worthless sons of bitches who should have been tarred and feathered and castrated and everything imaginable would have been all right.

Though he found some comfort in the south end bar, it was located in a white neighborhood and he soon grew frustrated with racial slurs and harassment by police. He decided that he had to tell his family and gain more freedom to travel in his own neighborhood and among his own people.

After six months of deliberation, I told my mother. And much to my surprise, she didn't have a heart attack or tears didn't flow. She told me she had her suspicion of me, in her own way of speaking, and I was still her child and whatever I do, try and have a little class. After that, things went a bit easier. Some of my friends, at first were taken aback by it, but some of them stood by me 100 percent. That in itself should have been the acceptance I wanted, unfortunately it wasn't. And running with a complete gay crowd, drinking was a part of every day. You know, I guess we had all beaten down these feelings that we were less than normal or less than people or less than what society had programmed us to be. And drinking became a part of every day then.

(Was the drinking to deal with those beaten down feelings?)

Yes. You know, because today's gay individuals don't have the pressure that we had. I even look at some of my friends and myself for that matter who chose to get into drags. We always went someplace where we could do it secretly, where nobody would ever recognize it was us in drag. Whereas in relation to today, they can do it any kind of way they damn well feel like it. They can go to the doctor and get those false titties put on their chest and everything. If their money calls for it, they can have an operation, it's more of an accepted thing now than it was thirty years ago. Even though they have gay bashings today, they are far and few between in comparison to then.

And the only place that I can honestly say that even though we were still a minority, during my stint in prison, we were very much in demand. This alleviated, so to speak, the sock in hand routine among the fellas. If they could find someone who was gay who was willing to have a relationship or just to get their nut off. And because of this, whereas in the street, there might have been name-calling or possibly fighting, in prison, it wasn't like that. We were little jewels, so to speak, pleasure vessels for their purposes and they more or less protected us from any type of verbal or physical abuse that might come our way. Other than that, society at that time did not think it fashionable for Mr. America to be known as having dealings with a gay person.

Getting back to drinking, yes drinking. I can honestly say, I'm almost certain that if I hadn't been gay, I probably wouldn't have been alcoholic. Or for that matter, I probably would never have really and truly become a dope fiend. But being gay and the lifestyle in which we led, drinking became a very important part of it. We no longer secluded ourselves to gay bars then. We used to go to straight bars and cluster around; it was a form of release. We had more freedom in the black north end than our counterparts in the south, where it was still a very, very clandestine situation. . . . Blacks as a people are very loving and they don't get bent out of shape as much as Caucasians. If you research any of the gay bashings, it is usually done by whites. Very, very seldom, you know it's a rarity to pick up a newspaper where blacks have gone out of their way to be destructive to another individual on account of his lifestyle.

As I listened to John tell this part of his story, I pondered his ironic message. Only in prison, only with men defined as social outcasts and undesirables was John able to feel a sense of his own specialness or importance. Harassed by the police and by the white population at large, he found protection from physical and verbal abuse once he was behind bars and in the "company of thieves." This man with the refined voice and scholarly bearing who had given up hopes of college and who had been coerced first into trade school and then into the military, could only experience himself as a jewel, as something precious and desired by others, in a prison cell. For once, there was a role and sense of identity for him within his immediate community. For once, he was accepted and able to feel connected to other men. In the relish with which he told this memory, John poignantly conveyed the tragicomic dimension of the drag queen depicted in Manuel Puig's play, *The Kiss of the Spiderwoman*.

By the early sixties, John had entered fully into the gay subculture of Hartford and explored the expression of both his sexuality and his sexual identity. Now part of a community, he continued to struggle with how to maintain a sense of meaning and importance in it.

The whole gay experience came into full bloom, get dressed for Halloween or parties at somebody's house, playing mind games with yourself that you really were a lady, and it was all right to dress up in women's clothes whenever you felt like it. The no-longer-standing-up-at-the-urinal-but-sitting-at-the-toilet syndrome. I can look at some of those things today and I want to laugh, but it is so. It hurts to know that I was playing mind games with myself to think that the prettier I looked with a dress, the gayer I was or the closer I became to the real deal. And yet still waking up with a thing swinging between my legs just like any other heterosexual male—it took me a long time to come to grips with that. You know that until ten years ago, I never related to myself as a male, I was always she or Miss so-and-so and I always referred to my friends as Miss Sammy, Miss George, it was never just a plain George or Sammy or Wesley. This was a delusion that we all suffered from and I guess as we became more comfortable within ourselves, we were able to stand back up and use the urinal and drop the prefixes. And the wigs and the makeup and whatnot were put away forever. And I guess it was an accepting process of ourselves. No longer with the shame and the guilt that we had lived with for so long, but at the same time the shame and the guilt had made me an alcoholic and a dope fiend.

John's involvement with the drag world and the exaggerated emphasis on the femininity and ladylike qualities of its participants stand in interesting contrast to recent scholarly writings on male homosexuality. Cabaj states emphatically that "the vast majority of adult gay men are not effeminate," and Israelstam and Lambert describe an active movement toward a more macho and athletic image in gay men in the last few decades.[5] It is not hard to imagine that the outright rejection and humiliation experienced by John and his peers in the fifties and sixties led them to feel a sense of otherworldliness and isolation that promoted the creation of an alternate society—a literal "velvet underground." The competition to outdo each other in being ever more effeminate was, in its own way, a process of finding communion, of creating a community with decorum, standards, and defined roles. To the mainstream society, it must have seemed bizarre and perverted, but so much the better, since the straight society had made it clear that it wanted no part of these gay men. Though the last twenty-five years have allowed for advances in acceptance of gay sexuality (and clearly John experienced a greater self-acceptance because of these changes), there is still evidence of a cross-dressing subculture in many urban areas of the country. The recent film, *Paris Burning* (1992), depicted the popularity of cross-dressing balls, though the participants' sexuality varied across the board from gay to bisexual to heterosexual. The majority of the individuals depicted in the film still lived alienated and outcast lives, often functioning as hustlers or prostitutes.

In addition to John's ability to find a community of men during this phase of his life, I was curious if he had developed any more sustained intimate relationships. He described one long-term relationship that lasted from about 1958 to 1970. He felt very ashamed of his behavior to his partner. Despite his partner's loyalty, John frequently cheated on him and demeaned him. He would take money and gifts, but gave back little in return.

I didn't respect the relationship at all, until it was over and I then realized I committed a great injustice, a great injustice because it was during our relationship that he exposed himself to his family. I didn't respect that; I cheated right in his face. I didn't respect the relationship because it was my first one. . . . I was so self-centered and the only thing I wanted then was *what I wanted.* I used him for materialistic things. He had two jobs and he provided me with all the liquor I wanted. I was still drinking at the time. Later he provided me with money for drugs, for awhile.

By the mid-sixties, John was drinking daily and frequently drunk to a point of passing out. He was still able to work on a steady basis and maintained his very active social circle. Things might have continued on in this way for quite a while if it had not been for the death of his mother in 1965. In the years since his coming out, they had maintained and even deepened their relationship. They played pinochle every Monday and often attended church together. They talked around the kitchen table and she encouraged his brothers and sisters to accept him. They followed her lead, because no one dared buck her authority. After her death, John experienced a deeper loneliness and hollowness than he ever had before. More alcohol did not fill this void, but heroin did. He first started with snorting, but soon developed nose bleeds. He switched to skin-popping and finally began to mainline. With heroin, "The world was all right. Nothing mattered once I was there."

He soon found that his life was changing, adjusting itself to making heroin the center of his concerns. There was never enough money from work to support his increasing habit. For a short time, and ironically, given his adolescent resistance to trade school, he felt that if he could get a factory union job, he would have enough money to meet the demands of his addiction. He trained as a tool maker, but detested the work.

It wasn't fashionable being gay to be a tool maker and come home with grease all under your fingernails, chips cutting your hands, and possibly cutting your face. It was just an unfeminine thing to be and I hated it. I left that and I went to hairdressing school which was more my cup of tea. But at the time I was deep in heroin, and though I did manage to get my state license, I had only worked a year when I was arrested for selling heroin—sales and possession. That was in '70; I came out in '72.

John did well in the maximum security prison and went through his first drug program. He eventually became the coordinator for other residents at a prison halfway house. He was in line for a state job as a rehabilitation counselor when his supervisor told him that because of his sexual lifestyle, he could not be given the position. John took this rejection very hard. He had never ventured to make it in the heterosexual world without alcohol or drugs to soothe his anxiety. Now after hard time and hard work, he had taken steps to be himself and be sober in the mainstream world. As he saw it, the response was—you may be sober, but you are still a freak. Not only were his efforts at communion undermined by society's homophobia, but discrimination against his sexuality attacked his sense of agency as well.

Fully aware of the self-destructiveness it symbolized, he took up the needle (like a flag of surrender) and said "Fuck it." Through the next few years, he battled heroin and even went through a very miserable eighteen months of methadone treatment. When he wasn't using dope or methadone, he was back drinking wine. Once again, his life was changed when he sampled a new drug—intravenous cocaine. This became his principal addiction from the late seventies on. Knowing the expense this habit entails, I asked him how he generated his funds.

Basically, the term we used was "hanging paper," which meant writing false checks. I didn't choose to deal too much because my love for the drug was too much. I would always owe more than I would sell. So you know, I went to hanging paper, credit cards, or whatever scheme I could.

I was briefly involved in prostitution when I lived in New York. And it was a very fashionable thing to do at the time. I am heavily endowed in the front so I was able to keep good East Side customers. So rather than push dresses up and down the garment district, I would go out without underwear, so potential customers could see what they were buying and that's how I supported myself while living in New York. In Hartford, there was not much of a business for it unless you were in full drag. One of my brothers had gotten wind of me in full drag working the streets and he came to me and explained that he would kick my ass if he caught me, so I didn't.

John went through countless jobs during these cocaine years—short order cook, busboy, shipping and receiving clerk. Keeping with his self-image, he tried to avoid manual labor jobs, but took on anything else he could find. Finally, in 1981, he entered treatment again at Blue Hills Hospital in an effort to kick his habit. He had a successful admission and was so well-liked that he was recommended for a nursing assistant program. He completed this training at the top of his class and even gave the address at the graduation ceremony. He took on a job as a nursing aide and remained free of heroin and cocaine, but continued to drink in a more controlled fashion. Though he enjoyed the work and felt a sense of pride in helping his patients, he still could not prevent his drinking from affecting his performance. He eventually was caught under the influence of alcohol at work and forced to leave this position.

He rebounded from this setback by discovering nursing temporary agencies. He found this day-to-day arrangement well-suited to his addiction; he could work in short spurts when he felt able to do so and just claim that he was too busy when he did not feel like taking a job. The money was good enough to allow him to resume his more serious drug habit and by the mid-eighties, he was back into intravenous cocaine and heroin. John's descriptions of his cocaine use in particular are very instructive. Israelstam and Lambert have written about the different meanings of alcohol and cocaine in the social and sexual habits of gay men. They have suggested that alcohol may serve a disinhibiting effect to remove the anxiety and guilt associated with homosexual acts. Yet, they suggest, that alcohol is more the primer or catalyst, while cocaine serves to release individuals into a full expression of their sexual desires. If alcohol is the initial remover of barriers, then cocaine is the aphrodisiac.[6]

Cocaine was my love. I think of all the drugs I used cocaine gave me the most freedom. The rush, the bells, the removal of all sexual inhibitions, you know. I was just totally free under the influence of cocaine. It seemed like all my hang-ups dissolved, you know, and I was just able to be Johnny with no remorse, no regrets, no guilt, no shame.

(What were you when you were Johnny?)

I don't know, I really and truly don't know. It depends on how it would hit me. I would say I was a sexual tiger when I was Johnny, due to the feeling I got from cocaine. . . . It allowed me to remove all barriers that might have stopped me from functioning because of guilt or shame. I used cocaine to make prostitutes of others who wanted portions of my cocaine. I would explain to them that under the influence of my cocaine, I became sexually aroused to the point of, you might say, freakishness. However, if you participated in shooting up my cocaine, you have to participate with me in whatever sexual deviance I desired for the time being. Don't get angry, just don't participate if you don't feel you can pay the price.

Actually we were prostituting each other, they wanted it and I wanted it and that's the way it was, you know. Most people are extremely receptive to it. So coke was like a cure for me in a sense. It helped satisfy my sexual hunger and at the same time I used to think of myself as a good Samaritan because my coke helped satisfy their cocaine hunger. It was an exchange situation and if it wasn't, I didn't have no use for you when I was doing my coke. Not every time I did cocaine, but it hit me often in that sense. You were forewarned that "hey, this is it."

By this point in my interview with John, I had come to understand more about this alter ego of Johnny. Johnny was the uninhibited aggressive and sexual imago of John, the vehicle of his demoniac rage and unrestrained destructive agency. Johnny was the sexual tiger filled with ferocious anger and stalking the pleasure that was prohibited him by society at large. Johnny was also the biting tongue that could lash friend or foe if threatened or disrespected. In John's language, Johnny is dominated by oral imagery, most evocatively expressed in his phrase—"sexual hunger." There is a theme here that resonates with many other stories of drug use I have listened to from the men of the Pines. The pursuit of pleasure as a primary goal in life is essentially an autistic one, a residue of an infantlike greed for satiation and sensual bliss. There is an eerie parallel to the stupor an infant slips into after gorging on the breast and the nodding satisfaction of a semiconscious, sated addict.[7] Yet Johnny's sexual demands took the use of cocaine to another place as well. The equation of drugs and sex became a mutual exploitation— a dehumanizing of each partner into a mere vehicle for the other's needs. Here the tiger sprang to life and the sadistic-aggressive dimension of Johnny's oral hunger surfaced. The same mouth that sucks and is satisfied could bare its teeth and bite. There was anger and hatred in Johnny's pleasure—there was a self-loathing that the next hit from the needle was unable to banish. It was the fundamental nature of Johnny's hunger that his appetite went unfilled. Finally, John endured the consequences of all that Johnny had done.

And it was through cocaine, I believe, more so than through my sexual encounters that I became HIV positive. And this led me through a great denial period, "next time they take blood they're going to realize they made a mistake." I just wouldn't accept it. And not accepting it, I felt I could drink my HIV status away, to the point where it seemed like I was in and out of detox every other week.

(How did you learn of your status?)

I wasn't practicing safe sex or being concerned who used my needle or whose needle I was using. And one day somebody I know says, "I know somebody who can buy us some coke." It was a program called "Project Coke"; they take your blood and let you know if you are HIV positive or not and they pay you for it. We went, got twenty-four dollars and a token. Cashed our tokens in, got some wine, took thirty of the forty-eight dollars and bought half a gram of cocaine and proceeded to get high. We took the last fifteen dollars and bought more cocaine and then got a few more dollars somewhere to buy a quart of wine. Three weeks later, out of curiosity I called the program and they said they wanted to talk with me. That's when I found out I was HIV positive.

As John turned to the final chapters of his life story, his hand gestures slowed and he sat more upright in his chair. He conveyed the sense of wisdom and directness that had inspired me months earlier to ask to hear his story. The teasing lilt in his voice and the ironic distance were gone. He spoke to me now in open and unadorned language. His eyes met mine and were not fearful, but insistent that I hear what he had to say.

I went into a denial period, drinking, drinking, drinking, taking drugs, drinking, drinking. That is what brought me to the Pines. It is not being able to cope with being HIV. Since I've been here, I've been going to a support group for HIV-positive individuals. The van takes me down to New London. There is a twelve-step program similar to AA, though it relates to HIV positiveness. This is support, an opportunity to sit down and talk about things that are pertinent to me. I no longer see it as a death sentence, because when I first found out I had it, the first thing I did was to start calculating how to kill myself through an overdose of drugs so it didn't look like I was committing suicide. . . . But through going to AA at the Pines and the support group and the AIDS clinic, Johnny has had a great turnaround in his life.

No, I am not celibate, but my drive is not as demanding as it used to be. For one thing I'm aware that I can be perceived as a genocide tool if I don't practice safe sex. And right now, I practice no sex other than I have two novels that are sexually oriented and when I feel the need for sex I get my novel and go to the bathroom and that's that. Sometimes I do lack companionship, but the support groups and individuals at Lebanon Pines help me to talk about my feelings and frustrations that I relate to my disease.

The Pines has helped me look into me and start removing some of the bullshit that has been so dominant in my life for the last thirty-three years and I'm bringing about slowly a great deal of change. I don't feel as bad about myself as when I first found out, but then again I don't feel as fearful about life as when I first found out. In fact I sometimes see this, in a way, as necessary for my higher power to talk to me, because at that time when I was drinking and drugging, I wasn't listening. And I grew up in a very religious setting and I had thrown all that away, you know, for the sake of a good time, or what I thought was a good time, drinking and drugging.

John's return to a higher power represented more than a spiritual presence in his life. It was a way for him to find his way back to the community and family setting of his youth. Whether he "threw away" this background or was instead first discarded by the members of this community is a point of contention; nevertheless, he found a way to reconnect to his upbringing and to decrease his lifelong isolation. The pursuit of a "good time" was slowly yielding to a gathering sense of self-acceptance and peace in his life, manifested by a deeper sense of communion and social responsibility.

At the Pines, I'm apprehensive about them knowing I'm gay, but I don't have that problem really, because there are some people there that know what's happening and have elected to keep it amongst us. And when we're not in a crowd, we laugh and joke about it, without any companionship or sexual shenanigans, because at this time it would get in the way of things. The next person I involve myself with I would prefer them to be positive, even though I realize that they could give me something or I could give them something. And I would continue to practice safe sex. . . . I think I am humane enough to know that in the moment of passion anything could happen that would prevent safe sex. I know the formula is to put some cocaine in my hands, a couple of dollars in my pocket, with a quart of vodka on any corner in America and I could find someone to accommodate my sexual needs, but right now that is not my main priority.

John's priorities at the Pines, according to his counselors, were his meetings, both AA and HIV support, and helping other men through listening and talking. When he spoke at meetings, people gave him their attention and knew he was unlikely to play to the group for laughs or pity. He applied the same gentleness he had learned as a nurse's assistant to some of the younger black men at the Pines, tutoring them in reading and writing skills, helping them to fill out the endless succession of health and assistance forms. With his glasses, angular elegant features, and satiny voice, he seemed every bit the professor to many of the men at the Pines. As we finished our talk, I asked him how his period of sobriety at the Pines felt.

I don't know if I could use the term "sobriety" because I ain't never been sober so I don't know what it is. I feel within myself that I was drunk long before I took my first drink. That's why I hear people say very often "oh I took my first drink when I was twelve" and I tell you I took my first drink when I discovered I had a need to be accepted in general and by any and everybody, those above me and those below me. And right now I'm working on being accepted by myself. I can attribute my time at the Pines to being constructive and getting me to think about these things. In the street I was always too busy and when I wasn't too busy, I was in denial. Now I have the disease of HIV positiveness and I'm trying to do something about it.

John ended his life story the way he began it, by emphasizing the importance of acceptance and communion in his life. In the four significant domains of his life—his sexuality, his race, his addiction, and his unusual sensitivity—he always felt at odds with the world. Sobriety now meant acceptance of each of these aspects and no longer denying himself what made him unique. Acceptance of our identity and the limitations that inevitably accompany the acknowledgment of who we really are is difficult enough for anyone. For John, living in a society of homophobia and racism, it was a struggle that he resolved through an addiction that literally cut short his life. Yet, as his final words indicated, he achieved some triumph in this struggle; he found a way to himself and through his final example and actions, a way to reaching others. Closing in on death, he stopped running from life and faced its demands for authentic engagement more honestly and completely than he ever had before.

John remained at Lebanon Pines for another six months after this interview and continued his attendance at AA meetings and his support group. He was able to obtain an apartment in New London through an agency that provides subsidized housing for people suffering from AIDS. While living in his apartment, he maintained his sobriety and remained committed to his groups. I heard word of his positive attitude, but also of his worsening physical condition. Ultimately, he succumbed in August 1993 to pneumonia, secondary to his disease, approximately sixteen months after this interview took place.

The message regarding the importance of identity in a man's life emerges very clearly in the story of John Brown's life and death. Extruded from society because of both his color and his sexuality, John Brown struggled to find a sense of communion through his connection to various subcultures in the gay and drug-using communities. Though able at times to achieve a sense of love and friendship through his membership in these communities, he also paid a social price in discrimination and, ultimately, his own physical destruction. Though John engaged in thoughtless and sadistic behaviors at certain stages in his life, he was also a person capable of giving care and aid as a nurse. At the end of his life (ironically only after he had voluntarily elected to abstain from expressing his sexuality), he was able to display a significant amount of generativity through counseling younger men. He also found a way back to a spiritual grounding in the community of his childhood years. Unfortunately, the price he paid to reach this point of acceptance was his own life.

By considering John Brown's identity and not simply his addiction, it encourages us to place his life and death in a larger social context. Although John's addiction was indeed a biological and psychological problem that differentiated him from the majority of people in the society (including most gay and lesbian individuals), his vulnerability to developing addiction and his obstacles to lasting recovery were clearly aggravated by the social rejection he experienced because of his sexuality.

Responding to these pressures, the number of AA groups dedicated to the recovery of gay, bisexual, and lesbian alcoholics has increased dramatically in the last two decades. These groups are helping men and women make the connection between societal repression and their difficulty with recovery and self-acceptance. Treatment facilities are increasingly showing more sensitivity to men's sexuality during their detox and rehab stays. During my work at SCADD, I often saw fellow clients display direct and indirect signs of disapproval when sharing groups or common spaces with gay or bisexual individuals. Though our staff displayed zero tolerance for any kind of homophobic behavior, there is much more that could be done for men as part of their longer-term rehabilitation programming. If men are going to live together over several months, as they do at Lebanon Pines, a group on sexuality and its relationship to addictive problems might open up a lot of minds that have been previously shut out of fear and ignorance.

The solution to addicted gay men's struggles to find a sense of identity extends beyond the kind of recovery and treatment options available to them. To help young men like John Brown avoid the path of addiction, men of my age—teachers, professionals, fathers, community leaders—need to step forward and voice active support for greater freedom in the development of masculine identity. If men had been available in John's life to accept him for who he was and to encourage him to pursue, rather than deny, his self-expression, I am not sure that his life would have ended up in addiction and premature death. John Brown's story is a testimony to the pivotal role a sense of communion and acceptance plays in a man's life. The courageous and generative way in which he met death leaves the legacy of a question to the rest of us—how can we help men like John Brown feel a freedom of identity in open society rather than finding solace behind prison walls or in the injection of a drug?

4. THE BOYS OF SKIPPER'S DECK
Drinking Circles in Chronic Addiction

> "... the norm of non-interference, a certain placid acceptance of things
> as they are, and a good deal of gregariousness without the development
> of bonds of friendship. ... The curious, callous indifference which
> surrounds acts of violence, assaults, robberies, and so on in the Bowery
> bars and on the Bowery streets is the product of a fundamental denial
> of the creation of causal responsibilities.
>
> The Bowery man is, first and foremost, not his brother's keeper, nor
> does he admit any keepership relationship on the part of anyone else."
>
> THEODORE CAPLOW, HOMELESSNESS
> PROJECT STAFF MEETING[1]

I remember my first conversation with Tommy Reilly, one of the drinking circle of Skipper's Deck. He was about to leave the detox, still pretty shaky and by no means ready to embrace the virtues of sobriety. With what must have sounded like a bit of melodrama in my voice, I asked him what he was going to do. He put his thick red hand on my shoulder, winked, and said, "The boys will take care of me."

I'm not sure if I understood fully what he meant at that time by either "the boys" or how they would "take care" of him. Over the years, I came to identify a band of close to a dozen men who constituted a community of drinking buddies.[2] With arrests and treatment, though, all twelve were never actually together in one place.

I also grew to see an ironic double meaning in his phrase, "take care of me." The boys would help him through his withdrawal by sharing a bottle of vodka or a wine jug with him. In this sense, they would provide him with aid for his physical distress. On the other hand, there is the more sinister meaning implied in the words, "to take care of someone." When I was a child stretched out on my favorite couch and watching gangster movies from the 1930's, there would be a scene in which the "Boss" (George Raft or Jimmy Cagney) would say to one of his oversized henchmen (Mike Mazursky or "Slapsie" Maxie Rosenbloom) that some other bootlegger was horning in on his territory. The henchman would give a knowing nod or wink and say, "Don't worry, Boss, I'll take care of him," which, of course, meant that the rival was going to be machine gunned or run down by a black sedan in the next scene.

Ever since Tommy Reilly used that same ominous phrase with me that day, I have periodically contemplated its meaning for his boys and the manner in which they live. Was Tommy saying to me not just that his drinking buddies would give him the booze that would take the edge off his detox, but that they would also be giving him the poison that had been slowly killing him? Regardless of his ability at that moment to acknowledge the destructive implication of his boys' proffered care, I often wondered about this irony in my work with the men who formed his circle.[3]

As I became familiar with the faces and names of men who would repetitively cycle through the detox, treatment program, and Lebanon Pines, I felt increasingly frustrated with our approach to their sobriety. If we knew that one man in the drinking circle was actively drinking and was renting a room, it seemed almost pointless to admit another member of the circle to the detox. I can even remember episodes when two men from the circle would bring in a third man who had gotten too sick or incoherent to manage. At these moments, I felt like we were simply helping him to get back into adequate shape so that he could rejoin the party.

Some of the members of a particular drinking circle had become so interwoven into each others' lives that it made little sense to think about treating each man on an individual basis. The message they conveyed to me through their actions was that they had found a community apart from the sober one we were offering, and whatever its destructive aspects, they either felt unable or unwilling to let go of their place in that community.

My goal in this chapter is to explore the meaning of this destructive communion. I call it destructive because despite the putative communal values it offers to its members (friendship, dialogue, unity), it also perpetuates their addiction and isolation from more authentic and genuine intimacy. To understand the drinking circle, I have chosen to trace the route some members of a particular circle have traveled to arrive at membership. I also examine what they gain and lose from their participation in the circle. Finally, I suggest potential strategies, based in an analysis of identity and meaning, that might help them break away from this community that confines them.

Skipper's Deck

New London, the boyhood home of Eugene O'Neill, was once an important New England summer resort. O'Neill's family's summer cottage, called the Monte Cristo (after Eugene's father James O'Neill's most famous theatrical role, the Count of Monte Cristo), was a modest version of the much more elegant homes and estates that dotted the banks of the Thames River and Long Island Sound. Ocean Beach with a boardwalk and amusement park attracted thousands of visitors all summer long. Inns and motels within blocks of Ocean Beach also accommodated weekend and summer guests.

Though Ocean Beach still offers a striking vista of the Thames River opening to the Sound, New London has long since lost its standing as a fashionable resort. The once brightly painted and well-kept motels near the beach have been converted into rooming houses rented by the week and are often occupied by an indigent and addicted clientele. Skipper's Deck[4] with its cramped efficiencies and rickety porches plays this role for many men from Lebanon Pines. The residents would joke that they "wintered" at the Pines and "summered" at Skipper's Deck. For seventy-five dollars a week, they could get a room to flop in and access to hot water and facilities. Once one of the men was in a room, and staying sober enough to hold onto his monthly city check for the rent, a group would form to play cards. These games would carry on, virtually twenty-four hours a day, with men arriving, leaving, passing out, and dealing in at all hours of the night and day. The package stores opened at eight, and, as they passed the jug to still the morning shakes, the first hand of the day was dealt.

On a particular summer night in July, Danny Doyle, Tommy Reilly, Carl Sobilesky, and Clark Grady ante up their nickels and check their cards. They pass the jugs of wine and keep up a steady round of insults and profanity.

Arthur Drum is the only man not in the game. He is pacing slowly back and forth in the kitchen, taking deep drags on his cigarette. Arthur's most telling physical features are the two tattoos on each side of his forehead. One says "Eat Shit" and the other, "Fuck Off." He had come by that morning shortly after the package stores opened and the game had already commenced. After getting some good drinks inside him, he had ventured out and scored some cocaine, which he had parceled out to himself throughout the day. His supply finished about an hour ago and he is coming down hard. He has no money left and has quit the game and retreated to the kitchen. Arthur is not a regular member of the drinking circle. He had come to Connecticut from Missouri, hitchhiking to avoid problems with the law that had built up there. He had met some of the circle in the detox and found his way to the motel with the hope of scoring money or drugs. He slowly rocks his body as he keeps an eye on the players and the game.

Danny Doyle

Danny Doyle is having a good night at the table, perhaps aided by the fact that he is slightly less drunk than the other players. At forty-one, and after roughly thirty years of continuous alcohol and drug use, he can barely take a drink without quickly getting sick or going directly into a blackout. He still needs to consume alcohol steadily throughout the day to keep away the headaches, shakes, and sweats, but he has actually begun to control his intake. He finds it laughable to think about himself engaging in moderation, but he has grown tired of vomiting and cramping. If he is not exactly a controlled drinker, he is at least a controlled drunk.

A good night of winning only amounts to about five or six dollars; no one gets rich at these games. Still, Danny has already begun to think about what he might do with the money. He could use it toward the next booze run, but he won't be drinking more tonight. He'd rather save it and actually have a decent meal tomorrow for lunch after sleeping in for the morning. He is thinking about going to the "Royal" downtown, a classic chrome diner with a not-half-bad meatloaf dinner that gives you mashed potatoes, carrots, coffee, and pie. Thinking about sitting in the booth, having cash in his pocket, gives Danny a good feeling; he is part of the human race again—just another guy taking a break from work to have a hot lunch. He thinks back to his last real job, driving a truck for Southern New England Brewery, delivering to the markets and liquor stores all around Hartford. It set him back awhile to lose that job; the boss had been an alcoholic himself and had been pretty tolerant of his drinking. Danny had done well and had been maintaining himself on methadone and keeping his drinking more or less under control. Though he kept pulling dirty urines at the methadone clinic, they were only for alcohol and not for drugs and they hadn't kicked him out. They were looking for a reason to let him go, though, and when he missed a payment for his methadone, they seized the chance and started the withdrawal process at a rapid rate.

Danny is a small and wiry man with a wispy mustache and goatee. Despite the drinking and the hardships of street life, he still looks young for his age. He has a narrow face, and half-lidded eyes that give the impression he is high or stoned, even in cold sobriety. Like many of the men at the Pines, there are small white crescent scars on his face and arms, reminders of fights, cigarette burns, and car accidents. It isn't difficult to see the edge he carries around in most of his interactions with people. He doesn't convey a lot of patience or trust and seems to hold the working assumption that most people in the straight world are assholes, and it usually doesn't take long for them to prove him right.

Immersed in the game all day and now into the evening, Danny has managed a deep, protected buzz that has pushed all other problems to the side. He has had good luck with his cards and enjoyed the company of his boys. By the looks of the nodding heads of Carl and Clark (Clark Grady's story is told in Chapter 10), he should be able to play a few more hands and then pocket his winnings in anticipation of his feast at the Royal tomorrow. The only potential obstacle to a pleasant ending to an unexpectedly pleasant day is Tommy Reilly sitting next to him. Tommy is the large, ruddy Irishman, who first told me about his "boys." He has had a bad day of cards and has barely seventy-five cents left to play. Danny knows Tommy's temper and is hoping that it won't go off in his direction. For the moment, Tommy has grown quiet, but Danny knows it can be just a matter of time before he lets go of his fury.

In the tribal world of public high school, there have always been names for the distinct clans of students. In the seventies when Danny and I went to school (he was just three years older and we both went to high school in Connecticut), there were four distinct groups. There were the preppies or the snobs, the better dressed and wealthier kids who were popular and took the social leadership of the school—they ran the yearbook, controlled the student government, and planned the prom. There were the nerds or grinds or wonks, universally dismissed by their fellow students and loved by the teachers; they won the academic awards, and went on to private colleges or received full scholarships from the public ones. There were the jocks (and in particular, the football team), who had a certain kind of hold over the entire school, like decadent robber barons. And then there were the heads. The heads were the students who looked perpetually stoned, who smoked marijuana and tobacco in the lavs and the courtyards, in their cars and on the football fields, at the bustops and on the buses, who in fact never seemed not to be smoking something.

Danny had gravitated to the heads after finding little success academically at school. His poor performance especially frustrated him because his father was a teacher in his school. By the time he was in junior high, he had become a class clown and on a couple of occasions had stolen money from the pocketbook of one of his teachers. He felt like a loser and a nobody until he joined up with a group of kids who were drinking in the woods.

. . . The first time I drank I stole a bottle of beer from my father. I liked it. I was about eleven or twelve. There were a lot of older kids in the neighborhood that we knew. And we started making homemade wine when I was twelve. And I really got into drinking that. We used to put it in the woods a lot. We had forts in the woods and we were always hanging there. We got drunk in the woods and I liked it. By the time I was fourteen, we were buying beer from a friend of mine whose older brother was drinking beer a lot.

. . . The way I felt when I drank it, I felt good. I felt energetic, I had no fears, you know . . . I think that's when basically everything started. I felt like the king of the world.[5] I wanted to keep that feeling like that, so any time there was mention of beer or getting some, I wanted to be there. . . . Eventually I started to smoke pot. I felt the same way with that. I felt good . . . I felt in control. I felt like I was kind of a leader, people looked up to me. . . . I don't know if they did, I felt that way. Because there was something different, you know. I got into it, it's considered the heads, that people, you know—heads, drug addicts, you know, I felt like I belonged to something.

. . . I felt bigger than the kids I was hanging around with because they weren't really into it yet. I kind of hung out with two groups. I kind of drifted off to the kids with the drugs, and eventually I lost the old friends I hung with. I still hung with them, but I didn't see anything in common with them anymore. I just wanted to get high all the time, you know. . . . When I couldn't get marijuana, I got really depressed I couldn't find it . . .

For the first time in his life, Danny had discovered a sense of belonging and even community. He was one of the heads. By defining himself as a member of this crowd, he accrued some degree of agency as well; he gained status for his dope smoking and a sense of empowerment through his association with the other drug users. In these early adolescent years, the seeds of his connection to a drinking circle were sown. As he began to craft his own life story, the world of drugs was invested with a power to help him feel located and wanted in a group. Danny's words suggest that the taking of drugs not only gave him a physical pleasure, they allowed him to experience a sense of identity through his linkage to a community. This community was in opposition to the mainstream culture and was predicated on his sense of being an outlaw or rebel.

Before Danny turned eighteen, he had been asked to leave the high school, due to truancy and various problems with drinking and smoking pot on school grounds. Shortly after leaving school, he tried heroin and loved it. He recalled how his girlfriend at the time had found out about his heroin use and given him an ultimatum to stop. In a revealing and pivotal moment of his identity formation, he chose to continue his drug use and gave up this intimate relationship.

In desperation, his parents intervened and sent him to the Institute of Living, a private psychiatric hospital. Danny stayed nine months and received treatment both for depression and substance abuse. Even after the lengthy stay, Danny continued to drink and get high at every opportunity. Everyone else he knew drank or smoked and he felt he was just like everyone else. His parents and the hospital were making too big a deal out of his drug use.

Danny still lived at home, but eventually ended up in a rehab program because of a DWI arrest. Some of the friends he made at the rehab gave him pointers about how to scam doctors for narcotic pain killers and sedatives. For the next few years, he kept himself constantly drugged either by conning doctors or using counterfeit prescriptions. He also had a job delivering packages that allowed him access to people's houses. He would ask to use their bathrooms, particularly if they were elderly, and then pilfer their medicine cabinets for sedatives and narcotics. He eventually piled up a series of arrests for both prescription forgeries and thefts.

From the early eighties on, he alternated between rehab programs and halfway houses, mostly as alternatives to going to jail. He also began to attend methadone programs, once again to avoid jail and minimize his use of other drugs. When he was kicked out of one of his early methadone programs, he even did nineteen months at Daytop, a therapeutic community that emphasized confrontation by his peers of his "dope fiend" attitude and the "false self" he had created with drugs. Danny ultimately liked this program and experienced his longest period of sobriety since age 11, but when he left, he immediately started drinking again and soon picked up drugs once more.

I got to the point that I was so used to being in a program and told to do things, that being outside felt kind of lonely, because of not being around the people I was with all the time, I had made a lot of friends in there. I could have very easily gone and visited them, but I didn't. I got institutionalized, I guess. I didn't know how to deal with things outside. Kind of looking back, "I gotta do this at a certain time, because I got to be back there." And then all of a sudden I got this freedom, I don't know what to do with it. And it kind of threw me off guard.

Danny is clearly expressing the central importance in his life of belonging to a community. In fact, the role of drugs was secondary to his need to be part of a larger group or organization. Danny felt comfortable in the therapeutic community, even though he was drug-free. Guided by the institution and his friends in Daytop, he was able to feel a structure to his life. What was hardest for him and most overwhelming was "freedom"—the demand that he actively engage in choices and intimate relationships in his life.

One of the attractions of the therapeutic community or the drinking circle for Danny is not only its communal value, but its ability to "take care" of his struggle with agency. Having never formed a strong sense of either agency or communion, he has yet to figure out how to function alone in a world that expects self-mastery and responsibility. When confronted with these demands, he experiences an anxiety and despair that must be deflected. Enlisting blind habit, he returns to the circle of his drinking peers. The familiar routine of his addiction can then divert any claims upon him for active and responsible agency.

As if unconsciously seeking another institution to structure his life, Danny ended up going to prison for a year after further probation violations and petty offenses. He then resumed the methadone program in 1984 and managed to stay out of any significant trouble for the next four years leading up to his truck driving job. His escalating drinking during this time eventually led to the loss of this job. This setback marked the shift in his life from living at home and marginally functioning in the work world to homelessness and perpetual rehabs and programs.

I managed to hang out with people that were in the same boat as me, so there was always somebody worse off than me. But compared to what I was at, I knew I was on the way down. And the way I was feeling about myself and the way, you know, I was as a person, I was going way down.

Danny eventually made it up to Lebanon Pines and has cycled through there on six different occasions. By spending so much time there, he became an integral part of the drinking circle that would eventually take up residence at Skipper's Deck.

I think we are all basically the same way. We try to tell somebody who isn't using how we feel, and you know, you can't really get along with somebody who hasn't been there, as far as telling them where you're at. . . . We know how we are, and we basically gravitate to each other. I guess what it comes down to is they're your friends at heart. Whether you get along, I mean, half the time we're ripping each other off, but everybody seems, we always seem to go back there, because that's all you know, man. . . . We're the only ones that will put up with each other, no one else will.

. . . I think sometimes we compare how we are with somebody else who uses. These people will have more physical problems than me, and I'm worse off than some other people, as far as money, you know, I got nothing.

. . . Also you're not alone when you're with these people. It's better than sitting all by yourself. They're your friends, whether you like them or not, or whether you get along with them. You like them, you feel for them. I do. I think I've come to like a lot of them, whether they rip you off or not, they're still your friends.

. . . And I'm no better than they are when it comes down to it. I go through the same shit they do. I could be just as ornery, if not worse, but people haven't given up on me.

. . . People who don't drink don't understand this. They'd say, "Why do you keep doing it?" That's the way it is, we're alcoholics. We're addicted to it; it's all we know.

When Danny declares that "there is no one else who would put up with us," he is articulating a fundamental ingredient of the drinking circle relationship. Many men over the years have expressed this sentiment to me. In the circle, each member holds more or less equal status, but outside the circle, they feel inferior and ashamed of their lives. It should not be surprising that the men of the Pines scour the arrest logs and obituaries each day to see what ex-residents of the Pines or acquaintances from the detox have made the morning newspaper; it's not very different from college graduates who go through their alumni magazines to compare their respective status to their peers.

In acknowledging his comfort inside the drinking circle, Danny is able to express his discomfort with the sober world, especially AA.

Well, there's no excuse for drinking if you can control it or if you can stop, there's ways to stop. But sometimes you *choose* not to. Some of the feelings get so overwhelming that you don't want to stop. You can talk to some stranger in AA about your problems, about how you feel, they might listen for an hour, but after the hour, a lot of times, they won't even pick up the phone and talk to you if you call

them. I know the phonies in AA too. That comes to trust. . . . A lot of people I
don't trust.

Even though he sees drinking as a choice he is making, the idea of choosing a different life is both desirable and overwhelming to him.

It's hard to do. But I guess there comes a point in life where you have to. I'm not saying forget all your old friends, but sometimes you gotta reach out and start trusting
. . . because if I don't, I'm going to be back to the same place. I don't want to go
there. I like these people, I consider them the people I ran with, and I know them,
but I can't be with them forever. . . . It will go on and on. And a lot of these people
that I know, have died. They were in the same boat as me. They just didn't want to
stop. Never had enough, you know. Maybe they were suicidal, but I'm not.

Danny is able to articulate the danger of remaining in his circle, but he has
no clear sense of how he can break out of this world and avoid the lethal fate
of many of his friends. In all his forty-one years, he has never had a relationship
for longer than a couple of months. He claims that he is not ready for one, a
couple of nights here and there was good, but he doesn't want to answer to
anyone. He also does not allow himself to grow closer to his family.

My family loves me. I hear my niece and nephew always ask about me. And I seen
my niece a few months ago. I had just got out of jail, and she doesn't know I was in
jail, she's twelve, she doesn't know, she doesn't even know I'm here. Christ, I saw
the kid and all she could do was kiss me and hug me. . . . And this is what I'm running from, you know. I ask myself why I am running from this, people love me. I
love them too. . . . Because I don't feel comfortable. Why not? I feel like the black
sheep, why? My family, they love me to death. I don't know why I feel that way.

Tommy Reilly

When Tommy Reilly suffers ambivalences about the life he has chosen for himself, he has found he can quickly lay them aside with another shot of booze.
The only problem is that at age thirty-nine his body has already begun to break
down. Tommy has a reputation in the New London facility for the ferocity of
his detoxes. He has seizures, becomes violently sick, and drifts into a psychotic
paranoia. He stays in bed for three to four days and does not really emerge
from an incapacitated state until the fifth or sixth day of his stay. His face tells
the story of his alcoholism—the blotched red skin with tinges of blue from
damaged capillaries beneath the eyes, his nose swollen, red and porous, his

cheeks jowly and his lips cracked and raw. Yet completely incongruous with his face, and perhaps a key to his own state of mind, is his long, reddish-copper hair. He wears it in a seventies rock star cut—with a short bang in front and far down his shoulders in back, tapering slightly. With his alcohol-ravaged face, his 6'1" size, and a pristine white Celtics warmup jacket, his carefully groomed mane of hair makes for an unnerving appearance. He looks a bit like an aging roady for a rock band of the seventies who has fallen asleep at a keg party, only to regain consciousness two decades later.

Tommy, himself, might not reject this last comparison to a seventies roady. His favorite part of life is the early seventies, the summers before he started work at Electric Boat. He really has never wanted to get any older or to have more responsibility than that—just getting a buzz and hanging out with his girl at Waterford Beach. For him, the beauty of being high is that he can give up any active role in a relationship, any sense of being accountable to another person.

I never grew up. I was afraid to grow up, still am. Always ran from responsibility, ran from anything too tough. Didn't want to be tied to one thing. Wanted to be a free bird. Obviously the drinking was just way out of control. I knew it was years ago, but I really didn't care. I just didn't think that I'd live to be old, and I didn't really care about that either. I was almost on a mission. . . . To be the biggest partier. It's sick. Just thinking like a kid. I would stay in 1972 forever if I could. Things were perfect then. I hung at the beach every day and I had Peggy. I was in love, she was beautiful. My little cheerleader. I'd play ball, we'd drink some beers, partied some. Well, by then I was already out of high school. I just wasn't ready to mature. . . .

And I'm almost forty now, and I've been living the same way all those years. I moved around a lot, made a lot of money. Spent it all. Most of these jobs, I would quit. . . . I would just quit to go party or just to move. I was getting arrested a few times, I was getting hot, I'm out of here.

The girls were there for my needs and to have someone. I liked them to be there, but I didn't like ones that talked too much either. I wanted them to be there when I wanted them to be there, because I didn't want to be alone. My greatest fear was growing old alone. People have called me on it in the past. You want to live in the past, or you have to forget the past, or you can't keep thinking about the past. . . . That's all you ever talk about. I said, oh. But I don't want to be forty years old. You know I look at my brother and he's got the nice house, and the job, and the family. I say I want that on one hand, but on the other hand I say, God that's boring. Although what I'm doing now at the Pines is not exactly thrilling. It's not exactly fun. It's easier. All I do is make a couple of meetings and play cards. . . .

But it's weird. The first couple of times I went to rehab, I'd have visitors. I don't get phone calls, visitors, or anything any more. Everybody's just kind of said, hey, forget it. When he grows up. It's almost unsaid that when I grow up and when I get it together, they'll be there. But for now, it's like, you're on your own. Part of it should have been a long time ago, but I don't think it would have made any difference because I was going to do what I was going to do and nobody was ever going to tell me what to do. That was my thing.

Tommy's words clearly reflect his attitude toward communion. He does not want to be lonely, but he also does not want any binding responsibility or compromise in his relationships. Drinking companions provide an effective solution to this demand. By finding a circle based in minimal expectations (sharing material resources and monitoring each other's physical well-being), he can address his fear of loneliness without any demand that he make any personal or intimate connection.

Even with his heavy drinking, Tommy had managed to maintain a fairly steady and lucrative working life for several years. After the golden summer he described, he became a highly respected draftsman at Electric Boat. He worked there for six years, leaving during the strike of 1979 to become a freelance contractor, working mostly for shipyards down south. He did short stints for various outfits, making $1,500 to 1,600 a week and living in motels. By the time he left E. B., he was a full-blown alcoholic, drinking every day from morning to night, as much as a quart to a half-gallon of whiskey a day.

I didn't worry about anything. I was just carefree, and fun loving, and having a good time, well that's not true. But I would drink and all my ambitions would go away and I would seem like I didn't care about anything and at the time, I didn't. So it was just masking all that. I didn't have really any feelings. I just didn't care. . . . So I would just drink, get drunk, and have a good time, and laugh. People are attracted to that. I don't know if they want to be like that, or they just like it in other people. We'd have fun. But, of course, eventually the fun stops. It's not fun anymore. You're just drinking to make yourself feel normal.

Tommy especially liked working and drinking in the south because he found the society to be more traditional and male-based. Along with his emphasis on fun and lack of responsibilities, he very much wanted women who would be compliant to his wishes and place him at the center of their concerns.

I used to meet them at work, so I wouldn't be drunk. And I'd always treat them real well, at the beginning. But I was kind of a shithead. I'd try to mold them to get them just the way I wanted them and it worked for a while. But then they'd find out what's going on after I'd get drunk and smack them around a couple of times. That would kind of end it. . . . I'd just tell them the way I wanted them to do things. How I wanted them to dress, not dress. You compliment them on certain things just to make sure they did it that way or I could be a real shit and flat out tell them I didn't like this or that. . . . I found out that most women want to be led. Not so much anymore though. This was in the seventies.

When I asked Tommy to provide me with a self-defining memory, it also concerned an incident in which he struck a woman in the face. I asked Tommy more about this and he explained that he had been hitting women all the way back to his teenage years. In fact, it seemed that the more he cared about a woman or the relationship, the more likely he was to end up striking her until she left him. As he grew older, he would consciously choose partners whom he didn't particularly like in the hope that he would avoid getting angry and becoming physical with them. Eventually he found that it did not matter; he would end up hitting them anyway.

Tommy's violence with women and his ambivalence about it suggests another reason why a drinking circle provides such an effective refuge for him. He is less likely to get emotionally invested in his drinking friendships and stirred to the point of violence. On the other hand, when he does become violent, he can feel a sense of justification and freedom to express his aggression. In fact, he even finds that violence gains him a certain authority and status among the circle.

In the early eighties, Tommy intensified his travels both north and south, as well as taking trips as far west as Tacoma, Washington. He always managed to find work and money, but his drinking continued, with daily drunks and blackouts. Remarkably, he did not have his first detox until 1983, when he was twenty-eight, after ten years of daily heavy drinking. It did not slow him down, however, and he estimated that he was arrested forty to fifty times in seven or eight different states for alcohol-connected offenses— drunk and disorderly, DWI, breach of peace, criminal trespassing, destruction of property, assault, and domestic violence. He never did more than a night in jail and always found a way to avoid serving time for these charges, either by leaving the state or negotiating a fine or probation. At no point did he make any serious attempt to curtail his drinking.

I knew something was wrong, but not so much about people. I didn't care. Fuck them, I still had money. . . . It was bothering me when I woke up, and I wasn't really sleeping much, but I would sleep for an hour or so here and there. I would just start thinking, damn, and I was getting sick a lot, and I was vomiting blood. I was hurting because I wouldn't eat. But I'd have a few drinks and I'd say, fuck them, I don't care now. Finally I knew I had to get out of the motel I was in because I had no idea how long I'd paid for it. And I was so paranoid that I wouldn't go out unless it was at night. I wouldn't let the maid in to clean up the place. The place was a mess. I'd just sit and drink. Turn on the TV and just sit there and drink until you pass out, then you get back up and drink until you pass out. You have a few drinks to try to get your legs steady enough to try to take a shower, and then you just sit there and drink some more, pass out. I guess I was in that motel for a few weeks. I'm not really sure.

From this particular motel room in New Orleans, Tommy called SCADD and asked them if he could come back to New London for a detox and his first long-term program. From that point on, in the four years that followed, Tommy went through thirteen different rehab programs, ranging from fourteen days to six months in duration, as well as another thirty to forty detoxes. He became acquainted with the various men of Lebanon Pines and eventually joined the circle at Skipper's Deck. Life with the boys took the following shape.

It starts out crazy because, well, nobody really sleeps, at least I didn't. You sleep for a few hours or a little bit, get up and have a few drinks, just try to make it through the night. I had an apartment. Danny had an apartment on the second, Clark on the third. Danny would be knocking on the door three or four in the morning and I'd let him in and we would have a drink and there might be two or three other people there passed out. Squirrel[6] would stop by with some Percosets. Somebody else would stop by, have some crack. Whatever anybody had they would just kind of put it on the coffee table and everybody did it that was there, that was awake.

In the morning, the thing was we had to make the run to the liquor store at 8:00. So I was the only one who had a car. So first usually someone would walk up to Sammy's, that was the liquor store, but we never knew when it would be open.

. . . And we'd get to the liquor store and we'd buy a few half gallons and we'd buy some mix and we'd go back. And we'd just drink for a few hours so everybody started feeling normal and nobody was sick anymore. And then Squirrel might run and get some coke or something. That was their idea. If it wasn't there, I didn't care.

The joke was that the ambulance used be there at least twice a week to take somebody. We were playing cards one day and this guy, Will, he just rolled over backwards in his chair. I don't know if he had a seizure or passed out or what. We just called the ambulance and had somebody else just sit in to play cards. We'd just keep going. We trashed the apartment. I ripped all the cabinets off the walls, broke up all the furniture, smashed the little window that goes out to the patio. We just trashed it. I don't know why. We got in a lot of fights too.

. . . The cops were down all the time because we were so loud. They were always being called because somebody was doing something stupid all the time. Somebody was stumbling around drunk, breaking mailboxes. . . . The parties would be loud and we'd have the door open. We'd be barbecuing out back and it'd be snowing out and everybody'd be all drunk.

Ironically, in this mixture of adolescent "good times" and malevolent violence, Tommy finds a way of being that comes most closely to his understanding of himself. He can give up all responsibility for his actions and think no further than the next deal or drink. Though he squashes any sense of loneliness (by having contact with his boys virtually twenty-four hours a day), he is never expected to reveal any intimate aspects of himself, nor does he ask for intimate self-disclosures in return. The refrain that he repeated throughout his interview with me, "I didn't care," finds no resistance or confrontation among the drinking circle. Other than sharing good times and resources, he is not expected to care. If he becomes violent, there may be physical injury, but there is no emotional consequence. In contrast, he knows that in the few intimate relationships he has had in his life, his violence has cost him the love of someone for whom he actually cared a great deal. With the boys, he can abdicate any deep emotional commitment or moral responsibility.

Both Danny and Tommy accept that they might lie or steal from each other; their expectations of relationship with each other do not extend to these minimal codes of conduct. However, as Danny explained, their lives have led them to expect no better, so they cease to question the ethics of their circle's actions. In such a world, Tommy finds a troubled, but familiar, kind of comfort.

Carl Sobilesky

Unlike Danny Doyle or Tommy Reilly, Carl Sobilesky did not start drinking at a young age, and without one shattering incident in his life, it is unlikely that he would have ever become an alcoholic.

After Carl graduated high school and completed two more years in trade school, he took a mechanic's job for ArtCo Tool and Die. He was married at age twenty-one; both he and his wife were still virgins. They bought a house

in Montville, Connecticut, near New London, and settled into the routine of
fifties suburbia. Carl's passions were bowling and fishing. He would bowl in
a league on weeknights and fish on weekends and vacations, as much as possible. His wife would make tuna sandwiches on thick hard rolls and they
would picnic on the boat.

When Carl was twenty-seven, his whole life changed in the course of one
evening at the bowling alley. Two weeks earlier at the same lanes, he had had
a ferocious headache that might have been a warning of what was to come.
This particular night, he was in the midst of a game when he reached for a
ball and tumbled over. He was bleeding from his mouth, ears, and nose. He
had suffered a massive cerebral hemorrhage and went into a coma. He
remained in the hospital for eighteen weeks, hovering between life and
death. Finally, the doctors decided to risk surgery and were successful in
reducing the cranial pressure. He recovered over time with virtually no physical impairment, but he suffered from a severe change in his personality.

Carl returned to his daily life after his stroke unable to work or even to resume his old hobbies. He would lie in bed for days on end and then display odd
impulsive behavior. He would run out into the street and make threatening statements. He would make up stories or slip out of reality into mostly incoherent
fantasies. He no longer engaged in a sexual relationship with his wife, and
showed no caring or affection toward her. After a series of frightening and erratic behaviors, such as telling a neighbor he had a gun in his pocket (which he
did not), he was admitted to Connecticut Valley Hospital. The physicians
could find no lesions or evidence of brain damage to explain his behavior, but
they elected to medicate him with thorazine. He continued his pattern of impulsive actions, despite the medication, and even with high doses was un-
changed. He remained in the psychiatric hospital for over a year (an amount of
time that was more common then and would be almost unheard of now) and
felt depressed and cut off from his wife and family. Despite their efforts to reach
out to him, he pushed them away, behaving sullenly and cruelly.

Carl truly believed he could never get well, never learn to work and love
again. He wanted to protect his family from the crippled and destructive
person he felt he had become. He begged his wife to divorce him. He sat
wide awake in his hospital bed at night, feeling the full vacancy of his life.
Without his trade, without his capacity to be a responsible husband to his
wife, he had lost all sense of identity or meaning and wished with all his
heart that he could simply die.

In the last six months of his hospitalization, he met a female patient who
was an alcoholic. She had money and methods of smuggling wine into the

residence hall of the hospital. Carl finally discovered something that gave him pleasure and eased the pain of his humiliation. He began a relationship with this woman that was based in their drinking together as much as possible. A new doctor ultimately confronted Carl about his drinking and also took him off the thorazine. He put him on an antidepressant and within a month Carl was finally ready to leave the hospital. He left with a drinking habit that soon became the central activity of his life. Though he returned to his wife, they were divorced within a year and he took to the streets of Hartford.

Suffering from what was most likely a combination of mental illness and alcoholism, Carl lived a life of homelessness, shelters, rooming houses, skid bids,[7] and detoxes for the next fifteen years (from 1969 to 1984). During that time, he managed to have one period of almost four years of sobriety, in which he married a fellow client from a rehab facility and fathered a son. He could never bring himself to love this woman, and, after a layoff from a job, resumed drinking.

During one seven-year stretch, he claimed to have lived in an abandoned car in a parking lot in Hartford.

Up the street from the Hartford Hotel, heading towards the Hooker Hotel, there was an Amoco transmission place on the right hand side. Well, there was a 1966 Ford four-door sedan parked up against that building. You could only get in one door of the whole car. That was home for me for seven years. And I'll tell you the truth, when I went in there at night, no matter how early or late, no one followed me. I didn't give that one up. And I was in a truck, a railroad truck, underneath the railroad station for two years before that, but I got kicked out of there. I got arrested in there.

Yeah, that car was sweet. My bottle was my antifreeze. That's no joke. I had two or three blankets. I'd keep an empty wine bottle in there for my bathroom during the night. . . . And if I didn't have wine, I'd drink aftershave lotion, cleaning products, canned heat. That's sterno—you'd squeeze the liquid out—pure alcohol. Mix it with grape Kool Aid; horrible tasting, but it does the trick.

Carl collected cans and bottles, received vouchers for food from missions and social services. He scoured the dumpsters and the alleyways near night clubs and bars for unfinished beer cans and liquor bottles. He stole and panhandled when he grew more desperate. Through all these years, he lived a solitary existence, gliding in and out of various drinking circles, but never making a sustained connection with a particular group. He had one simple guiding principle that defined this time in his life, a total surrender of agency.

You're walking down the street and you wonder why people are heading over to the other side, literally. They see what's coming. I think the whole key to this, Doctor, is that you finally, you eventually, or you even start out with one philosophy and the only philosophy: You just don't care. And when I say you don't care, I also say that you get to the point where you don't care if you live or die. So you will just stand on the curb with your jug in your hand and walk across the street. You don't care what's coming.

One of his major sources of pain was that he had lost all contact with his family at this point. After too many drunken phone calls, embarrassing incidents, and bail fees for his various arrests, they had changed their phone number to an unlisted one and told him never to come and see them unless he could demonstrate he had achieved a lasting sobriety. His parents had been loving to him, but they had no experience with alcoholism and with his mental condition. They were proud working people set in their routines and could not make sense of Carl's behavior and his refusal to help himself.

Eventually Carl was able to get a monthly SSD check, which allowed him to stay in cheap boarding houses, which he shared with other alcoholics, prostitutes, ex-cons, the indigent elderly, and, on a few odd occasions, traveling circus performers. By 1980, he had migrated back south from Hartford to Middletown and found a room in an old hotel.

For most of that decade, he would pull together enough money for his wine for the day and then sit by the banks of the Connecticut River. He would wait for the warm current of wine to channel through his body and then let his mind take him where he fancied.

I dreamed a lot. This is very important. I dreamed a *lot*. The moment I got a jug in my hand, or even without one, no matter what time of day, I had dreams. Some of them crazy, but they were dreams. You could stand in back of the Sears and Roebuck parking lot overlooking the Connecticut River with Harbor Park down to your right and the rocks you can drink on to your left, and the birds and ducks, and the sunrise. I'd stay there three or four hours. The cops don't bother you. They leave you alone, as long as you're off Main Street.

. . . I've always dreamed of owning a log cabin on about 9,250 acres of land that's all mine, you know fenced in, posted with a trout stream that has maybe 12- to 14-inch trout all through it. A pond, ducks, two dogs, a cat. All the fishing equipment for me to fish with, a gun. Self-sufficient, no electricity, a kerosene lamp. Also a long porch, a rocking chair, the whole thing. Also heroes—not the supermen, karate type or the good cops, doctors. But sports, hockey, baseball, things I could never do. Coach little league. There's all kind of things I'd dream. Food, food! I'd be sitting there with a goddamn Saltine cracker in my hand, wishing it was a steak. Not too bad, not too really bad, you know.

Similar to Danny and to Tommy, Carl relishes the release from agency and responsibility that drunkenness can bring him. He is free to dream of great acts without engaging in any movement more complicated than raising the bottle to his lips. Sitting by the river, he is free of any entanglements or expectations that relationships might place on him. He is able to let the routine of his alcoholism guide his days. He rises with the opening of the package stores, drinks until any demands or worries dissipate. As this morning buzz wears off, he takes action to find bottles and cans until he has enough to buy a jug for the afternoon and evening. Nighttime brings on the last few drinks and the foggy descent into sleep.

Carl had his first admission to the Pines in the early eighties and found that its log cabin country atmosphere was not so different from his daydreams. Here was a place that for the first time since his cerebral hemorrhage allowed him to feel a modicum of self-respect. He was able to work, attend groups and meetings, and participate in the holidays and celebrations of the community. Lebanon Pines gave him the prospect of becoming an active contributor to life again; he could step away from the alcoholic passivity that defined his street life. He could allow himself to take the risk of seeking communion through friendship, dialogue, caring, and identification with Lebanon Pines as his "community."

He had two prior long stays of seven months and two and one-half years before he returned for a stay of five years. He became the store manager at the Pines and one of the men who defined the old timers' relationship to the place. He was fiercely loyal to Bill Sugden and the other staff of the Pines. Though he continued to display eccentric behavior, had poor hygiene, and tended to ignore social boundaries about ending casual conversations, he was well-tolerated by the staff and residents. He even managed to fulfill one of his fantasies by serving as the pitcher for the Lebanon Pines softball team on occasion. In contrast to his time on the street or among the drinking circles of Hartford or Middletown, he felt a genuine sense of reciprocal relationship and nurturance.

At the very end of the five years, the frustrating unpredictability of mental illness caused his impulsive and erratic behavior to escalate. His hygiene and social appropriateness declined. He could no longer manage the store and grew despondent over the loss of his position. Despite many interventions by the staff at the Pines and the outpatient psychiatric services, he was unable to remain a resident and was discharged to a sheltered living situation. He soon left there and returned to the drinking circles and walking the streets. For the second time in his life, he exchanged a life of meaning that combined agency and communion (his role as store manager and community member of Lebanon Pines) for the routine of the street alcoholic. Back on the streets and drinking, he increasingly found his way to the rooms of Skipper's Deck. By seeking out the boys, he could at least re-create for an evening the sense of fellowship he had found at the Pines.

Finishing up the Game

As the evening of poker at Skipper's Deck turns to night, Tommy Reilly has gone into a blackout. The room is slightly blurred, but almost mechanically, he can assess his hand and make the appropriate bid. His hands have an irritating tremble to them and he continues to sip at the vodka in front of him. He looks with suspicion at the other players around the table. Danny is continuing to ride a winning streak and is doing his best to hustle the deal along, wanting the game to end soon with his streak intact.

Tommy Reilly watches Arthur Drum as he moves in and out of the kitchen shadows, and then turns back again to survey the others at the table. It is getting closer to eight at night, closing time for liquor stores in Connecticut. Tommy is feeling he is going to need to make one more run, but he has 25 cents in front of him and nothing in his pockets. Danny has already used his earlier winnings to buy two half gallons and he isn't going to do any more drinking tonight. Clark has fallen back to the couch and is now fast asleep. The table before Clark's chair is clear of change and Tommy knows for certain that, by this time in a day-long drunk, Clark has given away any other money he might have. Carl is also nodding off, but this is different. He is new to the games and is sitting there with bills in his front shirt pocket. Tommy can't tell for sure, but it looks like maybe there are four singles. Carl has taken money out of a beaten up brown wallet and stuffed it in his shirt pocket throughout the day. As Tommy eyes Carl, Arthur says to no one in particular, "I feel like shit. I got to mellow this shit. Bag of dope to coat my slope."

Tommy starts to get that twisting in his gut that will quickly rise into a vice-like headache. It is always how his paranoid thoughts start. He knows where this scene is heading. So does Danny, who wastes no time in scooping his majestic sum of five dollars off the table and into his pocket. The game is over. Tommy sweeps the cards off the table on to the floor with his thick red arm and lets out a long low "Fuck." Now his eyes are all on Arthur, whose eyes in turn have located Carl's pocket. Tommy says another "Fuck Me" to himself for having let a busted cokehead come and spend the day.

Then it happens. Arthur has moved from the kitchen toward Carl, leaning in toward the pocket of bills. Just as his body lunges forward, it is flying faster backward, blood spraying in the air, bits of glass sleeting down, amidst the red. Without rising from his seat, Tommy had backhanded the ashtray into Arthur's face and broken his nose.

Arthur slumps back against the cabinet below the kitchen sink, semiconscious. Danny jumps up and runs into the kitchen, grabs a dish towel and places it over Arthur's face to slow the bleeding. He shouts to Tommy, who still has not moved from his chair,

"Fuck, Tommy. Why'd you use the fucking ashtray? Jesus Christ." Tommy looks down into his hand, which is also bleeding and splintered with shards of glass.

"He was going to take my money for his fucking dope." Tommy then reaches forward and takes the bills from Carl's pocket and then slowly drags Carl to the couch and plops him down next to Clark. He reaches down into Carl's backpocket and takes out the brown wallet. When he sees that it is empty, he feels a sense of righteousness. He has fought for what was his and there had been nothing else to share. He turns to Danny.

"Let's throw this bag of shit in my car and bring him to Doc Alpert at L&M.[8] I'll go to Sammy's after and be back here with the jug."

Danny and Tommy lift Arthur, who is breathing hard and still dazed, and drape his arms across their shoulders. They leave the room, as his feet, dragging behind him, scrape across the linoleum floor of the hall. Inside on the couch, Clark and Carl draw breaths with phlegmy wheezes. As they sleep sitting upright side by side, Carl's arm has fallen forward over the shoulder of Clark in the manner of an affectionate embrace.

Leaving the Circle of Skipper's Deck

What would it take for Danny, Tommy, or Carl to leave the drinking circle and find an alternate identity and membership in a sober community? We have already seen some clear indications in the lives of both Danny and Carl. Both men are capable of staying sober and functioning effectively in institutional communities. Danny managed nineteen months of sobriety in Daytop and more than two years of sobriety at Lebanon Pines (if we put together his six different stays). If we combine Carl's three stays at the Pines, he logged over eight years of sobriety while living there. It should be clear from these extensive periods of sobriety that their return to drinking is an expression of their despair and confusion about living in situations that overwhelm them with feelings of freedom, responsibility, and isolation.

The critical factor of the drinking circle for Danny and Carl is not the access it offers to alcohol. Rather, the drinking circle affords them a way of counteracting the loneliness and purposelessness they feel in their lives divorced from institutional structures. Without meaningful intimate relationships or ongoing employment to anchor their lives, the drinking circle provides a ballast that holds them in place. It is a source of amusement, routine, gossip, in some cases sexual fulfillment (though this particular group of men did not acknowledge this function), material support, and perhaps, most critically, identity. If I am nothing else, at least I know I am one of the "boys."

When we consider that the standard treatment approach places a man like Danny or Carl in a twenty-eight-day program and then at best into a halfway house (there are long waiting lists in New London County) and more likely into outpatient counseling and AA, we can see the daunting task they are hoping to accomplish. I can only guess what it would be like for me to give up my marriage and my job as a professor with no clear prospect of how I would replace either one. This analogy is at the heart of Fingarette's argument about heavy drinking (see the Blind Habit section of Chapter 2) as the central activity of these men's lives. Asking them to stop means stripping them of their fundamental means for knowing who they are. Once cut loose from an institutional structure and without the drinking circle, they face an emptiness that is literally too much to bear.

Having stated that Danny and Carl can maintain sobriety in institutional settings, I am well aware that this fact hardly answers the question of long-term sobriety. Neither the state nor the federal government is willing to support these men for the next three decades of institutional living. What their success at Lebanon Pines suggests is that their treatment must offer a gradual transition over extended time from institutional reliance to self-reliance. It must also continue to surround them with peers who have a healthy attitude toward all aspects of sober life (e.g., self-sufficiency, employment, intimate relationships).

If Danny were to take part in the encompassing experience of a therapeutic community, he would need to make a slow movement out of the program to a highly structured halfway house, assisted at all points in time by a case manager. A case manager is a mental health or substance abuse professional who would be assigned to Danny or Carl and would aid them in procurement of all their basic needs—housing, clothing, work rehabilitation, psychotherapy, medication, and finances.

Beyond the men's individual treatment needs, it would also be important to reconsider the strategies of how we work with members of a drinking circle. At present, we tend to avoid having members of the same circle in a treatment program at the same time. We also discourage their rooming together after they are discharged. The reasons for this approach are that members of a circle can reinforce each other's resistance to an authentic commitment to sobriety. They can provide mutual support for blowing off the program or mocking the efforts of individuals who are sincere in seeking sobriety. Even if they both leave with the intention of living together and keeping each other sober, once one relapses, the other feels the freedom to give up as well.

Yet with effective confrontation of the drinking circle's negative uses of communion, it is possible that all of these disadvantages could be turned into advantages. Assuming we explicitly sought to have as many members of the circle as possible come through the program together, the counselors could directly address the role the drinking circle plays in their lives (positive and negative). With the topic of the drinking circle front and center, the group of men could identify ways in which the circle hurts them and collectively think about more constructive alternatives.

One of the most successful therapeutic communities, Phoenix House in New York City, began in 1967 when a dozen heroin addicts, recently discharged from a detox, pooled their welfare checks and restored a tenement apartment. They built a new circle based in a mutual commitment to self-preservation and sobriety. Within ten years, this effort had grown to an organization that maintained an annual residential population of more than 500 individuals.[9] This success story emphasizes that the individuals can change through collective action, and that a few key leaders of a circle may have a dramatic influence. It also suggests the possibility of assigning case managers not simply to individuals, but to a given drinking circle (though how one would define the exact membership of any particular circle would pose a challenge). The case manager could then broker services for a group of men who had stated and maintained a commitment to sobriety and mutual support.

From the bottle gangs of the Bowery[10] to the drinking circle of Skipper's Deck, many chronically addicted men have somehow found a way to come together and forge a community out of their despair. As Danny Doyle stresses, it may be a community that is killing its members, but at least it is *something,* a place to which they can belong and feel at home. Though we would like to believe AA could be the replacement for this destructive community, it has too often been a source of disappointment or shame in their lives. When a man does not feel good enough about himself or trusting enough of others to walk through the accepting doors of an AA meeting, there are few other avenues to which he can turn for solace. Predictably, he turns back to what he knows best and rejoins the drinking circle. For this reason, it may be more powerful to try to bring the drinking circle along as a whole rather than extract one member and place him among AA members with whom he feels little in common and no small amount of distrust.

Interestingly, once Carl connected to the men at the Pines and began to feel a sense of belonging with them, he also began to feel more comfortable and invested in the AA meetings held at the Pines. It is a vital question whether or not one's sense of community in AA begins at the doorway of a meeting or has already been forged by one's prior membership in agentic and communal aspects of society. If the latter is true, a man's ability to feel at home in a meeting will depend not only on the good will or intentions of the group, but also on his prior history and capacity to connect to and understand the implicit values shared by the group.

With this in mind, one can understand why Tommy Reilly hated AA and felt coerced into going to meetings. His nihilistic approach to life was in clear conflict with the spiritual uplift and prosocial attitude of the AA steps. To help Tommy break away from the destructive effects of the drinking circle, we would have to confront him with what he is hiding by participating in the circle. He would have to slow down from his constant escape into intoxication to look at what sparks his violence, his hatred of women, and his overwhelming concern for control. Unlike Danny or Carl, Tommy's personal myth includes the very destruction of communion at its core. He joins drinking circles to avoid genuine intimacy and connection. Much more than the other two men, Tommy's escape from the drinking circle depends on his ability to use individual counseling and psychotherapy to explore these painful and destructive features of his individual personality. For Tommy to leave the rooms of Skipper's Deck and find a home in the rooms of AA, he will need to find a way to *care,* both about himself and others.

As I list these suggestions for future treatment, I am sure a game is on at this very moment at Skipper's Deck near Ocean Beach. The cards are making their way around the table along with the jug. A radio is booming and the room is filled with cigarette smoke. The boys are joking and cursing, and, in the best ways they know how, taking care of each other.

Part Three

PROBLEMS

WITH

AGENCY

5. WHEN THE DEVIL
GRABS YOUR ANKLE
Poverty's Line of Despair

In the previous two chapters, I have asked what happens to chronically addicted men's sense of identity when their efforts to find communion are thwarted. I have argued that their difficulties with communion are a function not only of their addiction, but of destructive social or personal circumstances that contributed to their drug and alcohol use and now continue to impede their efforts at recovery. In the next three chapters, we look at men whose troubled sense of agency is similarly a problem of both addiction and the social conditions that fostered and now perpetuate their battle with sobriety.

In each of the chapters in this section, the factors that block the development of a healthy sense of autonomy and achievement—poverty, materialism, a life based solely in athletic glory—are familiar culprits in our society. For example, the destructive effects of African-American urban poverty have been well documented by political scientists and social critics such as

William Wilson, Andrew Hacker, Jonathan Kozol, and Alex Kotlowitz.[1] Films like *Boyz N the Hood, Clockers, New Jack City,* and *South Central* have depicted in graphic and emotional terms the violent and toxic relationship of drugs and poverty in African-American lives. Similarly, plays like *Death of a Salesman* by Arthur Miller or *Glengarry Glen Ross* by David Mamet (both later made into films) demonstrate how the American Dream of material success can betray men, leaving them isolated and empty in spirit. We need only to hear the taunting refrain of "Glory Days" in Bruce Springsteen's song of the same name or read John Updike's *Rabbit Run* or Irwin Shaw's classic short story, "The Eighty-Yard Run" to register the image of the athlete who has failed to develop a life beyond his sporting triumphs.

These works of social analysis and artistic statement describe clearly and eloquently the problems of poverty, materialism, and an overvaluing of sports heroism and celebrity for American males. My goal in each of the next three chapters is more modest and specific. Through the life histories of four men from Lebanon Pines, I hope to provide a psychological analysis of how these persisting social problems interact with addiction to affect the capacity for agency and overall identity formation in chronically addicted men. In doing so, I shall make an argument that these men's addictions cannot be understood simply as a disease process or personal moral failing. Dispiriting social conditions, whether they be poverty or excessive materialism, lead to many types of alienated and confused responses for men in this society. Some men compulsively accumulate possessions. Some men become workaholics, constantly vying for the next promotion or milestone of success. Others move through a series of transitory and unsatisfying relationships. Others tune out through endless absorption in television, sports teams, or the Internet world of computers.

For certain men who face a biological vulnerability and/or extensive exposure to parental and social modeling of drinking or drug-taking, their sense of dislocation and despair is expressed through substance abuse that eventually blossoms into addiction. Since addiction ends up generating much more apparent and easily quantifiable costs to the society (criminal activity, medical expenditures, public displays of intoxication, risks of motor vehicle accidents, etc.) than material greed, hours of television, or failed relationships, we are more likely to recognize and categorize addiction as an unhealthy and maladaptive response to the problems of alienation or meaninglessness. In identifying individuals simply as addicts, we are less likely to dwell on the possible continuities between their alienation and the other less pathological forms of disenfranchisement that exist throughout our society.

As the men's addictions progress and eventually pull them further and further away from the trappings of middle-class convention and morality, it becomes increasingly easier to see these men as fundamentally different from the rest of us—weak, greedy, immoral, and ultimately evil. And there is some truth to this perception. Lives that begin in distorted and alienated fashion are further twisted by the effects of addiction until the men in their adult lives seem to have little connection to the positive communion and agency that organize the rest of our lives. It is no wonder that chronicles of urban poverty often make their protagonists children; they suffer from, but have not yet become, the corrupting agents of the street. Similarly, in middle-class memoirs of single-parent children and adult survivors of alcoholic families our hearts open to the survivors' suffering and resilience rather than to the inner worlds of the absent or alcoholic fathers who "created" these dysfunctional systems.

I am not interested in waging a war of sympathy for these men. In the next three chapters, we hear about men's choices that, even if placed in a more enlightened context, do not seem particularly laudable or even well intended. The men themselves make no bones about acknowledging their negative and destructive behaviors. Nor is my goal to offer excuses for these men, but rather to achieve a deeper level of understanding that allows us to make better sense of their troubled lives. From engaging with their life stories, we learn what it means to a man's sense of self when he succumbs to the street world of poverty. We learn what it means to a man's sense of identity if he thinks that the size of his house or the cash he carries in the trunk of his car defines his self-image. We learn what it means to a man's sense of purpose when his life has been based in constant adulation by others, and suddenly that adulation ends.

We may not like who these men have become through their addicted lives, but their words and life stories allow us to see them in more complex and three-dimensional terms. They cease to be the monsters of our imagination ("crackheads," "cold-hearted dope dealers," "deadbeat dads") that have been forged through political rhetoric and "Just Say No" campaigns. Once we recognize their essential humanity, it may encourage us to work harder at helping them find new solutions to their fundamental alienation from authentic relationships and agentic contributions to the society.

Not surprisingly, at the heart of the story for all four of the men discussed in the next three chapters is the issue of fatherhood. Fathers are the primary models of agentic behavior for their sons. All four of these men's fathers eventually left their homes and three of the four fathers suffered from substance abuse. The inability of fathers to demonstrate responsible behavior in the society plays an enormous role in communicating antisocial and alienated messages to their sons. These problematic messages are then communicated to the next generation as the chronically addicted men struggle with their own inadequacies and delinquencies as fathers to their own children.

Let us begin this examination of the problems of agency in chronically addicted men's lives by looking at the story of two African-American men raised in impoverished areas of Hartford and New Haven, Connecticut. Though both men ended up addicted to drugs, their lives are characterized by different responses to frustrated agency and despair. Rolando Diggs, addicted to crack cocaine, often abdicates responsibility and surrenders any constructive agency. Thomas Turner turns more actively against the sober world, gaining a sense of self from his drug dealings and acts of violence. At times, his behavior exemplifies the destructive agency of Kierkegaard's "demoniac rage."

> Even if at this point God in heaven and all his angels were to offer to help him out of it—no, now he doesn't want it, now it is too late, he once would have given everything to be rid of this torment but was made to wait, now that's all past, now he would rather rage against everything, he, the one man in the whole of existence who is the most unjustly treated, to whom it is especially important to have his torment at hand, important that no one should take it from him—for thus he can convince himself that he is in the right.[2]

Either option, surrender or rage, always deposits each man at a greater distance from lives of positive agency and communion, from lives that would allow them a sense of respectability and uprightness in the society. The ground they lose is not easily regained and their chances of returning to constructive lives diminish as they advance in years. In his self-defining memory, Thomas Turner is haunted by the death of his mother on Christmas Day. He still hears her voice in his head long after her death, and his helplessness in response to her calls speaks in mute eloquence about his life of thwarted agency.

Thomas Turner

Thomas Turner was born in New Haven in 1940, the third youngest of four children. He is a tall, trim, and handsome man. There are flecks of gray in his hair, but he still conveys an air of physical strength and power. His voice suits his stature, gravelly and deep, capable of commanding your attention without raising its volume much above a whisper. I first met him in the detox in New London, as we were preparing him to move up to Lebanon Pines. Even in that first meeting, he told me about a series of deaths in his life that had left him troubled and tormented. As he accumulated more days of sobriety, these "ghosts" literally spoke to him in dreams and during the day. I could offer him little comfort in response to these memories, but encouraged his pleasure as he described his children's and grandchildren's joy about his current efforts at recovery. In the subsequent year of his stay at Lebanon Pines, he sought me out periodically, at first with increasingly positive news about the benefits of sobriety in his life, and later on with his frustrations concerning the persistence of past voices despite his hard work in the program.

Thomas grew up in housing projects during the World War II years and immediately after. His father worked at the Winchester Arms factory off Prospect Avenue in New Haven, and his mother did cleaning work. She kept this work secret, since the housing rules stated that only one person in the family could work to maintain eligibility. His father drank heavily and eventually left the family when Thomas was in his teens. Many others in his family had problems with alcohol and one of Thomas's earliest memories is of seeing his mother's mother killed while she was drinking with a lover.

She always liked to flirt around with men. She had us in the hallway, sitting on the stairs in the cold weather, watching. And she was upstairs drinking with this one guy and this other guy came up the stairs and he looked at us, I'd seen him there before. And an argument broke out, she was saying "I'm giving you my money and ain't gonna have you threatening around here." And the guy who had come up the stairs told her with a sharp voice to shut up. And he had one of those flat irons, you know the flat iron they used to put on top of the stove and heat. He hit her in the head with that. She fell out of the doorway, and I'm on the stairs looking at her, and my sisters and brother started crying. When I seen my mother cried, I cried, but not before. But it didn't bother me, because the neighborhood I came from, at that time, there was a lot of killings going on.[3]

To convey to me how common violent death was in his neighborhood, Thomas took a moment and counted up the number of people with whom he had grown up who had been killed. He came up with the figure of forty lives.

I used to say, "I'm in the wrong place at the wrong time." My little sister, she seen a guy killed. The guy got hit in the head with about ten different bottles. She had nightmares for a while about it. We used yell, "Shut up and go to bed, go to sleep." She'd come out into the street, hollering, and the neighbors would get mad and say "Get back to bed and stop that." She used to say to me, "I seen that guy get hit in the head again." I used to tell her, "There ain't nothing you can do about it. You can't keep screaming or they'll come up here and get you." Me and her usually talked about that. My baby sister, I loved her. I guess that was the way coming up. Part of life.

Though Thomas tried to accept the omnipresence of violent death as simply "part of life" growing up in his community, many psychotherapists feel that early exposure to these traumatic experiences has long-ranging consequences for the child. Yalom writes,

> A child who is harshly confronted with death before having developed appropriate defenses, may be severely stressed. Severe stress, unpleasant at all times of life, has for the young child implications that transcend transient dysphoria.[4]

Many of Thomas's subsequent choices and actions may be understood in the light of efforts to avoid an overwhelming anxiety about death that confronted him nakedly at an early age. The presence of death is a central part of Thomas's personal myth; it becomes the fulcrum around which the rest of his life story is constructed. Whether he will once again be the victim of death through the loss of loved ones or the agent of death as he inflicts violence upon others dominates all other questions regarding agency and communion in his life. Drugs, both the dealing and use of them, are his principal response to the incessant question of death in his life.

I seen drugs and alcohol every day. My father drank seven days a week. And I seen it in my neighborhood. If I had to go down the street and get a loaf of bread, I gotta go through it. And you'd see guys drinking in the alleyways. I used to watch drug addicts—I'd climb the fence and sit on the back porch and watch the drug addicts shoot up. . . . In my neighborhood, if you didn't drink, if your father didn't drink, something was wrong. I used to have a baseball game every day. My father used to come through the school yard where we played, we had to stop the game, help him through the school yard. A couple of times, in the winter time, he almost froze to death because nobody seen him. I used to get in a lot fights about that. I was a little tough kid when I was coming up. Everybody's father was like that. But their fathers didn't come through the school yard. Mine did.

Thomas's father was drunk daily and needed to be hunted down on paydays by the children to avoid losing all his wages to the bars. Thomas's family faced the continual threat of eviction and hunger as his father's alcoholism worsened and his working habits became more unreliable.

The awful thing about it was when my daddy didn't come home from work on payday, she used to send us to meet him to make sure he get home. But he used to go out the side gate sometimes. Now she got to worry about feeding us because she shopped Friday from Friday. And by Friday, the refrigerator started getting low. . . . She'd be standing in the doorway and see us come home by ourselves, without him. "You were out playing, you missed him." We would tell her, "Mom, we were sitting right there." She would get mad. A couple of times she beat us. But she was really angry at him. She knew that all week she was gonna have to do something to keep us eating, to make sure we had food.

Thomas's father finally lost his job when his drunkenness at work led to a small explosion and fire. He had been separated from the family for a time before that and afterwards had moved up to Middletown, Connecticut. He died there when Thomas was nineteen. He died the way that Thomas had always feared—of passing out in the cold and freezing from exposure.

Somebody wasn't there to watch him this time. . . . Because my mother used to send us out to look for him on the cold days.

School, Sports, and the Street

Despite the disruptions caused by his home life and his poverty, Thomas eventually turned these trials into toughness and speed on the football field.

I remember one time my mother made me put on a pair of red sneakers and she got them at the secondhand store for fifty cents in New Haven. I wore them, and they were girls' sneakers, thinking I didn't have nothing else to wear to go outside and I wasn't going outside barefoot. . . . It was just like clockwork, to quiet them down, one at a time, I beat them up so they wouldn't laugh at my sneakers. I tried to play ball and I know they be laughing and snickering. Those little red sneakers made me run fast. But when I'd catch it from those kids, it made me want to beat the hell out of them.

. . . I loved to play ball. I loved to play tackle football when I was in school. I loved the contact. Running and hitting hard. At times, I felt I could hear my heart beat. I loved the sport because of this. And my coach used to say, "I wish I had plenty of players like Thomas here. Whatever I tell him to do, he'll do it."

In Thomas's embrace of the physical contact and the hitting hard, we can already detect early signs of how he turns the violence that pervades his life into an object of pleasure and not only pain. Thomas played football at Hillhouse high school and was in the same backfield as a player who later went on to play professional football. He told a number of stories with great enthusiasm about his relationship with this player, and how Jim Brown, the Hall of Fame running back for the Cleveland Browns, once came into the locker room to speak to them both. Unfortunately, Thomas tore ligaments in his knee in his junior year and was unable to continue playing. Though he had already been drinking with friends for several years, his interest in getting high and drunk escalated after this disappointment. He soon quit school as well.

Under the influence of alcohol, his friends and he would dare each other to steal from the local stores and neighbors' homes. After leaving school, he took a job at Winchester Arms, where his father had worked. For the first year of working there, he felt extreme pride in bringing home a paycheck to his mother and being sure that she could buy food for the family without stress or worry. He even bought her a little freezer and she would store up meats and vegetables, as she put it, "In case some rainy day will come."

As Thomas told this story, I could see the obvious affection he felt for his mother. He talked about her cooking—sweet potato pie and apple pie—and how she would promise a fresh-cooked pie after a hard day of work. This was clearly a good period of his life, but always lurking in the background was the violence of the streets. There also seemed to be something inside him—an enjoyment of the violence—and a sense of power that it gave him. He recounted an incident in which a boy had beaten up his father and stolen his liquor. He tracked the boy down and beat him up badly.

I had hunted him down and I did a good job on him. Such a job that the boy's mother came to our house and said, "You didn't have to do that to him." I did that until I felt satisfied. And it was wrong, I know it was wrong. But somehow I liked it. That's why I was so angry with myself.

Just as he enjoyed the physical contact of football, he enjoyed the physical punishment he inflicted on this boy. As Thomas narrated his story, he was able to identify a critical element of himself—his capacity to embrace violence. Overwhelmed by death and violence at an early age, he experienced a traumatic sense of powerlessness in the face of these forces. Only by becoming violent himself and taking control of the aggression that surrounded him has he been able to regain some degree of power or influence over his life. His violent behavior allows him to change from passive victim into an active agent of destruction. Adopting this aggressive stance, he takes a stand against the so-called proper society that neglects him and exposes him to terror. His violent power affords him, though only for limited periods of time, a more direct sense of agency than he has been able to find through any other more positive channel.[5] At such moments, seeking violent retribution for violence done to those he loves, he adopts the imago of "Thomas, the avenger." This avenging imago responds to the omnipresence of death in Thomas's personal myth by paying back others for the pain he has suffered. Simultaneously, he pays a price for the brief sense of power and control he gains.

Thomas lost his job at Winchester for exactly this reason. He ran into a man in the cafeteria at work who had once beaten up his brother. The man taunted him about this episode and Thomas took the bait. They ended up in a fight and Thomas was fired. After losing his job, he was determined to get some quick money. He took to forging checks, breaking into homes, and robbing people on the street. He was arrested and convicted of forgery, and given a two-to-five-year sentence. He served a small portion of this time, but after a brief release, was re-arrested for armed robbery. He was then sent back to prison, this time for five years.

Prison and Dealing

Thomas found himself removed from normal life during prison, but he swiftly adjusted to the value system and day-to-day urgencies of that world.

In prison, it was like everything stopped. Inside them walls, it stopped. But I fit in to what was going on around me. There was fighting. Anything that's yours, you keep. So I kind of had that when I was coming up. To tell the truth, I was real comfortable with it. . . . When you get there, you have to fight your way up through the ranks. There was a guy in there from the streets and I got challenged and I rised to the occasion. I would love it, you know. It was a shame to say it, but I fit right into that at that time.

. . . If you want to keep your cigarettes, or your chicken, or your food at the table, you better learn to fight. . . . I think I made it through there because that lifestyle of being in jail kept me on the edge. From the time your light go out until the time you get up in the morning, even though you was in jail, you didn't know what event could happen. . . . It was like a mystery. Who was going to get who? Who was going to knife who? There was always something going on. I got into boxing. I was pretty good at it too. You got people with 106 attitudes in jail, you got 500 people or more than that, that you come into contact with on a daily basis.

Once again as with football and street fighting, Thomas points out both the omnipresence of violence and his comfort with this violence. He fit into this world of intimidation and retribution. Within the prison world, he allowed Thomas, the avenger, to dominate his sense of self. Though Thomas had been seeing a woman before he entered prison and she had given birth to his daughter, this relationship did not survive through his prison sentence. He became reinvolved with his daughter later in his life, but for this period during the middle sixties, he lost contact with her.

Thomas came out of prison in 1965 and found some part-time work. He married in 1966 and bought a house with his wife. He soon began to deal drugs to pick up money on the side. Though he had continued to drink, he stayed away from the excessive drinking that had killed his father. Instead, he began to abuse Percodan and later on moved into heroin. At the time though, he was experiencing a streak of prosperity from his drug sales.

It got to be a pretty good business. I was making more than I did when I was on the job. Money was coming back fast. And my brother was putting his daughter through Catholic school, private school. I bought her a car. Everything was going all right.

For roughly eight years, Thomas lived a stable life with no further arrests. He worked at a supermarket warehouse and successfully sold heroin to great profit. He gave money to his family members and his mother, but she did not want to take money he had made from drug sales.

We used to lie to her and tell her, "We bought a bedroom set, but we can't fit it in our house, we want you to have it." But it was really for her. She would take things. But if I walked up to her and handed her money, she would not take it. She'd look at it and say "You can't bring that in this house." But I would go over there and drink coffee, eat, take a nap. And that was all right. Now and then she would tell me "I'm hearing things about you. I got some friends out there in the street. I'm hearing things and I don't like them." I say, "Mom, you're just hearing things. I'm all right. She'd say, "I'm not worried about that. Look at the clothes you are wearing. Look at this and look at that. I'd say, "Mom, I work." She'd say, "Yeah. OK. You think you're fooling your mother, but you're not.

She often asked Thomas to find his brother and he would track him down in the "shooting galleries" of New York City. He had become a heroin addict and eventually was killed along with his wife over a drug transaction on the street in New York. Though his mother did not like Thomas's involvement with drugs, she still saw him as the son who had remained near her and on whom she could depend. Because they had remained so close, the next event in Thomas's life changed him and raised the specter of death to an even more profound place in his life story.

It was Christmas Day in 1974 and Thomas had been partying heavily and was busy negotiating with his drug connections.

I was supposed to go to her house and that year I missed. . . . I talked to her at a quarter of six, telling her that I wouldn't be over . . . that the kids would be over with their toys. And she said, "This is the first Christmas that I remember that you weren't here." I said, "Yeah, Ma, but we'll have some more together." She said, "OK." And my wife said, "You're not even going to take the time to go over there." And I said, "I've already explained it to you." I can still see the way she looked at me when I went out the door. At five after six, my mother was dead. Stabbed by a robber. They found her. She used to have a habit of sitting in the house in the dark. That's where I get that. The darkness is my best friend. I like the dark. She used to sit there and light up the Christmas tree. I loved that myself. I thought about committing suicide. We buried her the day before New Year's.

After his mother's death, Thomas reached out to drugs in a way he had never done before. He gave up any pretense at respectability. He embraced with both arms the anger that he had discovered inside himself during the violent moments in the street and later in prison. He was now fully Thomas, the avenger, bent on destruction and retribution.

I got angry and then I got past anger. I had rage inside of me. I wanted to strike out. I didn't care about my way of living, morals, or anything. . . . A lot of things come with drugs. Things you don't want to have to do. Killings. People get killed. It's a vicious circle that I liked. I liked the edge out there because I felt as though I fit right in. . . . If a challenge came up to me, I welcomed it. After the death of my mother, I didn't have no feelings.

In explaining this side of himself to me, Thomas was quick to qualify his words. He gave examples of how he continued to help family members through money and gifts. He also told me a story of how a woman offered him her daughter for sex in exchange for dope. He gave the mother two bags of dope and then put the daughter on the train to Bridgeport to live with her aunt. Even so, he moved immediately from that story to other stories of his violent ways.

I liked carrying a gun. I like the smell of gunfire . . . I knew I was wrong. But I felt comfortable with what I was doing. . . . I know many times I felt like O. J. Simpson, past angry to rage. Anger wasn't doing it. I wanted to see blood or something. And I used to get so angry, it's something I have to do. I'd close my eyes and open them up and see red. But I used to medicate myself and I was all right or at least I thought I was. Sometimes I'd rather go back to what I was doing. That way I don't worry about any kind of feelings. That's a bad thing to say, but I feel like that. . . . I took up for people that people pushed around. I never had nothing. But when I did have it, I tried to spread it to other people. I see kids in the store going to buy bikes around Christmas time and I'd give them money.

Throughout my interview with Thomas, this other qualifying voice would always emerge when he would describe the acts of Thomas, the avenger. He could not simply state his love of destruction without reassuring me that it made him uncomfortable or that he could be a loving or kind person as well. I am convinced that part of Thomas's descent into addiction grows out of this ambivalence. He is unable to occupy the role of antisocial destructive agent without feeling extreme waves of remorse and conscience. It is no coincidence that his self-defining memory is the Christmas Day death of his mother.

In this memory, he describes himself engaged in drug-dealing activity, essentially playing the role of a powerful, though negative, agentic force. Having chosen this destructive route to agency, he then discovers himself utterly powerless to save his mother from a violent death at the hands of other negative agents. His sorrow and remorse over this irony are acute and return incessantly to his waking and dreaming mind. No matter how much vengeance Thomas inflicts upon the world, he always seems to find himself at the receiving end of another loss; he always seems to be turning the corner and finding death in his path.

Addiction and the Problem of Sobriety

In the next decade of the eighties, Thomas built up his heroin dealing business. Though he rarely took heroin intravenously, he snorted it and smoked it enough to develop a strong habit. He did not want to think about the deaths and disappointments in his life, and heroin smothered the feelings for him. On top of the previous deaths, his youngest and favorite sister contracted AIDS and he used to visit her in the hospital.

I knew my sister was going to die. But I didn't want to face it. I used to tell her lit-tle things. I used to tell her, if you see Mom, tell her I'm sorry for what happened to her. And she'd say "Let that go." I said, "Well, if you see her, and you know you've got a shot at getting there . . . if you see her, you tell her I'm sorry for what I did." Then she would scold me for whining at her so much. Then I would go get back in my van and drive down to the park and get high until that feeling would leave me. And it was all right when it was gone.

Christmas time I used to go find her and my sister and me, we'd be together. And we would talk and when that time came the conversation would cease and there would be quietness. We'd get through it. My sister used to say it's over with. I'd watch the clock and then I'd say, "It's over."

Thomas made big money from dealing, despite spending a portion of each year in jail on various petty charges. He managed to avoid arrest for drug sales. He explained a little of his business practices to me.

I would pay $250 for a brick of heroin and I would make $1,000–$1,200 off that. So each time I would go out, I would buy more and more. And then I would have people working for me. They would sell a bundle [ten bags of heroin] and make $200 [twenty dollars per bag]. They got forty dollars for each bundle that they sold and they would bring $160 back. And it worked very well. I recall from a Thursday to Sunday night, I made $21,000.

It came in fast. But in order to do that, a lot of stuff come along with that. Shooting people. Sometimes, other people have been killed. There are some very ugly situations. But I felt comfortable in doing that. And when somebody's behind needed to be waxed, I felt comfortable doing that. Although I've been held up. Shot by different people. People owe you money. You don't worry about a couple of hundred dollars. But when they start hooking you for $1,600, then you got to get them in line. It helps you get everybody else in line. Don't go messin' around with this package here.

Thomas stamped his bags with his trademark, the professional football team logo of his old running mate from his high school days. Periodically, he would change stamps to avoid competitors putting bad dope in bags stamped with his trademark. His reputation depended on the quality of his product, the same as in any sales business. He also learned which policemen would accept payments or access to women in exchange for looking the other way or arresting his competitors. With the advent of crack in the late eighties, he diversified and began to sell both dope and crack. He would take drives down to Miami and return with five or six kilos of cocaine. As he moved into crack sales, he had to become more conscious of the distinct territories where gangs sold their wares.

You got to know where the welfare people are at. They spend a lot of money. Plus you got to have a good spot near the workers. Where they spend money. And if you got these spots, you might have twenty houses in your area where you're knocking off six or seven hundred dollars a night. You damn sure don't want to be threatened by anybody. And you go out there and put your mark. Gold tops— Twenty Love; Fifth-Ward Nation had pink tops. And it was that way all through New Haven.[6]

In a similar way to the big supermarket chains driving the corner grocery store out of business, the gangs soon left Thomas without the means or market to make his sales. He began to suffer from the large habit he had built up and could no longer support. He tried methadone for a while and was in and out of detoxes with increasing frequency. The more sober periods he had and the less involved in the drug business he became, the more his thoughts turned to his losses and the bitter turn his life had taken.

I was locking myself in the house. I was contemplating suicide. I had a nine-millimeter. I sat there and I wouldn't let nobody in. And I started crying. Something wasn't right. The dope wasn't numbing my feelings.

He called his son and his son convinced him to try a longer stay at a treatment facility. He came to Lebanon Pines and found the first thirty days there the roughest period of his life. He began to look at himself more openly for the first time. He began to talk to people and express feelings he had never shared. He even cried in his counselor's office; he had never cried in front of another man before.

As he took steps to working on recovery, on creating a new way of being in the world, he also found himself haunted by his remorse over his mother's and sister's deaths. These recurrent self-punishing thoughts began to take the form of voices speaking to him and calling out to him, especially at night. His roommate at the Pines told him that he sometimes talked in his sleep and had woken up screaming one night. Without the role of Thomas, the avenger, to strike out at the world and without drugs to block the remorse, he was more naked and vulnerable to the presence of death than he had ever been in his adult life.

Thomas managed to stay at the Pines for a year's time and presented a very positive figure to many of the younger black men. He attended meetings regularly, spoke in favor of recovery, and of the value of starting a new life. He grew closer to many members of his family, who had shied away from him during his heavy drug dealing and using years. I remember one session we had in which we exchanged stories about our weekends and he told me about the pleasure he had in taking his granddaughter fishing.

Even as he had these moments of new life, he could not subdue the voices. New memories of acts of violence he had committed began to return to him. A few months after his interview with me, his thinking turned increasingly paranoid and no amount of medication seemed to soften the harsh recriminations of the voices or his suspicions about the other residents and staff. It was as if his avenging imago had turned upon itself, accusing him and berating him in the voices of his sister and his mother.

In the first year of his time at the Pines, he had never displayed any act of temper or threatening behavior. In his last days there, he became belligerent with a few of the men over trivial incidents in the lunch line or in the television room. The staff began to feel that perhaps he had stayed too long at the Pines, that he was regressing rather than building on the positive ground he had gained. Thomas moved on to a sober living situation, but no one felt sure he would stay sober much longer or that he would be able to fight off the auditory hallucinations of a deepening psychosis.

Thomas told me that he felt his problems started before his addictions. He grew up in a family and in a neighborhood where fighting and drinking were all he knew. On the other hand, he said to me, his old running-back partner grew up in the same neighborhood and never took a drink. Thomas felt he had had the opportunity to make choices and that he had made the wrong ones. He wanted to blame the white population for all the "evil and hatred" he developed, but he felt that this is not sufficient to explain his life either. He returned also to that moment almost fifty years ago when he could not cry at his grandmother's death.

Sometimes I still wonder why I didn't cry when my grandmother was killed. Because she used to rob our piggybank and get money for her liquor that way. But I feel sorry for her because she's at the top of the hill.

At some point, in his youth and early adulthood, Thomas had traded in tears for rage. His answer to the complete lack of agency and power he felt in his life (as those around him gave into addiction or died) was to strike back with violence and anger. When the socially sanctioned channel of sports ceased to be open to him, he gave in completely to the destructive invitation of the street to quick money and the instant power of violence.

In describing the kinds of personal myths individuals construct,

McAdams draws upon the work of Agnes Hankiss, who has suggested we fashion four different narrative patterns. In the stories we tell of our lives, a good past can lead to a good present ("dynastic"), a good past can lead to a bad present ("compensatory"), a bad past can lead to a good present ("antithetical"), and a bad past can lead to a bad present ("self-absolutory").[7] Each of these patterns can be recruited to explain or justify the outcome of one's life story. Certainly, individuals in recovery rely upon the "antithetical" framework—their bad past of addiction has led to a better present of sobriety. For men suffering from chronic addiction and living in a bad present of active use or relapse, the compensatory and self-absolutory strategies of narrative construction are the most relevant.

For example, Carl Sobilesky's story from Chapter 4 is clearly a compensatory story. He began life in a positive fashion and then after his cerebral hemorrhage suffered a continued decline into his present difficulties. His drinking can be justified, in part, as a way to block out the memories of his youthful happiness as a successful husband and employee.

In a different way, Thomas's story of a past overwhelmed with death, addiction, and violence that leads to a similar negative present of despair can be characterized as a self-absolutory story. As McAdams puts it, in this story the individual is "paying the price" for previous failngs or errors.[8] Hankiss argues that individuals employ these narrative strategies in an effort to make sense of the complex events of their life histories. This need for sense-making is even more fundamental than the desire for happy or self-affirming endings. As Thomas constructs his story, his need for coherence requires that there be an accounting for the violence he has witnessed and committed in his life. The connection of the violence done to his grandmother to his own violent behavior (bad past—bad present) allows him to see meaning, albeit a tragic and remorseful one, in his current life.

Why and What Can Be Done?

The two thoughts that always return to me when I finish listening to the life stories told to me by men from the Pines is why did this happen to this man and what can be done to help him? These questions twist and turn in my mind for days with no satisfying answer to either one. The story of Thomas is no exception. With Thomas, one could answer the "why" by noting his genetic loading for addiction. He claimed relatives on both sides with alcoholism, and at least two of his siblings used drugs extensively. Yet, Thomas reported that he could take or leave alcohol, that he never became a dependent or chronic drinker. He was addicted to painkillers and later on, heroin. This variation in his addictive pattern extends our understanding of the genetic contribution of addiction to mean an overall vulnerability rather than addiction to a specific agent or type of substance. Thus far, the research literature has not established nearly as strong links for the genetic inheritance of drug addiction as opposed to alcohol addiction.[9]

Leaving aside issues of genetic vulnerability, we then turn to the circumstances of Thomas's life. His two most vivid memories from his past are the death of his grandmother and his mother. He chose his mother's death on Christmas night as his self-defining memory. This memory became a traumatic vision that replayed before his sleepless eyes at night, that appeared to him in daylight while he worked outside on the grounds of the Pines. This memory reminded him first and foremost of violent death and its omnipresence in his life. The loss of his mother was also tied to his failure to protect her. By choosing his drug world over visiting her home, he was unable to intercept any potential robbers. He attributed much of his drug use and anger after that incident to his urgent need to avoid feeling remorse. In either a heroin-induced nod or a state of rage, he could minimize access to sadness or overwhelming anguish.

Besides the repetitive nature of this memory, he linked it to other similar memories of the deaths of his family members. In describing his father's death, passed out drunk in the snow, he commented on how he was not there to help him. When his little sister died of complications of AIDS, he was not by her side. He claimed the nurses told him that her last words were to call his name. Toward the end of his time at the Pines, he turned to thinking of men whom he had shot in order to protect his territory or his reputation on the street. All of these images and voices of death filled his head and he felt unable to stop their demands on his conscience and peace of mind. Counseling and psychiatric medicine were no longer helping to still this riot in his brain. It was as if there were a worn out audiotape in his head and as much as he tried to record new information over the older tracks, the previous recordings would slip through, the old voices and muffled half-sounds interspersed with the new.

When we consider the "why" with Thomas, we touch the toxic conditions of poverty—exposure to crime, addiction, violence, despair. Without support from every direction possible, relatives, school, church, social services, and community organizations, boys like Thomas, witnessing violent death and substance abuse almost from infancy, will always be vulnerable to medicating their pain with every means possible. Frequent exposure to violence at an early age may not only traumatize children but may desensitize them to its effects, and may, in some cases, help comfort them due to the release of rage it allows. We know from the classic studies of violent modeling[10] that children who witness adults engaged in aggression will model their own behaviors after what they have observed. Thomas showed a great deal of insight at the end of his life story when he declared that something was wrong long before his addiction, that even his love of contact sports reflected something awry in his psyche. It is unsettling that a boy already weaned on violence was egged on by school authorities to express physical violence in a more "legitimate and healthy" outlet.

Once injured in football and deprived of his most accessible outlet for achieving immediate status as a man, Thomas struggled to regain this status. Relying upon his violent background once again, he turned to fighting and crime. His violence lost him his job and his criminal activity landed him in prison. Once inside there, there were no longer ambiguities about the role violence could play in his life. It was now his strongest card and his means to survival. He was free to express his demoniac rage at the world.

After his prison time, he took advantages of connections made there to build up a drug dealing business. His status as a man, not satisfied by low-paying jobs, could be amplified by his standing as a powerful and prosperous drug dealer in the community. By this point, his reputation for violent retribution was his greatest financial and personal security.

I grew close to Thomas in the time that he was at the Pines, and up until the last few months, I saw the positive effect he was having on other younger men at the Pines who had shared his background. I saw also his pleasure in living a clean life and in reconnecting to his family. Despite hard work in counseling, despite frequent adjustments of his medication by his psychiatrist, he seemed to slip deeper and deeper into the past, losing touch with the day-to-day demands of his life. He began to dress more sloppily and talk out loud to himself. Perhaps his long drug use had masked an underlying schizophrenic condition, or the trauma of thinking soberly about the unremitting violence in his life was inducing a psychotic state. No one could say for sure. What I do know is that we seemed to be losing him toward the end, and in a way that I feared he would not reverse.

Whether or not Thomas could one day regain himself and his sobriety remained unclear, but I find a chilling message in his decline. In our culture of can-do technology and self-help transformations, we tend to hold out the optimistic credo that no matter what you have been through, you can make it back. If you receive high-quality care, give yourself to the loving support of a Twelve Step group, and commit yourself to making good choices one day at a time, it can work out. What Thomas's story warns us is that this isn't necessarily so in every case and for every man. Like all living things, human beings can endure only so much injury before they may succumb to the weight of their trauma. As a society, we have no right to ask children and young men to endure the flood of violence that Thomas experienced. When someone like Thomas lapses in his recovery, we often say "he must not have wanted it enough" or "he did not work his program hard enough." Sometimes we need to step back and ask what are we expecting out of people who have been born and raised in a world of furies?

The "why's" are not always irrelevant to the "what is to be done's" for men suffering from chronic addiction. Many men are counseled to let go of their pasts and live for the present day. Thomas has not set aside his past to build a sober future. There may be pasts that simply cannot be forgiven, renounced, transcended. The Twelve Step culture holds to the concept of rebirth, of each day as the first day. Memory is not always inclined to accept the cleansing dictums and ready fellowship of AA. In some men's lives, memory is a witness that will not let go, despite the most agonized pleas for peace and repentance. Perhaps the human condition requires some of us not to move on from these events, even at the expense of our sanity. There may be no forgiveness, no new day, only the repetitive acknowledgment of what happened, of what was done, and what was not. The redemption Thomas can find may no longer be in his individual life, but in what his life can say to others. His own tragedy and loss can become a testimony to the injustice that poverty breeds. His story can serve as a cautionary tale of how violence begets violence and how the womb of despair seldom bears hope.

In Thomas's story, we have seen one manner of response, destructive agency, to the violations of positive agency that poverty inflicts upon masculine identity. In the next section of this chapter, we turn to a different, but equally despairing, response to the disruptive influences of urban poverty and drug use. Rolando Diggs's story demonstrates how the surrender of agency can become intertwined with addiction in a man's life and block meaningful efforts at sobriety.

Rolando Diggs

Before I interviewed Rolando Diggs, I had both heard about him at the Pines and causally joked with him in the corridors. He was a talkative, charismatic presence among the men. He was quick with laughter and good-natured teasing. He clearly liked to be liked and had no trouble achieving that end. At 6' 5" and 240 pounds, Rolando towered over me in our interview. When we began his life story, he confessed to a little nervousness and was at first unsure how I wanted him to proceed. Within a few minutes, when he saw there were no rules or right ways, he relaxed and then talked openly and fluidly for great stretches without a break. Though many men whom I interviewed had described for me the ruthless trap of crack addiction, none was more eloquent or clear than Rolando in depicting his own personal hell.

Rolando Diggs was born in Hartford in 1957. He is the oldest child and only son, with four younger sisters. He grew up in a modest apartment, a block away from a large housing project called Stowe Village. It was still fairly new and clean when he was a boy, but he recalled there was a lot of drinking and the kids from Stowe Village were very tough and angry. By the time he was a teenager, Stowe Village had turned into a place where living conditions were declining and drug deals were common. When I asked Rolando for his self-defining memory, he recalled the most significant incident from his childhood.

This is not hard for me to do because the memory I always think about was when I was seven years old and that's when my father left my mother. My mother was pregnant with my baby sister. And it really hurts me because of the fact that we almost ended up out on the streets. If it wasn't for the kind-hearted landlord that we had in the apartment building we was in, we would have been put out on the streets. So it's something I never forgave my father for because from that point on I had to become a man instead of living out my childhood. I couldn't live out my childhood because I had to help out my mother. And then my mother eventually had to go to school to become a nurse's aide and then she had to work two jobs to support us, so nine times out of ten, I was in the house most of the time, taking care of my sister. . . . I was really a studious person. I loved school, but then as time was passing by, I had to deal with the streets to protect my sisters and my mother.

Rolando's self-defining memory of his father's departure from the home captures each of the key themes that organize his life story. His sense of hurt and rejection by his father remained with him as a fundamental feature of his personality. Later on during his military service years, he described himself as having no ego, literally no self-esteem. Often children from homes in which parents have separated interpret the one parent's absence as a commentary on their personal worth (e.g., "If I had been better behaved or more lovable, he or she would not have left").

In recalling his memory, Rolando claimed that he lost his childhood because of taking on the responsibilities of being the man of the house. He watched his sisters for long stretches of time while his mother both worked and attended nursing school. His mother's need to work two jobs also left him without parental supervision after school, forcing him to learn how to deal with the streets. In Rolando's story, the mention of the streets always reflects the world of violence and substance abuse in which he participated. Finally, his self-defining memory stressed how the streets pulled him away from school and his studies, despite the pleasure he took in learning.

Considering this memory dynamically in the context of Rolando's life narrative, certain revealing themes emerge. For Rolando, from the age of seven responsibility became linked with a powerful resentment. The text of this resentment goes something like this—my father cut out on me, robbing me of economic security and my childhood, therefore all these efforts I make at being responsible (taking care of my sisters instead of playing outside) have been imposed on me by his irresponsibility. The act of responsibility for Rolando is associated with feeling out of control and powerless—the very reverse of what we would expect in the healthy development of positive agency. This reversal is reinforced, of course, by peer pressure from the street. As long as Rolando acted responsibly and did not fight back in the street, he felt isolated and impotent. Once he stood up and fought against the other kids, he was accepted and initiated into their drinking circles. In an additional reversal, the model of masculine agency in his family was not in fact to be responsible, but to step away and leave in pursuit of greater pleasure. Rolando was often caught between being the man his father had not been (i.e., providing for his mother and sisters) and being the man his father actually was (i.e., not being constrained by responsibility, and doing his own thing).

Though Rolando's family struggled with poverty, he was still looked at as better off by the kids who lived in Stowe Village. They would approach him in groups and shake him down for money on the way to school. Despite his large size (he was already over six feet by his early teens), he was very shy and passive, and unwilling to fight back at first. Things changed when he stood up for himself.

Matter of fact, when I took my first drink, it was in Stowe Village. That's when I finally got accepted because after taking all the jumpings and beatings that I took, I finally decided to fight back. And what really changed my aspect then, was that when I fought back, I won. . . . So that's when my lifestyle started to take a real change. That's when I started to get really a little more bolder and I started to hang out a lot.

After a brief flirtation with membership in a street gang, Rolando took a more positive step and devoted himself to sports. Similar to Thomas, his athletic career offered him structure and positive feedback that helped forestall his more negative approach to agency. He became a star athlete, first for Fox Middle School and then for Weaver High School, both in Hartford. He was selected two years consecutively as an all-state player in both football and basketball. Though he drank and smoked marijuana with friends, he managed to maintain a good academic record as well as excelling on the playing field. With his principal's backing, he was contacted by some colleges about potential athletic scholarships. Though his teachers urged him to consider these offers, he decided to enter the military service.

This choice continues to haunt him with regret, but at the time, he felt that he had to do something to generate more immediate income for his mother and sisters. Though his mother attempted to persuade him otherwise, he could not let go of this responsibility.

My mom even talked to me about it, too. She said, "We can manage, we can manage." And I said, "But Mom, you're working too hard, you're doing too many jobs. There are too many of us for you to be takin' care of and running yourself ragged." 'Cause my mother had high blood pressure. So I had my mind made up to go into the service. But as I grew, as I was doing my time in the service, I did regret coming into the service. I wanted to go to college. As a matter of fact, I would meet people that came into the service after slight careers in professional leagues and I was envious, and I was jealous. 'Cause I would say to myself, "Damn, you know, I could have been there." . . . I had a big resentment toward going into the service after a while and a resentment toward myself. I said, "Look at this shit, you just made the dumbest mistake you could make. But it was too late. And then that's where the liquor started flowing.

In Rolando's decision to join the military, we find the perpetuation of his distorted sense of agency first identified in his self-defining memory. Though Rolando's choice to enlist was made in the interest of acting as the man of the family and asserting his sense of responsibility and competence to earn income for the family, he continues to experience the decision as "giving in" or "giving up." For Rolando, being responsible is bound up with self-denial and putting his own desires or ambitions on hold.

There may also be a way in which he was fearful of taking the risk to act on his ambition. By choosing the secure route of the military, he did not have to face the possibility that he would fail in sports or in college. Without a strong supportive male in his life, he may also have been prone to more self-doubt about his capacity to fulfill his more demanding aspirations for himself. Whatever the combination of reasons for his choice not to attend college, Rolando soon felt a sense of thwarted agency and regret over his action. His primary response to this regret was to drink and pursue pleasure in an open rejection of so-called responsible living.

Rolando spent six years (three as a medic and three as part of the military police) in the Army. He had started off as a model soldier and met enough success that he decided to reenlist. As the years went on, he felt an increasing lack of purpose or motivation. When he entered, he had felt like the male head of his household and responsible for his mother and younger sisters. Far from home, and sending them money, he felt cut loose from these responsibilities and the result was boredom and loneliness. He increasingly filled his time with drinking, which was a major activity of many of the enlisted men. The liquor was inexpensive and there were many bars that catered to the soldiers from the bases. He became increasingly undisciplined, engaging in bar fights, disobeying orders, and returning late to base.

While I was in the service, I was just miserable. I just thought I had no purpose, my self-esteem was down. You couldn't call me egotistical, because I didn't have no ego. All I wanted to do was get drunk, get rowdy, laugh, joke. I treated life as a joke. Because I think, after I graduated from high school, I had to play the role of the adult. . . . My mother made me feel responsible, because I was still responsible for my sisters. I had to still protect them, protect my mom. But once I got in the service, all those responsibilities was gone, because all I could do was send money home.

I mentioned that when I had first encountered Rolando, I had already heard of his reputation for teasing and creating laughter among the men at the Pines. In describing his behavior in the military, Rolando is defining for us a central imago in his life—Rolando, the joker. Hidden behind this persona of an easy-going fun-loving drinker is Rolando's profound sense of despair over his surrendered agency. Feeling without purpose or motivation, he says "Fuck it—Fuck me, I might as well drink." In expressing this sentiment, he is simultaneously declaring his liberation from the shackles of a prematurely imposed responsibility that has shaped his entire life.

With his escalated drinking, life became quite rocky in the service. After a series of violations (Article 15s) for misbehavior, and after losing rank, though he did regain it, he was encouraged to accept a deal to leave the army immediately with an honorable discharge. Given how chaotic and dangerous his behavior under the influence of alcohol had become, he felt lucky to have the offer from the military and soon returned to civilian life.

By this point in Rolando's life, his ambivalence about his responsibility to his family and his anger against his absent father were disrupting any positive development in his life. Having short-circuited his own college ambitions because of his desire to replace his father as the male provider in the household, he had run smack into his own resentment about this choice. Stuck in a service career that held no interest for him, he was foundering in a sense of meaninglessness. Alcohol removed this dilemma and diverted him into a short-term pursuit of good times and pleasure. By the time Rolando came out of the service in 1981, he was suffering from a serious drinking problem.

He married that same year at the age of twenty-four and had a daughter later in the year. He told me that he had convinced his future wife to have his child and then married her after she became pregnant. He had somehow felt that by becoming a father he would find a positive structure and sense of responsibility that he had lost in his years in the service. He was determined to be a better and more reliable parent than his own father had been.

Within a few months, he returned to his pattern of drinking until morning and gambling large sums of money with friends. Though he always managed to have a job, he would spend his paycheck from Friday to Monday and have nothing left for his family. He would also lose jobs because of absences and showing up high for work. After a series of evictions for unpaid rent, his wife had had enough and they were separated and then divorced in 1985.

Rolando continued to find employers willing to hire him. Rolando, the joker, had a winning personality to go with his honorable discharge, and it was not difficult for him to find new work. However, the same routine of alcohol abuse would set in and he would only last a few months at most and need to move on. In the same way, he was initiating a series of relationships with women, convincing them to invite him to move in with them. He would live with them and take advantage of their apartments or houses until they would become fed up with his drinking and kick him out.

What was particularly painful about this period of his life was that he was beginning to lose the respect of his mother and sisters. He had been the responsible male to them for so many years, through his entire childhood and his years in the service when he had dutifully sent them money. Now he felt them backing away from him.

I started losing self-respect and that's when the family started to shy away from me too. Because when I was taking care of my sisters, the love, the bond between me and my sisters and my mother was so tight, nobody could penetrate it. Even when I was out there protecting my sisters, they would come to my aid too. I remember one time I was gettin' jumped by two guys and my sister came and jumped in too, so you know, we finally got a nickname for being together, "the Brady Bunch," but my sisters would be there for me too. And that was another thing that tore me apart, that I was beginning to realize that I was losing their love. I know I was losing their respect. Especially when I got addicted to crack.

Rolando's loss of self-respect was centrally tied to his recognition of his surrender of any positive agency in his life. Though in his childhood and military career, he had resented his role of responsible agent for his family, it had allowed him to feel a sense of identity and contribution in the society. Once he abandoned this ambivalent role and gave in fully to his "Fuck it" attitude, he lost a critical connection to positive masculine self-esteem as defined in this society. His introduction to crack only accelerated this process.

Rolando had been sniffing cocaine on nights that he was out drinking and finally a friend offered to teach him how to make crack and smoke it. He quickly developed a liking for it, but only allowed himself to do it on weekends, since he could not afford more than that. He called himself a "minor league baser" until he landed a job doing appliance deliveries in 1989. The appliance company allowed him to remove the old appliances and sell them for cash to pawnshops. This gave him a daily supply of money and he soon turned into a "major baser." He was living at his mother's home, eating her food and living rent-free, despite all his promises to help out. Meanwhile, his three sisters had all moved away and established their independence. In fact, his youngest sister, who had electrician and plumbing training, had managed to buy a house in East Hartford. One of his other sisters moved in with her. Though he felt resentment that his sisters had a house and would not share it with him, he also felt acute shame that the females in the family, all younger than him, were making it on their own.[11]

I went back on all the promises I ever made to my mother. I told my mother, I said, "Mom, I'm gonna get you your own house" and all that. And somewhere in my life, and it's still hard for me to figure out or find the exact spot, I just took a complete turn. You know, I went from the dutiful son to just the pain-in-the-ass son, always wanting to come around, always blowing his money type person. And it hurt. I was killing myself inside, and the only way I could fight this emotional pain that was flooding inside of my body was to compress it with the drugs, was to just wipe it out of me.

Within a few months of crack use, he was no longer welcome at his mother's house and was unable to work at all. He was reduced to running errands for teenage drug dealers in exchange for drugs. All pretense of autonomy or agency was now destroyed.

I would run to the store for them in a blizzard or just watch their backs, watching out for the police, or telling them where their customers were. I couldn't believe it, these kids, you know sixteen, seventeen, and I'd probably do almost anything for them.

. . . I didn't want life. All I wanted to do was get high on crack. All I wanted to do was be out there, runnin' back and forth. I got to the point, it was so embarrassing, that if I were to go to the store, I stunk, and had the same thing on for so long that the store owners wouldn't serve me. You know people would be in the store, and just turn their heads, but it didn't bother me.

He would panhandle to get food, but if he didn't eat it right away, he would end up selling it to another drug addict or exchanging it for more drugs. Then he would come down from his high and realize he still had not eaten. At 6' 5", his average weight was 230–245 and he had dropped to 170 pounds. The next few years of his crack addiction were a blur of schemes to raise money and of broken promises to family members. From a minor car accident, he was able to get an insurance settlement that covered his drugs and necessities for some months. After that, he took up with a woman who also smoked crack and after she sold her house, they moved to California for a new start. After a month or two out in the west, he picked up crack again and ended up back in Connecticut. From there, he moved to North Carolina to live with sober relatives. They found him a job at a turkey processing plant. He stayed clean for a short period, but hated the back-breaking work of lifting frozen turkeys over his head and hanging them on hooks. He was bored and lonely so far from his home and once again relapsed. Throughout this period of his life, the only thing that gave him real pleasure was the first hit from the crack pipe.

When I take that first hit, it seems like every tense moment, every feelin' I have, no matter how down I feel or how angry I feel, all that just comes out, as soon as I exhale that hit. And all of sudden, my whole body is just tingling, it's such a pleasant feeling, it's like havin' sex man, just right after you finish, after sex you're relieved and you're floatin', and my head's just clear and empty, and I'm just feeling tingling all over. But it lasts seconds. So in order to keep goin,' once it dissipates from your body . . . your body tells you, "Oh no, we gotta get more, we gotta get more, because I'm startin' to feel my same old way, startin' to feel tired, startin' to feel all my burdens. I'm startin' to feel all my emotions." Inside, everything is just running amuck, runnin' wild. I need to get that hit to calm all this down, to sort all this out. It seems like everything just flies like a bat and stays there when I get high.

For Rolando, who had never been able to establish any positive purpose or constructive sense of meaning in his life, crack reduced his life to a clear single purpose, the chase after the next hit. All of his time and his money were devoted to this mission. He had surrendered his agency to the pursuit of the drug. His sense of self, his feelings of power, the structure of his life— all of these aspects of agency were now defined by his addiction to crack.

He ended up living in the Salvation Army dormitories on four different occasions from 1990 to 1993, working for them and earning a few dollars a week. Despite staying with the Salvation Army for periods of six months and four months, as well as shorter stints, he always ended up sneaking alcohol or crack on the sly, and each time was asked to leave. After each dismissal, he resumed the full-scale chase for cocaine.

You go back to the chase, the full blown chase. . . . You're doin' more chasin' than thinkin.' You rarely have time to think when you're chasin.' And when you do have that time, it's just but for a moment. All that pain and anguish, and sorrow and hatred you feel comes out in that moment, that's when you start to realize that these people are hurtin' you, they fuckin' with you, that's when you have outbursts of anger and stuff like that. But then as soon as you get another hit, I'm amazed by this, because now I can look at it, as soon as I get another hit of cane, I'm not mad at them no more. And I don't want to work no more, and I don't give a damn about this or that no more.

. . . In the chase, every single thing, every single moment comes at you as soon as your body realizes you don't have any drug in your system. . . . All that bullshit in your head, the people you love, you ready to cry, get angry, be sad. Before you know it, you're snappin' at everybody, "Yeah, I'm sick of this, I'm tired of getting high, I'm ready to quit." All that comes to you. But then, as soon as you get a hit, you can forget all that, all of the preachin' you did, tellin' everybody, "I don't know how long you're gonna do this, but I'm gonna quit, I'm gonna find help." You forget all that. . . . We'll sit there in a group, gettin' high, all we do is just look at each other, we might get up enough courage inside of us to play a game of cards, and we like, "I'm tired of this. I smell, man, I'm ready to go back to work. I miss my daughter." We talk about the loved ones, we talk abut how we love this and that. What we miss in life, playin' ball and stuff. Matter of fact, when I was gettin' high off of crack, in my chase, I didn't play no more sports, as much as I love sports. Didn't play no more sports. I liked to write poems, didn't write no more poems.[12]

Rolando's words express eloquently the terror that sobriety had come to hold for him ("All that pain and anguish, and sorrow and hatred you feel comes out at that moment"). Confronted with these existence-wrenching emotions, the crack pipe seems almost like a necessary antidote. All sobriety could offer was the naked acknowledgment of the neglect and failure he allowed to dominate his life.

In 1993, for the first time, he began to get arrested—for sleeping in abandoned buildings, for shoplifting, for conspiracy to sell drugs. His body had also begun to break down because of neglect and exposure. He was back to running errands for the young drug dealers and forced to endure a brutal winter.

I'm walking a mile and half from the convenience store just to get these boys a bag of potato chips. And I don't have no winter attire, the sneakers I had on had holes in the bottom, all in the side, my feet soakin' wet. My feet had foot fungus, so thick I could peel chunks off. Matter of fact, people thought I got hit in the leg, my feet were so bad if I touched a little pebble, I was screamin' bloody murder.

Facing the possibility of going to jail for the first time and with nowhere to live, he was very grateful to come up to Lebanon Pines. When I spoke with Rolando, he had been there for four months, and was filled with an enthusiasm about his recovery. However, he had taken a few passes and experienced strong cravings; he still felt unready to make it outside of treatment. On the whole, he felt more hopeful than he had in years. He had even visited and spoken with his daughter, who was now twelve years old. Though he was only in the earliest and most fragile stages of his efforts at recovery, I asked him what message he took away from the story of his addiction.

Never to give up hope. There was a point that I gave up hope. It was the point that I wanted to die, the point that I didn't want to wake up. But I said (I learned now, that I said to myself), "Lord, if you are goin' to continue to wake me up, then I must do better." Know what I'm sayin'? I must strive to do better. Because I don't want to wake up no more in the world that I was before. I don't want to create the havoc I did in my life that I already did. I done as much damage as I think I can survive, so I'm not goin' to do any more. I'm prayin', one day at a time, that I can stay clean and sober.

The Surrender of Agency

As we consider Rolando's story, what are the limitations in applying the disease model of addiction to his chronic addiction? Unlike Thomas, Rolando did not suffer from any strong genetic loading for addiction. Neither his mother nor his father was a drinker and none of his sisters developed any problems with substance abuse. Part of Rolando's shame was that he was the only one in his family who abused alcohol or drugs.

If we do not place a strong emphasis on his biological vulnerability, then we can consider two other factors less emphasized by disease concept proponents—aspects of his personality and aspects of his environment. It is not always well-received in AA circles to point to the psychological makeup of the alcoholic as a contributor to the addiction. Alcoholics feel enough shame and self-loathing; the acceptance of the disease concept can free them from "beating up" on themselves. On the other hand, it is hard to look at Rolando's life up to this point and not see aspects of his personality that have contributed to his current predicament. At each juncture in his life, his ambivalence about the responsibility that had been thrust too early upon him led him to reject it rather than find better ways to accept it. For example, having assumed the roles of husband and father, he immediately felt encumbered by them and resentful of their daily demands. It was almost as if a part of him was saying, "Why should I be a husband and father, if my father wasn't willing to do this?" He felt more empowered when he was out with his friends. He described to me how they would tease him about staying home.

They'd say "Oh, you can't come out, man, you gotta go home to your wife" and so I defied that.

His gambling served the same purpose as drinking—to give him a momentary sense of autonomy, of heightened freedom and power; feelings that conventional responsibility only seem to squash and deaden. With continued use of alcohol leading to the loss of his marriage and daughter, he became the man he both desperately did not want to be and wanted to be—his own father. Once cut loose from any responsibility of wife and child, he buried himself in his crack addiction. If accepting responsibility felt suffocating and destructive, then abandoning responsibility felt equally noxious. From the "dutiful son to just the pain-in-the-ass son" was a bitter transition for Rolando and he began the process of "killin' myself inside" and fighting the pain of this slow death with ever more drugs. Whatever other factors contributed to Rolando's chronic addiction, there is certainly a traceable path between his crisis in meaning over becoming an adult and the perpetuation of his addiction through the full surrender of his agency as a man.

Rolando's humiliating descriptions of his role running errands for teenage drug dealers captures the depth of his self-destructive crisis. He paints a picture of an adult reduced to serving boys, the absolute reverse of his original memory, in which he was a boy taking on the role of an adult. If he once suffered deprivations from his excessive responsibility, he now suffers greater deprivations in the service of a drug that promised relief from that burdensome responsibility. Rolando, the joker, has become in the eyes of these boys and in his own eyes, Rolando, the joke.

What I am suggesting is that there is a coherent theme in Rolando's life story—his ambivalence about agency made the world of drinking and drugging particularly seductive to him. I asked Rolando his own understanding of how he had ended up trapped in an addictive cycle.

I know it's rough growin' up in the inner city, and there ain't no jobs, but I got a job, I got a good education. So, no I got to be truthful, the problems that supposed to be on the so-called black man didn't affect me at all.

. . . Matter of fact, I will not blame anyone. I had a resentment of my father because he left us, but the way that I had choices in my life, I chose the wrong choices.

If I do good, then I can praise that I did good. . . . I want to say, "Rolando, we did it. We did it. Me and my inner self, we did it." So that's what I'm strivin' at. I made all the wrong decisions, now I have to see if I can make the right decisions.

Rolando's words suggest that he has no difficulty acknowledging that his own personality and choices have played a role in his addiction. However, even though I want to emphasize the role that struggles with identity can play in addiction, I cannot accept Rolando's reduction of his problems to simply a question of his internal characteristics and personal behavior. As I have outlined in the previous chapters of this book, identity is a psychosocial construction; it is crafted out of who we are (biologically and psychologically) and what our familial and societal circumstances have presented us. The contribution of biological, psychological, and social factors is what Erikson meant by "triple bookkeeping" (see Chapter 2) in the formation of identity.

In forfeiting responsibility at many critical points in his life, Rolando did indeed make bad decisions. Sustained sobriety will require making better decisions. Conversely, I find his complete rejection of the influence of social conditions on his life equally problematic. Rolando says that if he does better, he wants to know that it is him and his "inner self" that are responsible. In asserting this desire, he also refuses to acknowledge the role of his poverty or his absent father in his current problems. This embrace of a "new age" formulation of his addiction is as bereft of a social analysis as a genetic or disease concept explanation would be.

Rolando's surrender of agency is a function of who he is as a human being with a unique "inner self," but it is also determined in part by the very social factors he dismisses. Though in his current concern with "one day at a time sobriety," Rolando's past may not hold much bearing for him in his life at present, for those of us interested in reducing levels of addiction, his past should still capture our concern. The combination of poverty and fatherlessness, as well as his proximity to housing projects with many troubled kids, increased his vulnerability to developing an addictive habit. The economic pressures on his mother kept her away from home and interfered with his development through childhood.

Research has demonstrated that children without adequate adult supervision are more susceptible to the influences of peers and more likely to initiate and continue substance abuse.[13] The lessons he learned in the street and indirectly from his father's absence were taken deeply into his own sense of self-worth and understanding of masculinity. The influence of these social factors on Rolando's adult choices to use drugs does not absolve him of his responsibility for his choices, but to disregard his life circumstances as contributing influences to his choices makes little sense. Unfortunately, this ideology of selfhood without context is too often promoted by Twelve Step groups and self-help movements. As Greenberg writes in his incisive analysis of the tendency of the recovery movement to detach the self from its relationship to personal and social influences,

> Redemption is no longer even a matter of coming to terms with one's own parents, and with the limitations posed simply by being the kind of being which bears the inscription of a particular family's history. Instead it is to be found in becoming the parent of one's own inner child, freed from the constraints of history and the "contamination" of external events. . . .[14]

I am concerned that a recovery ideology that teaches that the past or that particular social circumstances do not matter ("anyone can become an addict") leaves men like Rolando with no context for how to make the future better. Yes, he must avoid the alcoholic tendency to dwell in the past and wallow in resentment, but he can also learn productively from the past. He can attempt to understand the kind of man his father was and why he made the poor choices that he did.[15] History can teach us lessons that will guide us to better choices in the future.

Similarly, an acknowledgment that growing up in urban projects makes the surrender of agency more likely opens the possibility of a political consciousness. Men's responsibility in this society entails more than simply not drinking and going to work. For men in this society, whether recovering addict or non-addict, black or white, responsibility also means social responsibility—a commitment to changing the social circumstances that make young boys like Rolando vulnerable to drug and alcohol use.[16] Boys like the one Rolando once was are still making choices every day, good ones and bad ones, but we, as adults in the society, should do everything in our power to make those choices legitimate ones. When a seven-year-old had to choose between being the man of the house or joining a street culture of destructive "freedom," does it make sense to think about his subsequent problems as only a product of an undeveloped personality or "bad choices?" I am not sure "choice" is the operative word.

Concluding Thoughts—The Line of Despair

Once when I was in ninth grade, I needed to take a bus from my home in Woodbridge, Connecticut, to the downtown of New Haven. The total distance was no more than five or six miles. I am embarrassed to say I had never done it before. Though I traveled to New Haven fairly regularly, I always did so in the thick comfort of my parents' Volvo station wagon. Woodbridge is an affluent bedroom community that sits on a forested hill above the harbor of New Haven. It is also a segregated community; there were perhaps four black students in my graduating class of 530. In contrast, New Haven is among the ten poorest cities in the United States and nearly 87 percent of its public school students are black or Hispanic.[17]

Riding the bus to New Haven that day, sharing my trip with a mixture of white and black passengers, I remember feeling a surge of sentimental brotherhood. The words of Walt Whitman, whose poetry I had just discovered, passed through my mind.

> *The armies of those I love engirth me and I engirth them*
> *They will not let me off till I go with them, respond to them,*
> *And discorrupt them, and charge them full with the charge of the soul.*"[18]

Ironically, on the ride home on the bus, I took the wrong route and found myself traveling through a series of barren projects only a few miles from the border of Woodbridge. Now I was the only white rider on the bus and felt acutely how separate my world was from the world of the other riders.

In the years that I worked at SCADD, I took another bus ride, not entirely dissimilar to my New Haven ride of twenty-five years earlier. I traveled in my meetings with men and women to places that I would not normally go, learned from their memories and images about the bleakest aspects of poverty. Always though, I was a mere visitor, able to ride home to safer places and to turn my thoughts to less distressing concerns. I did manage to learn that a multilayered world exists within what I long ago saw only as "the projects." I came to understand that there exists more than a line between poverty and privilege or black and white. There is also a line of despair among those in poverty, a line that the vast number of people living in the inner city fight powerfully to avoid crossing.

Let us think for a moment about this familiar metaphor of the poverty line, the defining line that people live either above or below. In Woodbridge, up on the hill where I grew up, this vertical imagery of being above or below a line had real significance. Black people seldom came up the hill and whites only descended to specified places. For the most part, the line between Yale University and the adjacent Dixwell Avenue projects where Thomas grew up was just as uncrossable, though only a city block and no hills separated the two.[19] We would like to feel that with the advances since the civil rights legislation of the sixties such lines among us are gradually fading, but the economic rise of black individuals in this nation is still agonizingly slow.

What I saw the day I took the wrong bus line home was only this most obvious line—the line between "us" and "them," the line between rich white and poor black. What I have come to learn most deeply in my years of working with people who live in poverty—white, black, or Hispanic—is that there is yet another line that exists within poor communities. Beneath this line of despair, impoverished individuals resort to hustling, gang life, crime, drug dealing, and prostitution. Beneath this line, alcoholism and drug addiction become commonplace solutions to the persistent presence of death, alienation, and hopelessness in impoverished lives.

Between these two lines, the line marking privilege and the line marking despair, lives a diverse community of hard-working poor. As Jesse Jackson pointed out in a recent speech in New Haven (May 31, 1996), he is tired of the fact that our all too familiar image of the black man in the media is of a "gangsta" wearing a backwards cap and baggy pants, and sporting a gold chain. My fellow bus riders that day and the vast majority of economically disadvantaged black clients I have treated over the years have had little in common with that stereotype.

Limited economic opportunities caused by discrimination, inadequate educational resources, lack of health care, limited access to mental health and counseling services—all of these factors make passage out of poverty an arduous climb for those below the line of privilege. On the other hand, the omnipresence of drugs, crime, and multigenerational unemployment makes the descent below the line of despair difficult to resist. One frustrated man who repeatedly relapsed and returned to the drug scene put it like this, "I try and try to break free, but it feels like the devil has got me by the ankle and won't let go." Poverty is that devil—the person in its grip is lucky to stay above the ground. To rise up and break through to the world of privilege is an extraordinary accomplishment.

Since my work at an agency treating addiction inevitably brought me into contact with people who had slipped below this line, I often found myself unable to condemn or dismiss these people. Sometimes by making the necessary point that the majority of citizens living in poverty are not involved with drugs or crime, we inadvertently malign those who are. Listening to the stories of Rolando and Thomas, coming to know them in the brief way that I did, I cannot deny their humanity or their capacity for feeling pain or love. They were the first to acknowledge their bad choices, their lost chances. Despite Thomas's penchant for violence, there existed in him such a highly demanding sense of right that it was literally driving him crazy with remorse. These men were indeed accountable for the lives they harmed and for the children they brought into this world. Society correctly shows a respect for their manhood by demanding they suffer consequences or make restitution for their maleficence. However, their accountability does not remove their right to be listened to, to have their stories known, to be part of the human dialogue.

Nowhere is this idea better expressed than in the Gospel according to St. Luke.[20] Two thieves are nailed to crosses next to Jesus's cross. One cries out to Jesus that if he is indeed Christ, he should save both them and himself. The other thief cautions the first thief that he should be careful to invoke God, since they indeed have earned their punishment, even if Jesus has not. He then turns to Jesus and, addressing him as "Lord," asks to be remembered when Jesus comes into his kingdom. Jesus answers, "Verily I say unto thee, Today shalt thou be with me in paradise."

By accepting the consequences of his wrongdoing and acknowledging the possibility of a transcendent world, the thief will join the man he calls his lord in a better world. The message of this passage is a radical challenge. If Jesus, a symbol of purity and goodness, will share paradise with a thief, who are we, with our multitude of pettinesses, vices, and dishonesties, to wash our hands of other human beings?

In listening to men like Rolando and Thomas, in opening up, however momentarily, to their worlds of pain, I return to those words of Whitman that I recited in my first bus trip and think about them in a new light:

> *The armies of those I love engirth me and I engirth them,*
> *They will not let me off till I go with them, respond to them*

When I began my work at SCADD, and asked the men and women there to tell me their stories, I came to realize that their stories demanded a response. This response begins in the recognition that simply getting off at my stop and walking away implicates me in the conditions that engender their troubled lives. I am more astonished now than when I took my ride those many years ago about what we allow, what I allow, to exist in our society. It is no wonder we draw our lines so steep between the Woodbridges and the projects so close by. We would rather not know, not see. We would rather consign the problem of drug addiction in the inner city to a category of disease or a moral weakness than recognize its origin and perpetuation as a social problem.

The benefit that I see from looking at addiction through the lens of identity and meaning is that such an analysis requires a linking of the self to the society and of the past to the present and the future. When individual lives are placed in social and historical contexts, we cease to see addiction as a problem within the person, resolvable only through medical intervention or self-help. The corruption of agency that characterizes the lives of Thomas Turner and Rolando Diggs necessitates a response that goes beyond the individual. We are forced to consider our collective responsibility to create a society in which the legitimate prospect of positive agency is available not only to boys from Woodbridge, but to those of Dixiwell Avenue in New Haven and Stowe Village in Hartford.

6. LUST AND GREED
Addiction and the Empty Self

In this chapter, we meet Doug Richards, a self-made millionaire. Despite his great success in work, his addiction to drugs and alcohol perpetually brought him to depths of despair and self-loathing. Though he worked hard and reaped the benefits of money, status, and power, he still ended up penniless and a resident of Lebanon Pines. Doug Richards's life illustrates how the materialism and consumerism of our culture can twist the legitimate pursuit of agency into greed and reduce meaningful communion into impersonal lust. As all of us, addicted and non-addicted alike, attempt to find a sense of identity through agency, we face a society that often substitutes instant gratification and magical transformations through consumption for the building up of self-respect and autonomy through diligence and public citizenship. Doug Richards's manic journey from rags-to-riches-to-rags expresses clearly what Philip Cushman has dubbed the problem of the •empty self' in American society.[1] By first examining the destructive influence of consumerism on identity formation, we can see how Doug Richards's addiction is not simply a biological disease or a problem amenable to Twelve Step treatment. His addiction reflects larger social forces that make the attainment of meaningful agency problematic for all of us.

The Empty Self

In his book *Constructing the Self, Constructing America*, the psychologist Philip Cushman presents a historical analysis of how psychotherapy, both as a clinical practice and a cultural discourse, has became a central part of American society. Critical to his argument is a depiction of the modern self as based in the twin activities of acquisition and consumption.

Cushman argues that our understanding of the self is bounded by particular sociohistorical periods. There is no immutable self that can be defined by certain fundamental structures or properties. For example, the psychoanalytic conception of a self consisting of competing psychological structures (id, ego, superego) is a product of the Victorian culture in which Freud studied and developed his theories. The sexually repressed culture of his time made Freud more likely to understand the "hysterical" symptoms of his female clients as a response to inhibited sexual desire. Though Freud conceived of his discoveries as universal truths about human nature, we can look back now and see the cultural boundedness of his pronouncements.

Cushman's concern with how theories of the self reflect the social and political themes of a particular historical period is part of a larger hermeneutic or "interpretive" enterprise.[2] Hermeneutics denies that an objective world can be known with detachment and impersonal precision. The researcher always brings a cultural context to the subject of study and the object of study is always embedded in social and political relationships. Only within a "hermeneutic circle," can interpretations emerge, and all interpretation can do is to shed light on how an object discloses the pressing concerns or conflicts of a particular society or culture. With regard to his analysis of the self through the hermeneutic lens, Cushman writes,

> The self embodies what the culture believes is humankind's place in the cosmos—its limits, talents, expectations, and prohibitions. In this hermeneutic sense the self is an integral aspect of the horizon of shared understandings. There is no universal, transhistorical self, only local selves; there is no universal theory of the self, only local theories.[3]

Cushman's perspective supplements McAdams's emphasis on the life story as an entry into individual identity. In the hermeneutic inquiry, the goal is not to "read" individuals, but more to stand behind them and decipher the "cultural text from which they themselves are reading."[4] What about our culture then, according to Cushman's analysis, might be read in the "text" of Doug Richards's chronic addiction?

Though Cushman supplies a sweeping historical survey of changes in the construction of the self up to the present era, what is of most concern in understanding the relationship of the self to chronic addiction can be traced back to developments in the nineteenth century. As I discussed in Chapter 2, the new members of the fledgling American democracy, freed from religious and ancestral hierarchies, confronted the possibility and anxiety of forging a personal and unique identity. This freedom to create the self was linked to what the historian Frederick Jackson Turner called the frontier myth, the idea that Americans lived on a boundary between the untamed interior of the country and the stifling traditions of the old world. The mythic challenge of creating American society was to find a way of negotiating this tension, of bringing order to the wild without forsaking the "enchantment" and passion that differentiated it from the crowded and corrupt cities of the east and Europe.[5] The cowboy, a rugged individual, liberated from social conventions and free to roam the open prairie, became the archetypal symbol of the American self. He is also the ultimate emblem of agentic power and autonomy—John Wayne—tall, strong, and self-made.

Parallel to this vision of an idealized frontier was the concept of the "enchanted" psychological interior. Victorian society saw the need to reign in and control all irrational impulse and passion; the self required external structure and discipline to succeed in capitalistic bourgeois society. Though a strong current of moralistic and self-denying ideals pervaded American culture throughout the nineteenth century, Cushman suggests Americans also began to develop a contrasting vision of the self as an untamed natural force, possessing a spiritual value and passion similar to the open prairie. The popularity of Mesmerism in America with its emphasis on animal magnetism and an inner mystical truth reflects, according to Cushman, an American optimism about the transformative powers of the self.

> Simply put, the human interior was conceived of as neither dangerous, secular, nor controlled by external events, as Europeans believed; instead it was inherently good, potentially saturated in spirituality, and capable of controlling the external world: it was an

enchanted interior, a fitting partner for the enchanted geographical "interior' that spread westward to the Pacific. It follows that whereas in Europe the path to wellness was through control of one's interior, in America wellness was to be found in liberation of one's interior.[6]

The American prairie was a vast space in which one might forge a bold new society. Similarly, a psychological interior, released from authoritarian traditions, must have represented a daunting challenge to the citizen of American society seeking to construct a stable and meaningful sense of self. Ultimately, Americans tamed the west by releasing the engine of American capitalism; they laid down railroad tracks, cultivated the prairie, mined mountains, drilled oil wells, and built up commercial centers. They turned its wild resources into vehicles of material success and wealth that left the aging and cramped world of Europe far behind. In complementary fashion, Americans increasingly defined their inner sense of identity through the goods they accumulated and the monetary success and social status they achieved. By harnessing his internal resources—talents, skills, energy, initiative—the average man could reach a level of prosperity that would have been inconceivable in traditional class-based societies. Even more, this success was based on individual mastery, an agency not beholden to an authority beyond himself. The key to a successful future was to unlock the potential of the self (just as golddiggers mined the hills of California to make their fortunes). The fulfillment of the self's potential, the "pursuit of happiness," as manifest through material well-being, now became the primary purpose of life, as opposed to allegiance to a particular community or transcendent belief.

By the end of the nineteenth century, as the American economy shifted increasingly from a rural economy to an industrial and business base, the requirements for the successful cultivation of this interior self also changed.

> Capitalism was moving into a new phase of its history. An emphasis on producing goods through hard work and honest labor was being replaced by an emphasis on sales and consumption of goods and services, predicated upon the effectiveness of a sales technique and/or the attractiveness of the individual salesperson.[7]

Cushman argues that this shift to an emphasis on personality as the vehicle to success led individuals to turn to the developing fields of psychology and advertising to guide them in their efforts at self-cultivation. Individuals, determined to keep up with the demands of business and an increasingly consumer economy, looked to the science of human behavior and the advice and recommendations of magazine articles and advertisements (and later, radio and television) to help them to determine the proper conduct, appearance, and attitude to achieve success. If Americans grew ever more dependent on the selling of themselves to make a successful living, then any information or products that could enhance the self by making the person more confident, attractive, skillful, persuasive, powerful, and so forth would be a prized commodity in the society.

Here then is the relationship of the empty self to a capitalist consumer society as it has progressed throughout the twentieth century. The self is filled and formed by selecting and consuming products that have been endorsed by scientific "experts" or role model celebrities. If advertising can convince individuals that a better personality and subsequent success will result from the acquiring or consuming of a product, then their purchases of these commodities will keep the wheels of capitalism spinning. Even better, if the expression of individualism or self-definition can be achieved by consuming a particular product, individuals will actually see buying a product as a way of being themselves. Finally, if these products are finite and used up rapidly through planned obsolescence, the self soon feels empty and in fact, no longer itself, until it can purchase and take in more of the self-transforming product.

For example, Cushman describes a beer commercial in which the very average character is turned into a "party animal" simply by drinking the right beer.

> That's what consuming can do: It can transform the empty individual into a new, nondepressed, sexy, popular, rich, altogether happy and satisfied person who attracts others.[8]

He adds that it is no wonder that adolescents and young adults seek out drugs as a way to respond to negative experiences and frustrations in their lives.

> Of course they think that purchasing and ingesting a commodity will transform them; they have seen it happen for years, day in and day out, in television commercials.[9]

The reliance of the empty self upon commodities or psychological expertise (including psychotherapy) is a consequence of our emphasis on unbridled agency. By making our model of the individual an autonomous agent, separated from tradition, unencumbered by the past, we create an individual lost in space, depending on an "inner truth" that is ultimately defined (whether they know it or not) by the cultural ground in which they stake out their particular figure. Greenberg articulates this problem.

> A self in search of well-being, in a society which holds that "well-being" as its only common understanding of the good, cannot be distinguished from its background. Its conversation with that background is hampered by the concealment of the horizon's otherness.
>
> Such a self *thinks* it is free, but it is only "free" against the backdrop of a social world that has already defined freedom as a certain set of priorities. "Recovery" may be the freedom to buy and proudly drive a Mercedes, but this understanding of freedom is already constituted by some ontology. This understanding, which may be thoroughly concealed, gives its subjects the sense that having a Mercedes is intrinsic to the good life, that they ought to want to be the kind of person who can buy one. This in turn might make that person hold the concern with getting the car as a priority over, for instance, a concern with how the money is made to do so, with what societal practices and/or institutions are perpetuated by this pursuit.[10]

In rare moments, when we have reached an obstacle to consumption or been confronted by death or isolation, we may suddenly see how we are bound to a hollow and nihilistic culture. Despair may rear up and fill us with dread at the sense of emptiness we discover or the false heroes[11] and questionable values we have embraced. With frightening speed, we rush back to our blind habits and routines, quickly filling ourselves up to avoid these naked visions of the world we inhabit unknowingly. We return to the pretense of agency and independence, blocking out any problematic relationship we hold with others or society in general.

As we turn to Doug Richards' story, we shall see how his material success belies a corrupted agency based in a detached and empty self. In all the important ways Cushman has outlined for us, Doug Richards is clearly a product of the consumerist culture we all share. Like a buoy in a rocky cove, his story quietly alerts us to the dangerous waters in which we all travel.

Doug Richards

Meeting Doug Richards, sober and humbled at Lebanon Pines, you could never picture this man as salesman of the year, owner of eight insurance and real estate offices—as a big man around town. Balding, with long wisps of hair combed across the scalp to bridge the bare patch in front, slumped in posture, his gray-colored eyes barely revealed by his hooded and puffy lids, he looked at best like a drugstore clerk or the shoe salesman that he originally was. When I interviewed Doug, he was clearly depressed and very close to leaving the Pines. He knew he wanted to drink and that he had little intention of stopping. He knew this even though it was painfully clear that as long as he continued to drink, he could never regain his moneyed status or his prior success. Drinking had simply become a way to kill himself ("Fuck it"), to make his leaving this world an act to which he could remain as oblivious as possible. Sobriety for Doug Richards only brought awareness of loss and the hopelessness of his current life.

For Doug, alcohol and success, whether social or financial, have always been intertwined. The self-defining memory he chose to tell me makes this parallel relationship absolutely clear.

I was a very shy, withdrawn person and when I started to drink, that changed. It seemed like I belonged to the world all of a sudden. I became a part of what was going on, and that was, it was like black and white for me. From that point before, being the skinny little runt of a kid with crew cut haircuts, and not really having a lot of luck with girls and even with men relationships, and all of a sudden being the camp clown when I drank, and being very outgoing, and willing to take any kind of risk, and being one of the crowd for a change, instead of being a geek.

. . . I was a very conniving, manipulative person, so I was able to, as a way of building up my self-esteem, was able to get the booze. I got it from friends, from their parents' houses, and I always knew how to get the booze. I was the one who had it, so I was the hero. And I was the one as summer camp progressed and I became the camp program director, I was the one who controlled the partying. I said to everybody when work was all done and time to party. I told them where to party, I told them how to party, and the drinking went along with my success.

In this memory, which is rather startling in its frankness, we see Doug articulate his personal myth of consumption as an act of magic transformation. Taking his first drink could be likened to the moment Clark Kent enters the telephone booth and emerges as Superman. In alcohol Doug had found the immediate solution to his social awkwardness and negative self-image. With alcohol as his ally, he could not only gain self-confidence, but through offering and withholding of alcohol, he could gain control over others. By having power over this self-transforming commodity, he could wield power to transform others. From this early memory onward, alcohol, power, and success have become fused in Doug's understanding of himself and of his social relationships. With alcohol in his system, the imago of Doug, the invincible hero, charges forward from the telephone booth.

Doug's father suffered from alcoholism and abandoned the family before Doug was twelve. He would go away and come back periodically, with big promises, but leave drunk within a few days and not return for months or even years. Their family was very poor and as the oldest, Doug went to work at an early age. He also cooked and cleaned for the family. Life stabilized a little more after his mother divorced his father and remarried when Doug was thirteen. Though his stepfather was very strict, Doug and he got along reasonably well and he served as a positive figure in Doug's life. At the same time, a teacher at school took an interest in Doug and helped him catch up on his school work. Due to the chaos at home, he had entered junior high barely able to read. By the time he finished high school, he was an excellent student and won an appointment to the Air Force Academy. At this point his drinking was still confined to weekend parties and summer camp. On the night before his formal interview at Stover Air Force Base, he got drunk with a bunch of other potential cadets. It did not make a difference in the end, because he turned out to have a visual defect that pre-empted his chance of flying planes. Once he learned he could not become a pilot, he withdrew his candidacy and went instead to a state college in Connecticut.

Doug finished three and a half years of college with a "B" average, but began to escalate his drinking. Though he had a high school fiancée, he had initiated an affair with the summer camp nurse, who was also a heavy drinker. He broke off his engagement and eventually married the nurse, moving in with her and her three-year-old child, after she divorced her husband. Needing more money, he worked as an assistant manager at two different shoe stores, clocking fifty-five to sixty hours a week in addition to school. He learned to tell the managers anything they wanted to hear about his commitment to selling shoes as a career. His friend worked next door at a clothing store and helped him steal some clothes so that he could look good enough to go on interviews to insurance company jobs. With his sharp appearance and glib tongue, he landed an insurance sales job at age twenty-one, beating out several other applicants who were ten and twenty years his senior. The lesson learned by this early success is exactly the point Cushman was making about the shift in American capitalist values from an emphasis on honest labor to the magnetism of personality.

> Personality was shaped by attending to and manipulating others, not
> by following moral codes or adhering to religious ideals. Poise and

charm, rather than adherence to a moral code; personal grooming and health, rather than hard work and self–sacrifice, were the important behaviors to learn.[12]

With regard to McAdams's major categories of agency (see Chapter 2), Doug Richards places a premium on success, status, and achievement, with little concern for the self-discipline or responsibility that should also accompany positive agency. As he accumulated successes in his insurance work, he was also increasing his intake of alcohol, the elixir of his success.

I started working at National Consolidated in 1970. There were men there I considered my mentors, Rick Mahoney and Tim Hopper. They did well, partied well, they could sell. Our typical day would be, we worked 'til 4, then we'd go to the Maui-Maui to have drinks, and I would drive home at 9, 10 o'clock at night, drunk, sometimes have accidents. That was my life and I was doing what these people did. Working hard, playing hard. I couldn't do any of that without the drinking, because it's not my personality. It just gave me the nerve. . . . It gave me that false courage and I was able to do things that weren't me. It seems like I was acting it out all that time.

(If you could put yourself back in the mindset of those days, what was driving you, what were your goals, what did you want for yourself at that point?)

I wanted not to be poor like my parents. Money was my driving force. And that's what I lived and worked for. To have a nice car and a nice home. And I was beginning to have those things. . . . And I was a homeowner; my parents never owned a house. I had a car, I had a good job at National. I was in the top ten salesmen all the time.

My boss knew I drank a lot. He knew we all did. But we'd say, "Look what we're doing." We'd come back from the bar and had to make phone calls to make appointments. And me and Tim Hopper could get appointments in ten minutes. What would take other people two hours to do. As long as I was producing, which would be a theme throughout my career, I could always justify my drinking, or being absent, or not being on par, because I always did well the other times. The insurance business and drinking fit perfectly because I could work my own hours basically. I had nobody to tell me, "Come in at 9, leave at 5." And this is what I got used to all my life, that's the kind of job I did all my life.

Doug left National for other underwriting companies that offered him more money and he continued to excel as a top salesman. His pace became even more frantic, both at work and at the bar.

I went to work at United States Underwriters and that was a madhouse. I would literally talk on two telephones at the same time. I was a maniac, manic producer. I was non-stop. I would go in at 8 and work until 8 at night. And at that point, not drink during the day, only occasionally, but just work. Now the money was rolling in. We had started something new, advertising insurance on radio and people would call, and call, and call for quotes. We had the big insurance companies working with us and we would write a Corvette as a '62 Chevy and they would take it as that because they wanted the business and it was all cash. I was making $500–600 a week and getting four- and five-thousand-dollar monthly bonuses back in '74. And I was loving it. I loved making the money. One month I got that bonus and I went out and bought a new Z, a 240 Z, paid cash for it, went to Hawaii, started building a new house, all the time drinking like a fish. But it wasn't a problem.

As Doug described these years, I could see his face come briefly alive and I could see the aura of excitement and confidence he must have generated over the phone or in a meeting with a customer. Just as he had been the "party czar" at camp, Doug, the invincible hero, was now controlling the commodities that others could purchase to achieve their own sense of security.

On the other hand, as he told his story of his success mixed with drinking, he spat out the phrase "It wasn't a problem" with a biting irony. His mocking of this false assurance that he gained from alcohol became a kind of refrain throughout the interview. He is no longer under any illusion about the way in which he had relied upon alcohol to achieve his sense of agency, to transform his empty self. His problem now is that, without his alcoholic hero imago in place, he has not yet conceived of another way of being or of finding a sober self that he can accept.

Doug began to suffer migraines and went to see a psychiatrist. When confronted with the possibility that drinking more than a six-pack of beer every night might be contributing to his tension and headaches, he dismissed this advice as an overreaction. A few months later, this same psychiatrist killed himself, proving conclusively to Doug that this man had been a complete fraud.

I was justified in drinking. He was a nut, see, he didn't know what he was talking about. I'm OK—I'm still alive and he's dead. So everything he said just went pfff. He was a quack. He went to a hotel room and killed himself. See, he was a quack.

With money continuing to accumulate through the seventies, Doug built a house designed specifically for partying. It had a thousand square foot open floor, connecting living room, dining room, and kitchen with no intervening walls. They would have 200 people for a Christmas party, the house would be overflowing with bottles and the smell of pot was everywhere. On

Sundays, when the liquor stores were closed in Connecticut, he had found an under-the-table supplier. Just like his days at summer camp, people would call him up looking for the party and alcohol.

His wife continued to be his drinking partner. Though they argued, they still partied with each other and enjoyed their sex life. He described how they would drive drunk and stark naked to x-rated drive-in movies, have sex, and drive home, still unclothed. However, during blackouts, he became abusive to her, slapping her and running out of the house to the nearest bar. He also engaged in destructive behavior that he could not explain, breaking the antennas on cars, smashing windows and mailboxes. Though Doug could not account for this behavior, it seems to me to have great symbolic meaning. Here was this man entrusted with insuring the homes and automobiles of his customers and he was destroying the same property he protected. It is not a far leap to suggest that an unconscious, self-condemnation and unfulfilled hunger for meaning were projected outward as anger at the naive customers who helped perpetuate his lifestyle. Gaining profit could not fill his empty self and he struck out at the world in frustration.

In 1975, Doug's life took a turn that brought him more success than he could have ever anticipated. He left the ranks of the Willy Lomans to become a player in his own right, the CEO of his own company. His boss from U.S. Underwriters had come to him one night and told him that his cash flow was gone and he could not pay him. He asked Doug to work for him under the table and collect unemployment until he could pull himself out of financial problems. Doug told him he would think about it, but he had already hatched another plan. Into the phone booth and out again comes Doug, the invincible hero.

At 1:00 in the morning, I called Rick Mahoney and two other gentlemen that worked for him. At 3:00, we met at my house, at 4:00, Security Associates was forming. No money, no clients. It took the biggest balls in the world to do this. Tell this guy at the biggest agency in CT to fuck himself. Rented a space in Wethersfield, got filing cabinets, had no clients there, no insurance companies, had nothing to sell. I went out and got insurance companies. I was the mouthpiece for the company and I got us AETNA and I got us Travelers just from sheer talk. Just from telling them what we could do and how good we were going to be. Nobody said we could do it, and we did it.

When I talked to AETNA, I remember I was hung over. Still I sat there and told him that we were four young guys who were ambitious. I told him what I had done at National and at U.S. That we had marketing tools, that we could go on radio and advertise and we could write for a million dollars the first year or they could cancel us. . . . My partners were good, but I really ran the show. I was the one who went to the bank, again they said we were too young, but I convinced them to loan us four thousand dollars. We were able to pay that back and open up a large account then.

Though Doug was now the owner of his company, this increased responsibility did not slow his drinking. He continued to drink daily and heavily; he continued to drive while drunk and had a number of minor accidents. Despite these mishaps, no one could convince him that the drinking "was a problem."

Nobody could tell me it was a problem. If I did something, I was in a bad mood, or then I shouldn't have drunk Kahlúa that night. I should have stuck to vodka, or I shouldn't have drunk beer, I should have drunk wine, or I was tired. It was never the booze.

I started thinking and doing some reading. Maybe it was like a Hemingway thing. I was able to do things because of the drinking, like a poet. I was able to think and create new ways of making money in this business and create a new advertising scheme, because of the drinking. It enhanced my creativity. I was totally convinced of that. I still think it may have had something to do with it; it certainly gave me the nerve to do things a lot of people wouldn't do.[13]

Though Doug clearly worked hard, his remarkable success was based, as he was the first to admit, not only in alcohol, but in his ability to con and scheme. Why was he so good at this; why was he able to reach and exceed his goals of generating millions of dollars in insurance revenues? I am convinced that a major component of Doug's success was his ability to connect his own sense of emptiness to the emptiness and hunger in the selves of others. Given his fundamental loneliness and sense of inadequacy, he learned how to exploit this weakness in others to his own advantage. The society has no shortage of individuals seeking quick fixes that will transform their isolation and insecurity.

> The post–World War II self thus yearns to acquire and consume as an unconscious way of compensating for what has been lost, and unknowingly it fuels the new consumer-orientated economy; the self is empty, and it strives, desperately, to be filled up.[14]

"What has been lost" is meaningful agency located in unalienated craftsmanship and stable human relationships. "What has been lost" is a sense of place in a community and public space, a way of belonging beyond one's immediate and ephemeral circumstances. Doug Richards, a product of a broken family and raised in poverty, abandoned by his alcoholic father, knew this sense of loss and dislocation acutely; the difference for him was he had learned how to exploit this vulnerability in others. Through the transforming promises of advertising, he had learned a way to attract individuals and offer them one form of immediate relief from the overwhelming anxiety of living in modern society.

By 1979, Doug had bought out his partners and gone solo. He also made a new friend, Dick Manning, a helicopter pilot, who had served in the Vietnam War. They drank and smoked pot together and Doug decided to set Dick and his wife up in the insurance business. He trained them, helped them pass the licensing exam, and opened up a second office in Waterbury. Dick in turn introduced Doug to cocaine and this quickly became a passion as great as drinking for him.

I did those first lines, and I came up and Dick looked at me and he said, "What have I done? Oh my God, what have I done?" Because he could see that I loved it. I did. And that was the beginning of the end of my first marriage. I started doing coke and I started drinking with it, and the coke would lead me to longer runs, all hours, twenty-four hours at a stint.

Doug became very involved in visiting massage parlors in Hartford and getting to know the people who worked there and the people who ran them. He claimed there were many other white-collar types like himself there— attorneys, business owners, newspaper people. He would stay all night, drinking and doing coke with the women and the owners.

I would bring cocaine there and do it with the girls. At one point, I was having so much sex that my penis swelled up. I thought I had some venereal disease. I went to the Hartford Clinic and saw a nurse. I dropped my drawers and she looked at me and she was on the floor, hysterical. I say, "What's the matter?" And she says, "It's swollen from overuse. Just give it up awhile and you'll be all right."

His late hours and sexual escapades took their toll on his wife and she finally asked him to leave. It was when he mentioned the breakup of his marriage that I heard for the first time about their daughter, who had been born in 1971. Doug's comments about his relationship to his daughter say a lot about the focus of his life.

I don't like to admit this, but my children aren't part of my story, because I really didn't have a lot to do with them. They were just there, a pain as far as I was concerned. My mother and father were distanced from us, and that's how I was with my children. I really didn't want children. I really didn't care for children. So they were there. Whatever we did, they were there. We were partying in one room, they were playing with the neighbor's kid in the other room. They were just part of the scene; we had to drag them along because they belonged to us. My daughter would spend a lot of weekends with my parents, so we could go to a party.

(And there was your adopted child too, the son?)

Right, right, and I cared less for him because he wasn't mine. I mean I got further away from him, and he became a problem. Discipline problem; he was just a rowdy kid. He ran away when he was fourteen and he never came back.

In his description of his relationship to his children, we hear how he holds them in less esteem than the commodities that dominate his life. His children were "there," but they are not part of his self-narrative; they hold no transforming power to grant him material gain or success. They are not related to him or part of him; he describes them only as objects that "belong" to him, that get in the way of his efforts at consumption.

Once his first marriage was over, Doug had even less reason to put the brakes on his cocaine use. Despite his heavy drug use, his business continued to thrive and he opened several more offices around Connecticut throughout the early eighties. The cocaine also brought him in touch with drug dealers and people who were fugitives from the law.

Now the partying got even more intense. I started hanging around with people who carried guns, people from the underground, hiding from the law. People were extorting money from me. I didn't fit with these people; they were gangsters and hoodlums, carrying 57 Magnums, and they would tell me before I go to the beach for the weekend, give us $400 or else when you come back, your office will be burned to the ground. I couldn't go to the police and I had to give them money. I was getting into real trouble. Drinking and doing coke. The coke kept me out of blackouts, kept me awake and out of car wrecks. And again, the coke seemed to enhance my life. It seemed I was more energetic, could do more things, was more creative, would take more chances. I was opening up more offices.

Doug quickly married again to a woman from Rhode Island. He increasingly spent time there and began to diversify from insurance to opening up real estate offices. At the time of his second marriage, he was worth a couple of million dollars and earning a salary of $500,000 a year. As Doug told me about this period of his life, I could hear echoes again of that first self-defining memory from summer camp—how his discovery of alcohol had led him to become the party director, the don of intoxication and pleasure for others, Doug, the invincible hero.

I even did a little drug dealing in my office. Bankers, insurance people, attorneys, they would come in the office and I would have it in my desk, they would hand me a check, which I would take for the drugs, and I would hand them the drugs. And I thought at first they were coming for insurance. And I was doing a lot of radio advertising and they told me at the radio stations that I was starting to be called "Coke Man" at the station, so I stopped doing that—my name was getting around in too many places.

But I would literally ride around in my car with bank bags in my trunk of ten to twenty thousand in cash. I'd be at the bar and if you were at the bar with me, I bought the bar. People knew that when Doug was coming, that drinks were on Doug, for as long as he was able to do it.

All the money I took was in cash. The books were a mess at work. Always a hundred grand in the bank, but nobody knew how much Doug had in his car. As far as everybody else was concerned, I was the gravy train they were on and they weren't going to give me a hard time, always protected, taken care of . . . they would lie to my wives for me. Eventually, they would take me to rehabs.

With his new wife, Doug became well-acquainted with moneyed people in the beach resorts of Rhode Island. He parlayed these relationships into a growing real estate business in beach front cottages. He was still the guy with the fancy car and the nice clothes, and the great pitch. The big joke of those years was that Doug spent another summer on the beach and never got a tan; he was too busy shmoozing in the bars, putting together deals or simply partying.

I'd buy cottages on the beach, go to the bank, just with our signature, get the money. Spend Friday giving a guy fifty grand for a cottage, spruce it up, get a couple of people to paint it, put a new couch in it, the following Friday sell it for sixty-five thousand.

In addition to the cottages, Doug bought a motel and other properties. His life continued at this pace, working into the night, drinking, and doing cocaine. He owned a Mercedes (see the earlier quote from Gary Greenberg), a BMW, and a Jeep Cherokee. He was drawing 200–250 thousand dollars out of the business just for his personal use—for cars, clothes, travel, restaurant and bar accounts, and drugs. He was now drinking openly in the morning, not making it in to work, and doing cocaine despite promises to his second wife to stop. One of the starker memories from this period involved his daughter. She was fourteen and happened to open a door to reveal Doug with a dollar bill up his nose and a long line of cocaine spread out before him.

And I was so messed up at that point that I tried to convince her that she was dreaming. I kept on telling her that. It got to the point where she had to go to see a psychiatrist because she was so mixed up, and finally figured out that she wasn't dreaming. The more I told her that she was dreaming, the more I believed it myself. That it didn't happen, that she didn't catch me.

Soon, after repeated prompting from his wife and other family members, Doug broke down and came home from a bar, crying. He told his wife that he needed to do something, that he needed to go to a rehab. At this moment in telling his life history, Doug became teary-eyed and choked up, needing to pause from his narrative. This was striking for me, because up to that point, and soon after that point, his voice hardly wavered from a flat matter-of-fact account of his story. I needed to know why he was moved at this particular moment—what was digging deep into his stoic despair and opening up some vulnerability?

It's painful. It's a time where, it's happened so many times since—I guess I feel sorry for myself that I didn't see then that it could have been the only time, cause it doesn't seem to matter as much as it used to, as it did then. I guess it's just, all the people I hurt, my parents, my wife, my daughter. That was the beginning of it, and it got worse.

In these words, I hear Doug saying that his first attempt at recovery offered a window of insight, an opportunity to reflect upon his life and the way in which alcohol and drugs removed any genuine meaning or emotional attachment from it. In that first moment of insight, he understood the problematic agency he had constructed in his life and all the emptiness that it hid. When he did not avail himself of that moment of clarity, it somehow never returned. There was never a second chance to stop the rush to oblivion, to hold clearly in his mind the possibility of a deeper and more substantial life without alcohol. His tears seemed to say to me that everything after that first effort has been anti-climatic. In McAdams's terms, this memory was a nuclear episode that contained a turning point, teetering between redemption and despair. When Doug relapsed, he felt his life tip in the balance.

He completed his first rehab at a highly respected hospital in Rhode Island in the summer of 1985. He was thirty-seven years old and one of the most successful insurance underwriters in Connecticut and Rhode Island.

He came out of the treatment filled with the slogans of AA, in touch with a sponsor, and determined to attend his meetings. After sixty days or so, he had a fight with wife. Then, as he always did when people were mad at him, he gave her $500 to go antique-shopping. As he sat alone at his office desk, he strongly felt an urge to drink. He called names from his AA list and could only reach a former rehab buddy who happened to be drunk when he called. They both agreed that sobriety was too hard and Doug opened up a bottle of wine, and they commiserated together over the phone.

He had little sobriety again for the next year and a half until 1987, and then he stopped drinking for almost a year. In looking back, Doug saw this period of abstinence as a last bit of panic about the direction of his business. He did not stop with the help of AA or a sponsor. He threw himself into his work, seven days a week, twelve hours a day. He opened up more insurance offices and bought more real estate. He pushed the business's cash intake up to 10–12 million dollars a year. He had eight offices in two states, and bought homes for himself in St. Martin, Virgin Islands; North Stonington, Connecticut; a ski community in Vermont; and on the beach in Rhode Island. His monthly mortgage payments totaled $5,400. Without alcohol to consume, he filled the hunger of his self through more and more material extravagances.

During this time he had found an AA sponsor who was a fellow insurance agent with many years of sobriety. He ended up hiring him as a consultant, paying him $1,000 a month just for business advice. This turned out to cost him dearly when he suffered his next relapse. It was mid-1988 and he was driving to Waterbury hospital to visit his mother, who had experienced a return of cancer.

I'm driving, and I pull into a package store. I can't go to a hospital and see my mother without having a drink, nope. So I got a car phone and I'll call my sponsor. Well, I don't and instead I have some vodka mixed with club soda. And finally I call my sponsor and I said, "Drew, I drank." He says, "Listen, Doug, let's keep this between the two of us. I don't want to upset your wife. You drank, but you don't have to worry about it. Go back to what you've been doing, get back on the right track, and we'll keep it between the two of us." Years later I found out through counseling what that was all about, I didn't want to lose him as a consultant; he didn't want to lose me for the $1,000 a month I was paying him. So we compromised and that gave me the green light to drink on the sly and to try to get away with it.

In this next stretch of drinking, as Doug turned forty and there seemed no end to the demands of his business and the power of his addiction, he made the first of what became several suicide attempts. After an overdose of pills while drinking, he was hospitalized again. In the course of the hospital-ization, he met a new woman, who loved drinking as much as he did. Soon he was heavily involved in a new relationship and his second marriage quickly came to an end. I asked Doug how with all his drinking, cocaine, and hospital visits, he could possibly be carrying on his business and making money. He explained to me that he had an office manager named Donna, who had become his chief enabler. He had signed over power of attorney to her and she took care of all the payroll and creditor transactions. He would call her once a day, often drunk, and she would assure him everything was running smoothly. Sometimes she would drive him to the rehabs and she would constantly cover for him and lie for him. As I listened to his descrip-tion of Donna, I imagined that she was a lonely woman in love with him, who had made the business the center of her life.

No, Donna loved to help me to rehab, and she loved me to drink, because when I was away she could take my American Express card and buy what she wanted and steal money from the business, which is what she was doing. She embezzled hun-dreds of thousands of dollars.

With Donna holding down the fort (or taking it over, as the case may be), and the constraint of his second marriage over, Doug ceased working at all and simply drank and partied with his new girlfriend. They would leave for St. Martin on the spur of the moment. He was hiring limousines all the time now. They called him the "limo guy" because he used the limo services so much. When he wasn't with his girlfriend, he was hanging out at the beach bars in Rhode Island, buying the bar and offering coke. He was surrounded by a bevy of women looking for free cocaine and this group of girls became known as "Doug's girls" by the regular patrons of the bar. At this manic mo-ment of his life, he was a balding shy man, who had grown up in poverty, liv-ing out his fantasy of the American dream, of what it meant to have success—money, power, and women. It was as if he had become trapped in a fantasy beer commercial (such as the one Cushman described) looping over and over again—the geeky-looking loser picks up a Budweiser in an empty bar and suddenly beautiful women surround him, celebrities shake his hand, and the bartender smiles with benevolent approval. For the thirty seconds of the spot, all is the way it should be—he is popular, sexy, and in control. Then he wakes up and before the sickness and the black despair can set in, he sets out to drink and coke himself up, so the thirty-second spot can begin and play over and over, until he blacks out or gets kicked out of the bar at closing.

From the early 1990s on to the present, Doug's story became one of increasing debts because of divorce, legal fees for drunk driving arrests, and unpaid taxes. He also continued to make at least a half-dozen more suicide attempts through overdoses of pills. His relationship with his new girlfriend was a tortured affair of violent blackouts, breakups, and costly reconciliations through presents bought with credit cards he could not afford to pay off. Still in the dark about the true nature of Donna's "help," he had put the business in trust to her. She had convinced him to do this because the twenty-eight employees were fearful about its stability with him as its chief financial officer. Finally after returning from a rehab, he learned from a fellow employee about Donna's large-scale embezzlement from the business.

I hire this managing accountant to help me out and he literally takes over the business. I fired Donna, but we didn't have enough money to prosecute her. We had a payroll service and she would pay everybody, but make out separate checks to send to the IRS for withholding tax. When I went through her desk, she wasn't sending them in; she was just pocketing the difference. I owed the IRS $340,000 in back withholding. Now my life is totally shit. I'm drinking again, there's no way you can tell me I haven't a right to drink, cause if you had the shit I had going on, you'd be drinking too, all right! And I starting drinking with a vengeance.

The accountant he hired managed to keep the business solvent and income-generating, but he had Doug sign an agreement that he would have absolutely nothing to do with the business. In turn Doug would receive a monthly check for $800. Doug took this money and then after awhile found a sales job with one of the big Connecticut insurance chains. He managed to hang on to this job for the next couple of years and even was able to generate a good income and large bonuses. He eventually could no longer manage to make it into the office or to his appointments, and quit.

He next moved down south to try to straighten out by living with his brother, who had become a devout Christian. Doug had a brief stint of church-going and sobriety; he even managed to find an insurance sales job down there and started to make money again. Before he knew it, he was drinking, on the run, and heading back north. This same pattern repeated itself for the last year or two before he came up to Lebanon Pines. By the end, he had, like so many of the other men, resorted to living in shelters and church-supported missions. After a rehab in Hartford, he went up to Lebanon Pines for the first time in 1993, but lasted no more than a month. He found an insurance job and left, but only managed to work a few weeks before he started drinking again. He made it back to Lebanon Pines in July of 1994 after his most recent suicide attempt (this time with a razor on the wrists) put him into the hospital. He had been at the Pines for approximately two months when I interviewed him.

I had met Doug at least a year before the interview and we had had a few different sessions over the year before we sat down to talk at the Pines. When I first started to get to know Doug, I had trouble believing that this depressed shy man could have achieved the phenomenal success that he had. Ironically, I had a patient in my private practice who had worked in the same insurance company as Doug. One session this patient, who himself had a drinking problem, began to tell me why he thought his problem was not so serious. To convince me, he began to describe in detail Doug Richards and the wild roller coaster of his success and failure due to his alcoholism. As I listened, I thought to myself that Doug had indeed told me the truth and that in fact his story was probably a well-known tale among the local insurance salesmen.

It is a sad and depressing story and one that Doug told with a matter-of-fact frankness and a haunting pessimism. When I asked him what he thought the theme of the story was, he spoke with the same pessimistic tone.

There was a time when alcohol was fun, and I did have fun with it. And there was time that it did me well, and now it doesn't, but it still has a very important part in my life, and it still, I'm not afraid of it, I'm not ready today to say I'm going to stop either, even with this last thing [the most recent suicide attempt]. I mean the theme is that what you may call consequences, I just call them part of my story, part of my life as an alcoholic. And me being here is part of the story and I don't know where it's going to go and where it's going to end, and I'm not afraid to die, I'm not afraid of it, I'm not afraid. I used to think, maybe you have too much fun, you have it all at once, then it's all over with, that's the way it was for me. I lived my life the way I should. . . . Before all this happened, I was going to meetings, and doing all that stuff, so that's not the answer. I mean drinking is just so much a part of my life and now that it's different, it doesn't make it any less a part of my life. And when I get depressed and that anger comes, all that anger inside of me that I have had all those years, it still works to take a drink for me to get rid of it.

When Doug describes drinking as part of his life, whether he is drinking or not I believe he understands that the need for instant transformation is a fundamental part of his identity. The process of building a sense of agency through daily toil and a sense of communion through intimate, reciprocal relationship remains foreign and baffling despite his sobriety. The depression and rage he feels is less at the poverty of meaning in his life than at the fact that the transforming powers of alcohol and cocaine no longer seem to work their magic for him. Rather than providing him with fun and success, they now only bring him sickness and the bleak sobriety of detoxes, rehabs, and the Pines.

Only a few weeks after the interview, Doug's girlfriend showed up with a bottle of vodka in her car and he left the Pines a second time. He has not returned since.

Lust and Greed

From the first drink at summer camp to his latest binge in a motel room, alcohol always provided Doug with a way to be other than himself, to erase the fearful, impotent person he felt himself to be. The cost of becoming Doug, the invincible hero, through alcohol was a toll of behaviors engaged in without conscience and consciousness, and the resulting sense of dissipation, both physical and psychological. Similar to many other men of the Pines, Doug found no sustained answer for his alcoholism in the fellowship of AA or in the rehabilitation programs he received at expensive private hospitals. Acknowledgment of his alcoholism and acceptance of his inability to control his drinking brought him no closer to a sober life.

How then can we begin to understand what has happened to him, why, at the end of the interview, he seemed poised to drink himself to death? Once again, some workers in the addiction field might point to the heavy genetic loading of alcoholism in his family; both his parents were heavy drinkers and his father's life followed an alcoholic decline similar to Doug's. Psychodynamically oriented psychologists or psychiatrists might argue that Doug suffered from a narcissistic personality disorder created out of the inadequate positive mirroring and nurturing he received as an infant.[15] Certainly his grandiosity in response to intense insecurity and self-loathing, as well as his exploitative and callous relationships with wives and children, as well as business associates, all locate him within this diagnostic category of the DSM-IV.[16] More hard-headed reality-oriented therapists could simply say that Doug continued to do what he liked to do—drink, spend money, have sex, and hide from any other contingencies and responsibilities in his life. Though he suffered consequences from these activities, he did not find or could not imagine any other course of action in his life that could replace the immediate pleasure he could obtain from drinking. Simply put, he lacked the image of a better world than the one he lived in.

All of these explanations—the biological, the psychological, and the pragmatic—are plausible and none should be excluded in an effort to construct a comprehensive understanding of Doug Richards' life. As I have articulated throughout this book, there is another piece that often gets overlooked in our efforts to reduce human motivation and behavior to medical symptoms and psychopathology. Doug Richards is part of a larger society that provides a system of social structures and values to guide the lives of all its citizens. Faced with the existential challenge of anxiety about death, freedom, isolation, and meaning, our society's major message is to engage oneself in relationships and achievement. Through work and love (agency and communion), men and women will find comfort and meaning in their lives.

As Cushman and Greenberg detail, the concepts of meaningful reciprocal connections to another person or to other people and of contributory and honorable work are no longer simple givens in this society. If we live in a society that through economic and social forces undermines our capacity to form ethical and meaningful connections with others, if we live in a society that confounds our efforts at ethical and honest work, structural complications in these twin pillars of our personalities are likely to ensue.

The most unsettling aspect of Doug Richards' life is not his genetic loading for alcoholism or his lonely self-serving narcissism. It is the fact that for more than twenty years he was an unabashed material success in our society. Even more frightening is that his wealth grew primarily out of his ability to provide people with protection of their lives, homes, and automobiles. Who were the citizens of this society who were supplying him with his multi-million-dollar income? It is relatively easy to dismiss Doug Richards as a troubled alcoholic, but what does it say about our society when so many people entrust the most precious aspects of their lives to a business run by such a damaged soul?

Of course, Doug Richards' biology bears some responsibility for his alcoholism, and it is much more comforting to put Doug Richards in a cubbyhole as a defective machine that simply needed Prozac or Paxil to function more effectively. Of course, he demonstrated defective ego strength and a poorly developed superego and it is more comforting to us to recommend that he receive intensive psychotherapy in conjunction with AA meetings. Of course, his personal choices implicate him in his self-destructive course, and it is more comforting to hold him completely accountable and leave his destiny in his own hands. All of these explanations conceptualize his chronic addiction as an individual problem and offer solutions that do not ask us to examine society's role. They leave out our social structure's complicity with his self-destruction.

Right from the beginning of his drinking, Doug was sized up as someone who could "get the booze." His fellow campers egged him on, relied on him for their connection, gave him attention he had never previously received. Doug's shyness and responsibility prior to his drinking located him as a geek and social misfit, but Doug, the invincible hero, the party commander and drug supplier, found a crowd willing to accept him. We could dismiss this dynamic as simply the fortunes of the adolescent war for peer acceptance and popularity,[17] but the problem is that Doug continued to be rewarded for his drinking at each phase of his life. His employers knew he drank, but as long as there were results, they let it continue ("As long as I was producing, which would be a theme throughout my career, I could always justify my drinking, or being absent, or not being on par, because I always did well the other times"). The disconcerting implication of this statement is that as far as the insurance business was concerned, his alcoholism was only an issue if it affected his productivity as an employee. Doug himself was a commodity that provided money for others; he became expendable once he could no longer produce the income upon which his company depended.

A similar problem can be detected if we think about how Doug managed to become successful. From his first interviews for insurance jobs through-out his career, he was taught that appearance (confidence and clothes) as well as the right "pitch" were the ingredients of money-making. He stole the suit for his interview; he portrayed cars as different from their actual models in order to provide lower insurance rates; he stole clients from his former employer; he conducted drug deals from his office.

Interestingly, none of these actions had anything do with his personal demise. In fact, it was clear from his narrative that he continued to feel pride in these hardball tactics of business. These actions only brought rewards from the people around him. He made bags and bags of money; he was the pal of radio disc jockeys who played his ads and shared cocaine with him. The big insurance companies were eager to join in on his action and send policies and cash his way. He was loved by the limousine companies and the clothing stores. He had no trouble finding a succession of one-night affairs ("Doug's girls") and even involved three different women in long-term rela-tionships with him. He was never turned down when he bought out the bar. He kept his sponsor on a thousand-dollar retainer. His office manager and other employees tolerated his antics for more than a decade, as long as their income continued to swell. If work were simple honest work, if we all looked each other in the eye without a wink and a nudge, and all put our shoulders to the wheel each day, would it be possible for men like Doug Richards to succeed? I am reminded of a movie from the seventies, *Paper Moon*, about the confidence game, starring Ryan and Tatum O'Neal. At one point, Ryan O'Neal explains to Tatum O'Neal that cons work because there is always a little bit of dishonesty in every person and the confidence man simply exploits the tendency of all of us to want something for nothing. In the climate created by American society, we are all hungry and eager to have needs filled by goods, thrills, and glamour.

For Doug Richards to have been a success suggests that many people around him were looking for quick fixes, for ways to get more for less. In his characterization of person after person in his own life, we hear the lonely cynicism he feels about what others thought of him. He said to me at one point that "I was the gravy train and as long as the money kept coming in, no one said anything." The greatest problem with the emphasis on personality over substance in our consumer society is not that it allows some people unfair advantage because of their appearance or persuasive powers (there will always be inequity in the world), but rather what it does to the integrity and authenticity of human achievement. The ennobling and self-defining aspects of agency as defined by McAdams, and discussed in Chapter 2, are transmogrified into a meaningless acquisition of money, status, and power—in a word, greed.

As we were finishing the interview, Doug told me that it had become impossible for him to work in sales any more. He found that within a few weeks he would begin to make good money again and then his drinking would start up. Within a few weeks more, he would cease to come to work and fall back into the oblivion of daily drinking. I wonder if this relapse pattern was not simply the biological progression of his disease, but also reflects a problem of meaning in his life. With increased time in sobriety, he is confronting an existential crisis between the impulse toward an authentic and engaged life and the demands of the inauthentic, dissembling world of sales. He might deny my moralistic analysis and point out how happy he had been in his work. This happiness would still leave unexplained his impulse to destroy property when he was drunk and the anger and depression that surfaced in him even before his recent sobriety.

Many years ago, Arthur Miller captured the contradictions of our consumerist society in *Death of a Salesman,* where he pitted the life of Biff Loman, the prodigal son, against his father, Willy Loman, the washed-up salesman.[18] Biff's fundamental problem was that he had seen the hollowness and hypocrisy of his father's world of sales—the emphasis on charm and a good line, the ruthlessness of the company managers, and the secrets of life on the road (he walked in on his father during a one-night stand). Knowing this world, and confronted with own moral weakness, born of overpraise and vanity, Biff could not fashion an alternate world in which to live. He had wandered the west as a day laborer on ranches, but had been unable to accumulate any money or a future. (Biff, in an ironic spin of the frontier myth, could not find a home in either the old world of his father or the open spaces of the west.). By the end of the play Biff was struggling to find a route toward honesty, but this self-scrutiny revealed only more self-loathing. Biff, despite his own internal weaknesses, was a powerful anticipation of the alienation of American youth from the conformity of the fifties that came to full fruition in the 1960s.

The problem is that these contradictions, far from disappearing, have only worsened into the 1990s. Our economic climate is more competitive and coldly profit-oriented than ever, especially because of the recognition that we are now engaged in increasing international competition. How does any man find a way to work in an atmosphere that is congruent with values of decency and honesty? How does a man find a way to feel respect both for himself and for his fellow participants in the world of commerce? Doug Richards's story in its contemporary echo of the struggles of the Lomans articulates the dilemma faced by all men in our society, not simply those who are struggling with addictions to drugs and alcohol. Work, which should be a central safeguard against existential despair and meaninglessness, is too often a setting of moral compromise and spiritual bankruptcy. The forms of agency offered to males in contemporary society often do little to build a genuine and comfortable sense of identity.

Unfortunately, Doug Richards' story also tells us about the distortions that the corrupted American dream can create in the realm of personal relationships, both romantic and parental. In reflecting on Doug's description of his various relationships throughout his life, I found few mentions of moments of tenderness or intimacy with his wives or lovers. His reference points are to sex, shared drinking, and amounts of money spent. Often in his speech there is an equation of women to acquisitions or indications of his success or potency. At one point he described with pride how he was warned by a nurse that he was having too much sex. When he was spending money freely and distributing cocaine with abandon in the Rhode Island bars, he acquired a steady group of women followers. Now, our knee-jerk reaction might be to say that anyone with the slightest bit of sensitivity would see his behavior as superficial and a poor substitute for meaningful contact with a wife or partner. The fact that he thought this is wonderful, we might say, is just a sign of either his narcissistic nature or his addiction, or both. Normal, healthy people would not engage in one-night stands or frequent houses of prostitutes. Yet once again, I would ask that we restrain our impulse to explain his behavior away by only attributing it to his individual pathology.

Who were all the other professional men he would meet at the massage parlors? To a man, were they all suffering from personality disorders and addictions? Returning to my metaphor of Doug finding himself trapped inside the fantasy of the beer commercial, how many images in the media are there that remind us that the right car, the right clothes, the right wine will bring beautiful women to our feet? Even in our "politically correct" times how many jokes do you still hear about women looking for rich husbands? Among a group of men, how many stories are still exchanged about the number of conquests and whether a guy "scored" or not? In our society the communion and love that we are striving to achieve are perpetually at risk to be turned into commodities and acquisitions, distorted into measures of self-worth and power. In these cases, love can simply become the physical act, lust without any deeper intimacy or attachment. Reduced to these terms, it can be purchased like any other commodity.

The love in "communion" is not only about romantic love, but about connection to family, children, and community. Of all the emotional casualties rendered by Doug's distorted participation in a culture of lust and greed, none is more chilling than the neglect his children suffered. In a world view that centers on money, power, drugs, and sex, what place do children hold? Doug was clear in his answer—none whatsoever. Recall the language he used to describe them, "We had to drag them along because they belonged to us." This last statement reflects the translation of a flesh-and-blood bond into a legal and proprietary obligation. It conveys the same obligation one feels when asked to move one's car because it is blocking another car's entrance to or exit from a parking lot. One has to move the car because it belongs to you; one has to bring one's children along because they belong to you.

This understanding of children as an annoying obligation is captured most painfully in Doug's story about attempting to convince his fourteen-year-old daughter that her discovery of his cocaine use was a dream. In manipulating her understanding of reality, Doug was expressing his lack of interest in her integrity as a human being with independent thoughts and feelings. He saw his daughter solely in functional terms; she was a threat to his continued concealment from his wife that he had returned to cocaine use. If the consequence of this was the destruction of his daughter's sanity, he was either willing to pay this price or oblivious to this damage. This is a harrowing picture of how greed and addiction can drain the compassion out of human relationships.

Unfortunately, this indifference to others can be pushed one step further when one feels no sense of belonging or proprietorship in relation to a child in the home. In the case of Doug's adopted step-child, he could not even summon up a sense of narcissistic connection ("I cared less for him because he wasn't mine"). Since there was no blood link, he could not truly be considered part of Doug's emotional portfolio. The result is that he simply ran away and disappeared from Doug's life, like a neighbor, barely known, who chose to move one day and left no forwarding address. There is an eerie echo here of Doug's father, who left his family when Doug was twelve and from whom Doug heard not a word for the next nine years. He reappeared briefly for a night and went out drinking with Doug, made promises to bring him to his land in Maine, and then vanished again without a trace.

Where is Doug's adopted son, now a young man, and what does he recall of his childhood years? How does he understand the meaning of attachment or the role of money in life? Has he become a drinker or drug user himself? I think of him as Ishmael, the castoff son, wandering the American landscape with a growing number of other Ishmaels, the offspring of a society that tells us to find love, to find work, and happiness will result. Yet contained in the structure of this society are corrupting forces that make it ever harder to love and work in a way that will give birth to beloved Isaacs (sons of laughter) rather than a nation of lonely and empty hunters, of exiled and alienated Ishmaels.

Doug Richards's story is not simply an insider's look at what alcoholism can do to a life. Unfortunately, it offers us a glimpse at how fragile our mutually shared American dream can be and how susceptible it is to becoming something far different from our rhetoric. The very engines that drive our economy forward, the pleasures of acquisition and consumption, as well as the media that display the attraction of these pleasures, may infiltrate into the most private spheres of human intimacy. They may twist love and work into a lust for sex and money, into a hunger for more and more, without an examination of whether a deeper hunger for meaning and relationship is ever sated by the types of goods we purchase and consume.

Reconfiguring the Empty Self

Is there a way to step away from this cycle of consumerism and its destructive influence on agency and communion? Since it pervades the very way we construct reality and our understanding of what we need and want to live, there is no simple way to set it aside or enter into an alternate world. What an advocate of hermeneutic interpretation like Cushman would suggest is that we strive for sustained periods of awareness, of vigilance that allows us to locate the hidden meanings of our cultural behaviors.

In teaching the subjectivity of perception, psychologists often rely upon the black-and-white illusion of a figure that changes depending upon the way the eye configures it. If you look at the figure in one manner, it resembles the profile of an elderly peasant woman. If you look at it again, reversing the angle of orientation, the drawing now becomes the face of a young woman. The hermeneutic challenge is to help us to have the power to see as many of these configurations as possible and to understand the implications they hold for our personal understanding and social behavior.

How do we enhance this awareness? Cushman suggests that we must introduce a "third person" into the therapeutic work we do with clients suffering from psychological problems, including addiction.

> The third player I refer to is the ever present interpenetrating social realm. By "three-ness" I intend to convey that the individual, the dialogic partner, and the historical-cultural context are inextricably intertwined, that moral understandings are a foundational aspect of culture, and that our discipline needs to be concerned with how various psychotherapy theories affect political structures and activities.[19]

Therapists and proponents of recovery must look at how their theoretical understanding of the self and their potential remedies may reflect the same problematic ideas possessed by their clients. If we see addiction as a problem of consuming the wrong substance, as opposed to a problem of a self that depends on consumption, we are unlikely to emerge with a useful solution to Doug Richards's troubled life. If we locate Doug Richards's problem solely in genetic vulnerability, we will make no effort to change the structures that leave us emotionally hungry and desperate for magic transformations that consumption can provide.

> [The desire to consume alcohol] is thought to be caused by the biochemical structure of our genes—human nature—not the particular political arrangements of twentieth century capitalism. Thus it is foolish and ultimately ineffective to blame, and then advocate resisting, current social structures.[20]

Recovery groups begin with the assumption of powerlessness over the commodity (drugs, alcohol, food, etc.) or behavior (sex, gambling, codependency, etc.) in question. The response to this helplessness is to turn one's will over to a higher power. This higher power still remains outside oneself and beyond the social or political structures in which one conducts a life. In either case, surrender to the substance or to a higher power, the individual's capacity for meaningful positive agency in a sociopolitical context is negated.[21] What is missing from the recovery movement is to make the connection that individuals may turn to drugs or money-making or multiple partners, not out of a biological compulsion, but out of a need born of their particular sociocultural context. Their problem is not simply one of individual constitution, and the solution is not solely to be found in individual surrender. Though recovery groups create a profound sense of fellowship and community, they are inherently private (hence the modifier, "Anonymous"), as opposed to political. Only through a recognition of our public commitments and our responsibilities to each other as community members and citizens are we likely to extricate ourselves from the individualistic world of consumption that isolates us from each other.

> We have difficulty solving our political problems today in part because we do not experience ourselves as political beings. Our cultural clearing is configured in such a way as to exclude the social connectedness of the commons, the public meeting place where citizens exercise political obligations to their community and experience a sense of group purpose and group solidarity.[22]

My job as therapist or as citizen is not simply to teach people how to become better consumers of our nation's products—a fitness trainer for the psyche who slows down the intake of toxic substances and encourages healthy acquisitions (of relationships as well as material goods). My job, it seems to me, is to ask why we have lost the capacity to place public caring before private gain, or mutual concern before personal well-being. The third person of social-historical context must enter into our dialogue about addiction or else we endlessly transfer the problem of filling the empty self from one kind of consumption to another. Doug Richards might gain sobriety someday, but who will teach him how to question a society that leads him back to emptiness? Once sober, will he still haunt the highways with bags of money in his car, while his daughter and his son feel the widening emptiness inside their own hearts?

7. WHO WAS INSIDE
MICKEY MANTLE?

Addiction and the Heroes of Sport

The path we are traveling in the exploration of the relationship of identity to chronic addiction should now be more distinct. By confronting us with the most extreme difficulties in identity formation, the stories of men's chronic addiction allow us to see fundamental problems with achieving agency and communion that may touch all men in our society. An identity based in love and work can be undermined at various points by destructive social practices (e.g., homophobia or racism) and social conditions (e.g., poverty or a culture of materialism). Individuals may escape into substance use and addiction as responses to the obstacles they encounter in their efforts to achieve a sense of agency or communion.

On the other hand, there may be ways in which their successful attainment of agency (as defined by our culture) leads them to substance use. Achieving status, power, and prosperity in this society may actually have inherent costs to the creation of a lasting and meaningful sense of identity.

Billy Zeitel's story of his trip to the major leagues is an example of this latter dilemma. The confluence of drug use and professional sports exemplified in his life may reflect a problem of an excessive agency rather than a deficit. The fact that Billy Zeitel's baseball career was the best possible preparation for his subsequent identity as a drug dealer and addict speaks to intrinsic difficulties with the messages our culture offers, and that young men absorb, about how to achieve agency in this society.

The status we grant to celebrities (e.g., athletes, movie stars, rock musicians) through constant media attention and distorted wages is one example of the confusing messages we send to young men about the importance of certain aspects of agency. Recently, a star baseball player for the Florida Marlins signed a contract that will pay him $60 million over the next ten years (when we consider that this player is not even the best player in the league and that his team is not the best team, this figure is even more staggering). Jim Carrey, the film comedian, reached a point a couple of years ago where he could ask for and receive $20 million a picture. Why does our society reward individuals with these unfathomable sums for the ability to play a game or amuse us for a ninety-minute interlude?

First, we need to acknowledge that their salaries are paid by astute business people who would not pay such high sums if they were not making several times more from the labors of these stars. So even before we ask why certain celebrities receive tremendous payments, we need to consider why sports and entertainment are such money-makers in our society. Clearly, their ability to provide amusement and distract us from ourselves is serving a vital desire in the society.[1] The responsibility of work and agency that so many of us accept must weigh on us in such a powerful way that we value diversion as a necessary compensation. Trying to be agentic selves—to establish self-mastery, status, achievement, power—preoccupies and worries us to such a degree that a chance to think about a sports score or watch an amusing video gives us precious relief from that burden.

Society supports these forms of diversions with great relish and reward because they are much less socially disruptive than an escape through drugs or alcohol. However, we are seldom successful at disentangling completely our love of sports and celebrities from recourse to substance use. For example, in a content analysis of more than two years of network programming for sports events, researchers found that during sports events there were more commercials for alcohol than for any other type of beverage. Even more, these commercials often depicted the use of alcohol in ways that violated the Surgeon General's recommendations for responsible use of alcoholic beverages. Not only were viewers exposed to alcohol commercials (primarily beer), but they also received hundreds of hours of exposure through stadium billboards viewed in the background of sporting events, as well as event sponsorship by alcohol beverage companies. The stereotype of a man guzzling a beer and slumped on a couch watching a televised sporting event may be *the* archetypal image of late-twentieth-century American masculine identity (e.g., Homer Simpson from the animated series, "The Simpsons").

Aside from the diversion that athletes or film stars offer to our lives, they also hold a symbolic place as exemplars of what the self can become. As representatives of skill, attractiveness, and glamour they demonstrate individual talent and potential and how self-expression can lead to material success and fame. In recent decades, much psychological and social theory has highlighted how the quest for self-fulfillment or self-actualization has replaced the location of value in an external entity (whether God or country or family).[2] One of my students recently commented to me that the Army's slogan has changed from "Uncle Sam needs you" to "Be all that you can be." Since military service is no longer compulsory, individuals are encouraged to join up as a way of enhancing the self and expressing their future potential.[3]

In all walks of life in American society, individuals no longer do things simply because they are supposed to, or seek to fulfill others' expectations. People strive to act in ways that are "true to themselves" or that will maximize personal potential. Where once we might have relied upon religious belief or family tradition to guide our decisions, most of us now look inward as well. In language similar to Cushman's from the previous chapter, Baumeister argues that in a world bereft of traditional and hierarchical guides, individuals rely upon self-expression as the highest value.

> To live one's life properly and achieve the highest forms of human fulfillment, it was once considered necessary to know about God. Now it is considered vital to know about your self instead. On the crucial question of what to do with your life, the answer no longer comes from God (or from the station in society where God placed you). Instead, the answer supposedly emerges from deep inside yourself.[4]

As discussed in the previous chapter, the task of determining who that inner self is and what truths it urges one to follow is no less difficult than discerning "God's wishes." For this reason, individuals who have achieved fame and success hold an endless fascination to us. Through knowing the details of their lives, we believe we might be able to find clues to unlocking the self-actualizing potential that exists within our more mundane selves.

. . . [P]eople want to hear a famous football player describe his hobbies or his feelings about children, or they want to hear a famous actress discuss her political views or her experiences in redecorating her house. People may feel somehow that these petty details will reveal how this person managed to achieve fulfillment.[5]

In their moments of glory or supreme beauty, celebrities seem to hold a message for us about how we might transcend our all too familiar human weaknesses. As they appear to us on the playing field or movie screen, they seem to have achieved the supreme agency of status and self-mastery we all are taught to admire. The millions they receive begin to seem less outrageous if we contemplate the possibility that they are satisfying our hunger to know what a "true" self is or what the "real self" has the capacity to express.

In one of the more striking examples in recent decades, Tiger Woods, a twenty-one-year-old golfer, won the prestigious Masters tournament in his first year of professional competition, outdistancing the field by the largest number of strokes in the tournament's history. Given the expectation and media hype he had endured before the tournament, the complete domination he achieved was a symbol of human competence displayed under extraordinarily stressful conditions. The attention and adulation he received was, in part, an expression of our culture's deep commitment to mastery and achievement as one of the highest values of the self.

In society's rush to celebrate achievements of the self (accompanied by slow-motion montages and surging music), individuals often do not take sufficient time to ask questions about the moral value or larger meaning of that accomplishment. Sports fans admire Tiger Woods for the greatness of his self-expression (and he will be paid millions for his achievements), but the majority of his admirers do not step back and ask, "What is the point of a sport that involves hitting a tiny ball hundreds of yards on acreage that is invariably owned and used by the most privileged segment of our society?" There is little room in the moral equation of "successful self-expression = goodness" to wonder about the relative value of one type of self-expression over another.

Since successful self-expression in certain fields leads to celebrity in our society through media coverage (television reports, magazine articles, radio interviews, opportunities to write memoirs, etc.), more cynical purveyors of mass culture no longer care if this self-expression may be in direct violation of a larger moral good. A recent example of this phenomenon is Mark Furman, the notorious police officer from the O.J. Simpson trial, who managed to write a best-selling book despite (or perhaps because of) his overtly racist comments. Increasingly, the ability to become noticed by the media, to achieve "fifteen minutes of fame" is an end in itself; to gain celebrity is to announce one's self to the world, regardless of what the content of that self might be. People often feel that fame will ensure happiness.

> Thinking that you're great becomes a form of feeling fulfilled. People imagine that if their self-worth could be firmly, publicly established, they would have endless positive affect.[6]

There is yet a third and even more ominous way in which the professional athlete expresses an overinvestment in agency in contemporary American society. In a perfect turn of language, athletes have the capacity to become "free agents" in professional sports. Free agency refers to a severing of ties between athletes and their current teams. Up until the historic case of Curt Flood, a major league baseball player in 1969, professional sports teams would sign athletes to contracts that guaranteed exclusive rights to the player. The player was not free to negotiate with another team unless his current team released him or chose to trade him. Even if a player had been with a team for several years, he was unable to refuse to be traded; he could simply go to his new team or not play at all.

When the legal system ruled against the major league owners, players gained the right to declare free agency after an initial period of time with the team that signed them. They could also sign short-term contracts that allowed them to declare free agency periodically. After several years of service in the league, they could no longer be traded without consent. Though there have been a great many benefits to players that emerged out of this new system (substantially higher salaries and greater control over their destinies), there have also been some unexpected negative ramifications.

It is much rarer for players to remain with the same team for many years, and for a sense of allegiance or loyalty to develop on either the player's or the team's part. Players' performances are now so tightly connected to their salaries that they often emphasize individual performance in place of the team outcome. For example, in the closing seconds of a recent NBA basketball game, opposing players watched in amazement as a rival player raced the length of the court to score his fortieth point, despite the fact that his team was hopelessly behind. His selfish concern to reach the coveted forty-point plateau, even though the points were meaningless to his team, filled his opponents with such disgust that they did not even bother to try to guard him.

Though many of us recoil from this narcissistic display of agency, I am afraid that this self-centered mastery has a strong hold in our society. In the recent hit movie *Tin Cup,* Kevin Costner plays a stubborn golfer, nicknamed "Tin Cup," who refuses to "lay up" or play holes safe when confronted with a challenging drive. On the verge of winning the U.S. Open, he declines to play for par and attempts to hit a mammoth drive over a water hazard. Despite his long-suffering caddy's pleas with him, he continues to attempt the shot over and over, throwing away all chance to win the prestige and economic security that he and his caddy (who is also his best friend) have long coveted. Finally, on his twelfth and last try before disqualification, he clears the hazard and holes his shot. The crowd in the gallery bursts into cheers, his girlfriend embraces him, and all his friends, including his caddy, shout out with joy. Clearly, Tin Cup has displayed the invincibility of his masculine anatomy (hence his nickname) in a profound way; he has shown everyone that his spirit and will answer to no one. At one point before he decides to go for broke, he looks to his girlfriend (who happens to be a psychologist, as well as a former real estate agent) for counsel. She shouts out to him with a demented glee, "Trust yourself." In hitting the impossible shot, and making it, Tin Cup displays the value of expressing yourself without regard for the consequences to yourself or others. He is the ultimate free agent.

As we look to the free agents of sport with their multimillion dollar salaries and their commercial endorsements, they model a lifestyle unencumbered by responsibility or burdensome connection. Moving from team to team, city to city, they resemble modern guns for hire. They have little trouble finding female admirers, and some athletes have claimed thousands of different sexual encounters. They may have families and own homes, but they live mostly on the road, traveling in first class and living in hotels. They sleep at odd hours and forego the drudgery of a daily routine at the office.

Though the rest of us may hear about the great pressures and challenges they face, it is difficult to let go of the idea that their livelihood is based in playing the same games that so many of us loved to play as children. Similarly, people may disapprove of excessive drug use that interferes with their performance, but they may also envy their access to celebrity parties where it is assumed alcohol and drugs flow freely. In fact, some sports psychologists have suggested that professional athletes' use of drugs may be another way of asserting their freedom from management, a kind of adolescent rebellion in the face of restrictive authorities.[7]

I am suggesting here that highly paid maverick athletes may personify (in mostly unconscious ways) the destructive agency (I'd Rather Drink) that I defined in Chapter 2. Their ultimate freedom, which we value as the full expression of the American Dream, is simultaneously a celebration of the agency of the self and a rageful tantrum of despair against the bankruptcy of that self-expression. Broken loose from any meaningful communal structure or engagement in relationship, they resemble the privileged child who gathers his toys around him and then, with too great a show of enthusiasm, flaunts them against the other boys in the neighborhood.

Professional athletes' expression of free agency, an unencumbered self who is able to be masterful and powerful without any impediment or restraint, both attracts and repels the rest of society that witnesses their achievements and excesses. At the same time that fans support these superstars, they also hark back to an old-fashioned kind of sports hero like Cal Ripken, the shortstop for the Baltimore Orioles. Having played for the same team his whole career, he holds the record for the longest streak of consecutive games, breaking the record of Yankee first baseman Lou Gehrig. Prematurely gray and balding, his distinctly unglamorous appearance stands in contrast to the flamboyant orange-haired, cross-dressing figure of a consummate free agent, Dennis Rodman, basketball player for the Chicago Bulls (whose memoir is titled *Bad As I Wanna Be*). These two sports heroes offer a vivid expression of the ambivalence that exists about achieving agency in society. They exemplify the conflict between a mastery expressed in an essentially traditional context and a self-expressive mastery unbounded by even the most basic categories of physical appearance or gender.

Any young men (and, increasingly, women) who aspire to be professional athletes are likely to be confronted with all of the complex expectations I have detailed—to serve as a chief source of amusement for fans, to take on the weight of fame with the responsibility of achieving the self-fulfillment that so many in the society covet, and, finally, to make sense of the unbridled freedom and privilege that their celebrity and material success offer to them. On top of all these expectations that accompany success, they face one more challenge, even larger than the ones I have named thus far—how to handle and survive their failure of agency.

Failure comes in three major forms for the athlete—defeat, injury, and retirement. Facing any or all of these three crises, athletes are susceptible to using substances either with the hope of sustaining performance (e.g., amphetamines, steroids, painkillers) or escaping the reality of their demise (e.g., alcohol, opiates, barbiturates).

> Imposed or self-imposed career termination probably represents one of the most traumatic experiences for the pro athlete. The decline in status, social contact, and income can all have a deleterious effect on the individual. These problems are generally compounded by the residual effects of inadequate educational training, and for the average pro athlete, this means starting all over with little or no viable working skills.[8]

Some athletes, who have already found that drugs and/or alcohol can buffer their stress or ease their social anxiety,[9] may turn to substances to dull their fear about the future and their deepening sense of inadequacy and meaninglessness away from the sports arena. For some athletes, the loss of their athletic skill and career is a kind of death, and as we have seen, alcohol and drugs can offer temporary protection against this desperate awareness.

Billy Zeitel's story of addiction allows us to see how destructive both his success and subsequent failure in athletics have been for his development of a positive sense of agency in his life. Now long after his sports career has ended, what has become most clear is that not only was his educational training insufficient, but his training in making it through the daily demands of a normal life was also woefully inadequate. The self-mastery and achievement that won him celebrity and major league status, and which inspires profound envy in most men, turns out to have little to do with the day-to-day agency he requires to live an independent and responsible life in our society.

Billy Zeitel

There is a familiar argument that boys in school have over and over again—if you could be a star center fielder in the big leagues or a rock star touring in front of massive crowds, which would you choose to be? For me, it was never a difficult choice. I can barely carry a tune and have never learned to play an instrument. Yet hour after hour, I chased down baseballs on the hard pavement of Eastern Drive, extracting them from flower beds before the elderly lady who lived next door could confiscate them. Summer after summer, I hit high flies to the little kid on my block with the improbable nickname of James "the Giacco" Giacco. My room was filled with posters of Mickey Mantle and I lived and breathed by his ups and downs at the plate. In one of the greatest moments of my childhood, standing alongside my father at Yankee Stadium, I watched Mantle hit a grand slam into the right field stands. And as with the majority of American boys, a few prize moments in Little League were as far as my own baseball dreams were to carry me. Now, working at the Pines, I had heard in a staff meeting that one of the new residents had made it to the "show," had actually played baseball for the Pittsburgh Pirates (I have changed the name of the team for which he played). He had answered the call of one of my deepest fantasies—he had stepped up to the plate in a major league stadium and taken his swings against pitchers whose names I knew and whose records I could recite. What in the world was he doing at the Pines? How had he ended up so far from this moment of glory?

With the exception of a guy from my dormitory in college who went on to pitch for the Cleveland Indians, I had never personally known a professional athlete before Billy Zeitel, and I had certainly never spoken to one. My conversation with Billy was the first time I could say to someone—what was it like? Yet in experiencing this intense curiosity, I was also aware that this was, to a great extent, Billy's dilemma. How could he escape the box of being the object of others' fantasies; how could he get on with his life and not simply be the ex-professional baseball player in his own and everyone else's eyes?

As we began our interview, I found myself scrutinizing his appearance to determine if he indeed looked different. I asked myself, if I had not known he had been a pro, could I have told simply from the way he looked? After all, it was now almost twelve years since he had been in the major leagues. At first, I told myself no, he was only six feet tall or so, and he had a slightly bulging middle. He had a receding hairline, a scruffy beard, and his posture was not impressive; he entered my office with almost a slow shuffle, hardly an athletic grace. His shoulders were broad, but many of the men at the Pines lift weights, so this did not stand out with great significance. As he sat down, Billy shook my hand and it was at this moment, I noticed something unusual and striking. It was not the fact that he had big or strong hands. Again, many of the men at the Pines had worked lives of physical labor— road work, construction, masonry. I have shaken many a massive, callused, or beefy mitt. It was not his hands, but his forearms. They were the size of cinder blocks and looked every bit as hard. The muscular expanse from his wrist to his biceps was the legacy of his baseball years, of the thousands of hours of swinging lumber, snapping the bat head through the hitting zone to make contact between leather hide and the sweet part of the wood. He had traveled many miles from these moments in his life, but his arms still wore the badges of his labors in those fields.

How perfect that Billy was born and raised until age eleven in Brooklyn—a place of baseball legend, the land of Jackie Robinson, Pee Wee Reese, and the Duke. He had always played sports and always been good at them. From the age of six, Billy had been placed on older kids' teams and excelled. If sports were his paradise, his family life was a different story. His father was a drinker and a womanizer, who did not hesitate to use physical force to express his opinions to his wife and his children. He was 6' 5" and Billy's mother was nearly a foot shorter. He once beat her with a bowling trophy to the point of unconsciousness.

Billy's mother was Italian and her family was connected to both show business figures and organized crime. Billy's cousins included two well-known Las Vegas night club singers (in the Tony Bennett mode) and a former major league first baseman for a New York team. One day his mother's brothers showed up and threatened to resolve her domestic problems permanently, but she begged them to spare her husband and they reluctantly agreed. Billy recalled that his mother eventually could not tolerate this abusive treatment.

. . . She was crying all the time, you know, he was never home, never home. . . . My mother wasn't happy and all this stuff was going on, the beatings, and the sitting at the dinner table and having him throwing food at her and us, you know it was really crazy. He spit in my mother's face, man, I'll never forget that. I jumped on him, then, I was like eleven, ten.

This was not the last time Billy would fight with his father; I will return to another, more dramatic encounter a little later in his story. After these episodes of humiliation and violence, Billy's mother filed for divorce and decided to move to Connecticut to live near her sister. As was true in the stories of Thomas Turner, Rolando Diggs, and Doug Richards, Billy's father provided no positive model through which he might develop a constructive sense of masculine identity. Instead Billy fashioned a Father Imago that represented for him a substance-abusing, violent, and self-centered man who disappeared early on in his life. Unable to rely upon an image of a male as a stable and productive force in his life, Billy was much more likely to look outward for approval and role models. Without someone to imitate at home, he increasingly staked his sense of identity to the acceptance and acclaim he received for his athletic successes.[10]

His family moved to a beach town near New Haven when Billy was eleven. Thanks to his sports abilities, Billy made a very easy adjustment to his new school and life. He was the most valuable player in his Little League year after year, voted best athlete of his grade, and recognized by everyone in the school. He also excelled in his school work, managing a strong average and making the honor roll each year. On the other hand, life at home was still not completely settled. His mother had decided to return to school and pursue a career as a physician. She attended medical school in New York, leaving Billy, his two younger brothers, and a sister, to be watched by their aunt. Billy described himself as growing up fast and taking on a lot of responsibility for his younger siblings. He started to work as a busboy in a restaurant when he was thirteen and explained that he already looked old enough to tend bar. He told me with pride that he had started shaving before the age of ten.

By his senior year in high school, he was captain of the football, baseball, and basketball teams, making all-state selections in both baseball and football. He had learned to ride the wave of celebrity and status all these awards brought to him. He had developed the "Big Jock in Town" Imago, which he described to me as holding unlimited power, a sense of destiny, and an expectation of popularity and privilege.

I had a lot of friends and not really many enemies. I screwed around with a lot of women. I enjoyed it. I mean, I didn't treat 'em bad or anything, but, you know, I was in high school, the big jock in town, you know how that goes. I was a popular guy, and I had a lot of friends. And that kind of helped me out a lot later when I was selling drugs. It was really weird.

Billy's days of drug-selling were still far off from those idyllic high school years. As if his athletic and romantic conquests were not enough, he told me the story of the day he and a friend stumbled upon a barrel filled with money in the woods. It was hidden behind a restaurant that was known to have criminal connections. They found $20,000 and used it to buy clothes, throw parties, and to travel to visit his old friends in New York. Having this money fit perfectly with Billy's developing lifestyle. It may have been his father's influence or his mother's brothers, but Billy always liked to have the best of everything. When he turned sixteen, he bought a new car, a luxury LeMans, fully equipped and with custom features.

I'd wear silk shirts. I was from New York, you know. I dressed differently than the people in Connecticut when I moved there. People are going, "Who's this guy?" I mean I wore nice clothes. . . . I remember my fifteenth birthday we went to New York and had a blast. Yeah, it was wild. Everything was going like that most of my childhood. All of my childhood, mostly, except for a little bit with my father. You know, I try to forget that. You know, I really do.

Billy's account of finding the money and his parties in New York at the age of fifteen reflect how his identity was already conforming to the image of the free agent athlete—loaded with cash, well-dressed, and ready to party. The odd piece to this picture of unrestrained agency is his painful memory of his father's behavior toward him and his mother. He stressed how he tried to push this negative recollection out of awareness.

Finally, Billy confronted his father when he turned sixteen. Already well over 200 pounds from sports and weightlifting, he called his father and invited him to lunch at Central Park.

Yeah, I went to see him. I looked like Arnold Schwarzenegger when I was a kid. I used to work out with this guy who used to bench 500 pounds and I was benching 400 pounds when I was sixteen. I was almost twice the size I am right now.

In the park, Billy told him what he thought of his treatment of his mother and then jumped him. He beat him up badly and was finally pulled off his father by two policemen. He has had minimal interactions with him since, and recalled bitterly how his father had tried to see him after he learned that Billy was being scouted and offered signing bonuses by major league teams.

I asked Billy to tell me more about what this period of his life was like when he was contemplating playing professional baseball. He explained that he had received a number of athletic scholarship offers from, among others, the University of Florida, Rollins College in Florida, and the University of Connecticut. He preferred to enter the minor leagues and to begin his career immediately. Some major league scouts had actually come to his high school to watch a pitching prospect from the opposing team, and he ended up hitting three home runs and a ground rule double that same day.

After that, I guess everything shifted on me. I always did pretty good in high school. I hit for both power and average. A lot of teams look for different things. Like I got scouted by the Cincinnati Reds. They were looking for somebody with speed and I was fast. And they was looking for somebody that could throw the ball good, and I had set a record for throwing people out at bases that year, my senior year. But the Pirates wanted power hitters, they had always had a good offensive team, and I could fit right in with them.

At this point, he was drafted and began a rapid and fantasy-like rise through the minor leagues. He started in Winter Park, Florida, and I asked him what it felt like to know he was a professional baseball player.

It was unbelievable. There's nothing better than doing something you love to do, and getting paid for it. And I was a young kid. I had a little trailer I lived in. . . . Had my own car, and I went to work in the off-season and I worked out, you know, did what I had to do.

(Did you like the other guys?)

Oh yeah. They were great. They were crazy, man, you know. We road-tripped to UConn one time to see this girl and it was like *Animal House*. It was crazy—wild parties. Women, groupies, like rock stars. It was like being a rock star. I can equate it to that, equal to that.

Billy's memories of this early success reflected the images of unrestrained agency that are projected onto male celebrities. Billy thrived in his sport, but also attained a status of a "rock star" that allowed him entry to "wild parties" and a following of "groupies." Billy's mention of partying led me to wonder how much of a factor alcohol and drugs were in his life by this point.

I wasn't a drinker. I wasn't into going to keg parties. Beer made me feel bloated. I would have a few beers with guys after a game, but I was more of a lover than a drinker in high school. I liked the women, you know. I did liked getting stoned. I was getting stoned at thirteen and you know to be honest with you, I would get stoned every day or almost every day.

Throughout the interview, Billy would often return to his interest in women and how he saw this as almost another addiction. He told the story of how he lost his virginity at twelve years old.

At a young age, eleven, twelve years old, I used to like looking at older women. And I looked older for my age. My mother did something really weird, told my cousin to take me—(see I was chasing girls around the block. I mean I like good looking women. I dated a movie actress for about a year)—My mother had my cousin take me to a high-class bordello in Manhattan. There was this woman and I told her how old I was and everything, she kind of freaked out. She said, "Why are you so nervous?" I said, "Well, Geez, I gotta tell you something, you know, I'm twelve years old and my first time doing this, you know that's why I'm a little nervous." But it was something I never forgot, you know, it wasn't a normal thing to do.

Billy's obsession with women reflects a persisting theme throughout his life story. In addition to the pleasure he derives from contact with them, they seem to function as another external source of regard and validation that fills the emptiness inside him. As my discussion of Cushman's "empty self" perspective suggests (see previous chapter), Billy's success in sports and with women are mirror images of the same need to fill his emotional hunger for self-affirmation. Without constant adulation, he feels invisible; he lacks grounding in a family structure or community that would afford him a sense of self beyond his personality and accomplishments.

Continuing his progress through the minor leagues, Billy dated women and partied with his teammates. Though he smoked a great deal of marijuana, he still had not begun any extensive use of cocaine.

It was the early eighties and there was drinking and coke and you go to a party and there would be a dish of coke and a pound of weed on the table. And you can do it like out in the open, and it was just like, "Wow, how did you do that like that? You know, don't you have any conscience or any fear?"

In this fantasy world of women, parties, and sports, there was still the reality of Billy's baseball career. Yet even here, at least as he described it to me, everything came easily and life proceeded smoothly. Most players move in sequence from Rookie League or Single A ball to Double A to Triple A and, for the lucky few, to the major leagues. Billy went right from Single A to Triple A in his first year and a half. He hit over .300 with 30 homers in his first season in Single A and then followed that with hitting .312 with 18 homers and 80 runs batted in in Triple A. By May of the following year, 1982, he was called up to the major leagues from the Triple A team. I asked him to tell me about that first dream-like moment of joining the Pittsburgh Pirates team.

I was a little scared. I was nineteen, almost twenty, and I was just looking around at all the people. People saying stuff. It was real crazy.

(Did they haze you a little bit?)

No, no they didn't even know who I was. "Hey, who are you?" It was pretty cool. After you get a base hit, you hit a ball hard, and it was just the same thing. When I was a kid, I wanted to be a professional baseball player.

(So what happened as you came to bat that first time?)

I had my heart in my throat. I grounded out my first time. But I hit the ball good. I had a good eye.

(Was there a difference in the pitching once you got to the majors?)

Triple A to majors, a little bit of difference. A lot of guys threw junk. But I could hit a curveball. I could keep my eye on the ball. Watch the ball hit the bat. A lot of guys would pull their heads out. There's a lot of good baseball players in the minors, but they really don't get a chance.

I asked Billy to tell me about his first hit.

After five at bats. First I grounded out and flied out. I was trying to hit me a homer, man. I wanted to hit a homer for my first. We were playing in New York. I had my family there. I went 0 for 2 my first day at Shea Stadium. I had my grandmother there and my mother, and my brothers. First hit in New York. I got taken out the first game and then I went 1 for 3 the next day. I was a little frustrated the first day and the manager goes "Geez, you look nervous, kid." I'm saying, "I'm nervous, I'm playing in front of like 60,000 people. I'm nineteen years old. Know what I mean?" He goes, "Relax, relax."

Billy went on to play in thirty to forty games that year, hitting .250 with four or five home runs. His first home run was another highlight. He hit it off one of the better pitchers of his era, John Tudor, of the St. Louis Cardinals.

He was like a professor, that guy. He knew it was my first homer too. He's just shaking his head. I was running around saying, "Geez, nice pitch you gave me there for the first one! Geez, you handed it to me!" I told him, as I rounded second to go to third. It was like a curveball and he just lobbed it there and it was just like "Here you go, kid." That's how I thought it was, but then again, I don't know, maybe one just got away from him. I ripped it. It was nice. I always used a wood bat in high school and in Babe Ruth, 'cause I knew was going to be a pro baseball player. Always when I was a kid. I just knew it. It was weird. I used to see shooting stars all the time when I was a kid. I'm superstitious. The way I got dressed, I always got dressed the same way, when I was playing Little League and when I was in the pros.

As Billy told this story of his first home run and of his premonitions that he would make it to the big leagues, I could hear the pleasure and the almost childlike awe that this had all happened to him. With me there at the Pines, and with the twelve years that had passed since that glorious moment, it could have been another person we were discussing, another Billy. I found this aspect of our conversation particularly telling. There was a way in which Billy stood outside his own talent and was unable to account for his success. He knew he would be a pro baseball player, but felt this was due to fate ("shooting stars") as much as to his talent. Even though our cultural myths portray our athlete heroes as symbolic statements about the meaning of hard work and the determined cultivation of the self, Billy was expressing a strong lack of agency in his rise to the majors. Just as the film *Amadeus* contrasted the effortless genius of Mozart with the dogged mediocrity of Salieri, Billy reminds us that the success so many of us crave may have little to do with the self-actualization we attribute it to.

The pleasure Billy took in recounting his brief time in the majors soon yielded to his acknowledgment that there was no second act, no follow-up to his brief epiphany. He was injured and finished for the season, and for his career, three months after his first game as a major leaguer. He was playing the outfield at the Houston Astrodome. Its warning track before the back wall of the stadium was smaller than in other parks and because of the artificial surface not as differentiated.

I ran into the wall full speed. I backhanded the ball, caught it, and as I caught it, it was like getting hit by a train on the subway. I'm knocked out cold. I had this scar, see that [he shows me a thin line on his forehead], bleeding arm, two knees, one they had to dig up, and the other was arthroscopic, so it was shot. Broke my nose. But the ball's in my glove.

The injury, without equivocation, was the pivotal moment in Billy's life. He was on crutches for seven months. The Pirates waived him at the end of the season. His left knee was bad and his stock had plummeted. He tried to hook up with other teams, but without any luck. He was so desperate that he even took his brother's identification and went to the Mets' tryout camp.

They said, "Geez, let's give you a little check-up here, guy. I said, "O.K." "Oh, what's wrong with this knee. What happened to it?" "Oh, I cut myself." "Really? Let's take a little X-ray." And then, "Aren't you Billy Zeitel, who was with the Pirates?' "Oh, yeah." "Geez, you got a lot of balls, kid." Hey I wanted to play baseball, there's nothing wrong with me.

Despite his protests, it was over; no team would touch him. As Billy put it, this "really fucked up my head." He had gone from making $180,000 to nothing.

I'd look at a game on television, and I'd see myself playing. I would say, "That guy's making 3 million dollars a year, and I'm better than him. I could be doing that right now." I see a guy batting .220 these days, making 2 million dollars a year.

Billy went into a deep depression. His mood state was compounded by a brief bout of abuse of the Percosets they had given him to help with the pain from his knee operations. He felt he was part of a cruel joke. Despite his injury, he had lost none of his agility and strength. He could still play and no one would give him a chance. He worked out in the gyms with a vengeance and maintained peak shape. He was determined to prove them wrong and the truth is that he has never had a problem with his legs since.

It made no difference, though. From the pro teams' perspective, he was damaged goods; there were a hundred other players of his quality ready to take his place. For Billy, whose whole sense of identity was based in his accomplishments as an athlete, this unwillingness to let him practice his skills (even though he showed no decline in ability) left him in a bitter twilight zone. He was still Billy, the Big Jock in Town, he still had his gift, but the "town" did not want him anymore. In a literal and symbolic way, he was willing to give up his identity (assuming his brother's name for the tryout), but even this concession made no difference. The spotlight of interest that had always shone on him throughout his life because of to his athletic ability, this external light that allowed him to see himself, had been shut off. He was in the dark and he now had to figure out what he was going to do with his life after baseball.

Joining the Drug Trade

Initially, Billy went into construction work and played in semipro softball leagues. He made $50 or $75 a game and his team went on to win the state championship four or five times in a row. There was a lot of partying and drugs with this team. One of the sponsors was even arrested by the federal government for selling a kilo of cocaine to an FBI agent. It was through his contacts on this team that he got into dealing drugs. He was hungry for the big money he had tasted and for the excitement and recognition of being the key man. He found both, at least at first, by selling marijuana and later on cocaine.

Made me a lot of money. I had a lot of friends. I was good with people, I mean people used to go, "Geez, you should sell cars." . . . A lot of people knew me and I knew a lot of people and it just went off. I was treated like the big athlete. And I was always a funny guy too. I had a good sense of humor and made people laugh all the time. I had a lot of friends or so-called friends, you see who your friends are when you're down and out.

Billy had found a way to keep the buzz of celebrity and importance going—drug-dealing. Once again, he had a diversion to offer people that could allow them to escape from the demands of their daily lives. Through drug-dealing, he could surround himself with people and fill his evening with parties. By being the man with connections and trading on his brief celebrity, he could retain a sense of status and power among his peer group.

For those next five or six years, Billy kept up his high-profile life as a big man on the softball and drug-dealing scenes. He was living with a woman, and in 1986, they had a son who was born with three major heart defects.

He had two open-heart surgeries, and after he was better, she left me. He was in Yale for eighteen months straight. I seen so many little kids die. It was just crazy. I almost dove off a twenty-story building, man. I was working construction at the time and I just couldn't take it. They'd call me up and it was like, "Your son just went into a coma." I'm like "What?" I just couldn't take it. It takes a lot of balls to kill yourself. And I almost did it. I don't even know why I wanted to do it. I just couldn't take going into the hospital and seeing my son. PICU—little kids with pacemakers in, shunts in their heads, and . . . I can't take this no more.

What struck me as Billy described this terrible moment in his life was his emphasis on his own inability to tolerate the suffering and death he was forced to witness. When Billy told me he had contemplated suicide as his son lay in an intensive care bed, it clarified for me how unprepared Billy was to handle the actual events of life beyond the playing field. So many boys grow up idolizing athlete heroes, but the men they worship may know nothing about what it takes to be a man in the humblest sense—for example, how to support a spouse and child during a period of life-threatening illness.

Considering Billy's shame and fear about his inability to cope with life on its own terms, his deepening descent into addiction and his subsequent failure to see his son again become more understandable. Who had given Billy instruction or examples in how to endure a loved one's suffering, how to negotiate potential loss, or how to find empathy for others when his own pain threatened to dominate all feeling? Such lessons are not generally taught in the locker rooms or playing fields of professional sports. On the contrary, the athlete is continually turned back to reflect upon his or her own condition; performance, recognition, and money are the structuring forces of the self.

Billy first dealt cocaine for a few years before his own use of it overtook his effectiveness as a dealer.

This is how it went. I was selling so much pot that the guy goes, "Geez man, I wonder what he's doing with it. Here, see what you can do with this." And he throws a bag full of coke at me. So I got into that and got rid of it in three days and here's some more, and here's some more, and here's some more, and there we go. And I did that for three years. Made a lot of money. And I spent a lot of money. As I made it, I spent it, rented limos, front row at every concert, top price dinners. Boom—"Hey mom, wanna see $100,000 in cash? "What?" You know, stupid shit.

Billy continued to live the high lifestyle that perhaps he imagined he would have had if his baseball career had thrived. He bought a luxury condominium, two Lincoln Town Cars, a boat. He described going into a fine furniture store:

I needed a bedroom set. They said, "Oh, this is $9,000." I said, 'Yeah, well here's $20,000, lady. I want that and that. Now I don't want to wait eight months. I wanted it now. So they were just like whew, whew, whew, whew, everything taken care of.

In the familiar pattern of the stories I have heard of the dealers' fast lives, things eventually turned sour. Some of Billy's friends were arrested and he grew increasingly anxious. His developing paranoia was not helped by his escalating use of his own product. He was freebasing cocaine at an alarming rate and found he could not control himself. In six months from his first hit, he was broke, his girlfriend had left him, and he had sold all his possessions.

Freebasing cocaine. Pure cocaine. Hallucinating from smoking an ounce. I'd get two, three, four broads and go get a room somewhere and just go crazy. Women do anything for that. You'd be surprised. I mean good women. Just totally screwed up. . . . After that, I didn't care how it happened. "Wanna smoke this, come on, let's go take a ride. Get a couple of friends, come on."

Always in our conversation, Billy returned to the importance of money. He described it as a "power thing." He would see an old man on the street and take him into his limo, buy him dinner and put him up in a hotel room. Money let him do things for others, be the big presence in other people's lives. With money, he was again the Big Jock in Town that everyone knew, the center of attention, rounding the bases while the crowd cheered. With cocaine as his enticement, he was still the guy women would flatter and flock to see. The only problem was that his need for cocaine to maintain his habit and his profile burned up his money rapidly.

As Billy realized that his coke dealing had turned into a coke addiction, he begged his supplier to let him sell pot again. The dealer was no fool and told him that he knew what Billy would do with any money he made from selling pot. He was clearly trapped in his cocaine addiction and dealing other kinds of drugs was no answer.

One of the hardest parts of this period was his mother's response to his addiction. After the years of dealing with her substance-abusing husband and of trying to rebuild her own life, she was limited in what she was willing to give to Billy. She made a few initial efforts to help him, but when he went back to smoking cocaine and lied to her about money, she was through.

My mother's a tough Italian woman. She'll do anything for you, but don't lie to her, and don't screw her or else you're on the shit list. She goes, "I'll put a gun to your head and blow your head off to take you out of your misery." That's the kind of woman she is. "Don't even come around my house or I will shoot you."

After Billy lost his drug-dealing connection, his life turned into a single-minded pursuit of money to pay for his addiction. He moved into illegal scams—some as pedestrian as check-forging and some a little more ornate. He would put up signs to rent his apartment, ask for a deposit, keep the deposit, and then move out of town. Eventually in the late eighties, he was arrested for possession of narcotics and given an eighteen-month suspended sentence with three years probation. He eventually ended up spending a month in the North Avenue jail of Bridgeport for driving an unregistered vehicle and violation of probation.

I almost got murdered in my sleep in jail. I got jumped by ten black guys. . . . Somebody got killed, like a week after I got beat up in there. . . . They beat me up for being white, a racial thing. I have 70 stitches in my head. Broke my nose, my face. Lost some sight in my right eye. Cracked my skull. Ever see somebody die in a car accident? All the waste comes out of their body. But I just came back to life, for some reason. Somebody likes me up there.

Billy tended to blur the last five years of his story from the beginning of the '90s to the present. He hustled from job to job, losing them when he would not show up or was too coked up to work. He continued to get money through scams and shady dealings. Though he only attended one rehab, and that was in the eighties, he did go through twenty to thirty detoxes, mostly in the New Haven area. In the year previous to our interview, he was reduced to sleeping in shelters and relying on soup kitchens. Billy told this to me with frustration and pain in his voice. He told me that he wished his mother had a camera to photograph what lows he had reached; perhaps it would shame him into stopping his drug use. It might wake him up from the pervasive sense of "Fuck Its" that often overwhelmed him. He described how it felt for him, used as he was to silk shirts and top-shelf treatment, to go for weeks without showers and to be looked at like scum by people on the street. His worst moment was when he ran into a drunken priest in the streets of New London.

I knew the priest from going to the soup kitchen in New London. It was two in the morning and he was stumbling down the street. He had shorts on, looked like a regular Joe. Drunk as a skunk. I said, "Geez, Father Raymond, what are you doing?" I was high, but I was coming down and I didn't have no money. So I walked him back to his church, to the rectory part. He said, "You need a place to stay?"

He said, "Come on in, are you hungry?" I said, "Yeah." "Are you thirsty?" I said, "Yeah." I had a couple of drinks with him. He whipped out a half-gallon of Jim Beam, puts it on the table. He passed out. I grabbed his wallet; he had a couple of new things, like an air conditioner, a new VCR. I grabbed them, opened the door, put them outside. I went to the bank machine. He had the code in his wallet for the ATM machine. I mean how stupid. He had like $8,100 in that checking account. I didn't take it all, cause I couldn't. The machine wouldn't let me.

It was just totally degrading . . . really a shame, really playing handball on a curb. But I'm going to write him a letter. Apologize and see if I can make restitution when I leave here, and explain to him what I'm doing.

There is something almost archetypal about Billy's encounter with the priest. In terms of Billy's life story, it is truly a "nuclear episode" (see Chapter 2 for a definition of this aspect of identity). Within this memory, Billy, a debased representative of the contemporary agentic self, unconnected to any social structure or intimate relationship, encounters the drunken priest, a symbol of the deposed religious tradition in our society. Billy's depiction of the priest is both ridiculing and remorseful. He sees the weakness in the tradition the priest represents, but he also sees the equivalent evil in the pure selfishness that defines his act of thievery. This self-defining memory rings true as a metaphor for the contemporary self housed within many of us— hovering between narcissistic escape on the one hand and the potential hypocrisy of religious traditions on the other, we fantasize, just as Billy does, about making restitution to resolve this conflict, but have little sense of how to convert this fantasy into reality.

When Billy and I conducted this interview, he had been at Lebanon Pines for about thirty days; I asked him about his hopes or goals for his life at that point. He told me he wanted to be the person he had been before his addiction. I pointed out that he could not return to being the celebrity he once was. He responded that he just wanted to be able to walk down the street and be respected and looked up to, to have somebody say, "Hey, how are you doing?" I asked him if was ready to put the high profile lifestyles he once lived behind him, to let go of his past, and accept the daily routine of living his life, doing his work, being with family. He assured me that there is work out there for him to do and perhaps he might return to school. Yet as we discussed these prospects, he returned again to his memories of the first days in the big leagues.

I couldn't sleep at night, I was just so excited. I really didn't prepare myself for that when I was young, cause I kind of always assumed I'd be there. And I was there.

And I said to myself, "You know, man, people dream of coming here, and they don't do it, and I was here." Only for a short time, but that's the breaks, you know, that happens. Stuff happens. But it really did depress me.

Once again, Billy invoked the theme of fate rather than meaningful agency controlling his life. He felt no need to prepare for his stint in the big leagues; he assumed it would happen and it did. What he also did not prepare himself for was the rest of his life, a sober life of earning a daily wage and making a sustained commitment to a family and a community. Drugs allowed him to postpone the taking up of this "real work."

About three weeks after this interview, Billy was caught with another man from the Pines shooting heroin in the woods behind the barracks. He was sent on his way and none of the staff at the Pines felt optimistic that he would stop his drug use any time soon.

Heroes of Sport

Some months after I interviewed Billy, I heard the news that Mickey Mantle had died. Though their major league careers could hardly have been more different—Mantle was a Hall of Famer and Billy played for only half a season—they shared the problems of career-ending injuries and subsequent addiction.[11] Just as Mickey Mantle once served as an icon of athletic power and courage, he had now become a cultural symbol of how the world of sports can trap an individual in a public world that has little to do with the daily routine of living a life. If Mantle's life provided a tragic, highly visible example of this dilemma; Billy Zeitel, and thousands of other former athletic stars like him, are living out this same dilemma in less public, but no less troubling, ways.

Billy Zeitel's descent into cocaine addiction could be traced to factors beyond the culture of sports, to deep losses suffered in his childhood, and the various misfortunes of his life. Billy's father provided a negative role model of substance abuse, womanizing, and irresponsibility, both as a husband and a father. Even after his father had left the scene, Billy virtually raised himself because of his mother's involvement with her own career, far from her children. From early adolescence, long before he suffered an injury and his drug use escalated, he was already smoking marijuana on a near-daily basis. Because most professional athletes do not develop substance abuse problems, it would be unwise to use Billy's life story to imply a causal connection between any athlete's involvement in professional sports and subsequent addiction.

My thesis is both more narrow and more wide-ranging. I am suggesting that certain ways of constructing a sense of identity perpetuated by the culture of professional sports made Billy's vulnerability to addiction more likely to be expressed. Without that vulnerability, born out of biological and familial risk factors, it is unlikely he would have traveled the direction that he did. In this very specific sense, I am willing to argue that the culture of professional sports puts young men who are at risk for addiction at an even greater risk.

On the other hand, in a much wider sense, I am suggesting that the emphasis placed on fame and unbridled agency, exemplified by our sports culture, is problematic for all men's sense of identity, even if they have never touched a drink or drug. Over and over in Billy's narrative we heard about his investment in material displays of wealth, in the power and prestige that money can bring. We heard about the pleasure of parties and of sexual escapades. He was a man of some thirty-four years, yet his life story still centered on an adolescent's fantasies come true—easy money and wealth, public recognition, drugs, and sex. Most strikingly, we heard little about his private world, his thoughts or emotional struggles. His life was portrayed through recognition by others, through their appreciation of his athletic accomplishments or of his power as a purveyor of money and drugs. The one exception to this emphasis was his narrative of despair with regard to the medical condition of his son. Yet even here he told this story with an emphasis upon his own distress rather than his son's.

It is not surprising that Billy, an ex-athlete of the early eighties, would find his way to drugs and dealing. As I have heard from men in their thirties and early forties repeatedly in my interviews and work at the Pines (and as I experienced in my own life), the decades of the seventies and early eighties were a time of rampant marijuana use in high school and college. For Billy, the transfer of his sports celebrity status, built on public recognition and superficial contacts, to a similar power-oriented status as a drug dealer made a certain tragic sense. But what does it say about our culture that there can be a parallel relationship between the heroes we set up for our children and people who deal drugs?

On the surface, until Billy injured himself, he was an embodiment of the American dream. He was a handsome successful athlete with large sums of money and an unbounded future. Millions of American boys would have wanted to be in his shoes. Yet how does the society reconcile this adulation with the inadequate preparation this hero's role provides for living a life?

The problem is that boys do not see their sports heroes as living lives that are actually fraught with pressures and challenges. Boys, and, perhaps many men, have substituted the fantasized life of recognition, money, sex, and drugs for the confused and at times, barren, life of the actual athletes. It is my worry that there exists in some members of our culture the distorted fantasy that Billy's pre-injury life is a normative expectation for a young boy. In other words, all lives that do not reach this level of public acknowledgment are in some sense failures or inadequate.

What happens in a culture when the standard life becomes the life lived by celebrities of the media? Why do we have a cultural passion for talk shows that turn average people into momentary stars, that allow their flesh and blood to be translated into points of light that fill millions of home? I think the answer is that we have lost the sense of the inherent value of the nontelevised lives we live. Work stripped of meaning and endlessly responsive to the economic bottom line has caused many of us to feel cornered and at the verge of despair about our lives. Our investment in images from the sports world, music, and film allows us to escape.

The images of our sports heroes that fill the airwaves and the magazines are ones of vast sums of money, of entrepreneurial power, of freedom to seek any type of pleasure. I could say that they also model the value of hard work, but any boy who knows something about sports knows that the majority of athletes who work slavishly day in and day out never reach the pinnacle of sports. The greatest athletes are born with skills that surpass all others— they may work hard, but they have bodies and reflexes that are gifts and not won solely through effort. For this reason, they do not necessarily model for young boys the meaning of agency as discipline, responsibility, self-mastery. The admiration boys feel toward their heroes shifts to an appreciation of the inherent talent, the personality of the star, rather than the effort it takes to reach their level of skill.[12]

I do not think that the world of sports, so prized by American men, is necessarily a bad training ground for building character and values. Quite the contrary, sports in the Olympian ideal have the capacity to teach perseverance, teamwork, humility in victory, and acceptance of defeat. They also can teach one about the incalculable potential inside oneself—that the boundaries of achievement were wider than could have been anticipated. However, these lessons, I believe, must be mediated by older and experienced teachers, whether coaches or parents. The cliché that sports have become a big business has a significant meaning in this regard. When athletics no longer serve as a simple medium of pleasure, or as a vehicle for the development of character, or as an adventure in the discovery of the capacity of the self for achievement, they then devolve into another commodity of our culture, to be bought and sold without the mediation of meaningful relationships. The risk of this happening to the young athletes in our society is greater now than it has ever been. If the strong guiding presence of parents and ethical coaches is not felt, athletes will be prey to the public-dependent life that being a star creates. Billy could not remember the names of any of his minor league managers and he described his major league manager as a hard drinker with a vicious temper. After his injury, he was discarded by the major leagues. Ironically, he worked harder than ever on his physical conditioning, "to prove them wrong," but the bitter lesson he took away was that hard work is not enough. Baseball was about money and he had become a risky investment not worth the effort. As Billy put it, these kinds of interactions and experiences, "fucked up his head."

Billy Zeitel, essentially parentless, and innately gifted, did the best he could in embracing the athletic culture that offered him an opportunity for success. In return, the culture made good on what it promised him—money, praise, sex, and drugs.[13] Once injured, he sought a way to maintain these facets of his life that had become his self-definition. Dealing drugs was a convenient solution. For many poor and poorly educated boys in this country who lack Billy's athletic abilities, the movement into drugs or drug-dealing as a way to money and status is even more direct. I know that many people might not appreciate my drawing parallels between the world of sports and the world of drugs, but I fear that they both reflect the emptiness we have left our children to feel about the daily living of life. And this is not simply the problem of the poor. One only needs to think about the money invested and the attention given to my own state university's basketball teams (University of Connecticut) and then consider that for several years the university's library languished in a state of disrepair. We only need to consider the vast budgets of motion pictures made in Hollywood. We build our cathedrals of sport and film to find a desired pleasure and potency that we cannot uncover in our day-to-day lives.

Billy's story serves as a warning for other athletes, but it also cautions the rest of us about the burden we place upon our athletes and other forms of celebrities—what we ask of them in order to fulfill our cultural hunger for self-fulfillment, how we project our fantasies of immortality and enchanted youth on to them in response to our own daily despair and experience of meaninglessness. Once they have obtained these wishes, we also take our envy and frustration out on them. If they do not bear their celebrity with total grace, if they reveal mortal failings and nasty habits, we read of their troubles with prurient interest and ask for more. What Billy experienced as a boy and a young man was very similar to what Mickey Mantle lived through and what the athletes from the documentary film *Hoop Dreams* described, and what thousands of other young men (and more and more often, young women) face as they strive to fulfill their unusual physical potential.

In Billy's story, there is yet another key to understanding the lives of certain kinds of chronic addicts and many non-addicted men as well. The siren song of glory in sports seduces both participant and fan, causing each to imagine that winning leads to a life of paradise—of riches, sensual fulfillment, and freedom from concerns. In Vince Lombardi's oft-quoted words, "Winning isn't everything. It's the only thing." With this perspective, how do we learn how to tolerate disappointments, losses, and murky stalemates that are as common as victories in most of our lives? I believe the answer to this question can only be found in the cultivation of our responsibility to each other, in acknowledging our interconnectedness as human beings. The statement, "Winning is the only thing" is a logical absurdity—by definition, whenever someone wins, loss exists as well. The sober life Billy hopes to achieve will have to expand to include this full scope of experiences. The best thing we could do for him is teach him, as he was never taught, that he can fail and still be part of a community, that he does not have to be at the center to be included in the circle.

The Midrash is an ancient collection of stories and commentaries written by rabbis about the various books of the Hebrew Bible. In one story, "The Most Precious Gift," Moses tells the Israelites that God has offered to give the gift of the Torah to them and he asks if they will accept it, without knowing what it is. Having just experienced the miracle of freedom from Egypt, the people unanimously agree to accept whatever gift God offers. Moses goes up the mountain and returns some days later, but empty-handed. He tells the people that God will indeed give them the Torah, but He wants something as a guarantee that they will truly accept and live by the gift He gives them.

The people puzzle over this and finally decide to collect all their jewels and gold and present them to God. Moses, weighed down by these treasures, strides up the mountain to deliver their gift. He comes back days later, but still without the Torah. He explains that God wants something more, something that will fulfill the people's promise to follow the dictates of the Torah.

Once again, the people search their homes to find the appropriate gift for God. This time they settle upon beautiful creations made by their own hands, woven cloth, carved wood, and polished stone work. They send Moses on his way with the hope that these handicrafts will demonstrate their devotion.

Moses descends from the mountain for a third time and still does not have the Torah. He tells the people that even the work of their hands cannot serve as a guarantee to God. The Israelites stand speechless in dismay until a mother with a baby makes a tentative suggestion. Suppose, she says, we offer to teach our children the lessons of the Torah. Let this be our guarantee.

Moses climbs the mountain, holding only this promise and nothing else. At last, he returns holding the two stone tablets filled with God's words. The people rejoice and reaffirm the gift they have promised to God, to teach their children the commandments of the Torah, who in turn will teach their children, passing on their lessons to each new generation.[14]

The lesson of this story is that material wealth or even exquisite achievement cannot guarantee access to spiritual fulfillment. The route God requires is through the acceptance of what Erikson called generativity—the responsibility we all possess to safeguard the generations that follow us.

Billy's story raises the same question about what we need to do to ready our athletes (and ourselves) to become men as opposed to gods—men who live with death and physical decline, weekly responsibility and drudgery— men who live in worlds of getting up and doing what needs to be done without press coverage, extravagant rewards, and congratulatory banquets. In simple terms, Billy's story asks how we might teach men to convert their quest for agency into generativity.

Perhaps my boyhood hero, Mickey Mantle, never really had to enter this day-to-day world, but the price he paid was that his only livelihood was being a creation called Mickey Mantle, an icon that had hardened and aged with a tired and frightened man inside it. For Billy Zeitel, now in his thirties, his brief celebrity long faded, the choice is much simpler. He must learn to rise to his responsibilities as a man, to accept the duties of work and family, to become part of a generation that must teach the next generation, or he will, with increasing speed, give up his life to addiction, prison, and, very soon, death. As even the most casual reader of the sports pages knows, his story is not an isolated one. He is joined by many a proud and ambitious giant who, once carried on the shoulders of his teammates, now hides from them in the shadows of the streets and rehabs. If each of these men could be helped to see himself as a potential teacher instead of a vanquished loser, the battle against sobriety might suddenly seem less urgent and the prospect of sober life increasingly desirable.

Part Four

PROBLEMS WITH

IDENTITY

FORMATION

8. WAR ON MEMORY
A Vietnam Veteran's Struggle with the Continuity of Identity

War makes men like me, hollow men, men weighed down by memory, out of time and out of place, men who spend their lives trying to recover what has been lost, men haunted by the awful mystery that spared them, that left them alone, walking in empty spaces.

MICHAEL NORMAN, "THE HOLLOW MAN"[1]

A fundamental premise of the framework of identity I have applied in this book is that successful identity formation requires a linkage of past, present, and future.[2] In constructing a life story of identity organized around agency and communion, individuals need to see the events of their lives as woven into a unified narrative, as opposed to a series of discrete episodes or random occurrences. If a story grows out of an overarching set of goals or a unifying personal myth, then what we have done in the past, what we are doing now, and what we hope to accomplish will coalesce into a meaningful causal structure. Even more, this unified structure locates individuals in a community of time, connecting them not only to the present society but to others' stories from both previous and future generations.

For example, in my own personal myth, I see myself (with the touch of self-righteousness that characterizes many a life story) as committed to the "calling" of teaching at a liberal arts college. As I look to my past, I can see how my parents' academic careers influenced me, but even more I can identify the impact of the dedicated professors who taught me as an undergraduate at Amherst College. Their idealism and enthusiasm about the intellectual community of a liberal arts college helped answer my confusion about what career path I might pursue. My current work as a teacher and researcher still draws upon the inspiration they provided for me and the models they offered me in the classroom and during more informal advising. At the same time my past experiences working in troubled and impoverished communities, including my encounters with individuals suffering from chronic addiction, have widened my vision of the responsibility of a liberal arts college to the larger community. As I plan for my future, I anticipate growing as an effective teacher and scholar, but also continuing my work to build stronger relationships between my college community and the community in which the college resides.

I have chosen this example from my own life, not because I think it is unique or particularly laudatory. Rather, it simply provides a straightforward example of how my sense of identity formation relies on a narrative construction that establishes continuity over time. From such continuity, my identity finds a sense of coherence and a discernible direction for the future. Additionally, I am able to experience a sense of communion not only with my present community, but with both a tradition of intellectual service and the promise of generations that will follow me.

Individuals suffering from chronic addiction often feel the exact opposite way; they struggle with problems of incoherence and discontinuity with regard to the location of identity in a unified past, present, and future. Their difficulty with the continuity of identity may often stem from two compounding problems—trauma and the effects of addiction on a linear sense of time. Either problem in and of itself, trauma or addiction, can block an individual from developing a continuity of self, but both together are particularly devastating to efforts at stable identity formation and location in a community across time.

Combat veterans who are traumatized by their war experiences and then develop addictions face this exact dual dilemma. Having left behind comrades, alone and haunted by the past, they see no clear vision of how to escape memory and move forward. Some end up waging a war on memory through an addictive life.[3] Their war is fought on two fronts—in the short term a drink or drug dulls pain and consciousness of the past or present, and in the long run a life of addiction buffers them against future engagement with relationships and societal demands. As Michael Norman puts it, their addicted life allows them to live in the "empty spaces," a purgatory that is neither the hell of recollection nor the terrifying risk of new losses and sorrows. If we are to understand more about the problem of identity formation in chronically addicted men, we will need to learn more about how they can use their addiction to stay out of time and to avoid creating a narrative coherence in their lives.

The message of the story Tyler Casey tells in this chapter is not simply that war is hell and leaves horrible scars. Beyond these blatant truths lies a subtler insight about what the construction of identity demands from all of us, addicted and non-addicted alike. To feel that we are moving toward a desired goal in our daily activities, we look to our past for a coherent message about our previous experiences.[4] To trust ourselves to take action in the future, we need to extract a sense of meaning with regard to what we have done and what has been done to us. Trauma of any kind—war, abuse, disaster—challenges our capacity to make unified stories out of the events of our lives. The nature of trauma, its disjunction with any previous reality, stuns us and leaves us grasping for sense. When the memories of the trauma persist and we cannot integrate them into an acceptable framework, when they simply won't fit what we know of the world or want to know, despair sets in. A drink or drug relieves this despair, both by blotting out thought and by blotting out the need for memory. If we can understand this point, we can then understand that a Vietnam War veteran suffering from chronic addiction is not simply an addict with a traumatic past. He is a man who is caught up in a struggle to destroy his past and in this way release himself from any demand that he have a future. His problem is not that he has a bad story, but that his trauma and addiction drive him to become story-less: to let go of his identity and sense of membership in our society.

Getting Started

Tyler Casey had canceled twice before we finally did our interview. Though this fact should have tipped me off to his reticence, he came into my office at the Pines in an uneventful fashion. He took his seat by the side of my desk, as I sat with my chair angled toward him. As I watched his face, his eyes looked out onto the opposite wall, apparently studying the titles on my bookshelf. His eyes were a swimming-pool blue, though there was a cloudiness to their gaze and red lines in the whites. His hair was wavy, a little disheveled, and mostly gray, making him look slightly older than his forty-seven years. His frame was basically lean, but he showed the beginning of jowls and these were accentuated by a gray stubble on his lower cheeks and chin. He wore a white tee shirt and khaki pants, looking every bit like the carpenter he had been for most of his adult life. The only physical sign that something might be different about our talk was the beaded line of sweat that had appeared on his forehead, just below his hairline. He had listened to my initial description of the project and signed the consent form without raising any objections or comments.

The counselor who had recommended I speak to Tyler had mentioned that he was a Vietnam vet and that he had worked with the Veterans Administration (VA) hospital some years earlier to address his combat experiences. I had been asked to evaluate a number of Vietnam vets over the years at SCADD and had observed a wide variety of responses to what they had gone through, ranging from a complete unwillingness to discuss anything to do with Vietnam to the opposite—a compulsive retelling of experiences and a kind of frozenness in that time period. I suddenly sensed my own nervousness at commencing the interview, even though Tyler had not raised any concerns. After seeing numerous Vietnam veterans suffering from chronic addiction, I was convinced that I needed to include their stories in my project. However, I was unsure that my research justified asking them to retell memories they had tried to leave behind or had worked through in their VA treatment groups.

As I explained that the interview began with a self-defining memory, I found that I needed more words than usual to convey what I meant. Tyler told me he didn't have any memories that fit my request. On my third pass of describing how I would like him to recall any memory from his life that might reflect something significant about who he is, he told me, "Vietnam, it's always there."

I asked him if there was something specific that came to mind when he thought of that time in his life. The sweat showed through on the chest of his white shirt and under his arms.

Just about all of it, babies being killed, people being blown apart, friends getting shot. It's all there. It's not separate incidences, really, just all, by now, just messed into one big nightmare, so it's hard to differentiate between them. It's, ah, I don't want to talk about it. Maybe this isn't a good idea. I'm not comfortable with this. I'm really not. I'm sorry. I can't do it.

At this point I turned off the tape recorder and gave up any idea of doing the life study. I told Tyler he had nothing to be sorry about and that this interview was only something he should do if he felt like doing it. He stood up to go, at the verge of a panic state, and went as far as the door. Then remarkably, he stopped himself.

You know, this is what I have done for most of my life is cut out from talking about this shit. That's what they worked on with me so hard at the West Haven VA—to stop burying all of this, so I could finally move on. That's why I told Debbie [his counselor] I wanted to do this thing with you. I wanted to show myself that it didn't run my life anymore, that when I needed to, I could tell it as part of my life, and stop running to a drink or a drug. I'm going to get some air and try again.

I sat alone in the office, unsure if Tyler would return. After a few long minutes, Tyler knocked on the door and re-entered the office, his face splashed with water. He said,

"Let's try it again. I want to do this for me, show I can look it in the eye, even though the whole thing sucks. You ready, Doctor Singer?"

I was not at all sure I was ready, but I started up the tape recorder and we began our work.

Stopping Time

It would not make sense to tell Tyler's life story in the conventional chronological way. To stretch his life over the pages of the chapter, apportioning more or less equal time to each of his five decades, would be to misrepresent how his life has been experienced. If those five decades were laid out on a twelve-inch ruler, I would put a mark halfway and call the first six inches zero to eighteen years of age. I would then put a mark at ten inches and call the space between my two marks eighteen to twenty years of age (twenty months of military service). From ten inches to the end of the ruler, I would call, borrowing a phrase from Tyler, "the wasted years," twenty to forty-seven years of age.

In his pioneering study of the phenomenological experience of alcoholism, Norman Denzin called alcoholism a "dis-ease of time."[5]

> The alcoholic is simply uneasy in time. He is unable to deal with time on his hands. He cannot let go of the past and purposive actions that would commit him to a stance in the future are avoided. By drinking time comes to a standstill.[6]

Denzin wrote that for normal individuals time is both linear and goal-oriented. We think of the past as influencing our present actions and of our present actions as leading to our future objectives. Though we draw upon the past and look to the future, Denzin emphasized that most normal individuals orient their lives to the here and now, to addressing the immediate present concerns of daily work and relationships. Normal individuals react emotionally to the events of the present and experience a sense of self in relation to who they are at the present time.

In contrast, Denzin portrayed the alcoholic as living a life in time that is circular rather than linear. The past and the future have more hold over the individual's consciousness than the present. The alcoholic is perpetually pulled back into a past of negative experiences. The past's hold on the individual fills the future with dread, a dread that cripples the individual from taking action in the present. The alcoholic's consciousness stands the typical causality of time on its head—events in an anticipated future can influence the present rather than present actions leading to future effects.

For example, Denzin described a man who after a period of sobriety anticipates having a slip and drinking when he is visiting Toronto on business.[7] With this sense of resignation about his impending weakness in mind, he ends up drinking in the airport bar while waiting to board his plane. Using his knowledge of his past susceptibility to drink on business trips as a way of understanding his future actions, he allows his alcoholic sense of time to overwhelm his experience of the present. In the end, he enters a blackout from drinking and never boards the plane or makes the trip. The imagined dreaded future is erased and the present dissolves in an alcoholic haze. The next morning when he awakens, he experiences the present solely in terms of horror and regret at yet another drunken action of the past. Caught on a kind of hamster wheel, alcoholics seldom move forward in time, perpetually running ahead only to end up backwards or upside down.

In my experience with substance-abusing Vietnam vets, I have noted many men who display exactly this difficulty with being frozen in time. Though it may be twenty-five years since they served in the war, their hairstyles, vocabularies, and lifestyles still seem to reflect the atmosphere of the late sixties and early seventies. Though there are some non-alcoholic men who for the rest of their lives define themselves and draw their sense of identity from their military service in their youth, these vets suffering from drug or alcohol addiction seem an extreme case. More than simply associating their identity with that critical juncture of their lives, they are often unable to add new dimensions to their lives either in the realm of work or relationships. Despite efforts at marriages or careers, they find themselves remaining stuck in a period of time and in a youthful confusion, as if the rest of the society had sailed on and left them hopping from bar to bar in a ship-less port.

When I asked Tyler at the end of his interview what he thought the message or theme of his story might be, he told me

I know it would be a whole lot different without the war. I dream sometimes of what it would be like if I didn't go to war. . . . It's a fantasy, like winning the lottery, of course, but . . . I'm disappointed in my life. I'm disappointed in myself. . . . There's a lot of things I'd do different and a lot of things I wouldn't do different. It's hard, like I say, I'm on a kind of emotional roller coaster right now.

The war is an event of the past that maintains a hold over the present and how Tyler currently sees himself, as well as over what he expects for himself in the future. Despite the span of twenty-seven years, it still turns the future back upon itself, leaving him in a confused and uncertain state. As Tyler works at his sobriety, he will continue to rely upon the Posttraumatic Stress Disorder (PTSD) program at the VA hospital to help him find a way to build a life in the here and now. Though he cannot be expected to let go of or forget the past, he will be continually encouraged to see a tangible present and future that are not blotted out by either traumatic memory or efforts to destroy memory.

I think the big trauma for me was, I almost, to me, had an ideal childhood. My grandfather had me do a lot of things, but he taught me, he didn't push me, he didn't make me, he kind of encouraged me to want to do these things and learn how to do it. And then I went from playing sports into killing somebody in like a six-month period. I think that was the trauma right there. I'm walking around in daylight, and all of a sudden, I'm blind.

This "blindness" continued for more than two decades until Tyler began his PTSD groups at the West Haven VA. He described how, working with group members, he came to understand how he approached time after he left Vietnam.

But Vietnam was not something we talked about very freely. And that's another bad thing, because we all stuffed it. Instead of talking, having groups, if it got messy, oh, let's have a drink. A big time word, but I'm looking at it in a different sense, a different context now, is "wasted." That was the big word, or one of them back then. "Oh man, I got wasted last night," or "Come on, let's go get wasted." Boy that has so many meanings now, and that's just what we did basically. Literally wasted our minds, our bodies, our lives. I don't think any bigger word came out of the seventies than "wasted." "Yeah man, I got wasted . . ." Yeah, I sure did. Killing brain cells, that's not a waste? Your life, your family, your friends.

To make sense of what led Tyler into his "wasted years," we need to learn more first about the period of daylight, his childhood shared between Connecticut and Maine, and then about the beginning of his darkness, the memories that haunt him from Vietnam.[8]

A Boy's Life in Maine

Part of the compelling quality of Tyler's story is the idyllic way in which he portrayed his childhood summers in Maine. In contrast to almost all of the men who have shared their stories with me for this book, Tyler talked with pleasure and ease about his family life and friendships in his early years. There was no alcoholism in his family history, and neither parent took more than an occasional beer or glass of wine. Tyler's father's family was from Connecticut, the Bridgeport area, and his mother's family was from Maine. His parents met when his father was in the service and stationed in Maine. They moved down to Bridgeport and then to a smaller Connecticut town nearby, but each summer Tyler would travel up to Maine to live with grandparents.

I spent all my summer vacation there. I'd come back, maybe a week before school started. They used to have to come out and find me because I used to hide because I didn't want to come back. I mean I just loved it there.

The air is clean, the water tastes different, better. We had an outhouse and we had to get water from the well. I just thrived. And I went back Christmas vacation, winter vacation, whatever, after I got older, I went back myself. I would go hunting with my grandfather and my uncle. Go deer hunting way up on the Canadian border. And poor me [smiling], I ate lobster, and crab, and fish, and venison, and duck, all in season. It was stuff that we had caught or killed, not something that you bought at the store.

Although at the end of summer, he would cry as his parents drove him back to Connecticut, by the time he was halfway home he would cheer up thinking about the friends he would see and the new season of Little League and school sports he would play.

I played volleyball intramural, football intramural. I loved them all. We played out-side. There wasn't a day after school when we weren't playing something. What-ever the season was.

His father always encouraged his athletic activities and his involvement with the Cub Scouts, but he was not the kind of man to say "I love you" or show much emotion. He was not demonstrative in a physical way to Tyler or his sister, but Tyler felt his presence and his concern at all times.

I had a good childhood. I can't say it was a dysfunctional family at all. My father wasn't a gambler, wasn't a womanizer, was a hard worker. Though we didn't talk, he was behind me 100 percent in sports, he was behind me 100 percent in every-thing, he just didn't care for my lifestyle in later years.

In some ways, Tyler may have had an even closer relationship with his grandfather in Maine. When he graduated from junior high, he was given an outboard motorboat and he would use it to travel between the island where his grandfather worked as a caretaker and the mainland. Tyler made a point of stressing how much he appreciated his grandfather's trust in letting him manage a boat at such a young age. He was able to earn money running errands between islands and the mainland.

This early responsibility and taste of money may have influenced the course of his high school years. After his sophomore year of high school, he picked up a 3 to 11 job at a service station and threw himself into the work. He also began to date girls and found them another distraction from his studies. His blue eyes won him quite a reputation among the local girls and he was well-known for what they called his bedroom eyes.

His grades, which had always been in the A–B range, began to sink into C's and D's. Despite his parents' admonitions, he was too caught up in own-ing his own car and collecting his weekly paycheck to worry about school. Rather than finish out high school, he decided he could learn technical skills and continue to collect wages if he joined the service. Since there was a lot of talk about Vietnam and he was likely to be drafted (now that college was not in the picture), he thought he might as well enlist in the Navy. He loved the sea and figured he would be less likely to be in the line of fire on a ship than in the ground forces.

I got my GED in the service. I was all gung ho, like I said, I'm the man of the world now. I'm working in a gas station, pumping gas, I mean they haven't allowed me to change oil yet, but I'm a big guy. So four of us got together, they seduced us, more or less. Well, you go in on a buddy plan. You and your buddy go in the same time,

you go through boot camp. so there's four of us. We all went together, we went down and signed up.

In Country

After taking a series of aptitude tests, Tyler was offered the opportunity to be part of one of the elite divisions of the Navy, the Seabees. The Seabees were a construction battalion that assisted landing forces by building bridges, temporary air landings, roads or any other infrastructure need. John Wayne had glorified them in a World War II movie, *The Fighting Seabees.*

Here I think I'm going to be on a ship, sail all around the ports, you know, there's a babe in every port. These older guys, the officers, these guys have a swagger stick. Put it under their arm and they walk up and down the well, got a little brass band on their stick for each port they stop, Italy, Japan, Egypt. Oh yeah, so and so was here, this girl is here, and oh boy, I had three of 'em there. Yeah, that's what I wanted. Never saw it. Spent twenty months in country. Never once set foot on a ship.

It is always hard to know how much memory can alter the past or shape an experience to soften its edges, to fit it more comfortably with one's current understanding of oneself. Tyler's presentation of his leaving high school and ending up in the Seabees portrays him as a rather passive and naive boy, seduced at each step by the lure of money, manhood, and comic book adventure. It is not implausible that there might be another spin on these events. Could he have been frustrated with the outcome of school, and feeling inadequate in his uncommunicative father's eyes, joined the service to prove himself? Once assigned to the Seabees, he could not turn down the chance to be associated with what the recruiters called a "new breed of fighting man." Yet wherever the truth of his past may actually lie, Tyler, by all reasonable standards, deserved to be considered in the normal range of young men. At the time of entering the service, he had had minimal exposure to alcohol (by his own count, he had been drunk no more than five times), never been arrested, suffered no unusual childhood traumas, and shown no signs of mental illness. Today, we might have flagged his loss of interest in school and decision to drop out as a worrisome indicator of problems, but in 1965, though his parents did not approve, they did not see this move as a sign of pathology or imminent self-destruction. At the time, Tyler may have seemed like an action-oriented outdoor type of kid who simply could not tolerate the regimented structure or paper-and-pen work of a classroom. His father had been in the service himself, and it was possible that the experience of boot camp and complying with orders might help him to mature and to learn more self-discipline.

Some research has demonstrated that the veterans of the Vietnam War who have suffered the greatest problems with PTSD and addiction were individuals who came into the service already suffering from significant disruptions or traumas in their pre-combat life.[9] These findings seem quite plausible, but they should not lead one to dismiss the possibility that more or less healthy individuals, once exposed to the bare horror of war, are capable of developing significant trauma or scars. The ideological implications of associating postwar trauma and addiction with a prewar vulnerability are indeed troubling. They may lead us to reduce our emphasis on the destructive impact war can have on combatants; they may also lead us to place subtle blame on the individuals who possessed risk factors. If only they had been hardier before they entered the service, they would not be continuing to display symptoms and dysfunctional behavior in the years since the war.

In selecting Tyler's story from the many I have heard over the years, I do not want to imply a refutation of the previous research on prodromal factors in veterans' PTSD or addiction,[10] I only want to underscore the point that such prodromal factors may increase the risk for these disorders, but are not necessary for them to emerge. As we move into the horror that Tyler experienced in Vietnam, my goal is again to shift our focus away from an emphasis on Tyler as a flawed biological entity who was prone to develop trauma and subsequent addiction. Instead, to understand the full context of Tyler's life, I want to ask additionally how the trauma of combat could affect his capacity to achieve a meaningful continuity of identity and in turn drive him toward the despair of addiction. By understanding addiction as more than a physical malady and combat trauma as more than the expression of a psychological vulnerability, Tyler's subsequent struggle with a sense of identity after Vietnam may make more sense.

Now here I am, I was going to join the Navy, getting off a plane, in a war, helmet on, flak jacket, weapon between my legs, and the airport is under attack. . . . Now I'm dodging bullets. I messed myself. I pissed all over myself. Scared. And I saw a guy start to fall. I said, "Man, this is it." It was almost, "Mommy!" You don't know what else to do.

. . . And they could train you and train you for years, and put you out there, if you've never actually been, they could fire over your head, or around you, they don't come anywhere near you, but when you're there and you see people dropping and heads blowing apart, it's something else again. I didn't come from that. I came from Maine, and sports, and building a car, and being with my girlfriend.

In this statement, we hear the discontinuity that war and combat can create. One moment, Tyler is a naive and cocky teenager, the next he is soiling himself amidst an explosion of violence and bloody combat. How to connect this past to this present is the challenge that combat trauma raises to identity formation.

Along with many of the other soldiers, Tyler drank at the Enlisted Men's Club and sampled the omnipresent marijuana. He claimed to me that up to that point he had shown no evidence of a drinking or drug problem or dependence. He did try smoking opium a few times, but shied away from it, partly out of fear of it being deliberately poisoned.

In mentioning this worry, he referred to the fear and suspicion that the American soldiers developed with regard to the guerrilla tactics of the Viet Cong. He described prostitutes who would lodge single-edged razor blades in their vaginas, or bodies of mothers and children in the road that once lifted would detonate hand grenades.

All you gotta do is change their pajamas. From working in the field to the black silk.[11] You know, the farmer that waves to you every day and you wave to him, and see him at night, he could be sniping at you. Maybe he's got a mortar hid out there and he throws mortars to you, then he'll see you the next day, waving to you.

As Tyler recalled more examples of the enemy's treachery and betrayals, his speech sped up and his sentences became more fragmented. Finally, he described an incident that he would refer to four times in the course of our conversation. Each time, he would circle back to this moment of abject terror and violence, providing another detail or a more graphic image. It is a moment of his life that had not let go of him and with which his mind still wrestled to achieve some distance or control. It has become the moment that has trapped him in time.

But anything would get you nervous. You got nervous about everybody. Little kids. A little girl blew away one of my best buddies. He used to, when we were back in the rear, he'd go to the PX, he'd buy all the candy and gum and lollipops. He'd offer the candy, go down the village, and hand them out to the kids. It was a little girl, she couldn't have been more than eight or nine years old, took out a .45 and buried the clip right in his back. And I cut her in half. I could hear the mother and father, I just started blowing the village apart, the other two guys that were with me starting blowing the other side apart, a couple of Marines came up and pulled us away.

He described himself as having a breakdown after this incident, of being unable to calm down. He was hospitalized for two weeks, and then put on light duty for a while. In describing the aftereffects, he emphasized that at the time the trauma he felt he was for the loss of his friend. They had been through firefights together and had protected each other. He felt that the friendships he had made with his fellow soldiers were deeper and closer than any relationships he had formed before. In boot camp, they had warned him not to make buddies, that watching a friend get hit under fire could freeze you. It was better to stay more self-enclosed; it was safer. He had been unable to do this and when one of his best friends had been killed before his eyes, he had reacted wildly and violently with no thought of his safety.

We started to move on in his narrative, but his words circled back and he returned again to the incident.

We were about this far apart, we were five feet apart, not even. Just got through giving a little group of kids some candy, we're walking down, and all of a sudden, BAM, BAM, he went like that—"Oh"—right away. Of course, you look around, see where it is. I didn't know he got shot, until I saw the blood. She didn't even look at me. I don't know why him, she didn't even look at me, and I just lost it.

Something like that doesn't get written down. It wasn't a mission. We weren't under attack, we didn't attack. That's considered a little thing, and oh, well. It doesn't even get written down, it doesn't even go in the record. And, ah, how many things like that happened, you know, it's unbelievable.

Tyler's emphasis on the fact that this incident never became a part of an official record is quite revealing. It suggests another way in which the past preoccupies his present life. If the death of his friend and these villages could have become part of an official story, part of a record of the war, perhaps he could have found a way of locating the incident in time, of putting it to rest in the past. Without such records, these events exist solely in his memory, cut off from any communal acknowledgment. Untethered by history, they hover at the perimeter of consciousness until the current of thought sweeps them back into awareness.

After Tyler returned to active duty in the front, he found that his attitude toward the enemy changed. Fueled with rage and desire for revenge, he claimed that killing became "fun" for him.

It's a sick thing to say, but you see somebody running, it's like a squirrel or a deer, you know, a kid with a BB gun, you see a squirrel, you to try to get him because it's fun. It doesn't matter that's it human. And especially, if you lose a friend. You can't help but make friends because that guy saved your life, what are you going to do, hate him? Take a walk, screw you, no you become close. And it hurts twice as bad. Of course. It was, man, I need a drink now. After everything, I need a drink.

In Tyler's words here, we hear the emergence of the two major defenses against despair that would come to dominate his postwar addicted life. Tyler used drugs and alcohol to block out the hurt and memories of his combat experiences. In this sense, he passively hid from life and surrendered any sense of agency. On the other hand, he began to embrace an active stance opposed to life. In learning to enjoy the violence of the war, he turned toward a destructive agency in which the use of substances was an intimate ally.

At the center of his rejection of life was the memory of his friend's death. As Tyler attempted to move his story forward and describe his construction battalion, he veered back for a third time to a memory of the village.

But we had to go on patrol during construction, and if you just went out, into the village, that's when that incident happened, you know, it was supposedly a safe village. And it turned out not to be so safe, see, you never know, you don't know when it's going to happen, that's why the guys were, "Hey, smoke this, try it. How do you know you're going to see tomorrow?" That could have been me that got blown away. . . . And you get some, a survivor's guilt, you know, why did this guy die, and this guy dies, machine gun fire, and it didn't hit me. I didn't get wounded.

The guy just got through giving these kids candy. Why did she shoot him, and I didn't give her any candy? Why did she shoot him, and I'm five feet away and closer. Why not both of us? You get a survivor's guilt, too, and it all plays a big, it just all plays such a big role. . . .

After ten months in country, he was sent back to the States for further training. He attempted to go AWOL, but was brought back and threatened with serious charges. He decided not to make any more waves and accepted a second tour of duty back in Vietnam. He went back for another ten months and once again underwent heavy fighting. At one point his company was overrun, and of the sixty-six men, thirty were killed. After surviving a massacre like this, he would drink to forget his defeat and his losses, but also to celebrate that it was over and he was still there.

Between his two tours, when he was back in the States, he began to realize for the first time how unpopular the war was becoming. He heard about draft card burning and how people avoided coming to the war, and all of this made him extremely bitter. When he returned after his second ten months, things had even worsened. There were times when he was yelled at and spit on for having served in Vietnam. He was only twenty-one years old, but he had little in common with the peers he had left behind in the States. The one thing he could connect to was the widespread use of drugs in the society. He was offered LSD, speed, and downers. He was willing to try it all, anything that would block out the nightmares and memories that he had brought home with him.

I found out all of this stuff takes me away. It hides it, even if for a little while. For a while, my passing out was my only peace of mind. Because when I passed out, 99 percent of the times I didn't have any nightmares, any remembrances. Or I didn't think about it. Once in a while if I was by myself, everybody cries in their beer, but you try not to do that. I got real good at blocking it out, to where I was doing it and didn't even know it. And there's even times now that I lose my train of thought 'cause I don't even want to go into that area. It's an automatic defense system. They told me at the VA that I was real good at it. I said, "Real good at what?" Because I don't even know I'm doing it.

It doesn't necessarily have to be with Vietnam. It's anything bad, or something I don't want to hear, or I don't think I can do. I'd run and drink, or I'd run and do drugs. I've done everything there is to do, intravenously, smoking, drinking, snorting.

It was extremely difficult for Tyler to readjust to being home. Once again his sense of a continuity of self was jolted. As he described it, he was in the jungle and forty-eight hours later, he was in a bar with friends, but still with the same jungle mentality. He was jittery, easily aroused, and ended up getting in a lot of arguments and fights. As he was explaining to me how he disliked talking with other vets about Vietnam, he returned for the fourth time to the memory of the incident in the village.

Vietnam was not something I really liked to talk about, 'cause it's still right there, 'cause every time you mention it, you see the kid with his head blown off, or you see that little girl. I cut her just about in half, her dress might have been holding her together. My M16. I probably put forty rounds in her. I blew a hole right through her with the first clip. And I just kept her right up, dancing like you see on TV, that actually happens. I'm firing from the hip. On automatic, you don't have to aim because you are not shooting one round.

To avoid the thoughts of death and the guilt associated with these memories, Tyler perfected his automatic defense system of not thinking about the past, of not remembering.[12]

For so many years, I could tell you about the good things, no problem, my life in Maine, on the island, with the boats, with Greg and Doug, Bill, Tommy, and Steve,

I knew it all. But after high school, after Vietnam, things got really buried, I didn't even know I was stuffing these things. It's subconsciously, and some things are buried so far, I didn't know I knew 'em. Somebody would say a name, and I'd say, "I don't know that name." And then they'd mention an incident, and bing, I've got everything. I had forgotten all about it. It's a little scary.

In conjunction with his ability to repress memories from Vietnam, he relied on drugs and alcohol to catch and sweep away any of the past that managed to slip by his defense.

The reaction we got coming home from Vietnam, I was actually starting to feel not very good about myself. They were convincing me that I had done something wrong. And I had gone to protect my country, so to speak. That's when alcohol and drugs took off in my life. I drank to forget, to bury, anything I could do to alter that thought. And I must have done pretty good, 'cause like I said, some of them, are totally gone.

With the tactics of repression and substance abuse, Tyler engaged in his personal war on memory. Through this war, he subverted his fundamental sense of identity, of knowing who he was and who he might become. Although he practiced these tactics of forgetfulness ardently, my interview with Tyler suggests that this process of active forgetting was never quite as successful as he would have wished. Freud coined the term "repetition compulsion" to describe an experience that has not been sufficiently worked through psychologically. The individual feels overwhelmed or out of control with regard to this experience and has attempted to repress any thought related to its circumstances. Yet the unconscious, in which the memory of the experience is banished, struggles to resolve this unfinished business. As a result, we find ourselves returning either through dreams or unconscious acts to experiences that are similar or share an affective pattern with the original unresolved one. We are compelled to repeat what we have not worked through psychologically.

In his paper "Beyond the Pleasure Principle," Freud argued that this repetition might be in the service of mastery. By reviving the repressed material, we afford ourselves one more opportunity to change the ending of the experience, to make it better. Freud specifically related this point to an explanation for why combat veterans from WW I had recurrent nightmares about their battle traumas. If dreams were primarily an act of wish fulfillment, why would these men torture themselves to relive their private hells?[13] Could it be, Freud suggested, that only by reviving these memories in dreams, could their unconscious complete the work of physically overcoming the memories and reducing their discordant tension?

According to such reasoning, Tyler's decades of burying his memories were doomed to an equivocal result. Try as he did, he could never quite leave behind his nightmares or sudden flashes of what he had experienced.

It just became a way of life, but I was, for lack of a better word, I was happy in that life. Only because I didn't remember, or knew less and less. But the nightmares were still there, and it scared a couple of girls away. I'd wake up screaming and punching and kicking and soaking wet, and start to dry heave, and throw up. I mean, it was so real.

. . . I wondered if I was going nuts-o, am I getting crazy? And I'd start feeling like that, and, and, ah, let's grab a couple of beers. Just drown it. Or let's smoke a joint, whatever was there at the time as long as it took it away.

. . . There's very few veterans of the people I hung out with, and if there was, we didn't know between each other, because nobody said anything. Unless somebody else brought it up, "Yeah, Tyler was in Vietnam." I didn't even want to hear it. I didn't want people to ask any questions.

The Wasted Years

This circularity seems to be at the heart of the despair Tyler experienced in the next two decades of his life. Trapped like the hamster on the wheel, he would set off with drugs and drink to leave aside the past, but late at night, or through an unwanted conversation or a stray reference on the television, he would find himself spun around to his starting place, the past, one more time. As Denzin wrote,

> Locked in the past, the alcoholic fearfully confronts the present and the future through the temporal consciousness alcohol creates. . . . This uneasiness with time is manifested in the divided self the alcoholic experiences. Trapped within the negative emotions that alcoholism produces, the alcoholic dwells within the emotions of the past. The alcoholic approaches the present and the future with an anxious, self-fearfulness that undermines the ability to generate positive, emotional feelings toward self or others.[14]

Denzin's words make clear that addicted individuals are no longer simply trapped by the past, but also by the negative effects their addiction produces in the present. As Tyler's post-Vietnam life centered more and more around drugs and alcohol, he grew estranged from his family and no longer sensed his father's support.

They were behind me, but they didn't like my lifestyle. I'd go and visit, say hello, then my father and I wouldn't get along for a year or two, and my sister would be mad at me. I just tried to stay away. I didn't like it and they didn't like it.

He saw the same pattern in his relationships with women when he returned.

I always had a girl around. So I was lucky in that respect. And some of them really cared for me, and they left because of my use. But what I did care? I care now, you know, looking back, but what did I care then, there's so many girls around, you know, free love, free dope, you know, it didn't matter. And I was hiding.

For most of the seventies, Tyler drifted, driving up and down the east coast, crashing with friends, picking up construction jobs, and beginning to deal drugs. He took up with a well-known motorcycle gang in New Haven, the Huns, and was one of their best suppliers of pills and marijuana. He found himself frequently in barroom fights, and even worked on several occasions as a bouncer. Some of these fights led to assault charges; he also was arrested at different times for possession and sale of drugs. The longest period of time he did in prison was a year, but he mentioned spending weeks or months in various jails in at least six different states.

He had lost any interest in making his life conform to the middle class ideal that had been painted for him by his childhood in Connecticut and Maine. His goal was first and foremost to get high. He was actively choosing addiction over life.

But I had to get high. And it didn't even matter why, I just knew I had to. If I did this, I won't think of that. It just went away.

By the early eighties, the drug scene had become increasingly violent and the use of guns on the street had become widespread. After a friend of his was shot, Tyler found the parallels to his experiences in Vietnam were growing too close for him to block them out of mind. He backed away from the drug scene and began to limit himself to alcohol and marijuana. By maintaining a daily level of drunkenness, he was still able to avoid putting himself back into normal time; he was still in a twilight zone "out of place and out of time."[15]

When you're drinking, your mind just goes a thousand different directions. You're like a little kid, everything can occupy your mind at that second. And it can change in a second. Kids look at a lollipop, and all of a sudden you see something on TV, and there goes the lollipop, watching something on TV, and all of a sudden, I'm bouncing a ball out there, there goes the TV, go over by the ball, so when I was drunk, I was the same way. I was always occupied, my mind was always full. By this time, nobody was asking me about Vietnam anymore.[16]

Tyler married in 1980, was divorced in large part because of his drinking, and was married again in 1981. This second relationship also dissolved quickly; he has not seen his second wife since 1986. Whatever the legacy of his Vietnam experiences, he was now suffering the consequences of his flight into drugs and alcohol. Though Vietnam remained a negative feeling in the background of his consciousness, his more immediate problems were now connected to the adverse consequences of his addiction. He could not hold jobs or last very long in relationships. He continued to be belligerent to bosses, friends, lovers, and family.

In 1987, he was arrested for DWI and court-ordered to do his first alcohol treatment program. After twenty-eight days, he was back out and drinking, but some seed had been planted for him that had never taken hold before.

That's when I realized, wow, that one program took the fun out of getting high. I knew I was doing something wrong. But by that time the disease was so far advanced, that twenty-eight days is like a drop in the bucket. It's like a shot for somebody out of a quart bottle who is used to drinking the whole quart.

From 1987 through 1992, he bounced in and out of detox facilities and treatment programs, managing to put together some long stretches of more than a year of sobriety, but he always relapsed. Then in 1992, he was referred to the PTSD program at the West Haven VA.[17]

My counselor said, "I think you ought to go talk to someone else." And she explained about PTSD. She said, "I think you have two problems working here." And she was the first one that noticed it. She had worked with other veterans. And now they have a counselor there, in the detox and rehab unit, that works specifically with the Vietnam vets.

I felt safe there. When I got out, if I felt shaky, I'd go up there, talk to the brothers. They don't want to get high, and other guys were doing that. We'd just sit and talk, and that way we wouldn't get high, because we don't want to. And talking together, we don't reminisce. We know where we've been, what we've done. And that's nice. The groups I was going through made me relive this, made it come out again, made me accept the fact that this happened, and there's nothing I can do about it.

In the last few years, Tyler changed the trajectory of his life and has become committed to gaining sobriety. Yet he still has a long way to go. He continues to move between the West Haven VA, Lebanon Pines, and other detox and rehab facilities. He feels a bitter irony that having finally faced the demons of Vietnam, he now has to grapple with twenty years of substance abuse and dependency. At age forty-seven, he feels physically and mentally ravaged. The war on his memory indeed took no prisoners. I noticed that his train of thought wandered in our interview and that he showed some aphasic tendencies in being unable to find words for ideas he hoped to express. He still needs to be evaluated at some point to determine whether an alcoholic dementia or Korsakoff's syndrome are present. He suffers from swollen joints and peripheral neuropathy and other alcoholism-related symptoms (gastritis and water retention).

Psychologically, the "wasted years" have left him with little sense of how to function as an adult in society. He has yet to master the shift from adolescence to adulthood in which one accepts that daily work responsibility and committed relationships are the fundaments of adult life. He is still new to staying put with his feelings, as opposed to finding a way to run from them or bury them with substances. He knows he is not ready yet to pursue any new relationships in his life. He had begun one recently and ended it.

I broke it off because I have nothing to offer, what have I got to offer? Nothing. I have myself, and that's not even in very good shape right now. Until I get back on track, I'm glad the support's out there, but I don't really want to start anything until I know what I'm going to do.

When Tyler asks, "What have I got to offer," he is asking a fundamental question about the meaning of his life and his own sense of identity. Who is Tyler? He is no longer the ocean-loving boy of Maine. His identity as a soldier is filled with memories that undermine any sense of human decency or rationality. His life after Vietnam is a blur of intoxication, street crime and violence, and constant running away from himself. Yes, he can claim the labels society offers him—Vietnam vet, PTSD survivor, recovering addict and alcoholic—but none of these labels add up (at least not yet) to a unified sense of self, an identity capable of linking the events of his life together in a meaningful way. He cannot "start anything" with another person, because the ravages of his life have left him with no clear sense of what he is "going to do." Any of the support groups and treatments he attends can offer him structures for recovery and steps to take, but Tyler requires something more. He is still seeking a reason for going forward, an understanding of why he has lived his particular life and what direction he should travel in the future. His sustained recovery depends ultimately not on his capacity to identify himself in terms of the war or his addiction, but his ability to find his humanity beyond the scars these destructive forces have inflicted. Tyler can fill some "empty spaces" of his life with meetings and treatment, but in the long run his recovery will demand more of him. He will need to grow into a manhood that was cut short by his time in war.

To accomplish this growth, he will need, in my opinion, two critical ingredients, besides his AA involvement and PTSD treatment. First, he must find a way to reconnect to society by offering a tangible contribution of work or service to society. In other words, he must rebuild a positive sense of agency, independent of his status as victim of trauma and addiction. To grow into the manhood of which he was robbed, Tyler needs to feel a sense of competence and social usefulness. I am afraid that in our tendency to see men like Tyler from an illness perspective, we underestimate how critical this sense of agency and responsibility is to their ultimate recovery. I would urge any case manager assigned to him to pursue doggedly any prospects for rehabilitation that would allow him to re-enter the workforce or at least have a meaningful volunteer placement.

Second, Tyler needs to find a way of creating a sense of stable place and time in his life through having a residence he can call home. If he can achieve another stable period of sobriety, he would benefit greatly from having an apartment in a community in which he could establish meaningful connections and relationships, similar to the world he had found for himself as a boy in Maine. As he builds up time in his recovery, the opportunity to see the same faces at the market or the post office would begin to allow him to consolidate a role in a community and a sense of identity over time. His drifting over the years and his homelessness have only compounded the discontinuities in his identity and his disorientation from a stable sense of self.

Even before he builds up these stabilizing and positive features of identity, he will first need to come terms with the "demoniac rage" the war uncovered in him. Whether the war unleashed an instinctual aggression in Tyler or simply socialized him to find pleasure in violence is an unanswerable and age-old question, but regardless of the answer, he will need to work through and relinquish this aspect of his personality.

I enjoyed killing. That's a sin, that we grew up being taught it's a sin. But I don't know any little boy that didn't take their slingshot and try to kill a bird. . . . It's doing the wrong thing that seems to give us the most pleasure. If you tell the kid he can't have

a cookie, what's he going to do, he's going to try for three or four. "No, don't shoot that." "Don't shoot, says who?". . . . It's perverse. "Don't drink that, it's not good for you." It's good for you. I liked to do it. I can do it. It's topsy-turvy.

Our understanding of chronic addiction and perhaps how to treat it successfully may not be complete until we come to terms with this kind of defiance and rage. The moral and life-affirming possibilities of AA—Bill W.'s optimism and commitment to small-town values—have to find a way to address the destructive pleasure that can be found in addiction. McAdams' model of identity, and my own application of his model, must recognize the anti-agency and anti-communion strain that can come to dominate a life. In a combat veteran's case, the psychological consequences of war can go beyond PTSD to the cultivation of aggression and sadism. Tyler's recovery will require a moral compass that points him away from the "pleasures" as well as the horrors of war.

As Tyler finished the interview with me, he was exhausted, but pleased that he had told his story to someone outside the VA hospital. He hoped that this step was a sign that he has begun the process of bringing together his PTSD work and his efforts at sobriety. Still, he is under no pretensions that the struggle is behind him. He told me how he is able to steel himself and move forward, as he had done with me that day, but then he often feels an overwhelming fright and soon starts drinking again.

I asked Tyler if he felt that he was making progress in his efforts, despite the relapses. He pointed out to me that he has had more sober time in the last five years than in the previous twenty years combined. He is starting to remember things about his life, good and bad, that have not surfaced in his thoughts for decades. He cannot promise himself he would stop tomorrow or give up running away, but he is gradually learning who he has been and who he is. As this knowledge takes hold inside him, he feels he can make the tentative steps toward imagining who he might become in a sober world. Still adrift after so many years, he is still coming home from a place he has never left.

What the Wall Reflects

Tyler visited the Vietnam Veterans Memorial in Washington, DC, twice, for the dedication and then for the tenth-year dedication. I have thought about the image of him standing there, looking at the name of his buddy lost in the village that awful day. Part of the magical quality of the memorial is the reflective gleam of the stone. You can see yourself looking at the names. The reflection silently asks, "Why not you? And since not you, what way will you live your life, you who are able to stand and look at the names of people who have lost theirs?" In some way, the reflection in the wall reminds us of the challenge put to us by those who died—to make our lives amount to something, to make them matter in some way.

For Tyler, who endured the soul-injuring facts of war, this optical exhortation to seize life is more clouded. War does not burn clean; rather it leaves a black and oily residue that reaches back to poison the heart. Freud, in the same essay, "Beyond the Pleasure Principle," argued that the repetition compulsion reflected not only a need to master, but an impulse to destruction or a return to one's earliest state of nothingness.[18] Though his concept of a death instinct, or Thanatos, has achieved little scientific credibility over the years, there is little doubt that exposure to war can detach and dis-integrate the returning combatants from the social order they left. Hemingway's short story "Soldier's Home" captures this alienation perfectly. Krebs has returned from WWI and has moved back in with his parents. He sleeps late, avoids any relationships, and has not looked for a job. After some months, his mother has a talk with him at breakfast to express his father's and her concern. She tells him she is worried about him and that his father is waiting at his office downtown to talk to him about taking a job. She asks him if he loves her and he tells her no, that he doesn't love anybody. Crying, she asks him to kneel and pray with her. He says he cannot pray. She asks him if he wants her to pray for him, he says yes.

> So his mother prayed for him and then they stood up and Krebs kissed his mother and went out of the house. He had tried to keep his life from being complicated. Still, none of it had touched him. He had felt sorry for his mother and she had made him lie. He would go to Kansas City and get a job and she would feel all right about it.[19]

The experience of combat has steeped the soldier in the world of death and made access back to life an unfamiliar path. In existential terms, the intrusive influence of death experienced too blatantly causes the individual to disengage from life and withdraw from human interaction. Tyler's use of alcohol and drugs during the war and when he returned was a way of "deadening" his feelings and "burying" himself. Life no longer seemed his natural habitat—its demands were like stark sunshine to a cave dweller. He went from "walking around in daylight" to being "blind" and when he returned he was asked to regain his sight.

He returned to a society actively hostile to the sacrifices he had made. He gradually learned that the war had more to do with elections than protecting his country. He quickly came to hate his government. He took solace in an easy way of not-being—to light up or shoot up or drink up. He felt incapable of living life as an adult, not because he still felt like a child, but because he felt he had become an old man overnight.

I went from a child to an old man. Then the alcohol just made it from an old man to an ancient one.

He was ancient because death was all around him rather than his being surrounded by the future and hope. His combat trauma put him in a moment unrelated to anything before and impossible to connect to anything after it. It replaced the daily sensation of being alive with the sensation of death-in-life.

Damage was done not just to the content of his life, now filled with feelings of loss, betrayal and rage. He also sustained damage to his trust in time. He was upended and could no longer be confident that a step forward would take him to a place ahead. It might only bring him backward or to nowhere or turn him upside down so that he would be dizzied and disoriented and unable to find his feet or solid ground (the damn hamster wheel again). Tyler's solution, not a healthy one, but the best he could manage, was to wage war on time. His two weapons were repression and intoxication. By not talking or thinking about the war, and by drinking himself into an insensible blur, he could sabotage the past's hold over him. He could disconnect himself from history and leave aside his memories. But time is not easily defeated and, like a funhouse filled with mirrors, he would open a door of escape only to find his own macabre image looking back at him. At such moments of terror, more booze or pills could shatter self-reflection and give him brief peace by generating a blackout.

Barely surviving these repetitive skirmishes, he found no promise in the future; he had no trust in goals or plans. Not knowing who he was (since he did his best to forget this), he could put no stake in his capability to complete or accomplish what he set out to do. As he grew older, the past not only continued to terrorize him, it offered him an unassailable attribution for not taking control of the future. With the self-serving reasoning of a person caught up in addiction, his past and its linkage to the now widely publicized affliction of PTSD justified his life's paralysis and his relapses. With what he had gone through, how could he be expected to sober up? His weapons of repression, denial, drugs, and alcohol, aimed at destroying the past, could not avoid simultaneous annihilation of the future as well. He lived finally in a despairing and stagnant present—a man haunted by a moment in his life, fighting that moment, winning freedom momentarily, and then slipping back again into the same moment, only to flee it or fight it again.

History's narratives are often punctuated by accounts of wars; they provide crucial overlooks in the landscapes of nations. Yet for Tyler, his experience of war was ahistorical. He had lost the illusion of time as a forward-moving line; it had become for him a sphere spinning in place. And so when he told me his story, he would attempt to move the narrative forward and then suddenly we would be back with the candy from the PX, his buddy's sudden fall, the dancing girl in air, and the shower of fire he released that awful day.[20]

More recently, having finally acknowledged the influence of memory on his life, and having sought support through the VA and the recovery network (AA, treatment facilities, psychotherapy), he has begun the long road of constructing a recovery. His success will depend on his ability to find a positive meaning that organizes his life and propels him toward a sober future. Most important, he will need to let go of the positive association he has created between his use of a substance and a sense of relief and release from life.

When I feel better, I think I've got to use something. That's what I don't want to do and I've done it before [not used]. I know I can do it, so it's not out of reach. It just seems it at times.[21]

At forty-seven years old, Tyler has re-opened the question of the kind of life he wants to choose. His experience with the war will always influence his answer to that question, but the prospect of recovery offers him at the very least an alternative to the destructive path he had tried for so long. As he pursues sobriety through continued residential rehabilitation and AA, his involvement with his PTSD treatment will also be crucial. Although no amount of counseling can change the fundamental horror and irrationality of his combat trauma, his recognition of shared experience with other survivors and his involvement in leave-taking ceremonies (for example, the writing of letters to lost buddies and the burning of these letters with their ashes scattered at a memorial site) may reduce memory's power and its intrusive influence on current thoughts. With reduction of his PTSD, his impulse to blot out his thought through alcohol may also come under greater control. On top of this progress, his efforts to regain a sense of agency and to locate himself in a stable community might solidify his recovery process.

In time, he might be able to fill in the gap that has existed for so long in his life between "child and old man"—innocence and death. In working toward this goal of fashioning a coherent life story, he will recover more than his sobriety, he will recover a sense of identity that will finally make peace with memory and link it to a meaningful present and purposeful future.

9. THE TORTURE
Abuse, Addiction, and the Search for Authentic Identity

HELEN: *Can't you tell me where you're going? Will you write?*
(He shakes his head)
. . . But you must! How do you live?
ALLEN: *I steal.*
FROM THE END OF THE 1932 FILM *I am a Fugitive from a Chain Gang*

To achieve a sense of identity, we need not only a sense of continuity over time, but a sense of distinctiveness and uniqueness in relation to others. We may feel a consistent sense of self that connects past to present and future, but how do we differentiate ourselves from siblings, friends, or other members of our community? McAdams's life story theory of identity argues that the narrative we construct of our lives provides that differentiation and individuality. Inside the story we tell of our lives is the essence of our unique sense of identity.

Through our particular combination of nuclear episodes, imagoes, themes of agency and communion, and generative concerns, we gain ownership over a story that is authentically our own; it has never been told before and can never be told again. As this story depicts the personal myth of our lives, it comes to define us inwardly and to others. How often, when asked if we know someone with whom we are only casually acquainted, do we reply with the phrase, "I don't really know his story"? As we come to know the details and major episodes of this person's life, we can claim some knowledge of his identity, of what makes him both similar to and different from other people.[1]

In depicting the life story as a key factor in the differentiation that constitutes identity, McAdams has suggested that certain narrative properties allow one to see someone else's story as a "good life story." By goodness, McAdams does not mean aesthetically or morally superior to another story, he means good in the sense that the story is able to convey a sense of meaningful identity to the narrator and potential listeners. A bad story is a story that offers fragmented, incoherent, or contradictory views of identity. A bad story is a story that does not hang together or is so rigidly or simplistically constructed that it fails to account for critical turning points or decisions depicted in the narrator's life. From the listener's perspective, one cannot make sense of the story being told, nor can one fully believe it. As the narrative is presented, it loses its authenticity and tests the listener's credulity. Bad stories are stories the listener and, at some level, the narrator cannot trust.

In more formally defining a good life story that reflects the mental health and secure identity of the narrator, McAdams has proposed six standards.[2] Among these criteria, there are a few that focus specifically on the issue of authenticity. McAdams suggests that we must find a life story *credible;* "[it] should be accountable to the facts that can be known or found out." If a listener repeatedly feels a rising skepticism about the details of the story, this warning signal might point to something awry in the construction of identity. McAdams also suggests that the good life story is *differentiated* and reasonably complex, so that as the life story proceeds, it accumulates "more and more facets and characterizations." If, on the contrary, a story begins to take on overwhelming similarities across time periods and a certain repetitiveness in characterization (e.g., every female character is a bitch or every male character is a snake), one may begin to question the rigidity of interpersonal understanding that is driving the narrative. The good life story should also display *coherence;* "a story that lacks coherence is one that leaves the reader scratching his or her head, wondering why things turned out in such an inexplicable, puzzling way." If the listener feels the story has ended abruptly or with unanticipated shifts, one can only wonder what is missing from this depiction of the self—is the narrator hiding information or engaging in unconscious self-deception? Finally, McAdams suggests that good stories yield a *reconciliation* between conflicting forces, "harmony and resolution amidst the multiplicity of self." If a story ends too simply, without attention to a sense of closure and unity, the listener is left uncertain about how the narrator will fare in the future, whether the depicted identity will survive with stability and strength.

Drawing upon the work of the psychiatrist Robert Jay Lifton, McAdams has characterized individuals who are unable to fashion good stories as *protean men.* By this, he means they adopt a series of roles, tell multiple stories that accrue to these roles, but find no distinctive coherent narrative that unites all the parts they play.

> The protean man searches for unity to define the self, but, like the Greek god Proteus, his fate is to flip back and forth among the various guises he can so readily adopt. Unity and purpose remain outside his desperate grasp.[3]

My thesis in this chapter is that the problem of achieving lasting sobriety for some chronically addicted men is a problem of their ability to create good stories, stories that achieve a coherence and authenticity. Michael Cochran has no problem telling great stories filled with drama and intrigue; he is in fact a born storyteller. His deeper problem in relation to identity and lasting sobriety is his inability to take ownership of a good story that differentiates him in a lasting and convincing way. Without a clear means of knowing himself and sticking to a story, Michael is always at risk to drift back into the world of deceit and drugs that has characterized most of his life. Although he is able to weave tale after tale of insight and recovery, the solidity and permanence of each new recovered self is no greater than the single strand of a spider's web.

The combination of violence, drugs, and a lifetime of scams and lies has threatened to put Michael's authentic story beyond reach, not only beyond the listener's reach, but his own as well. The greatest injury Michael has endured may not be the abuse or violence inflicted upon him, but rather the way his identity has been damaged by that violence and his subsequent addiction. His capacity to reinvent himself, to "perform" in ways that allow him to fit into different worlds and to assume different roles, has left him with too many stories and with no story. When a life is based on the crafting of stories to gain confidences only in order to betray those same confidences, it may be nearly impossible to turn the performance off. Michael has paid a great price for learning how to adapt to a lifetime of violence and addiction. This cost, as revealed by his life story, is his protean ability to become someone else. Yet, free of substances, in cold sobriety, he has been repeatedly confronted with the overwhelming existential "freedom" of becoming himself (see Chapter 2 for Yalom's discussion of the meaning of this freedom). Rather than constructing a meaningful identity out of this freedom, he has uncovered terrifying memories and a sense of emptiness that have predictably propelled him toward another performance. Part of his emptiness is his realization that without performance he does not know how to participate in a community. He has no confidence that a more truthful version of himself will be accepted by sober society.

Home Life: The First of Many Prisons

I first met Michael Cochran in the detox facility of SCADD in New London. The head nurse told me that he had been through a rough detox, but was now requesting to talk to someone about some painful secrets from the past. Wearing the thin blue pajamas required for detox, Michael entered my office in bad shape—body tensing with each step, face blotchy, eyes half open. Given what I now know about Michael, I realize how unusual this moment of bodily and psychological defeat was for him. Michael is a confidence man—a talker and a dream-seller; looking like death warmed over is not his style. He is an extremely handsome man with light blond hair and blue eyes that meet your gaze and keep right on looking. He is short and fit and moves with grace. What is most captivating, though, is not his appearance, but his physical style—his speech, his movements, his attitude. He is a cocky rooster with a Jimmy Cagney swagger. He manages to convey the threatening toughness of a gangster and combine it with the open smile and enthusiasm of a boy on a fishing trip. He has Cagney's voice too, a rhythmic whisper that draws the listener closer. Even though he is forty-three, if you look quickly, he could pass for a young man of twenty-three. Only when you look more carefully do you see the broken blood vessels in his cheeks, the slightly swollen nose, and the scar tissue around his eyes.

After opening up to me in the detox, Michael went up to Lebanon Pines, but stayed only a few months. He left after some men came looking for him. He made it to a halfway house, but ended up picking up cocaine. After a one-week binge, he went back into detox and then returned to the Pines. He stayed at the Pines for close to a year and it was toward the very end of that stay that I asked him to tell his story for this book.

Michael repeated for me the secrets he told me in detox that first time, but he told them now with more detail and also added others he had not shared. Once he started, the stories flowed continuously from him and he seldom moved in his chair and only rarely shifted his hands from his lap. He would look with his steady blue gaze at nothing in particular and speak in clear, clipped sentences about the violent events of his life. Later on, when he came to describe his undercover escapades with the police, he showed more life and more expression in his voice. But the stories of his family, of his youth, were told with a blank stillness. The stories flowed out of his mouth in an almost mechanical way; there was none of the stopping and starting, evasions, or tearful releases that I associated with clients' revelations of previously undisclosed abuse.

As with so many of the men, Michael's self-defining memory laid out essential themes for the longer narrative of his life,

When I was approximately eighteen months to two years old, I was in a crib in the back bedroom upstairs. I was wearing red pajamas, the kind with the feet and a flap in the back. I had feelings of being really alone, abandoned at that time. I remember holding on to the crib bar and looking out the window and seeing my family out by the maple tree, my father, mother, two brothers, and my sister were out there. One sister was missing. They were all playing and having a good time. I felt really abandoned. There was a reason I was not out there. It seems like it was deeper than just nap time. It seems like this was happening all the time. I do not know why, but I think about this all the time. And that is where it ends, right there.

There is imagery in this self-defining memory that resounds in Michael's story—the sense of loneliness and abandonment, the enclosed and barred space of the crib, the idealization of the family playing by the maple tree, the missing sister, and perhaps most importantly, a deep inarticulate sense of his fundamental isolation from others. His memory suggests that there is something inherent to his nature that places the possibility of a secure communion with others (even his own family) out of reach. From this first recollection (clearly a self-defining memory that functions as a nuclear episode—see Chapter 2), Michael has laid down the ideological setting of a basic distrust in others that will repetitively color the sweeping and complicated narrative to come. In Eriksonian terms, the first stage of psychosocial development (Trust vs. Mistrust) left Michael unsure about the capacity of others to nurture him or offer him comfort from his fears. The subsequent incidents of his childhood turned that distrust into a naked recognition that putative loved ones could turn upon him with violence and rage.

Michael was born and raised in a wealthy town in Fairfield County, in a community well known for its affluence, its ties to the New York financial world, and its country club–boarding school style of life. His twin sister and he were the youngest of five children. His other sister was the oldest, eight years apart from the twins. They grew up in a thirteen-room house that had a rolling lawn, well-kept gardens, and polished floors inside. His father was an executive in an aerospace company and his mother did not work. As far back as he could remember, his parents drank heavily. The code of behavior was strict. He could remember no expressions of affection, no signs of love. To the world outside, there needed to be the appearance of perfection, of the happy family. There could be no complaints or speaking up. As I listened to Michael paint this picture of his family, I felt a sense of familiarity with this depiction. Many clients from more affluent, alcoholic families had told me similar stories of the strangling effort to keep up appearances while the family would sink into a deeper hole of alcoholic despair. I also felt the presence of memory's editing pencil—magnifying through omission and simplification what may have been a more mixed and complex situation. Nothing in these comfortable generalizations of mine could prepare me for the next part of his story.

From the time I was four years old to about twelve years old, my parents locked me in a walk-in closet. The average time was for three days to a week. In this closet, I was quite frequently sexually abused by my mother, older sister, and father. My twin sister, Patty, went through the same ordeal, but they locked her in the attic. I do not know if my brothers went through the same thing. I do not have any good memories in my past, in my childhood. I was always in trouble, in school, in kindergarten. I was always looking for attention from stealing, lying, making up stories, whatever it took.

. . . My mother and sister would tie me up and play with my penis. It was more like a torture thing. They were not trying to get pleasure, they were trying to torture and belittle me. It was a very humiliating experience. My father sodomized me. That is the extent of it, but it was very continuous. My mother and sister were very much into torture, they would do all kinds of things to me. I'd get burned, beat up, tied up.

In my work as a psychotherapist, I have heard many accounts of physical and sexual abuse. With the publication of several popular books and the explosion of coverage in the media, revelations of abuse have increased to such an extent that I would listen to accounts on almost a weekly basis among the clients I saw at SCADD. As work by the psychologist Elizabeth Loftus and others[4] has argued, the absolute accuracy of these accounts must be placed into question. I cannot say with certainty whether Michael's family members behaved with the level of brutality he described.[5] Yet what seems more important is the internal image he carries with him of these crucial caregivers in his life. Whatever their actual conduct, he experienced them as sadistic without explanation or remorse. In terms of the coherence of his life story, these incidents have no psychological antecedents. He cannot give an account of what might have led his parents and older sister to engage in such satanic behavior. He offers no information for the listener to derive a plausible reason for the complete lack of intimate, communal behavior displayed within his family.

As I listened, Michael continued to produce story after story of their abuse and violence toward him. He described how they would give him medicine to induce vomiting and then beat him for soiling the bathroom. He told of another episode in which he worked hard to do better in school and finally brought home a report card filled with A's and B's. His parents' response was to beat him and send him to the closet for proving that his previous grades were caused by a lack of effort. As he grew up in this atmosphere, he hated authority more and more and became more troublesome in school. He ended up in a boarding school by the age of thirteen, but was quickly expelled when he was caught stealing drugs from the infirmary.

As Michael related his story, the words flowed in a rapid, mechanical fashion out of his mouth. At times, I would interject a question, wanting to bring his eyes back into focus, perhaps wanting him to acknowledge my presence in the room. He continued on, telling me about how he was perceived as wild and rebellious by his upper-class peers. His quickness to fight and the rage he had built up frightened many of his classmates.

In discussing his relationship with his siblings, his story again turned to a series of troubling revelations, all delivered in his rapid monotone.

Now I will talk about my relationship with my other two brothers and my twin sister. My twin sister, I really loved her a lot. There were days when they would come and pick who was going to get it (I called it the torture). They would never take us together, always her to the attic and me to the closet. If something was wrong, it did not matter who did it in the family, one of us would get the punishment. I am pretty proud of the fact that I had some courage then and I went to the closet for her and took the blame. She could not deal with it, she was just a frail little kid.

My brother Philip is eighteen months older than me and I have no idea what he was like in childhood. . . . He reminded me of my father and I did not like him. Philip was a mama's boy. He kissed up to them and I fought them. He was probably the smarter one. My brother Danny is four years older than me. I idolized him.

He was everything I wanted to be, good at sports, intelligent, tough, good-looking. Danny and I looked alike and Philip was the opposite, very fair, blond. Danny sexually molested a girl in the neighborhood when he was fourteen years old and I was ten. I got the blame, this three-year-old identified me. I did not do it. The police were not involved, but I was severely punished and beaten. I was humiliated when the neighbors found out. I had to live with that stigma for a long time, but I never did it. From that time on I was confused. I could not understand why Danny did not own up to it.

(How did you know he did it?)

Danny and I looked so much alike, almost like twins, yet he was taller. There was nobody else in the neighborhood who looked like us. I knew he was guilty. Within a year or so, I found him having sex with my twin sister against her will. I tried to stop him, but couldn't. It was terrifying to me because I did not know what was happening, but I knew he was doing something wrong. My feelings changed. Toward the end I hated Danny.

In every sphere of family life, Michael returned to the same themes of sadistic rejection and cruelty. Even the most innocuous memories of Little League baseball took a demonic turn.

To give you an example of the love in my family, I played Little League baseball for four years. The last game of the season of the fourth year my father came. He used to go and watch my brother play football, but never me. He used to say that baseball was a sissy sport. I was a sissy. I loved baseball and I was good at it. This last game was for the pennant, we were down by one run and I hit the ball and made it home. Outstanding! The crowd went crazy, it was the best day of my life. I went around the fence to my father and he slapped me in the head and asked me why I didn't hit the ball over the fence. I will never forget that. That son of a bitch.

In these stories, one can begin to detect an imago of the Father-Destroyer, filled with agentic power, who cannot be pleased and is inexplicably sadistic. Michael's personal myth in response to this imago is to depict himself in the recurrent dilemma of achieving success only to find it undermined by this authority who responds with violence instead of acceptance. Michael's own efforts at agency (e.g., his success in the baseball game) emphatically do not have the power to liberate him from this destructive cycle.

By age thirteen, Michael began to deal marijuana and pills. He had made some connections in Bridgeport and sold their drugs to his classmates. He might have continued on in this way through high school, but a pivotal incident in his life took place the following year.

One day I came home and my father had my twin sister against the wall and he was drunk. He was slapping the shit out of her. Blood was coming out of her mouth and her nose. My father was 6'2" and he used to box and wrestle. He was a tough man. I saw my brothers, sister, a friend, and my mother standing there watching this happen. So I pushed Patty out of the way and then I was against the wall. He just took over hitting me. I only came up to his chest. I kind of hit him and half pushed him. I think I caught him in the shoulder. He backed up three steps, fell over, and he was laying there. I did not know what was happening to him, but he was in tremendous pain, though. At this time, I was not trying to hurt my father, I was trying to protect Patty, no one was helping her. I remember feeling bad that he was on the ground. At that point my family turned on me, even Patty. She said, 'Look what you have done to your father. How could you do this?' I was very sad and really confused. I never felt this alone, even in the closet. I was completely rejected.

It turned out that Michael's father had suffered a paralyzing stroke from his fall and never fully recovered. When I had first met Michael in the detox, he had told me this same memory. It seemed to be another crucially self-defining memory for him (similar to the crib memory). Fusing these two memories together, their imagery tells us that for Michael the crib or the closet was a lonely place, but to come out and interact with others was to risk the release of rage and of his own "badness." Even his twin sister, whom he attempted to save, could turn on him and condemn him as no good. Her response left him utterly isolated. He seemed to have no choice but to flee, as much from fear of himself as from the wrath of his family. This imago of himself as the "Bad Seed" paralleled his Father-Destroyer Imago. Defeating his father gave him no comfort; it only confirmed his own "evil" nature. As Michael probed in adolescence to create a sense of identity grounded in agency and communion, his sense of these two sources of meaning was turned upside down. Those individuals who should have provided the greatest source of communal resources had become his main providers of pain and abuse. Efforts to assert his agency and independence brought him explosive and violent retribution with a subsequent sense of rejection and defeat. The same night of that incident he was exiled from his home and, in yet another bitter twist, his mother made no effort to keep him with her.

My mother packed my clothes and gave me five dollars. It was the end of February, snowy and 9 p.m. I was told to leave and I left. I hitchhiked to Bridgeport and I slept in the hallway of the YMCA. I didn't have enough money for a room and the guy there knew something was wrong. The next day this guy, Tim Forbes, he was a black guy, looked at me and knew I was a fish out of water. Bridgeport was a rough city and I came from private schools. Also being in the closet I did not know what life was. I was hungry, tired, and kind of dirty-looking. So he approached me smiling; I was not fearful. He dragged me into the back of a restaurant and bought me some food. He did not know who I was and never even asked my name.

Forbes had a little apartment and I slept on the couch in the living room and he slept in his bedroom. He proceeded to raise me. When he was working during the day, I went down with him to the Y where the other guy, Jimmy Whitehall, was. These guys literally became my parents.

Though Michael managed to find some comfort from Tim, and perhaps one of his first experiences of genuine communion, he soon joined the street action of Bridgeport. Within a few months, he had found his way to an even more powerful sense of comfort, heroin.

I fell in love after my first bag of heroin. I felt no pain and nothing could bother me. I did stay with Forbes until the addiction got worse. When I was fifteen, I was having trouble with people in the neighborhood. People would talk tough in the city, I would take that as a threat and I would fight back. Forbes saw this and tried to work with me. Tim loved me, I know he did. But heroin was my cure-all, with it I did not care about anything. At fifteen, I got arrested for shooting a Puerto Rican who ripped me off for six dollars. Then heroin was two dollars a bag, he ripped me off. I laugh at it now. I was just a kid shooting at a Spanish guy in a Spanish neighborhood. I was lucky I didn't die. The cops were on me in a second.

This arrest marked the end of Michael's first years in Bridgeport. His family's attorney was able to step in and arrange for him to be sent out of state to Florida where his family had moved. He was told he could not return to Connecticut for five years and he was escorted to the bus station by bailiffs. Though he felt great hatred toward his family, he still headed to West Palm Beach, where they resided.

The strange thing is, as much as I hated these people, they were still my family. I still had feelings for these people; I never wanted to admit it, but I did. For many years I remember sticking needles in my arms thinking, "I'll show you, I'll show you." I thought a lot of the punishments I had gone through were my fault. I had done something wrong.

I got down to West Palm Beach and right away I started to live on the street. I'd run into people and live with them. By this time I had had a couple of years of street living, from blacks to Puerto Ricans to tough white people I had learned real quick. West Palm Beach kids were no match for me. The first heroin bust was in 1968, so they weren't even used to this. I started stealing doctor's bags from the backs of cars. They had morphine, morphine sulfate, meta-morphine. I was in seventh heaven. Doors were unlocked, no burglar alarms. Things were great.

I always had morphine. I couldn't get heroin. I did get arrested when I was sixteen. I had probably ripped off fifty doctors. When they arrested me I had a large amount of narcotics and I got five years in prison.

In the next part of Michael's story, there are eerie parallels to the torture of his childhood. It is hard to know how memory has acted on these two periods of his life. The emotional trauma and senseless brutality from his childhood seemed to have blended with this period of incarceration. At least, his imagery and his descriptions were frighteningly similar. In the stories that follow, there are always sadistic individuals (Father-Destroyers) who commit acts of violence against Michael. In turn, Michael, the Bad Seed, smaller and younger than his assailants, fights back and asserts his agency, but his efforts at retribution are never satisfying. They lead either to further punishment or remorse. Independent of the details of these stories, another defining imago repeatedly emerges from the narrative—Michael experiences himself as a Marred Survivor. He is someone who does what it takes to go on, to get through the next ring of hell, but each time, he comes out more bruised, more angry, more distant from any world founded on morality, trust, or authenticity. His journey through the prison world and criminal world is a dizzying one—any of the psychological and social structures that might provide him with a sense of safety, sameness, and communal reassurance are absent. There is only Michael on his own, doing what he can to survive and to feed his drug habit, the habit that allows him not to feel or think, either in the present or about the past.

I think the hardest was the first part. I spent eleven months in the county jail. It was before they had a thing called fast and speedy trial. I remember the first night I was in prison, I woke up around 2 a.m. and there were two black guys and a white guy taking turns sodomizing another guy. I remember putting my head on my pillow, crying and praying. I remember being scared to death. With my attitude and my anger, I was involved in many fights in those eleven months and I lost everyone. I was only sixteen; they were a lot tougher than me. I never gave up and I was never sexually abused. I know now that it is because I fought back.

When I went to prison, I was sold out. I plea bargained for probation because I was so young and it was my first offense in Florida. I copped to a lesser charge to get five years instead, but I was sold down the river, it was all bullshit, there was no plea bargain. So from the jail, I went to the penitentiary. I was liked there. I do not know why, but people always like me. There were some people there from West Palm Beach and they told me they would stick up for me, but I had to be tough and fight. So they told me the first thing you have to do is make a name for yourself. I remember I punched this guard right in the mouth for no reason; the poor guy did not do a thing to me. I don't think this guy even moved and he beat the living shit out of me. Right there I ended up doing eighteen months in there and after that I was sent to a chain gang. That prison was not a nice place. It was a hell hole. The first sixteen fights I got into I got terribly beaten up. I was in my first prison riot there. I saw my first people killed there. I saw four or five people die; there was nowhere to run. When I went to prison, it was segregated, blacks on one side, whites on the other. Our president got the idea to integrate everyone and all hell broke loose in there.

There were long-haired red necks and these were mean, nasty whites. Most of them uneducated and most of them hated blacks, Jews, or Italians. They were just a KKK type of person. I could be anything I had to be to get along with these people. I have three or four good size razor scars on my body from those prison riots. I've been stabbed and cut with a razor. A razor was a very handy weapon. At this time I got my first real taste of blood. I had stabbed four or five people by the time I left there. Prison got to be a way of life for me. I did not have to be the toughest to survive, but I learned real young how to stay on top of the situation the best I could. . . . I saw people get pencils punched right through their eardrums, throats slit. I saw a lot of violence. I was part of it. I can remember how I was when I finally came out. My twin sister, Patty, came and picked me up. I don't know how I got in touch with her. Wait, I do know. There was this woman, Lucy Moyers, whose job it was to help Catholic prisoners. She helped me find my sister. Patty picked me up and she took me out for pancakes. When they released me, they gave me five dollars. I remember two guards walking me to the gate saying "You'll be back." They were squeezing my arms so I would do something, but I did not. I wanted to, but I wanted my freedom. Prison had done something to me. I hated black people. I was stabbed two or three times by blacks. I remember a bus boy stepped on my toe when I was waiting in line when my sister was paying the check. It was a little black guy and I beat the shit out of him . . .

I registered a jarring irony when Michael described the guards giving him the five dollars; this figure was the exact amount of money his mother gave him when she sent him on his way (releasing him from another kind of prison). It also hit me that when Michael left the first time from his home, his savior at the Y was a black man. This time, after his prison experience, he left with hatred for blacks and cruelly beat up a black man for a trivial offense. All of these aspects of his story—the repeated parallels, the unrelenting violence, the feeling that he has told you the worst part and then another more gruesome detail is revealed—strain the credibility and differentiation of his narrative. They make me question the goodness of his story, make me feel a repetitive uncertainty about the authenticity of his narrative and, by extension, of his identity.

Before his moving on in the narrative, I asked Michael to go back and tell me about his experience on the chain gang. I had not heard a man of the Pines ever mention this kind of confinement and I was curious to know what it entailed.

We worked ten hours a day, six days a week. You could not talk to the guy next to you. There were ten guys to a chain. You were chained every morning. A lot of brutality. It was the worst place in Florida. We took care of the canals; we kept them clean. There were snakes, alligators were in there. We went into the Everglades a lot of the time and worked in the swamps. . . . I remember being on this crew with this guy, Boss Hardy, he would shake all the time, he had some physical problem. He was mean. One time I was talking to this black guy and you were not allowed to talk to anyone next to you. He hit me so hard in the chest with his shotgun that he knocked the wind out of me. He stood over me and he was going to smash my face in and he called me a nigger-lover.

One time there was a fight. Do you know what bush axes are? It's a pole with a pickax and it stands about five feet. It's almost like a baseball bat. The blade is a metal blade about twelve inches long, six inches wide and it hooks at the end. It's used to cut down branches the size of your arm. So there are ten guys on a chain. There is this black guy on the left of me and one on the right of me. I'll never forget this day. These black guys on both sides of me started "Motherfucker this, motherfucker that" and I was looking, and they were big, like 6' 3" or so. I'm only 5'7". I could tell these guys hated each other. They both had their bush axes over their shoulders getting ready to attack and I am right in between them. There was ten feet between one guy and ten feet between the other guy. They both lifted their bush axes at the same time and I fell straight back on the ground. They could of chopped my head off. One guy swung and the bush ax went right through the other guy's leg, completely through him. The guard shot the other guy, shot him with a shotgun, right in the legs. This all happened two feet on one side and two feet on the other side of me. This guy is screaming bloody murder, the other guy is screaming bloody murder, and the guard has his shotgun leveled right at me. I'm laying there and I even peed in my pants, that is something that I never told anyone. I did. I thought I was dead.

. . . Toward the end of my stay I was moved to a smaller camp and I had about eight months to go. There were about a hundred guys at this camp. It was a barracks situation with a guard tower in the middle. This guy watched us all the time when we were not working. This was still a chain gang. These guards there are like the bottom of the barrel. Your pay for work was two packs of rolling tobacco and a bar of soap. If you did not work hard, you were handcuffed to the back of a truck and then thrown in a hole. Out of my three and a half years in prison, I probably spent eighteen months in solitary confinement for fighting with guards or prisoners. I was always disrespecting a guard. I was nineteen years old and one of the youngest guys at the camp. They picked one black guy and one white guy to be liaisons to the guards and I was picked. I was the best talker. From the time I was arrested until the time I got out of prison I read over a thousand books. I used to read Word Power by Reader's Digest. I studied everything, only because I did not want to be like the other prisoners. Something in me drove me, and at least I accomplished that much. Now I see it really isn't that much, but I thought so then.

They picked me for this, because I was young, tough. I could speak, and I wasn't afraid. So I talked the whole camp into throwing a strike. I'm nineteen and it is a time of rebellion. I was going to talk them into it. There were six guards out there; we were in the middle of a medium security prison. I said we are not going to work until we get better conditions. Well, let me tell you, they have two holes, three cells; these are completely metal cells and they are in a building out in the middle of the field. There is a hole in the floor where you piss and shit. There are not sinks or water. A light burns twenty-four hours a day. The cell is four foot by six foot. They took me and twenty other guys and loaded up those cells to where you had to sit so crouched, we could not even move, butt naked. Let me tell you that everyone of those prisoners wanted to kill me. I had talked them all into this. I had not known they were on the phone with the sheriff's department. You never saw so many cops in your life. They swarmed the place. Needless to say we had to give up. I did not even have a weapon.

I blew this one big time. We stayed in there twenty days. Twenty days! They took away thirty days of my good time, which they did not tell me until the day I was supposed to get out. Just little mental things they do to you. I remember the first time I went to the hole when I was on the chain gang. They feed you peas and carrots. Two tablespoons twice a day, 5:30 a.m. and 5:30 p.m. Every third day, if they remembered, they would give you half a meal at noon time and that was it. A piece of chicken and a spoonful of potatoes and maybe a half of a cup of water with each meal. In thirty days, you would lose thirty pounds. This was designed to physically, emotionally, and mentally break you down.

The thing was, though, I had years of experience in the closet. I remember big guys talking about how scared they were. When I went, I adapted right to it, it was like being in the closet. I was laughing because there was no way they were going to break me, it was impossible. And it *was* impossible. I remember a guard coming one day just to antagonize me. I told him he could keep me in there forever and not break me. I told him that when I get out, his girl would be sucking black cock. This was a big southern guard. I was only supposed be in there for three days. He just smiled and closed the door. I couldn't understand why he gave up so easy. Days went on and days went on. There was a state law that you could not stay in there for more than thirty days. Great law! No one even knows you are in there. I was there for about fifty or sixty days.

(What did you do to pass the time?)

I did the same thing I did in the closet, the same thing. I would make up games. I would make up stories. I would just start by saying O.K., I'll drift off in a sail boat. Wait let's go back, let's build the sail boat and build it intricately. It might be months before I could even sail it. And these were the kinds of things that I would do. I would make up these stories that were so fantastic, and it would keep my mind going and they couldn't break me. They couldn't break me in the closet. I learned about five years old to start doing this.

Back to the guard. After fifty days I am weak. It was starting to get to me. I could not think of any more stories. It was so quiet and hot. And there was a horrible smell from where you piss and shit. And I am dirty and nasty. And I am hungry and I am angry. Because now all I am thinking about is the violence with my parents and I want to take it out on someone, but there is no one there. I remember the door opened and I went to get up and I fell back on the ground, I was so weak. This guard came in and beat the shit out of me. He broke my nose, some ribs, and knocked out some teeth. Then they dragged me by the head to the infirmary. I was there for about six weeks, because they beat me so bad. . . . When I got out at nineteen years old, six months later, I swore I would die before I would ever go back.

In a series of haunting repetitions, we find the same critical elements of his first self-defining memory of his crib, his childhood torture closet memories, and his last fight with his father. In his memory of the chain gang, Michael ends up imprisoned in a tiny room by a sadistic male authority. He is punished for his precociousness, and his rebellion only results in further violence. Michael's narrative whirls around and around, finding always the same limited plot, characters, themes. It lacks any differentiation or reconciliation that would allow it to grow or move forward.

After Michael left prison, he actually lived with Lucy Moyers, the Catholic relief worker who had located his sister. She became convinced that he was truly a good soul and that he had been led astray. She was determined to bring Michael back to God and attempted to incorporate him into her own family life. In Lucy, Michael provides another critical imago, the Healing Female, a trusting and forgiving figure who will repeatedly surface through his narrative. Inevitably, he portrays himself as disappointing and exploiting these well-intentioned figures. Unbeknownst to Lucy, Michael had found ways to use drugs (marijuana and pills) or drink (apple jack and coconut wine) throughout his time in prison. He had no intention of stopping his addictions.

She told me I was not like other boys, there was something special about me. I almost started believing this lady. . . . I lived with her and I remember just conning her out of all kinds of money and things. These people really tried to show me love and kindness. She had a son who was twelve and had saved two hundred and sixty dollars. I talked him out of that. I needed to buy heroin.

Michael left Lucy's home and began to live with a girlfriend. She was sixteen and he was nineteen. Though he did some construction work, his heroin habit deepened.

I could never get enough heroin, never get enough. My addiction was stronger than a lot of other addicts, I had a lot of pain to kill. I would break into houses. I was a con, a liar, and a rip-off artist. . . .

In another memory from that period, remarkable for its symbolic overtones, Michael stumbled upon the very guard who had imprisoned him in his chain gang cubicle.

I was coming home from work one day and I walked into this store and there is the guard who beat the living shit out of me. When this guy saw me, he turned white; he was big, an ex-navy guy. He was in his forties. I went over to the cooler, they didn't have plastic bottles then, and I grabbed a beer bottle and broke it on the table. I told him I was going to cut him very slowly and very thoroughly. I remember telling him this. He started crying and I couldn't do it. It was like hurting a kid. I couldn't do it. I put the bottle on the ground, then I remember getting real defiant. I walked back into the store and got a full bottle of beer. I stole that; I had to do something wrong. I drank it. I just wanted to show him I was tougher. It might all sound crazy, but this is what happened. So I did not hurt this guy. And I know that bothered me, for a long time that bothered me. I wanted to hurt him.

(What was it that bothered you so much?)

Because I had swore I would kill him if I ever saw him again. The beating he gave me was unmerciful. I could not just do it. So I remember driving home from that store and I was crying, crying, crying. My father was a big man and I always wanted to kill my father. But I didn't do it and something happened to me. I don't know, I let myself down at the time. I didn't know how to release the feelings I had. I just cried. I guess that was a release. I thank God today that I did not kill this man. In fact, I feel real bad for threatening him and making him feel afraid. But that's now.

In the previous chapter, I discussed Freud's concept of the repetition compulsion—how certain conflicts can repeatedly return to our thoughts or encounters until we find a way to master them. In Michael's story of his encounter with his torturer, there is a clear repetition of his earlier encounter with his father. The memory expresses Michael's enduring dilemma—he can only define agency in terms of violent destruction, but this power has no capacity to bring him solace. For Michael, to assert himself is simultaneously to destroy those to whom he feels attached. Assertion of his identity cannot be uncoupled from the victimization of others.

Michael continued to commit armed robberies in Florida and also cheated some drug dealers out of money and large amounts of heroin. He fled from his girlfriend's home in the middle of night and found his way back to Bridgeport. After finding work and staying clean for a while, he sent for his girlfriend; they were married by a justice of the peace who was also a pharmacist. Michael cased the pharmacy after the ceremony and later went back and robbed the place. His heroin habit resumed shortly after the marriage; he began by "chipping," using small amounts every few days. Soon the desire for daily bags kicked in and, not surprisingly, he again committed armed robberies. And in due course, he was caught again, but this arrest held a twist for him that affected the next twenty years of his life.

Well, I got caught breaking into this guy's office of a construction company. He was hooked up with the mob and I didn't know it. . . . They had me arrested. It was in Fairfield, right next to Bridgeport.

This detective came to me and I was in the holding cell, waiting to go to Bridgeport, where the county jail was. . . . He came and got me and pulled me out of the cell and brought me up to his office, gave me coffee and a cigarette. And he's talking and you know, and I'm still, I want to be defiant, but there's something clicking here, something's not right. What does this guy want, you know? Now at this point in life, in my times, I was born and raised with the fact on the streets, and in prison, that you don't rat, you don't snitch, you don't turn anybody in and you don't talk to cops. That's way that it is. Well, you know, I had already done some time in prison. By that time I was twenty-one, I had been arrested about twenty or thirty times. You know, my life was going nowhere and I can see this.

So it was time to change my value system here. So this guy says, he wanted me to come to work for the police. He said, "Now hear me out. We have a special group of police officers. It's called the Southwest Regional Crime Squad." They took one or two cops from every city; Danbury, Bridgeport, Wilton, you name it. And they took these guys, these rookies, and their hair was long and they trained them special and they trained them to be street narcotics officers. Called them narcs. And they said they would drop all my charges. I would go to work for them and I would get paid. I would get paid! They knew I knew a whole lot of people. And I made the deal. And my first officer was Carlton T. Pipes. He was twenty-six years old. I was twenty-one. C.T. was tough and he was cool. And we ran.

We did 142 cases between Bridgeport and Stratford. . . . This guy, C.T., would get twenty to thirty dollars a case. I'd make two or three cases a day. Plus all the drugs I wanted and dope. If we got a bundle of dope, ten bags, by that time I'm doing half-loads, fifteen bags a day. You know, I'd get three or four bags per case.

(He'd give you the drugs?)

Yeah. Oh yeah. Here's this, here's that. Everything was dishonest, illegal. Everything was entrapment. And I told him, you know, why don't you get some of your stuff out of your property warehouse that you guys seize from other guys. We'll put it in the trunk and make believe that we are boosters [shoplifters] and sellers, so it looks like you're a criminal and people are going to accept you more. And it went like wildfire. And we sold it and then we'd bust the people we sold it to and then keep the money and split it up.

So he was just about as bad as I was. He didn't shoot drugs, but he smoked pot and he did everything else. He used to take a wet match and rub the wet sulfur on his veins and it'd leave a track and unless you were real good, you wouldn't know. I'm the one who taught him to do that. Him and I got real close, we got real tight.

It was at this point in the telling of his story that Michael's attitude became noticeably different. Through all the incidents of his youth and all the stark accounts of his prison life, Michael spoke in a soft, matter-of-fact voice. There were only a few times where his eyes would look toward mine and where he would convey a sense of pain or sadness. Now, as he recounted his years as a narc and his access to money, unlimited heroin, and a sense of power, he became expressive in his entire body. His voice sped up and he laughed; he almost seemed to move to the edge of his seat as he painted a picture of setups, scams, arrests, and shootouts. I had a strange sense that this had all been a wonderful dangerous game for him—a way to have drugs and thrills, but still stay out of prison. In the language of despair that I have used throughout this book, he had shifted from using drugs as a surrender and escape to embracing them as an expression of his destructive agency. They now became a way he could stand safely above the rest of world and laugh at its gullibility.

The essence of this destructive role was to give up any effort at forging an authentic identity. His job was not to be himself—he was actually getting paid to pretend and dissemble. He could exploit his distrust of communion by legitimately betraying others in the interest of law enforcement. He exacted agentic revenge upon others, by setting them up, stealing their money and drugs, and watching the police take them away. In a macabre sense, he had found his calling. All of his previous cons and lies had led up to this realization of his adult persona—his most compelling imago—Michael, the Performer. He could now hide his conflicted and troubled identity behind a series of assumed roles and disguised selves. The only problem for him was that he began to need more and more money as his habit grew larger and more expensive.

I would go crazy when I couldn't find someone who was selling drugs. This was the early seventies. Everybody was selling drugs. But when I couldn't, I would give drugs to people to sell. If I had to make a case, I would give them three bags of heroin, and I'd tell them to sell it double the price. And he'd sell it double the price to the cop. And the cop didn't know it. The cop paid him. The guy paid me half the money, sometimes three quarters of the money. Plus I'd get paid for the case by the cop and by the town I did it in. So not only am I making half my dope back, I am making about 200 percent of my money. And I can't get arrested. So I found out that I could work for the police, do my drugs, make my money, have my power, people liked me, and I was in heaven. And I really got off on the danger. I carried a gun. It wasn't all legal, but it was O.K. And they loved me. I was making these guys look good. Well, I got burned out, so they wanted to move me up to another section of Connecticut. The Milford–New Haven area.

. . . I get excited talking about that because it was excitement. I was able to go into an area that I'd never been in before and pick people out, bust bookies, drug dealers, and do the same thing. You know, they were giving me a place to live and they'd give me food, they were giving me a car. I always had a weapon. . . . I lived a good life. I lived a good life for a drug addict. I was on top of the world. At that time, I had no respect for the police. I had no respect for drug dealers. I didn't give a shit about anybody but me.

(What happened to your wife?)

We were getting separated, 'cause of the drugs and stuff like that. She was still over in Bridgeport. And about every month, I'd stay with her for a weekend. It just wasn't working out. What got so bad was, I got up to 270 cases and I was making a lot of phony cases, setting up a lot of people that didn't have nothing to do with drugs. I'd convince these people, sell this to my friend I owe him some money so I can't sell it to him. I'll give you twenty bucks for selling it for me. . . . I don't give a fuck if you go to prison. I probably set up 500 people without exaggeration, but maybe only 300 needed to go. I did this for twenty years.

Michael eventually continued his narc work out of state, hooking up with police departments in Illinois and Florida. He was arrested himself for possession and went back to prison in Florida for another two years, coming out in 1975. Upon leaving the prison, he somehow managed to hear that his mother was dying in a nursing home in West Palm Beach. He went to see her at the home. As Michael recounted the story of her death, he seamlessly moved into his account of his last visit with his father. Both stories convey his confused need to hate and love his parents, to punish and embrace them.

I went to see her and it was awful. She was just as yellow as those lines in the street. She had cirrhosis of the liver and she was dying. She was dying. And I remember I would sneak her up Thunderbird wine. I hated this woman. . . . I remember sitting on her bed, giving her the wine she loved. She was all bloated. Her liver was just so yellow. But what I remember most, which I guess, which I'm almost sad right now was, at the time, I hated this woman. And I remember telling her she had had enough, and I kept fucking forcing the bottle down her throat. And I remember spitting in her face and I, she didn't know, she didn't know that she was going to die. She had no idea. She was fucking loony tunes and had no idea. . . . And I remember calling her a bitch and I spit in her face. Really hated this woman. She died. She died. I left and she died. She died on my birthday, July 22nd, 1975. What I remember was a weird feeling 'cause when she died I had a lot of anger in me. I remember beating on a tree, beating on a fence, going crazy. By this time my wife had left me and I was into heroin full blown again. And something really happened bad when my mother died. I don't know what it was. There is a whole lot differently that I feel about my mother and father. Right now I feel a lot of sadness for them, for their lives. . . .

What followed was more heroin. Till 1980, more heroin, more on the run. I ended up going to Pittsburgh, St. Louis, Kansas City. I worked for the police in every single city I went to. I approached them. I always did good. Always did the same thing. Then in 1983, I found out where my father was. And though he had divorced from my mother, he ended up back in West Palm Beach. I was in Illinois at the time. I was clean. I had gone through a program and was running a group. I was more like a counselor. Back then being a counselor was not a big deal. You graduated a program and became a counselor if you want to work with them. I had never done anything honestly in my life, not even these programs. And as a result, I ended up being high, not being able to live with my own lines.

So I found out where my father lived. . . . And I convinced myself, this is how sick I got, that I was going to kill my father. He was 6' 2", 220. I was to use no weapons. I set down guidelines. No weapons, no guns, no knives. I was to beat him with my fist. . . . The fact that he was in his forties and I was in my twenties, this made it fair. I figured I could take him on, beat him to death. You know for 1,800 miles I forced myself to think about all the times he sodomized me in the closet. I thought about all of the times he raped my sister. And I was just bubbling over with anger. And I went right to the address and I knocked on the fucking door. And my brother, Philip, answered the door and I knocked him out. I grabbed him, knocked him right out. I was very tough and strong at that age. He didn't stand a chance. And I went into the house, and there was all these closed doors in the house. And I wanted to kill the son of a bitch. I kicked in three doors, each one with the anticipation he was behind it and I was going to attack. One door left, I knew he was there. I remember breathing real hard. And I remember there was nothing that was going to stop me. I was going to do this. And I kick in this door, and there laying on a bed was my father. A hundred and thirty pounds. Just a sheet—naked—with a sheet laying over him. . . . The skin was peeling off his body. And he stank. This was my father. This big, tough, wealthy man, reduced to nothing. And I could not attack. I could not. It was the most pathetic, putrid scene I had ever seen in my life. I went over and I sat down on the bed and I started crying. I could not kill him. He was dying of cirrhosis of the liver, exact same disease my mother died of. I sat on the bed crying. But you know, he never lost his toughness. The son of a bitch looked up at me and he said, "What the fuck are you doing here?" That's what he said to me, that's what he said to me. . . . And I looked at him, and I'm gonna tell you now something that I've never told anybody. You know what I told this man? I told him that I loved him. I've never admitted this because it takes away from my anger. But I've lost a lot of that anger. And I can honestly tell you that I did love my mother and father. They were just sick people. They had problems. They weren't really—you know there was this big thing in recovery—responsible for their own actions. Bullshit. Some people I don't believe are responsible. They crossed that line. They had a sickness. So anyway, I got up and walked out and my poor brother, Philip, he was just waking up. And he got up on his knees and I hit him again and he went right out again. And I left. And I left. I didn't kill my father. I feel bad to this day that I crippled him. And I got on with my life.

Even in this gripping story of a quasi-reconciliation with his father, Michael's narrative includes comedic turns (e.g., the knocking out of the good brother, Philip, not once but twice; his father's deathbed greeting) that challenges one's ability to trust its veracity. Somehow Michael's Performer Imago, the fast-talking confidence man, slips in and leaves the slightest bit of doubt, even in this painful scene. It is quite possible that Michael does not intend to create this distance from his story; he simply does not know another way to be, a way not to perform.

The life that Michael continued throughout the eighties was one of more scams and setups working with different police departments. Along the way, he managed to marry two more times. In each case, he married women who hoped to turn him away from his drug habits and criminal ways ("Healing Females"). Despite long stretches of sobriety and church-going (in one case a couple of years), he ultimately found his way back to his drug habit and confidence games. Both marriages ended when his involvement with heroin and his need to stay one step ahead of both dope dealers and federal agents put him back on the road again. He would look for new small cities where he could offer himself as a contact to the police department narcotic bureaus. These activities lasted into the nineties, but at the same time his years of heroin addiction and the recent cocaine binges were wearing down his body physically. He also felt a loneliness for a relationship beyond the prostitutes and "coke whores" he could attract with his money and drugs. He began to pursue rehab programs, and claimed to have attended as many as ten different ones over the years.

So I would try rehabs and the first time I took it more seriously was in a ninety-day program I did in Providence, Rhode Island. I got into it. The only trouble was I could never talk about my past. I had to lie to make up stuff. I would never let them know I was sexually abused, or the kind of life I had. I never let anybody know I didn't have a high school education. I told people I had three years of college. I did this all my life. And as my lies got worse, to cover up lies, I couldn't stay straight. But each time I went to a program, my lies got less. I've probably been in ten programs, ten or twelve programs. And about twenty detoxes to go hide out. And to clean up. Kick dope, go back on, shoot dope, kick dope, go back on. Since the sixties.

Michael was finally arrested again for heroin use in 1991.

In prison I started shooting heroin and dealing heroin for the Latin Kings. I ended up ripping off the Latin Kings and turning them all in to get my sentencing reduced down to a year. That's where I got these cuts across my stomach. They were trying to kill me in prison. And they shipped me to this tiny cell by myself in Brooklyn, Connecticut. And guards, I turned in some guards. I turned in the Latin Kings and I got the fucking feds after me. My whole life has gone down the tubes.

And I'll tell you exactly what happened. I really started my recovery. It was about three years ago. I got on my knees. I'm in this cell, altogether I've done about seven years in prison. And I'm in this cell, all by myself in protected custody. And I've got child molesters, rapists, baby killers on all sides of me. These people are protected from everybody 'cause everybody wants to kill them. And they got me right in the middle. I'm even having a hard time being around these people, I want to kill them. Yet the guards want to kill me because I turned in some guards too. My life is over and I know I'm going to die. I know it. . . . So I got on my knees and I started praying. I just asked God to change my life, and it worked, it did. I met a guy, who was an ex-convict, who came there to the jail AA meeting. And he got to the warden and got special permission for me to go to more AA meetings. And I stayed clean, despite there being a lot of drugs in there. I stayed clean for nine months. And I went to a halfway house and I'm reading my AA stuff, and I stayed clean for fifteen months altogether.

Contained in Michael's account of his turn toward recovery are equal parts spiritual discovery and pragmatic expediency. He had burned every bridge that might lead him to further lucrative criminal activity. After twenty years, there was no one left to betray. As he had put it in describing his decision to become an informant, it was again "time to change his value system." He began an exploration of a new kind of narrative identity—the Recovering Addict. Though this role offered him another possibility of performance, it was not as easily adopted by him. It demanded an honesty about his past that he did not feel ready to invoke. The Fourth Step of the AA Twelve Steps asks that individuals in recovery make "a searching and fearless moral inventory of ourselves." Michael felt unable or unwilling to reach this point and found himself slowly stealing back to drugs and confidence schemes. He swindled a woman he knew in Florida out of a large sum of money by selling her land he did not own. He also cheated some local drug dealers out of some money and used his profits to finance his heroin habit again.

It was after a near-fatal overdose that I met him in detox and listened to his revelations about his past for the first time. He subsequently went up to the Pines, but left when some of his disgruntled business associates showed up to talk with him. After more running, he finally made it back to the Pines for his more extended stay.

There was only one loose end in his story that I asked him to explain. What had happened to his twin sister—the one member of his family for whom he had felt the greatest love.

Patty died. About four years ago. I was in Providence and I found her through a private detective. She was in Montgomery, Alabama. Her husband, a great irony, was a head of a drug rehab facility. But in the three years before she died, she had developed multiple personalities. The nightmares are what got her. It's funny; my nightmares did not start that bad until she died. So I called her and she thought I had died. She got a letter from Vital Statistics in Florida, saying that I was killed in prison. So she thought it was a joke. I had to convince her. I had to tell her certain things. I mentioned the closet and the attic and she snapped right to. She started crying. And she started talking like it was yesterday. The day I crippled my father. We were fourteen. And she's saying I'm so sorry. And I really understood. I understand because of all the years, the confusion, and the pain and the brutality. She didn't know. She didn't know whose side she was on, if there was a side. So I told her I forgive her and the only thing I wanted was a family and I loved her. She's the only one I cared about in the family. So I had a lot of money at the time. I had about eighty thousand dollars on me from running drugs. I was living in a fucking mansion near Cape Cod. World by the ass. I was gonna fly down, get her, bring her back up. And we were gonna start a family. Be a family. All dreaming you know.

Well, I hung up the phone and I got a phone call from this hooker that I knew in Brockton, and I had arranged everything with Patty. So I was just gonna go meet this girl, drop off some cocaine, pick up some money, get laid, then fly to Montgomery. Well, she was there with some of her girlfriends, and I spent about three days, and about four ounces of cocaine later, shooting cocaine and having sex. And just blew off Patty. It'll wait till Monday. It cost me about five thousand. But it was worth it. When I got back, my sister's son had called. He had got my phone number from her husband. She had had it on her bed when she died. Took an overdose of sleeping pills they had given her so she'd sleep with the nightmares. And he told me that she had committed suicide. It was the day after I hadn't shown up.

I flipped out. I went out at it hard and heavy. I never—I forgive myself now, but barely. Lot of pain, lot of hurt. You know, my mother and my father and my sister, wasted deaths, wasted lives.

Even with Patty, there was no satisfactory reconciliation; the same undifferentiated tale of family disappointment prevails. Always Michael reaches out to find a way back to communion, always his agentic self undermines his efforts and leads once more to violence and isolation.

The Search for an Authentic and Differentiated Identity

When Michael finished his story that day, both of us were exhausted. It was a story that did not seem possible and yet it was the living, articulated memory, the believed-in reality of Michael Cochran. I cannot go back and verify these details, each beating or abuse, each brilliant con or near-death escape. What seems more important than the veracity of each incident is that Michael had constructed this narrative of his life. He chose to present himself that way to me and perhaps to himself. In the story that he had constructed, his escape from the private torture of his coat closet led only to the same brutality on the street, in jails, and in prison. Most of his adult life had been lived as a con artist, playing the police and the drug dealers off each other. Lying, stealing, and cheating were the basic methods he used to gain his income and his drugs. His livelihood was to set up and betray people. Now this same story concluded with his redemption, his discovery of God and the AA tradition. Was it possible for someone like Michael to make the transition from a protean con man to a person who aspired to sincerity and commitment in relationships? Was it possible for him to find a way of being in the world that did not rely on false poses and dishonesty?

Besides the violence and criminal behavior, there was always the presence of heroin and cocaine. Drugs were initially a means of escape for Michael; pain and memory killers that could temporarily blot out his sense of abandonment and his recollections of abuse. As long as he was high, he could leave aside questions of his authentic identity, questions of who he really was. He did not have to be that terrified boy in the coat closet or that nineteen-year-old in a concrete box in the searing sunlight of the prison camp.

Michael also used drugs because they had become a direct expression of his destructive agency; they were connected to a livelihood that was both lucrative and exciting. In his stories you can hear the braggadocio of a boy playing cops and robbers, the fascination with violence, danger, and power. Drugs were his entry to this adventurous world and his only means of staying inside it. Given the popularity of gangster films right up to the recent *Pulp Fiction,* it is not hard to see the seductive aspect of this life to Michael who, by the time of his early twenties, had had little access to any other means of power or prominence. The more intriguing question is what happens when someone like Michael wants to step out of this world. How would he face the mundane reality of the daily work world? How would he cope with expectations of responsibility and honesty? In short, how would he live a sober life?

In retracing Michael's story, one can identify an evolution of imagoes—a series of self-images organized around themes of agency and communion. Beginning with the Bad Seed. Michael understood himself as someone unworthy of nurturance and intimacy; from the time of his crib days he felt doomed to isolation and abandonment. In the face of abandoning and abusive authorities (Father-Destroyer), he made failed attempts to assert himself, only to emerge as a Marred Survivor, wounded, bitter, and hustling for existence. Drugs and his own acts of violence seemed to be his only comfort in the face of these defeats and injuries. When the role of police informant was offered to him, Michael was able to take all of previous survival skills and destructive tendencies and channel them into a single role, creating his most enduring imago—Michael, the Performer. As an informant, he could exploit his desire to hide from his past, to avoid looking inward; he could turn his love of drugs and drug culture to his economic advantage; he could sadistically manipulate and victimize others rather than be a victim himself. Most of all, he could indulge his need to play roles and take on identities; he could receive official sanction from a law enforcement agency to be someone beside himself.

Despite the satisfaction he derived from these years of performing, he ended up, unsurprisingly, still isolated, still in a prison, and with no more viable roles to play. In this tight space, as he sensed the extreme anxiety of facing anew his own existential despair (isolation, freedom, death, meaninglessness) without any of his lifelong defenses, he found one more role, the Recovering Addict. As he soon discovered, this new role placed demands upon him that he had never encountered before in his life.

As a drug dealer and user, Michael did not expect to trust anyone and thought anyone would be foolhardy to trust him. The world of addiction in which he traveled is necessarily about "me" and not about "you" or "we." If I have some, I'll be glad to share. If I need some, I can think of no one but myself. In this sense, the addict's world was congruent with Michael's survivalist and self-focused way of being. There is no authenticity expected of a person and there is none displayed. In the most definitive sense, one's own personality and one's relationship to others are simply vehicles for allowing more drugs to enter one's body. Michael's shift to recovery asked of him a very different way of being in the world: recovery expected him to take responsibility for how he affected others and to be responsible in a honest way to himself. Suddenly, he was being asked to take ownership of a single life story—to form an identity that would not shift with expediencies. How he handled these new demands is very revealing about the problem of gaining sobriety when one's sense of a differentiated and authentic identity is very much in question.

From the time of our interview, Michael remained at Lebanon Pines another three months. During these months, he appeared increasingly religious and grateful about his recovery. In his soft-spoken and boyish way, he conveyed a newfound calmness and moral concern. Although he said and did everything that the Pines could wish for in a resident serious about sobriety, his counselor still felt concern for Michael. In their sessions together, the counselor could never be sure whether the connection between the two of them was quite real. Michael was so grateful, so open to the possibility of his renewal and growth that it seemed "too good to be true." The counselor, who was also a recovering cocaine addict, tried to explain to me that he felt like he could see himself in Michael, that their work kept leading them to find historical and emotional parallels. There was an uncanniness in Michael's bonding with him; Michael reflected back all the positive values of recovery without any rough edges or complexity.

As the counselor spoke, I was reminded of the old description of the "As if" personality. A psychoanalyst named Helen Deutsch coined this phrase to describe certain aspects of the Borderline Personality Disorder.[6] Individuals whose early upbringing had been filled with instability, threatened and actual abandonment, and confusing messages of extreme attachment and extreme rejection had learned to "play the emotional game," to portray themselves in ways that would assure their acceptance, their popularity. In a frantic effort at "fitting in" to avoid further rejection, they would become everything to everyone, behave "as if" they really were whatever the social climate or interpersonal environment asked of them. Beneath this outward appearance, this capacity to be a good girl or a fine student or a perfect spouse, was a certain emptiness, a vacuum of such intense fear and hurt that it repelled all attempts to enter it and fill the self with an authentic and fully expressed identity.

These ideas became even more relevant with regard to Michael when he suddenly revealed a change in his plans for discharge from the Pines. For months, he had discussed his desire to move to a halfway house in Seattle. He had investigated his possibilities thoroughly, including the particular halfway house, the AA meetings located near this house, and the local church affiliated with the same group as the one he attended while living at Lebanon Pines. He had gone so far as to put up a map of Seattle on the wall of his room and to mark each location with a stick pin. He had spoken to the halfway house manager and the pastor in Seattle. In all my years of working with men at the Pines. I had never heard of any man who had planned his transition so carefully, especially when it involved such a long distance move (his interest in Seattle was in part a result of his need to put many miles between himself and the world of betrayed associates he had left behind). Yet despite all of his planning, he went into his counseling session one day and announced that he had met a woman at his church and that they had been seeing each other the last couple of months. He had asked her to marry him and she had agreed. She also was in recovery and they planned to devote their lives and their marriage to a sober, spiritual life. She had a fourteen-year-old son from a previous marriage and he hoped to serve as a loving and effective stepfather for the boy. He had lined up a construction job and would be leaving the Pines in a couple of weeks. After they saved enough money in the next few months, they would make their move as a family to the West.

What were we to make of all this? Could we believe that Michael was truly on his way to recovery? After all, he had practiced much of what we counselors and therapists preach. He had let his demons out of the closet and he talked about his past; let his anger, his hurt, and his inexplicable love for his tormentors all surface. He had grieved and would continue to grieve for his lost childhood, but he would no longer be frozen in this phase of his life. In theory, this recovery had freed him to begin a loving and productive, as opposed to a self-loathing and destructive, life. It had freed him, in fact, to engage in a loving relationship with a woman, also in recovery, and her son.

Complementing these psychological and interpersonal advances was his spiritual awakening. He felt touched by a higher power, in his case by his Christian God, and believed that this spiritual blessing had moved him to a state of grace, removed from his past sins, lies, and evil desires. He described himself as literally washed clean and forgiven, ready to live his life in the hands of Christ. He counted each sober day with gratitude and as a sign of his relationship to his personal savior and guide in his recovery.

Filling out the picture of his recovery was his surrender to the tenets of the AA Twelve Step program. He had acknowledged that his life with drugs was unmanageable and out of control. He had recognized the pain he caused to others and himself. His goals were to take a clear and honest inventory of his transgressions performed in the service of his addiction and eventually to make amends for these acts. He planned to use his knowledge of the living hell of addiction to be of service to others and to give the gift of sobriety he had gained.

Michael presented these four forces—psychotherapy, entrance into a loving relationship, Christianity, and AA—as having transformed him and readied him for his new role as recovering husband, father, and productive citizen. Obviously, despite our good will for Michael and our hope, the staff at the Pines felt skeptical that this package could be put together in such a neat and rapid fashion. The abrupt change in plans and the embracing of new roles, new performances—the responsible bread-winning spouse and the loving stepdad—felt a little surreal to us.[7] In McAdams's terms, his story once again lacked coherence. Could this be another con, or could he be conning himself? Of course, when our thoughts went in this direction, we also felt a little guilty, as if we were denying the "miracle" of recovery and excluding him from this possibility.

Michael came back to the Pines to meet with me about a month after he had discharged. He was wearing his shiny new wedding ring and glowing with the good news of his life. He talked about his morning prayer sessions with his wife and new stepson and of the responsibility he felt to be a good father. He even talked about meeting the boy's biological father and receiving this man's encouragement and approval of his efforts to give his son direction. Michael was way too smart to think his past did not exist and that all would be perfect now. In response to my questions, he gave me heartfelt assurances about living one day at a time, about working his program, about keeping contact with sponsors and counseling. He acknowledged his weakness and his daily potential to fall backward and relapse. Michael was able to talk about his fear of the possibility of failure, but he also expressed his confidence that this risk was low. This was the life he had sought for so long, the family life he had always wanted.

We received a postcard from Michael a few months after he left for the West. His wife, stepson, and he had made it as far west as Arizona. He and his wife had each found work there and decided to stay there for the immediate future; Seattle still remained the ultimate goal, but he had found a construction supervising position in Arizona that he could not pass up. He remembered us all at the Pines and we were in his prayers. He was at seven months of recovery and counting—one day at a time (for the latest news of Michael as of the time of publication, see the Update at the end of the book).

More than any other man I interviewed, Michael's story challenged my own ideas about personality that I had pursued in my research at Connecticut College. The narrative perspective on personality to which I subscribe values individuals as the crafters of their life stories, narrators who bestow meaning and emotion upon a carefully selected set of episodes from their lives. This life story reveals a self, an author who has an integrity across time, a reasonable consistency and sameness despite developmental and situational influences. Even more, though this theory recognizes the role of the unconscious, the limits of self-awareness. and the pull for positive self-presentation, it grants narrators a certain degree of good faith and trust. In most cases, narrators of life stories are not only trying to inform us about who they are, but are making honest efforts to inform themselves as well.[8]

Michael Cochran's life story presents a particular kind of challenge to this perspective on personality. Since Michael, the narrator of the life story, had lived his adult life as a confidence man. I felt necessarily wary on several counts. If Michael's adaptation to his life's repetitive traumas was to shift his personality according to the survival demands of his circumstances, then his capacity for authorship of a definitive life story might have been severely damaged. That is to say, Michael might have become so used to surviving by fitting in that it was almost impossible for him to say with authenticity who he was. Because he lacked a unified self, his story inevitably would be ontingent on the social circumstances and needs of others. This possibility, an elaboration of the "As if" phenomenon mentioned earlier, requires a little more discussion.

Michael's capacity to leap out of his narrative and into his new family and his new role as husband/father highlights the performance dimension of crafting a life story. As participants in the creation of our life stories, we all engage in artistry, and the truths or realities of our lives may yield to the narrative conventions and characterizations we have inherited from our culture, including books, films, television, newspapers, and confessionally oriented self-help groups. As I listened to Michael, I could not help feeling the resonances in his story to icons of popular culture. As he portrayed himself, the rich outcast teenager, wandering the streets of Bridgeport, I could see drunken James Dean curled in the gutter at the beginning of *Rebel Without a Cause*. As Michael told of his chain-gang days, Paul Newman from *Cool-Hand Luke* hovered in the background. His long days in the hole with the sadistic guard outside conjured up Steve McQueen, pounding his baseball into his glove, heading off to his bleak cell, the theme music of *The Great Escape* accompanying each step. These images in the mind of the listener are not simply flights of my imagination. Michael, as storyteller, and I, as listener, share a way of knowing the world that has been filtered through the common culture in which we are both immersed. These archetypal images have been authored by our culture and they become part of the vocabulary we share in reaching a mutual understanding of Michael's story.

Similarly, as I have emphasized throughout this book, Michael's AA script of the destructive influence of abuse, the subsequent decline into drugs, and a final recovery through spiritual awakening and love reflects a cultural narrative of increasing familiarity in our society. Through AA stories, the vast recovery and self-help literature, and television talk shows, we have all inherited a structure for organizing these terrifying and potentially nihilistic life events into a narrative that offers meaning and a guardedly optimistic future. Is Michael any different from the millions of others who find their way to recovery by telling their stories? What Michael's duplicitous past and his startling transformation highlight for us is that his story cannot exist without the influence of prior stories and cultural narratives that give this story much of its form and structure. Just as Michael was able to inhabit and master the narratives of prison tough guy, of police "bad boy," he was now capable of locating himself in a narrative of recovery. If this is so, where do we find Michael, or anyone else, under the blanket of these influences?

The problem that AA presents for Michael is that it offers him another stage for the adoption of a precrafted role. In its emphasis on the airing of private stories in a public forum, it offers Michael the opportunity to display his new emotional release and new identity repeatedly for the eyes of others. By making his private redemption a public act, both his AA testimonials and his born-again witnessing at church may allow Michael to substitute communal displays of emotion and confession for inward change and self-knowledge. When someone like Michael "finds" himself in a room with others, I am not sure he can have a firm grasp on the self he is finding. The support and the praise he receives assure him he has done something right, but is there enough independent time and introspection for him to understand what he has actually found and what the implications of living a sober or a righteous life would be? For men like Michael, whom psychologists used to call sociopaths and now describe as suffering from Antisocial Personality Disorders,[9] the public forums offered by AA and church testimonials may actually facilitate an escape from the self and a further immersion in performance.

Though Michael's history as a confidence man sensitized me to look with more scrutiny at the credibility of his story, it also made me wonder about the factors that invade my own stories, my own narrative performances. The admonition, "Just be yourself" seems increasingly harder to follow in an age where the camera is always rolling. I wonder more and more how to locate those moments in my own life when my guard is down, when I am naturally and spontaneously responding to the world around me. Given the omnipresence of the mass media in our contemporary lives, there appears to be another facet of personality emerging in our lives. It is more than a distinction between a private and public self.[10] Traditionally, psychologists have imagined the public self as the self one imagines others see—the mask we put on, or what Jung called the persona. Our media culture now asks us to consider the televised or cinematic self—the character we become who inhabits stories heard not simply by a circle of immediate others, but by millions of others. When the reference point for our personalities is no longer simply our families or peers, but personalities observed on screens, the issue of authenticity or depth of self becomes even more problematic.[11]

Though it may be exceedingly difficult for any of us to locate moments free of performance or public influence, some individuals may be more prone to adopt roles that please others or at least produce strong reactions in them. For example, individuals high in the motivational theme of power, as measured by the stories they generate in response to T.A.T. pictures, are more likely to seek the spotlight and call attention to themselves. They desire above all to be noticed and to be in command.[12] The prominent personality researcher David Winter has found that individuals high in the power motive will tend to generate stories that reflect themes of characters trying to assert influence over each other. The resulting response from the characters who are being controlled may be strong negative emotions of fear and anger.

In looking at Michael's T.A.T. stories, three of his four stories were centered around conflict between characters; in fact he used the phrase, "making him do something he doesn't want to do" in response to two separate cards. There was strong imagery of violence in his stories. In response to the picture of a boy contemplating a violin, he saw the boy as having a cut lip, probably because of his parents' attempts to force him to play the violin. Though this picture can often invoke themes of tension between the child and parents' expectations, the projection of violence and injury into the card is much more unusual.

The results of this psychological test suggest that Michael was strongly inclined to control and influence aspects of any situation he entered. Such heightened sensitivity to power led to efforts to manipulate his self-presentation in order to maintain control over individuals whom he might experience as potential threats to his control. By controlling the story, he could also control how much of himself he would actually reveal. In this sense, his story could function as a protection, whether conscious or unconscious, to prevent the revelation of less crafted and more spontaneous (therefore more frightening and uncontrollable) aspects of himself. One could think of this performance aspect of his narrative as analogous to the patter magicians maintain in order to divert us from the real trick that is happening somewhere else (in this case inside the hearts and minds of the narrators).

Beyond his capacity to manipulate his narrative, Michael's adaptability in life turned any comfortable notion of a differentiated and authentic identity on its head. The rapid shifts in his life, his capacity to adopt new personas, to fit in, presented a disorienting challenge to my investment in seeing him as a real person, as someone I could trust and believe. I experienced this gap between Michael and myself as a genuine loss. Both the events of his life and the choices he has made left a rift that is not easily filed. How could he ever convince someone he was for real and how could he ever fully convince himself? These qualities of unreality and suspiciousness that had entered his very makeup loomed as a risk to any effort he may make toward recovery. Like the famous ending of the Orson Welles film *The Lady from Shanghai,* he lived in a hall of mirrors, and the shattering of each reflection revealed not his flesh and blood, but only another ephemeral image.

What compounds his challenge to an authentic and differentiated identity is that from an early age, as he described it, those around him, his parents and siblings, were also engaged in contradictory and disunited performances. In this beautiful Fairfield county home of the aerospace executive, alcohol abuse, incest, and physical torture may have taken place.[13] The brother whom he admired turned out to be a child molester. The sister whom he sought to protect from torture sided with her torturers. Michael clearly had no sense of others' authenticity or capacity to be anything other than individuals who act certain roles in certain circumstances. The whole structure of law enforcement at the city and the federal level was reversed for him; officers of the law fed him his drugs and shared in his corruption. Who among all these players in his life could teach him about commitment to his words, about staying still within himself, rather than leaping for the next role, the next way to gain advantage or momentary admiration?

In thinking about Michael, I have often returned to the first self-defining memory he described and have found yet another revealing aspect to its imagery. From the bars of his crib, Michael watched his family playing together without him. He clearly longed to be part of them and yet felt the nagging sense he had done something that had led to his exile. Sketched in this early memory is Michael's isolation and shame, but also his role as an observer, someone apart who watches and imagines a desired life inhabited by others. Throughout the rest of his story, he was often in this outsider role—in his closet, in the "hole," in the amber space of heroin, and in his undercover guises. His memory offers us a metaphor of a troubled individual, barred somehow from the natural activities of life, and from congress with his own flesh and blood. In exile, he observes the play of others, who themselves lead double lives, lives that have only a surface of intimacy and love, but contain beneath that surface confusing and destructive impulses. In this gap between himself and others exists his stories, efforts of performance that allow him to fashion links, coherencies that give him the capacity to belong to someone else's world. For now, Michael has replaced the solipsistic narrative of drugs and scams with a redemptive narrative of recovery; he is using this narrative to pull himself out of his personal cell and to enter the lives of his new wife and her child. If this new performance is to take hold in a different and lasting way, he will need more than the public displays of renewal and recovery that AA, church services, or even his married life afford him. He will need to look with cold sobriety into a mirror in a solitary room and say, "Is this me?" and not run from the reply. With a history of deception and performance in a society that increasingly confuses public and private worlds, Michael has many forces working against his ability to stay seated and survive that moment. If he does, he will feel the beginnings of a genuine ownership of his identity, of a story that finally steps back from dizzying reversals and holds its place.

What is the role of therapy, AA, or medication in this change? Only to help remind Michael that the fundamental question that shapes his life, or any life, is "Who am I?" and that we must find the answer, to the best that we are able, in authenticity and not artifice. If any of us hope to help men like Michael, we need to honor the complexity of the search for identity and to create conditions of safety and acceptance that allow a legitimate search to take place. As the many individuals I have known who have achieved a lasting recovery would attest, sobriety is a necessary but not sufficient task for answering the problem of identity. In a sense, the Twelve Steps only prepare the recovering individual to resume the large step all of us are perpetually taking, the crafting of an identity that holds credibility and meaning—a way of being in this world that is uniquely and honestly our own.

10. INVISIBLE MEN
The Absence of Identity

"Then I came to realize that men build themselves personalities as they build houses—to protect themselves from the world. But once they have built a house, they are forced to live in it. They become its prisoners."
COLIN WILSON, *The Outsider*[1]

When I first began to contemplate the problem of identity formation in men suffering from chronic addiction, the stories of abuse, violence, sexual struggles, and drug-dealing were the ones that captured my attention and influenced my thinking. Over time, I came to understand that although many chronic addicts told these more dramatic stories, there was another type of chronic addict, a quieter, less sensational one, whose story was actually a great deal more common.

This chapter addresses the stories of men who, either because of early effects of mental illness or the disruptive influence of early alcoholism (or both combined) have never embarked on the process of constructing an adult identity. Even though they have reached their late thirties or early forties, they have yet to sustain meaningful agency in the workforce or communion in their intimate relationships. Because of their inability to take on the challenges of either love or work, they remain at the margin of society and at the margin of adulthood, neither boys nor men.

Alcohol has become their primary means of self-medicating the anxiety and loneliness they experience in each attempt to function in so-called normal adult life. Though their alcoholism allows them to blend into a drinking world and avoid particular notice among their drinking peers, they remain essentially isolated, frozen in development and continuing to suffer from mental illness that is often untreated. These are men who never marry, never accumulate any property or savings, and who, more often than not, die unnoticed and alone.

An AA saying goes, "Alcohol is a great remover. It'll take away paint. It will take away pain. And eventually, it will take away your liver, your kidneys, and your life." For the quieter, solitary addicts, like Clark Grady (one of the sleeping poker players from Chapter 4, "The Boys of Skipper's Deck") and Seymour Harter, who tell their story in this chapter, alcohol has helped to remove their sense of isolation from their peers and from the human race in general. With the aid of alcohol, they can lose their self-consciousness and blend in with the world. In the dark corner of Ernie's Cafe on Bank Street in New London or at the counter of Dunkin' Donuts on Broad Street, they may feel momentarily enclosed in a force field of alcoholic safety. At such moments, with a good buzz on, alcohol can remove them from the critical scrutiny of others; they can relax and let go of their vigilance toward ridicule and rejection.

To capture the loneliness and quiet despair of Clark's and Seymour's lives, think for a moment of what it is like to eat a meal alone in a fashionable restaurant or even to arrive early and wait on your own until your companion arrives. When this happens to me, I sometimes make sure to have a newspaper or a book. Whether I have this external protection or not, I always rely on the internal protection of assuring myself that despite what anyone spotting me alone may think, I am really a successful person with a job, wife, and kids. These are touchstones that buffer me from a sense of marginality. In my roles as teacher, therapist, husband, father, son, life-long friend, I am a protagonist, a central figure, whose absence would not only be noticed, but felt forcefully and critically by a significant number of people. These reassurances remind me that, though I may seem momentarily alone, I have evidence in fact that I do matter, that I do count to others. Suppose however that your experience of being alone in a store, a restaurant, a movie theater is not an occasional oddity, but a daily fact. Suppose further that the sight of your aloneness cannot be internally assuaged by reminders of your connections to others and the reassurance brought by the roles you occupy in their lives. Your aloneness is not an appearance, but the fundamental fact of your identity. With this in mind, it is no wonder that invisibility becomes such an attractive feature of alcohol.

Remember Tom Sawyer and Huck Finn's comical crashing of their own funeral when the entire town had assumed they had been killed by Injun Joe. Twain was playing on the universal fantasy that we could be present at our funeral to hear the testimonials to the value of our lives and the positive influence we had on others. Often after the death of a head of state or a beloved performer, newscasters will report the number of people who attended the service and cameras will depict the crowds assembled outside the church or hall. I still recall with pride and a bit of astonishment that when my wife's mother died suddenly at age 57, a memorial service held a few days later on a Monday drew 900 people. In no way a public figure, my mother-in-law, a bookstore owner and the town doctor's wife, had lived a life grounded in relationship. She never lost track of a person who had passed through her orbit; she wrote cards, made phone calls, took the time to pay visits. Despite her varied interests and accomplishments, the true meaning of her life had been in the web of human connections she had woven in an unbroken skein among the periods and places of her life. Whether surrounded by family members or seated alone at a restaurant table, these relationships and her sense of secure belonging inside them allowed her to feel noticed, to accept being seen alone without feeling vulnerable and revealed in her isolation. Her connections to all kinds of people, from her immediate family to the customers at her shop, were the warm wool she could pull up around her to fend off the chill of despair that comes with knowledge of our essential separateness from others.[2]

When I think of the notice of her death in the *Boston Globe*, detailing her education, her record of work and community service, and the loving family members she left behind, I contrast these words with the notices I would read about men who I had known from the Pines (the nurses used to clip them and pin them up for us to read next to charts and memos at the nursing station). One notice in particular of a man from the Pines has stayed with me. His name was Willy Diamond and we had all known him for years. He had been through the detox and the Pines countless times. He had had moments of hope and success through our halfway house. At one point, Willy, with his Yankee cap and teeth like a jack-o-lantern, had even worked the telephones for us at the New London facility. Still, he had gone back out drinking and in his last years descended into living in SRO's (single room occupancies) and not even bothering with treatment or rehabs. He might come through for an occasional forty-eight-hour detox, but he was gone the minute his time was up, and then we might not see him for months. He died in his mid-fifties from a fire started in his room, after he fell asleep and his cigarette ignited his bed.

The notice told his age, that the cause of death was smoke inhalation caused by the fire, and mentioned the funeral parlor handling the arrangements. For the vast majority of readers of the *Day* (New London's daily newspaper) that particular morning, his death was an item they passed over or read with little interest. A transient, middle-age man, most likely an alcoholic, had died in a motel fire, and left no one to mourn him. The alcohol's magic had done its trick; it had turned a man of flesh and blood, of mind and heart, invisible. If we looked behind those lines of newsprint, uncoiling them like the white bandages of the invisible man, we would find the increasing emptiness of form, until what once seemed a human frame became a memory of shape, and then, effacing itself, thin air. Alcohol, the great remover.

Clark's and Seymour's stories explore how men can embrace alcohol to protect themselves from being seen. They also demonstrate the cost this invisibility inflicts upon their prospects for living soberly. They are not there to be counted or to be counted on. When expectations arise, they disappear. Like the lost boys who live in Peter Pan's Neverland, they never advance and never engage with the demands of adult life. A sober life based in family, friends, work, and community is a prospect more terrifying than their impending death from alcohol. They live passive lives robbed of responsible freedom and meaning. As a consequence, they continue to drink and relapse after repeated sober stretches of six months or a year in institutional settings like Lebanon Pines, rehab hospitals, and halfway houses.

Their stories raise one of the hardest questions to confront in our society: "How willing are we to commit to the principle that every life matters, every life is sacred, every person is worthy of love and notice, attention and patience?" Clark and Seymour have built lives of isolation, premised on the often accurate conviction that no one really cares too much about them or their future. This conviction was first hardened in their years of public schools, where the only solution to their experiences of social awkwardness and embarrassment was to withdraw. They learned at that moment that nobody particularly cared if they disappeared; as long as they avoided criminal or deviant behavior, as long as they engaged in their self-destructive behavior relatively quietly, it was of no consequence to the world around them. They could simply "get lost" and everyone else could get on with the business of finding work, partners, and families. They could float on the margin of the society, in roadside bars, minimum-wage factory jobs, boarding houses, and weekly-rate motels and no one took notice.

The problem of their sobriety, then, is not simply that men like Clark and Seymour must find themselves, that they must suddenly build an identity out of the responsibilities and relationships that they have never previously accepted. The equal problem is that we, as a society, must find them. We long ago absolved ourselves of the responsibility of integrating these individuals into our world. We colluded with them as they slipped away, unconsciously acquiescing with their quietness and withdrawal. As long as they were not causing disturbances on the playground, as long as they were not robbing or stealing, their silence and their absence went unremarked. Recovery for alcoholics who discovered invisibility at an early age is a daunting prospect. It requires full re-engagement of society in raising these boy-men to true adulthood. This task cannot be accomplished with brief visits to rehabs, AA meetings, and outpatient treatment. Anything less than a multiple-year intensive involvement would be insufficient to repair the internal damage they and the world around them have done. Of course, this type of intervention asks a great deal of resources from the society and from professionals responsible for their treatment. So, as we hear the stories of Clark Grady and Seymour Harter, please ask yourself, what can they do and we do about their lives? Can they find themselves and can we find them? And if so, how can these discoveries be achieved?[3]

Clark Grady

In the interviews I conducted with the men of Lebanon Pines, the responses to my requests for self-defining memories were revealing in a variety of ways. Most times, the self-defining memory clearly stated the themes of family conflict, loneliness, or substance abuse that were to dominate the narratives of the men's lives. Yet for some men, the self-defining memory was revealing in that the man selected it as an isolated example of how he wished the rest of his life could be—the memory was like a special place that he had found once and now lost, and was unlikely ever to revisit. I remember, as a child, traveling to the woods at the top of the hill where I lived and discovering, with a boy whom I did not know well, a tiny pond with reeds and large bull frogs. This boy did not come to play with me again, and I could never find my way back to this spot. It then became a place that I would find in dreams at night, gradually taking on an even more serene and magical character. Finally, I could no longer say with certainty if I had ever been to this pond in the woods; perhaps it had been part of my dreams right from the beginning and I had only wished it into memory.

Clark Grady told me a memory like that, that had given him a pleasure he has seldom regained.

Here is an event that has meaning for me because I've missed out on a lot of normal living. I've never been married. I don't have children. I never even owned a car. I've never had a job since '75 and here it's almost '95. So all my memories are nothing that has any real great significance because they're not something you'd want to remember, as far as childhood goes. I didn't have a father growing up. Well, around thirteen, I went with these neighbors fishing. And I've only been fishing twice in my life and both times was when I was thirteen and fourteen. I went in a rowboat out into the ocean and it was an experience and if somebody asked me if I ever had any amount of time what would you wish to do? And believe it or not, I would like to go deep sea fishing or learn to scuba dive.

My family in Hartford, in the city—we never went on vacations. So it was like being given a gift. "Clark, would you like to go the beach with us for two weeks in Branford, Connecticut?" It wasn't asked to me first, it was asked to my mother, then to me. This was prior to my ever having picked up a drink. I wasn't smoking cigarettes then yet either. I guess why I'd pinpoint this memory is that I was having the feeling of happiness, you know, running in the water, something I never did before, other than in a swimming pool and then that was going back to when I was ten. I guess it was something that you did together. It was togetherness, even though I wasn't really big friends with Mike again after that time. It was something for me, an experience that I have never experienced again.

The circumstances of Clark's life bear out the relative impoverishment of experiences that he alluded to in this memory. At the time of his interview he was forty-one, and he had spent the last twenty years of his life more often in rehabilitation facilities than outside them. Invariably, Clark is a responsible, compliant, and altogether pleasant hospital patient, Lebanon Pines resident, and halfway house occupant. He is quite trim and meticulously neat, to a point of obsessiveness. He wears white virtually all the time—white tee-shirts, white pants, and beautifully maintained white basketball sneakers. Having lost his hair in his early twenties, he prefers to shave his head. He resembles nothing less than a hospital orderly and is often mistaken for one by new patients or residents. He is pale and square-jawed, with dark eyebrows, and soft brown eyes.

He grew up in a working-class neighbor in Hartford, in a mix of Irish, Italian, and some black families. He attended Catholic schools up until he entered the Hartford public high school. His mother and father lived in separate apartments within the same apartment building and continued to do so well into his adulthood. His father was and is a heavy drinker, who never participated regularly in either raising the three children (Clark has an older sister and a younger brother) or providing much economic support. On weekends, around the time he was fourteen, Clark would leave the basketball court at the park and hop over two fences that enclosed a field. At the end of the second fence were the railroad tracks and a large weeping willow tree. Under that tree, Clark could find his father and a band of other men—Tracy Gafferty, a man they called "the Indian," and Chickie Regan.

I used to go collect the paper route money on Saturday and I would go see my father and I would bring him peanut butter sandwiches and cheese sandwiches. I would open up the weeping willow tree and it was all cleared out, except for in the middle there was a place where you could start a fire. You could walk right by it but unless you opened up the tree, you wouldn't know there was nothing there.

I was young and impressionable. It's like wanting to shave when you're nine years old, wanting everything too fast, you want to grow up. So my father, or my father's friends when he wasn't around, would give me a couple of beers. And I would go there on Saturday and see Indian or whomever, my father even. And they'd buy me a six-pack of beer from my paper route money and I would sit there, drinking a six-pack of beer, in my little fort.

With Clark's father not contributing money to the household, they were always struggling financially. His mother collected money from the state and worked part-time as a librarian as well. Clark took on jobs—the paper route, short-order cooking, and farm work. His sister attended a Catholic high school and they had little contact with each other. Clark was quiet and kept to himself in school, managing to advance each year without catching the notice one way or another of his teachers or the school officials. In the early seventies, he easily fell into smoking pot as well as drinking, and found a small group of neighborhood boys who would smoke and drink with him. By the time he was sixteen, he had started to feel a strangeness or difference about himself, as if he did not belong among the "normal" kids in school. His day-to-day feeling in class or the hallways was one of nervousness, of not fitting in, of being abnormal. He found that he wanted to drink to get rid of this feeling of strangeness, of being a misfit.[4]

Alcohol at that age was the number one thing to get out of that feeling, not for getting drunk, but just to get out of that normal way of feeling I had growing up. You
know, I didn't have any normal highs, some people got into athletics or school
work and can get high from that. I so easily fell into getting high on substances to
where it directed my life up to the present day, as to where exactly I'm going to
live, and what's going to happen.

Clark graduated from high school in 1972 and, with his aunt's help,
found a good job at a wire factory. It was a union lifetime job and he was set
up with a nice weekly wage. He was drinking daily at this point and began a
pattern of missing Mondays. The company sent him to a rehab in 1975, but
he resumed drinking shortly after he finished this program and soon lost his
job. He worked at another factory in that year, but barely lasted a few
months, before his absences led to his dismissal again. At this same time, his
mother kicked him out of the house, telling him that she had put up with
one drunk all her married life and she was not about to go through this a second time.[5]

Clark's swift and comprehensive descent into alcoholism marks him as
what Jellinek long ago called a gamma alcoholic.[6] According to this line of
thought, these individuals seem to be particularly genetically susceptible to
alcoholism and have little ability to control their intake of alcohol once they
begin to drink. This pattern most closely fits the stereotype of AA's depiction
of the man allergic to alcohol.

Unable to restrain his drinking, Clark distanced himself from his family.

So, I left the house. I had a lot of animosity back then—it was February—but personally I would do that to my own son, if I had one, 'cause I understand. I am an
alcoholic and I understand. If my blood brother is drinking and slobbering drunk
and he comes over, I'll make up a story that I have to go to the dentist. The following day if I see him and he's sick and shaking, I'll dig into my pocket and give him a
couple or three dollars, but I do not want to be around intoxicated people. And if I
can't deal with it, how do I expect Joe Blow down the corner to understand him? If
you're sick, I sit down and talk to you, but I don't care if you're five foot two and
your eyes are blue and you're stone naked, I don't want to be around you if you're
intoxicated.

One reason that Clark had no arrest record and had never spent a night
in jail was precisely because he gave such a wide berth to people that became
sloppily drunk. He would leave a bar immediately if he sensed that the
crowd was too rowdy or loud. He told me that he has a great phobia of being

locked up in a small space and is afraid a cell would drive him crazy. His only run-in with the police was when he was eating an ice cream cone in a restricted area of the Hartford Civic Center. The police tried to kick him out and he was slow to leave, so they brought him to the station house on a charge of criminal trespassing. He laughed in telling the story, thinking about how they had removed his shoelaces while he was waiting in the holding cell. Giving up his ice cream cone may have been an annoyance, but hardly grounds for hanging himself from his cell bars.

I asked Clark about any significant relationships during this period of his life, from his early teens to his mid-twenties. He said he had a girlfriend for a brief time, but if she drank one beer in an evening, he would drink six. He was always chasing a way to feel less different from other people, more comfortable with himself.

I might be open to a relationship now, because I feel, without alcohol, my life is empty. You know, I feel lonely. But back then, it was a selfish feeling. When I drank a couple quarts of beer, or a half pint of vodka, that was not drunk, but that was not feeling normal either. I could not see then what alcohol was doing to me. I just knew I somehow had to get out of the way I was feeling at the time. That was the priority over anything.

Alcohol took away that normal everyday feeling of never any bright spots. I would feel good after a game of basketball, but there was never any closeness in my life; I just never had any close male or female friends. . . . That's kind of a sad thing to say, but that's the truth. . . . I have had plenty of people that I know through association, but there is not any friends. Growing up, I called them friends, because we'd hang out together. But that's the last time I've seen them, when I was nineteen years old, any of the people I grew up with. I'm forty-one, that's twenty-two years ago.

After losing his jobs in '75, Clark ended up enlisting in the Navy with the hopes of breaking his routine of drinking. He found himself talked into joining by a very persuasive recruiter.

He starts telling us stories about these girls in Europe, how they think every American's got money and they damn near tackle you when you get off the boat. He was telling us how many times he got laid in the Netherlands and in Spain, and Jesus, like not only myself, but three out of the four men sitting there listening, decided to join the Navy.

After basic training, Clark was stationed in South Carolina, where his most graphic memory was of the beer machine down the hall from his duty station. He paid thirty-five cents for Pabst Blue Ribbon, and the local liquor store sold quarts of Bacardi Rum for five dollars a bottle. He was making more than $200 every two weeks with no bills or other expenses. He drank so heavily that he found himself in the base hospital with abdominal pains. They gave him an exam and ended up detecting tuberculosis in his right arm. He was treated with steroids and lost all his hair in about five months. For the duration of his convalescence at a medical facility, his only duty was to say "here" for roll call in the morning and recuperate the rest of the day. He drank heavily during this time, and eventually he could not even make it to the morning roll call and say "here." He was discharged honorably due to medical circumstances (his TB, not his alcohol abuse) and returned to Hartford in 1977.

From 1977 to 1982, Clark tried to resume civilian life and find work, but instead he spent more time in detoxes and treatment programs. He began to confront the basic fact that he did not know who he was without alcohol.

Using alcohol has been my personality. Taking it away is like taking away my personality, 'cause I have always conducted myself behind drinking. . . . When it's raining out, get under an umbrella. Whenever I had anxiety or fear, I would go out and get a drink and that would be my umbrella. . . . I call the regular people out there earth people. They're on the earth and living off the earth. I'm on some far-off land drinking and hiding. I'm not an earth person. . . . I was uncertain about everything, from going out on dates to job interviews. And alcohol provided me with, not gumption, but it provided me with a little backbone.

. . . I never had a pet, never had a dog. I don't mean to sound like poor Clark. I'm just trying to explain, trying my best to, explain how much, how easy alcohol came to be my friend, my only companion, 'cause it gave me comfort. I tried to get comfort in different areas . . . [long pause], but it seemed like when I started to try to do it, all of sudden Clark's lost his self-confidence.

This was one of a few points at which we had to stop our interview to allow Clark some time to collect himself. Clark told me that he had never told his story at an AA meeting and had only once before revealed this much about himself during an intake for psychotherapy. He had been sober for more than a year when I interviewed him and it is possible that his insights into his life history and his own sense of pain and loss were more clear and sharp for him than they had ever been. I could hear clearly in his words a mixture of fragility, passivity, and self-pity. He seemed stuck in a place that simply being sober could not repair. He somehow needed to gain the sense of his own efficacy, of his own capacity to function independently in the world. Yet how does anyone give this sense to another person, how can it be taught? It is one thing to increase self-efficacy in relationship to a specific behavior or fear, but what do potential helpers offer to a man when the basic steps of living his life appear to be overwhelming for him?

In what was now becoming a pattern, Clark's body collapsed again in 1982 and broke his cycle of drinking and rehabs. He suffered acute kidney failure and was brought unconscious to the Hartford Hospital emergency room. His legs were filled with fluid and he was unable to work. He ended up staying four months in the Newington VA hospital and then was sent in a wheelchair to a convalescent home in Rocky Hill. He spent almost two years at this home, working on recovering full use of his legs. His roommates were a seventy-two-year-old stroke patient and a man unable to talk or walk after being paralyzed in an automobile accident. Clark was twenty-nine years old.

Being the youngest man in the facility and slowly regaining his health, he soon became a favorite of many younger nurses who worked there. In particular, he grew close to one nurse who would spend hours telling him about her life and problems in her family. He was convinced that there was a real possibility of a relationship developing and they even had some moments of physical intimacy. However, Clark had found someone in the kitchen who would smuggle drinks for him, hiding them underneath a pine tree on the grounds. When he finally discharged, he took up his daily drinking, and though the nurse would call him on occasion, he could not bring himself to reciprocate her interest.

As with many men at the Pines, Clark found himself caught in the "Catch-22" of receiving SSI payments because of his physical disability; the checks removed his initiative to better his life or resume efforts at employment. Without the checks, he felt terrified about his ability to work and feared he would end up on the streets. From 1983 to 1986, he lived at a boarding house, collected his monthly check, and drank from morning until he passed out at night. He might have continued this way indefinitely, but he began to have severe seizures and was forced to move out. At this point in his drinking history, his morning shakes and sickness were so painful and overwhelming, he needed to have a half-pint of vodka to be able to function. After the second half-pint, he might feel sufficiently normal to get up out of his room and go outside for a short time. With nowhere to live, he finally came to Lebanon Pines in 1986.

His first stay at the Pines lasted only a matter of months and he was kicked out for smuggling in a bottle. After a few more years of boarding

houses, detoxes, and rehabs, and another short stay at the Pines, he managed to stay there from 1990 into 1991, a total of a year and eighteen days.
After this long stretch of sobriety, he felt he had to leave and test the waters
on his own. He got an apartment in Hartford and set out to live a sober life.

I'd wake up in the morning to a bowl of cereal. I'd make my bed. I'd take a shave
and shower. I'd look over at the clock and it's twenty after seven in the morning.
So I'd get dressed and I'd go get a paper and I'd read the paper from page one to
the end and, look up at the clock, it's ten minutes to nine. I had nothing to do. It
lasted three weeks. Then one Saturday, I said I gotta get a drink. I gotta do something and I did and I drank for a year and four months without any more treatments other than detoxes.

What Clark's words make clear is how a sense of identity buffers us
against the profound loneliness and purposelessness that is inherent in existence. By establishing a sense of meaning through work and relationship, we
are able to stave off the anxiety that consciousness of our own mortality and
fundamental insignificance awakes in us. Without love and work, or the
analgesic of alcohol, Clark is trapped in a state of existential despair. Compare his words to Camus's description of this same despair.

> Here I am defenseless in a city where I cannot read the signs . . . with-
> out friends to speak of, in short, without diversion. In this room pene-
> trated by the sounds of a strange city, I know that nothing will draw
> me toward the delicate light of a home or another cherished place.
> Am I going to call out? cry out? Strange faces would appear. . . . And
> now the curtain of habit, the comfortable tissue of gestures and
> words, wherein the heart grows sluggish, rises slowly and finally
> unveils the pale face of anxiety. Man is face to face with himself: I defy
> him to be happy. . . . [7]

After Clark's return to drinking, he began to suffer more severe seizures
and was again kicked out of his housing. He received a promise from Bill
Sugden that could he return to the Pines again on August 1st of 1993. This
meant he needed to live in the shelter for twelve days until the 1st arrived.
The shelter had strict rules about no drinking and Clark was determined to
abide by them; he had never slept in the street and did not want this to be
the first time. The shelter asked all residents to leave by seven in the morning and then reopened its doors at four in the afternoon. For that span of
nine hours, Clark had to walk the streets, sober.

In them nine hours, I've been on streets sick before and drinking before, but never on the street sober before. And during that time, I was trying to find something to do, and I was actually seeing what the streets were really like, soberly true, first time.

. . . And the thing that bothered me most, it wasn't that I was afraid, it was just flat out loneliness. That's what it was. I saw maybe half a dozen people that I knew in those twelve days. Maybe a couple of them waved to me and we talked for a little bit, but that was it.

. . . And when I'm feeling sick or if there is something I don't want to do, I think about them hours of sitting on them benches. Out of nine hours, seven were sitting on my ass with nothing to do. Just watching people coming and going—this is working hours—people going to work.

Clark sat on that bench and, for all intents and purposes, was invisible; his existence, his claim to life, felt nullified. In this story, we can identify the one sustained imago of his life; he is like an alien among earth people, an alien who cannot even be seen by normal human eyesight.

Despite a few stray beers over the twelve days, Clark managed to make his way back to the Pines and had remained there up to the time of the interview in October of 1994. The staff was determined that he make another effort at living outside the Pines and had set a deadline for Clark to leave in another three months at the beginning of February of 1995. As we finished the life history, Clark increasingly returned to his anxiety about what he would do when he left, how he would fill the time and avoid feeling his profound sense of loneliness. Since Clark had suffered so many failed attempts at halfway houses, the staff was reluctant to give him a bed in a halfway house that another more determined man might be able to use. Instead, they were recommending a less restrictive option, a three-quarter house. Far from ideal, it was better than an apartment on his own in Hartford, which was certain disaster.

What am I going to do in a three-quarter house in the boondocks? I am flat out scared. The first bus stop is two miles away. What am I gonna do? Here, people don't realize the commodity that Lebanon Pines has and that's company. You got 106 people here. You can get by the day playing cards or bullshitting or watching some program together on TV. When Clark's alone by himself, I want company. And the first thing I think of is drinking. . . . I want something to wake up to, and I'm not talking about a wife. Something to belong to.

. . . I know people who say "get into AA and you'll make friends and meet people" but it's easier said than done for me. It takes time. . . . For me to be able to conduct myself, and gives me a little electric shock to say this, but for me to start standing up and quit bending over and finding things wrong, would be a big deal. But it is something you got to work at and I'm just about one of the laziest sons of a bitches going around.

I would just like to have some ability to take care of myself. Skillwise, workwise. I had aspirations of becoming a great chef and I signed up to go to a culinary institution once or twice and that fell through because of drinking. So I don't have any skills to fall back on.

I have no family to send me dollars. I more or less divided myself from them by not bothering them with my problems. My brother and sister each have their lives. My parents are in their seventies and I just separated myself from them. I've been protected by Lebanon Pines, but Bill's the best. He said, "I don't want to be an enabler by allowing you to keep coming back here." What's that saying . . . shit or get off the pot! I am facing a whole new door and I don't have nothing to fall back on except making sure that I stay sober.

In response to Clark's words, I tried to make some encouraging statements about how it might work out for the best and how his counselor can help him develop a plan for his days. In my heart, though, I could feel his fear and my own. What protection or promise could I offer him against the long mornings of idleness or the lonely ticking of the clock at night? Clark's situation makes clear how vital a role AA can play for recovering men in providing them with "something to wake up to" and a place to go. Yet the problem for men like Clark is that they cannot allow themselves to feel worthy of the company AA offers. For Clark, AA is a repetition of the schoolroom class—he is with a group of people who, whether they show him kindness or not, are "earth people," while he remains the alien. He has had too many unsuccessful efforts at AA and no longer feels that he belongs among the members. It is ironic, yet sadly true, that even though AA is based in an egalitarian ethos ("we are all drunks"), there are many chronic alcoholics who do not feel they fit in with the group. Clark is comfortable going to the meetings when they are based in hospitals or rehabs and are drawing on men similar to himself, but once he is out in the community and attending meetings with people who have jobs or families, he feels hopelessly inadequate.

The one other emotion that is missing from Clark's story, and that might have surprised him to hear mentioned, is anger. Clark's helplessness and passivity in the face of his slow self-destruction invariably generates anger in counselors who work with him. His helplessness is re-experienced by each successive counselor as his or her own helplessness in trying to move Clark forward. In psychodynamic terms, this process is called *projective identification*.[8] The client is experiencing an extremely uncomfortable or unacceptable emotion (e.g., anxiety, anger, sadness, sexual desire) and is unable to acknowledge or articulate these feelings. In order to allow these feelings expression, the client unconsciously creates circumstances that create the exact same feeling in the therapist. The therapist first registers the existence of a strong and not fully explicable emotion. With sufficient alertness to the process of projection, the therapist can then express awareness of this emotion and place it in a more structured and verbal context. To complete the process, the client can then identify with the therapist's appropriate response to the threatening emotion. The client receives the modeling of how to experience and process strong feelings, feelings that terrified the client sufficiently to cause the projection of them into the therapist's psyche.

I suspect that Clark bears great anger over the desolation he experienced in his life. If he was indeed a lost boy, then he knows full well that someone lost him long ago. Imagine Clark living in the same apartment building as his father, but barely receiving money or attention from him (unless they were drinking together). Whether rightly or wrongly, Clark may still harbor anger at his mother for washing her hands of him when he was barely nineteen years old. Finally, Clark may reserve the greatest anger for himself, for his failure to take initiative, for his willingness to give in to the institutionalization that has been a persistent theme in his life since the mid-seventies. This accumulated anger is connected to his current state of powerlessness to change his circumstances and to begin the business of living a life.

Clark then has the capacity to project these feelings of powerlessness and anger on to everyone of the counselors with whom he works. Unfortunately, it is very difficult for any counselor working with him to move beyond this sense of enraging impotency and to model for him a more healthy way of dealing with these feelings. The result may be a sly (perhaps unconscious, perhaps not) victory by Clark over each of his prospective helpers. A supervisor of mine once described this process as the "power of powerlessness." An adolescent or young adult can paralyze a household by claiming to be incompetent or unable to separate from parents. The more the adolescent recites inadequacies and displays ineffective behaviors, the more the parents jump in with suggestions, solutions, and alternative plans. Defeated at every juncture, the seemingly potent adults are reduced to exhausted failures by the "powerless" child. For adolescents on the brink of independence and a substantial loss of control, the sense of control they can gain from thwarting their parents' efforts and expectations may be a reasonable compromise in reducing their anxiety.

The only way to break this deadlock is to work with the parents to step back and allow the adolescent to proceed on his or her own; their helping efforts only reinforce the adolescent's sense of inadequacy. The adolescent, in turn, must learn other ways of feeling power than the habit of thwarting helpers; he or she must experience examples of autonomous efficacy. In partnership with a therapist, peers, or older role models, these changes can slowly be achieved. The same will need to be accomplished with Clark, but he has been lost for so long and his sense of powerlessness is so entrenched, that the battle to gain this ground is that much more difficult.

The image of invisibility is relevant here as well. The invisible man has power over those who can be seen. He can affect the visible, disrupt their lives, but he glides on untouched and elusive. By drinking and retreating behind the force field of his alcoholism, Clark cuts off connections to his helpers, remains beyond their grasp. The control and mystery gained by this behavior have the capacity to frighten those affected by it. The Invisible Man, though more human than the other nineteen-thirties Hollywood horror icons, rightfully belongs in that pantheon with Frankenstein, Dracula, the Mummy, and the Wolfman; they all begin with human elements, but they grow to possess an otherness that we cannot fully understand or trust.

I will finish Clark's story for now with a look at how he responded to the T.A.T. cards presented at the end of the interview. His responses were particularly revealing of the frustrating passive-aggressive trap his drinking has created for him. The first card he examined depicted a boy sitting rather glumly in front of a violin. Most individuals grasp the achievement struggle inherent in the picture—does the boy want to practice or not; is he going to achieve any skill or expertise with this instrument? Clark indicated that the boy's mother wants him to play, but he has no interest whatsoever. He would like to please his mother, but "he's trying to find the easy way out." There is no resolution to Clark's story—the boy is simply stuck in this dilemma of wanting to please, but also wanting to avoid unpleasant effort.

In the next picture, of a man angrily pulling away from a concerned woman, Clark first saw the woman as a nurse (reminiscent of his relationship in the convalescent home). He then decided it was a married couple and the man has a drinking problem. The woman is trying to help him, but he wants to drink more than he wants the help. She really loves him, and even though he goes out and drinks, she will still let him come back. Clark described the look she gives to her husband as "too much caring."

The third card is more ambiguous and depicts a young man in the foreground with a dream-like image of what appears to be a surgical operation in the background. Clark described the boy as living in the past and filled with memories. He is recalling his illness and not focusing on the present. He is caught up in hoping that he will never experience this illness again and he is looking for something to take away his memories.

Finally, the last card displays the heads of two men, an older one beside a younger one. Clark saw the younger one as in a lot of trouble and the older man as his lawyer. The lawyer is explaining that because of his past behavior, he will have few choices about his future. He has to pay for what he has done in the past. I asked Clark how this story turned out and he told me that the young man goes to jail and loses everything. He ends up with hatred in his heart toward even the kindest person. He feels sorry for himself and wishes he could blame somebody else, but he cannot.

The consistent thread of these projective stories is that Clark finds no positive ways of resolving the dilemmas of his protagonists. There are loving characters present, but the protagonist of the stories can find no comfort from them and in fact is likely to continue hurting or displeasing them. This frustration leads to self-pity, anger, and a desire to blame others, as well as a strong wish to make these feelings magically disappear.

In powerful symbolic language, Clark conveys the agony of his passivity; he feels stuck in the past and unable to change the future. His stories emphasize the necessity of identity formation for the ability to imagine goals and future plans. By knowing who we are, by grounding ourselves in a sense of agentic purpose and communal connection, we not only recognize our origins, but inherit an agenda of activities and relational commitments for the years ahead. Without an identity, we are like the boy with the violin, who has yet to take up his instrument, thereby avoiding the daily practice of adulthood.

Clark left the Pines as scheduled in early February of 1995 and moved into the three-quarter house. As he feared, he drank fairly soon after his arrival and resumed his circuit from detoxes to boarding houses to rehabs. Though the treatment world only reinforced his sense of helplessness and immaturity, he has learned to find all other worlds full of terror and defeat.[9]

Seymour Harter

In contrast to Clark Grady's cherished memory of a fleeting experience of companionship and happiness, Seymour Harter recalled a memory that spoke directly to his sense of isolation and difference.

When I was three or four, I was always telling my mother I wanted to go to school because my older sister was going. I can always remember shaking on my mother's dress, "I want to go to school!" Well, then when I got there, I don't know if I really liked it; things didn't work well for me. I didn't have any idea what I was getting into. Fear set in, and I was in with all these groups of people and it just didn't seem like I fit in.

Within this brief recollection we can find a central recurring theme of Seymour's thirty-seven years. He always experienced himself as not as good as other people, as not belonging in their company. He told me at several points that he drank to find sufficient self-confidence to converse with other people rather than shy away from them. Unfortunately, he often became surly or argumentative when drinking, which only served to undermine his hopes of improving his relationships with others.

Right from hearing this memory, I wondered what it could be in Seymour's life that had led him to experience such overwhelming feelings of inferiority and inadequacy. He believed that one of the dominant influences was the fact that his mother had suffered from schizophrenia throughout his childhood and early adult years. Though he loved her very much and was her favorite among the three children (an older and a younger sister), he still endured great embarrassment and pain because of her illness. She made repeated visits to the state psychiatric facility in Norwich for weeks or months at a time. When she returned, she was more or less stable, but she would stop taking care of herself after a few more months and the illness would return. I asked Seymour to talk more specifically about the nature of her schizophrenia.

She was never violent, but she would always tell me that people were trying to kill her, the people on the TV, the newscasts were talking about planning her death. She used to get cigarettes from this guy in the Navy because they were cheaper, and she thought that he was putting drugs in her cigarettes to try and kill her.

When his mother would suffer a psychotic break, his father and grandparents would look after the children. His father was a policeman and a stern, quiet person. He did not show much emotion and Seymour never saw him cry. He was an attentive parent and made sure all of the material needs of the children were met. Seymour remembered that on weekends his father would throw pizza parties for the family and bring home pizza and soda. All of the children would get to sit on his lap and it was a very pleasant time. Nevertheless, the whole family lived in a constant tension over when their mother might lose touch with reality again.

When Seymour was around ten, his mother became fixated on an imaginary person named George who was going to come to their home and give them millions of dollars and wonderful gifts. There had been a real man named George at a factory where she had worked and she had first believed that this George was trying to kill her. This fear became so vivid for her that it may have been necessary to transform George from potential killer to loving benefactor. Through constant reminders about his mother's potential assailants, Seymour learned a substantial fear of people. As he continued on in school, his conviction that others would be mocking or cruel to him was borne out.

I always felt out of place. I never thought anybody liked me. I remember being fearful of people. In third or fourth grade, if I thought anybody was making fun of me, I would retaliate. I might tip over someone's desk. But after that, I seemed to go back inside myself and I would hold everything in. After fourth grade, I wouldn't talk to anybody too much.

I asked Seymour if he had ever tried to explain about his mother's condition to other children at school, or if he had received any social support because of her illness.

I told one friend and he went and told his parents. I was really mad. I was planning to beat him up, but his mother spoke to me and my mother, and promised it wouldn't go any farther. But people know . . .

My mother couldn't clean the house very well; she wasn't capable with her heavy load of medication. She was on the couch all the time. She smoked cigarettes and drank coffee constantly. She would get a good-sized jar of instant coffee and a gallon of milk a day, and drink it all. And not using any hot water, she would just put the coffee in the milk and stir it up. It was real sad. . . . She was very overweight and ended up with diabetes.

Besides his mother's schizophrenia, there were other areas in which Seymour felt an extreme self-consciousness. When he was a little boy, he fell face first off a porch onto cement and broke his nose. A few years later, he rebroke it again running into the corner of a building while playing kickball in the school courtyard. The result of these two accidents was that his nose was flattened out considerably and a little off center in the bridge. He was teased by his sisters and other children, who called him "nigger nose" and "toe nose." His first name had always been a source of teasing for children in school as well. He dreaded starting each new year in school and having to go through the first attendance roll call. He still remembers a time when the teacher said his name and a boy shouted out, "Who the hell is Seymour?" The whole class laughed at him and he felt himself cringing in his seat.

I asked where the name had come from and he explained that it had been his father's name and his grandfather's name. For a long time, he had suspected that it was related to his having some distant Jewish background, which he saw as another potential source of shame for him. Years later, when his sister had a baby, he was looking through a name book and saw that in fact it was an Anglo-Saxon name.

Seymour took some pains to explain to me that regardless of his mother, his nose, or his name, he also had a basic conviction that he would not make friends or become part of a group.

It wasn't *all* that; I just thought people didn't like me. I wasn't accepted. I didn't fit in. Even if I didn't know them, I'd just say, "That person doesn't like me." To myself. Nobody likes me.

Ironically, Seymour had his greatest success in school at exactly the point where he was first experimenting with drinking and smoking marijuana. He had joined the freshman football team in ninth grade and in order to remain eligible to play had raised his grades from D's to C's and B's. The following summer before tenth grade, he was even made a starter in the pre-season workouts. Yet he found that his interest in using alcohol and drugs far outweighed the motivation he had felt for football and he soon quit. I asked how it could be that drinking and drugging took precedence over an activity in which he was experiencing success and a modicum of acceptance.

I remember that first euphoric feeling. A friend and I split a pack of Budweiser and I just felt like the weight was lifted off my shoulders. I felt that I could talk to people and be compatible. I thought people would be my friends. I didn't have any fear of being rejected.

In the spirit of the times, Seymour quickly moved into other drugs besides alcohol and marijuana. Throughout high school, he used LSD, mescaline, mushrooms, and various uppers and downers. I wondered if his drug and alcohol use presented any special problems for him, given that his father was a police officer. He explained that he was stopped a few times for driving under the influence in high school, but when the officers saw who he was, they would drive the car home for him and leave him inside. His father also found a marijuana pipe in the family car one time, but did nothing more than have a talk with him about how hurt his mother would be if she found out. Seymour felt that having a father in law enforcement was a great enabling force for him.

His fear of people extended into a dread of dating and getting close to females in high school. He recalled two occasions in which he came close to having a relationship but was terrified to pursue it. In the first situation, he had been told a girl was interested in him, but he could not bring himself to speak to her or even to call her for fear of rejection. In the other situation, Seymour managed to get up the courage to ask a girl he truly liked to go to a Blue Oyster Cult concert with him. Once he was at the concert, he drank so much more than she did that they could barely communicate the remainder of the night. This parallels what happened to Clark Grady in his one failed high school relationship.

In 1976, Seymour graduated from high school and took a job at Electric Boat. For a young man already facing the beginnings of a serious substance abuse problem, there could have been no worse place to work. The ship-yards of Electric Boat (where they build nuclear submarines) are noisy, dirty, and dusty. The work involves grinding, welding, and the coating of metals with solvents, paints, and other chemicals. The workers there are often young men who have been attracted by EB's advertisements placed in news-papers all over the country. Much of the work does not require lengthy apprenticeships and can be accomplished by men with few prior skills. The shipyard accordingly attracts a rather rough bunch of transitory workers. What many of them have in common is that they are also hard drinkers.

Seymour worked as a chipper-grinder. He ground wells, cleaned and flushed them with solvents; he also cut angle lines in metal and worked at grinding machines. This kind of job was in the thick of the hottest, dirtiest, smelliest work that the shipyard had to offer. At lunch break, the workers would lead a virtual stampede toward the bars outside the yard. Seymour said his group of co-workers had a favorite table at a restaurant bar and before they reached their table, there would already be three or four pitchers set out for them each lunchtime. Seymour felt that part of the reason the men drank so much was that they were doing government contract work and once the orders for the submarines were in, they felt no particular pressure or incentive to perform.

No matter if you show up drunk, EB's getting paid. They don't care about produc-tion, this is how I feel. I would take two or three days off, go to the lake, get drunk. Most of the people there were able to maintain and get drunk. People sleeping, not doing nothing all day, just getting drunk and sleeping in tanks.

After two and a half years there, he was given a choice of quitting or being fired for lost time. He moved on to another job working at a textile mill.

After two years, just after his twenty-fifth birthday, he faced the same alternative, once again for missing work. In the midst of all his problems holding a job, his mother died in his presence.

I came out of my bedroom and she was face down in an ashtray, dead. One of those big ones. I picked her up and her face was full of ashes. And see, I knew my mother so well, I didn't know if she was playing a joke on me or not. She came into my room that morning and she said, Bud, do you have any cigarettes? And I said, "No Mom, I don't." And she goes, Come on, Bud, I know you've got a cigarette." And I said, "No, Mom, I don't." And she said, "Well, O.K. for you." And then she says, "I don't feel good, I don't want to walk down to the store." I said, "O.K., I'm sorry, I don't have any cigarettes." So she closed the door and I heard the door close that meant she was going outside to the store. It was only 100 yards away.

The thing is that I might have had some. I don't know. I might have been out drinking the night before. And where usually, if I was sober, I would give her anything just to make her happy. But if I was drinking, I might say, "I don't have any."

. . . And there she was. I thought she may have been playing a game on me, trying to make me feel bad. And I picked her up and I pinched her cheeks. I went to the faucet. I didn't know what to do. I was in shock. I threw some water on her face. Then I just called the police and the ambulance and I just knew that she was dead.

There was never an autopsy. I never received a death certificate. I'm sure my father has one. I'm sure it was a stroke or a heart attack. She was very overweight and she smoked five packs of cigarettes a day.

After his mother's death, Seymour's drinking grew even heavier and more overwhelming. He continued to move from factory job to factory job, now unable to stay at a place more than a year. He also found that he became increasingly belligerent and argumentative whenever he drank. His behavior led to some arrests for disorderly conduct and breach of peace. When he entered a blackout, he was capable of any unpredictable action. He once left his motel room to go to the bathroom, forgetting that he was nude, and then fell asleep in the lobby. Another time after a police officer kindly drove him home, he turned to the officer and told him that he was a fucking asshole. He was arrested for urinating on a car in a parking lot. Seymour expressed to me his confusion over his angry, aggressive behavior when he was drinking.

I would never want to hurt anyone. I hear people saying that when you are under the influence, that's how you really are. And I don't believe that. I don't believe I'm capable of being that rude or mean. Except for when I'm drinking. Maybe there's some anger there—I went through an anger group at the Pines. But I still don't think I'm an angry person, a real angry person. I'm the silent quiet type. . . . I don't even like killing ants or bugs or cutting trees down. Alcohol is just the devil, that's all I can think of. Brings out, for me, the devil.

In the mid-eighties, while working for yet another company, Seymour went through a series of twenty-eight-day rehabilitation programs. The owner of this particular company, in which they made laboratory instruments, liked Seymour a great deal and felt he was an excellent worker in periods when he had his drinking under control. He continued to hire Seymour back and to pay for his rehabs through health benefits. All told, Seymour must have worked for this company over a seven-year period with several interruptions because of his drinking and rehabs. Over all these years, Seymour also intermittently attended AA meetings. I asked him to tell me more about what role AA played for him.

I've been going to AA, off and on, since I was twenty-five. I think even my mother was alive the first time I attended an AA meeting. I feel better after I've left a meeting. I felt I had things in common with people. It helped me to grasp the concept that I was an alcoholic. I remember before I had gone to my first meeting how I was riding around in my car and I said to myself, "All I do is drink and work and spend all my money." And I started saying, "So what?" That's when I really didn't care.

I asked Seymour in that period before he started AA and rehabs if he was still feeling positively about his drinking. Was it a source of confidence for him or perhaps pride in how much he could drink?

I always felt negative feedback, because I made a fool out of myself when I drank. And I always tried so many different ways of drinking—just going out on the weekend, just bringing so much money with me—then I'd just end up going back and getting more. I'm only going to drink on Saturdays. I'm only going to drink once a year, but it never worked. It's the only thing that I knew how to do in my life. And how to be accepted, or how I thought I could be accepted by people. Today I know I was not accepted by people when I drank. But it gave me an illusion of acceptance.

Seymour's words about drinking highlight the theme of this chapter, "It's the only thing that I knew how to do in my life." His experience of agency or competence was tied up with alcohol, as was his desire for acceptance and communion from his peers.

By the late eighties, Seymour's life had become a blur of drinking, arrests, and detoxes. He told me that he had few memories of that period and that he had begun to experience greater fear of other people.

I would drink if I went out. If I didn't drink, I would stay home. I thought people were pointing at me, I thought people were looking at me. I was paranoid. I was afraid of people. If I had a drink, I could go places.

In 1990, his drinking took him back to the twelve-day in-patient program at SCADD and he then entered one of SCADD's halfway houses. He remained sober for ten months in the halfway house and then for an additional three months after he left. This thirteen months of sobriety was the longest stretch of clean time he had experienced since he was fourteen years old. Since that period, he managed to have other long blocks, of ten months and six months. His last five years up to 1995 were spent more sober than active, but unfortunately the majority of this sober time was in some form of institution, whether hospital, halfway house, or Lebanon Pines. His first visit to the Pines was in 1992 for five months and he moved on to the halfway house again after leaving the Pines. It was during this second stay at the halfway house in New London that Seymour came to see me in my capacity as staff psychologist at SCADD. He found that he was suffering increasing problems being around people and that he had experienced a few bouts of panic attacks.

Lumps in my throat, pains in my chest. And I've had these off and on through the years, but I just never knew what they were until I started getting really bad where I would see things move. But they weren't moving, I told you this before, it just seemed like I was seeing the world through Plexiglas and my heart was racing. It's awful. It takes all the energy out of you and you can't do anything and you just gotta lie down, if you can. Massive crying attacks, couldn't stop crying. I made it five months in the halfway house and I couldn't take it any longer so I had to go out and drink. People were starting to get to me again. The fears and the pointings and the making fun ofs, I used to kid with the guys because they had microphones down there on Howard Street, and you can hear them in the winter all over the town saying, "Please move your cars." And I was just kidding with them, saying they were calling for me on those microphones, and some of the guys still kid me today, "They're still talking about you down on Howard Street." So I left there and I drank and I ended up going to another detox.

Seymour was able to get work again at the same instrument company and lasted there for another year or so. The owner was completely aware of Seymour's alcoholism, but also felt that Seymour knew the business inside and out. So he would squeeze what work he could out of him until Seymour stopped showing up and then he would let him resign. It was an enabling relationship that Seymour saw as a mutually exploitative situation. Though he had employment and money, he knew that the owner would always push him harder and expect more until he would need to drink and escape from the situation. From the owner's perspective, he was getting expert labor at a cheap price and considered himself lucky if he could get six months to a year out of Seymour before the drinking overwhelmed his performance. What is striking in this pattern is that Seymour clearly displayed the capacity to be a fine worker and might have developed, without the destructive influences of his alcoholism and mental illness, a sense of agency and competence. With these factors at play, he repeatedly fell back in the opposite direction, experiencing a sense of inadequacy and failure.

By 1993, Seymour had reached such a point of desperation that he had made two suicide attempts through overdoses of blood pressure medication. After the second one landed him in the hospital, his sister and brother-in-law stepped in and offered to have him live with them on the conditions that he see a psychiatrist and not drink. He lived with them for approximately three months and during this time, he began to take antidepressants and Klonipin, an anti-anxiety drug.[10] He claimed that they were helping him to feel better and less anxious around people. However, after the three months, he ran into an old drinking buddy and decided to drink with him. In the course of the day of drinking, he took an overdose of his antidepressants and the Klonipin. He went into a coma for four days and was considered quite lucky to have survived. After that experience, he could no longer live with his sister and ended up back at Lebanon Pines.

Seymour was more positive about this most recent stay at the Pines. He continued to take his medication and also began to go to psychotherapy. He started to address the fundamental problem that he had no understanding of how to live without drinking.

The program didn't work for me because I still wanted to drink. That's the way it's been for me, I don't want to drink, but I get out in society and I don't know how to live. I don't know how to live a life of sobriety. All I know is how to drink.

. . . In my counseling, I've told that lady more about myself than I ever told anybody. I've told her, like I told you once, about the dogs. I could be 20 miles away and I would be talking to a dog, one of my sister's dog. I don't know why, a thought would come to mind. Like negative thoughts, like a guy on my shoulder always putting me down. "You're an asshole, you're no good, you're not worth it, why are you living on this planet, you're a waste, just a waste. And I would just yell out my sister's dog's name, "Sadie!" I would talk to the dog. Nothing special. I don't know why.

I always liked that little dog. I would say "Sadie, help me!" I've also started going to church. It helps put the Twelve Step program in perspective. I don't know if I consider myself a Christian yet or not, but I like the fellowship of Christianity. I believe in it. I believe that they are good, honest people. There are days that I know I am a good person and I know I'm honest. But there's days I have panic attacks still. I still have these crying binges. I get into the black holes. And I know I couldn't stay sober on the streets right now.

The black holes mean no hope. Might as well die, kill myself. Drink myself to death. Or shoot five or ten bags of dope, as much as I could fit in a syringe. You know, my last roommate here at the Pines shot himself in the head. He was my roommate in the house of four. I'm sleeping in his bed now.

Can We Find the Invisible Men?

The life histories of Clark Grady and Seymour Harter confront us with an aspect of addiction that does not lend itself neatly to the Twelve Step recovery model. The overarching theme for both men is that they had not developed any sense of adult identity, of responsible work or intimate relationships, before they found alcohol.[11] Alcoholism gives them a pseudo-identity, a way of both being in the world and disappearing in a crowd, and it gives their life a putative purpose (at first, to find a way to get drunk, and later, to find a way to get sober). With sobriety, they repeatedly experience the reality of their unformed identity, naive in the ways of relationships and of sustained work; they also feel no motivation or greater sense of meaning in their lives. It is understandable why within a few months of self-imposed sobriety (as opposed to institutionally imposed), they invariably flee back to drinking. They are finding their way home, back to the only clear understanding they have of themselves.[12] The shuttle from rehab facility to detox to rooming house to shelter back to detox and rehab is a familiar and, at some level, comforting world. They know the detox technicians, the nurses, and the fellow clients. There are few expectations placed upon them and minimal responsibilities. They may gain little self-esteem from these places, but on the other hand, they can compare themselves to men who are worse off than they are.

Both Clark and Seymour, in remarkably similar language, told me that stopping drinking was no longer the primary problem, the real problem is knowing how to live a life. Unfortunately, much of the recovery literature and rhetoric assures individuals that if they accept their alcoholism and maintain sobriety, everything will eventually fall into place and life will improve. For many successful AA participants, not drinking brings a return of loved ones to their lives, an increased efficiency at work, and a renewed sense of self-respect. They find their old selves again; they become the person they knew they were capable of being. Rather than repeated nights of bleary drunkenness, their new life of sobriety seems light-filled and pregnant with possibilities for growth and human connection.[13]

For men like Clark and Seymour, who as of yet have been unable to connect to AA, their not-drinking confronts them solely with emptiness and loneliness. They never embarked on the process of adult life and, now that they are in their late thirties or early forties, wonder if it is too late to begin. The rhetoric of recovery does these kind of men a disservice when it tells them that if alcohol is removed from their lives, all will turn for the better. When we strip men like Clark and Seymour of their alcoholic veneers, what are we offering them in return? If it is simply to sit in a cheap room with no prospect of work and little social contact, what do they have to protect themselves from the sense of inadequacy, isolation, and meaninglessness that predates their drinking and never goes away (except in moments of inebriation)?

Chronic alcoholism of the type presented in this chapter is not amenable to the current system of detox, hospital rehabilitation, followed by structured living situations (halfway house or three-quarter house). These men easily meet the criterion of suffering from dual diagnoses, both addiction and psychiatric conditions. Their capacity to make active choices was effaced early in their lives both by their difficult family situations and their embracing of alcohol. Clark's depressive passivity and Seymour's paralyzing anxiety are deep-seated emotional responses to the challenge of living; they are as potent methods of retreat and withdrawal as their addictions.

Yet the solution is not simply to get them sober and then treat their psychiatric problems with medication. As of the time of our interview, Clark had taken an antidepressant for almost twelve years (Elavil) and Seymour had had experience with Elavil, Paxil, and Klonipin. Both of them either went off their medications during periods when they elected to drink more heavily or used the medication to take overdoses. Treating Seymour's anxiety or panic attacks with medication and behavioral techniques did not address larger issues like his ignorance of how to ask a woman out on a date or how to adjust himself to the routine of working five days a week without absences or quitting. Sobriety and treatment of psychiatric symptoms are a beginning, but unless he received active help in learning the basic skills of life outside institutions, he would be likely to return to what he knows best—drinking.

Historically, there has been little integration of the mental health and addiction services at the state level. Often psychiatric facilities would refuse to admit clients if they had an active alcohol or drug problem. Similarly, supportive living situations for mental health clients would discharge clients if they were found to be drinking in their apartments or group homes. From the other direction, many addiction treatment programs were hesitant to admit clients with extensive psychiatric histories for fear that their staff, who were usually recovering addicts with little advanced training in mental health, would not be equipped to work with these types of clients.

The 1987 McKinney Homeless Assistance Act spearheaded a series of nationwide, innovative programs that attempted to provide more effective interventions to chronically addicted individuals who also suffered from psychiatric conditions.[14] Most relevant to the current discussion of men like Clark and Seymour were efforts to create *intensive case management* for the chronically addicted. Case management in general refers to the assignment of a client to a helping professional who is responsible for assisting clients in all facets of their recovery (e.g., housing, medical concerns, job retraining, counseling services, support groups, etc.). In most instances, the case manager does not directly provide services, but functions as a broker in the community to help clients navigate the social service and rehabilitation systems. Case managers ideally check in frequently with clients, serving as sources of support and information.[15]

Intensive case management means a much lower ratio of clients per case manager, more frequent contact, and more direct intervention to broker services.[16] Typically, case mangers for chronically addicted individuals may carry a caseload of thirty to fifty clients. Some of the McKinney Act demonstration programs achieved ratios of fifteen to seventeen clients per case manager. This lower ratio, in theory, allows for greater personal attention and follow-up than the average case manager can provide. For repetitively relapsing clients like Seymour or Clark, this involvement means a more careful monitoring of their tendency to isolate and slip back into destructive social habits. It means more opportunity to help these men build up the social skills and supports they will need to sustain sobriety. Finally, intensive case management allows the case manager to tailor the array of services provided in the community to the specific needs and problems of the client.

Going even one step further, one of the demonstration projects, Arapahoe House in Denver, Colorado, piloted a dyadic case management program. This program assigned two case managers to each client with the following goals in mind—availability to the client at all times, differing perspectives on the client, a blending of case manager strengths, and reduction of burnout and stress for the case managers.[17] Though this approach may sound highly labor intensive and expensive, the designers of the model point out that if it can remove individuals from the cycle of chronic addiction and sustained homelessness, the reduction of costs to the society would more than justify the initial expense.[18] Though a preliminary evaluation of the effectiveness of this model did not find stronger improvement for the dyadic case management clients versus clients receiving Arapahoe House rehabilitation services without case management, the authors of this study correctly point out that follow-up was only based on a four-month period, which is hardly sufficient to detect meaningful changes in a pattern of lifelong addiction.[19]

In addition to this intensive case management approach, an evaluation of various innovative programs emphasized that supported housing as opposed to transitional housing was a question of great importance.[20] Transitional housing refers to the residential care that Clark and Seymour have tried numerous times (Lebanon Pines, ninety-day programs, halfway houses, three-quarter houses). These housing options vary in structure and supervision, but all are stipulated to be temporary and not permanent dwelling places for clients. Supported housing refers to apartments or houses that receive some case management supervision, but are permanent homes for the clients until they elect to move out or can no longer function appropriately in such a setting. Evaluators of the homeless projects feel that this sense of ownership and permanency may make a significant difference in the commitment and stability clients feel toward their residences.

Even with intensive case management and a supported living arrangement, Clark and Seymour would need to develop more self-reliance and independence over time. In the long run, they would be expected to achieve a stable sober functioning without this kind of intensive management by others. The true success would be when men like Clark and Seymour can make the passage into adulthood and manage consistent employment and social relationships. What should be obvious from this discussion of innovative programs is that society must be willing to allocate considerable resources toward treatment and housing. Yet, despite the creativity and dedication of these demonstration projects, the federal government has not initiated a new round of funding for similar projects. In fact, with the passage of welfare reform, the federal and state allocations for services to the chronically addicted have been severely curtailed.[21]

Without these kinds of innovative and committed efforts to reclaim them, Clark and Seymour will continue to flounder, isolated and perpetually relapsing. Out on the streets alone, Seymour will call to the magical dog, Sadie, to protect him, and Clark will take refuge beneath a remembered willow tree, where under its safe umbrella, men and boys can pass their bottles in peace. Alcohol will continue to function as a magic potion, slowly erasing their lives, until they disappear in a world that had long ago lost sight of them.

Conclusion:
RECOVERING IDENTITY
AND MEANING

. . . {K}nowledge of others depends on my own identity. But this
knowledge of the other in turn determines my knowledge of myself.
Since knowledge of oneself transforms the identity of this self, the entire
process begins again: new knowledge of the other, new knowledge of
the self, and so on to infinity.

TZVETAN TODOVROV, *The Morals of History.*[1]

In the intervening chapters between Chapter 1 and this conclusion, I have
applied a life story framework of identity to answer two fundamental questions: Who are the men suffering from chronic addiction and what prevents
them from achieving sobriety? I have asked the men of Lebanon Pines to
answer these questions by telling me their stories, their life stories of identity.
Despite the diversity of the men—gay, straight, black, white, rich, poor,
mentally ill, athletically gifted; Vietnam vet, businessman, ex-con; alcoholic,
"crack head," opiate addict—they share the common fact that chronic
addiction has led to lives in which agency is frustrated and communion
thwarted. No longer able to define themselves according to the normative
expectations of society, they feel isolated and vulnerable to the forces of
existential despair—death, freedom, isolation, and meaninglessness. They
retreat from this despair through their defensive strategies that precipitate
their relapses—the surrender of agency, blind habit, and destructive agency.

Relying upon the consciousness-altering properties of substances to take them out of time and self, they escape from the unified and differentiated demands of meaningful identity. In so doing, they momentarily dull the pain and loss associated with their lives.

At first, I felt that this shared story seemed to answer my question about the identity of men suffering from chronic addiction. Yet I have grown to see that this narrative of thwarted agency and communion, and consequent despair, does not fully account for why the men are unable to achieve sustained sobriety. Much to my surprise, the stories the men told seemed to reveal a missing aspect from my model of identity that may play a critical role in their battle with sobriety. What emerged from collecting and analyzing the men's stories (and a theme to which I had not given sufficient emphasis) was the overwhelming sense of disconnection the men felt from not only the sober world, but from the world of recovering addicts. This disconnection, as it was expressed to me, went far beyond the sense of frustrated communion I had been primed to discover. The men's disconnection from the world is the articulation of what it feels like to be the person sleeping on the street corner whose picture I showed to my seminar on addiction (see Chapter 2). It is the utter horror of invisibility toward which Clark Grady and Seymour Harter appeared to be heading. As men sink deeper into the world of chronic addiction, their sense of no longer being part of mainstream society escalates. This sense of marginality hardens into a conviction of difference and separation. Their primary relationships are eventually reduced to only other fellow addicts and treatment providers. This separateness presents a massive hurdle to overcome before they can even entertain the prospects of accomplishment and relationship. For the men of the Pines to recover a sense of identity and meaning in their lives, they must first regain a sense of connectedness to the sober world. Becoming "visible" again means more than the ability to experience a sense of self-efficacy or knowledge that people care, it requires an experience of reciprocal connection felt by both the men in recovery and the non-addicted world. In sum, what is missing from the identities of men suffering from chronic addiction is a belief that their lives are embedded in the same world and reality to which the rest of us belong.

Aliens and Earthlings

Whatever the chronically addicted man's background, whether he has had great success in life or a period of intimate involvement with others, by the time he has reached the Pines, his fundamental experience of life is what Howard Bahr, writing about Skid Row, called *disaffiliation.*[2]

> As long as a man has viable social ties, i.e., has other persons bound to him by reciprocal rights and obligations, his defectiveness, is, at worst, partial. But the more disaffiliated he becomes, and the more powerless, the less "needed" or "expected" or "obligated" he is, and the easier it is for the adjectives "lost," "forgotten," "passed by," and "surplus" to be applied to the self. With the passing of obligations go also rights, and the new self-definition is imprinted via stigmatization, victimization, and discrimination in interaction with others.[3]

This sense of disaffiliation represents the end of the story that men suffering from chronic addiction construct of their lives. Filled with imagoes that portray destructive others and self-destructive self-images, their stories weave narratives of agentic and communal failures. Their ideological settings tend toward pessimism and a cynicism about their prospects in the sober world. Their personal myths capture themes of abandonment, loss, betrayal, and disappointment.[4] They have come to experience themselves as outsiders in a world unto themselves, or as Danny Doyle (Chapter 4, "The Boys of Skipper's Deck") described it, "We are the only ones that will put up with each other, no one else will."

Clark Grady (Chapter 10, "Invisible Men") called this sense of separateness the feeling of being aliens in a world of earthlings. Both the men's histories and their current pattern of relapses have combined to make them feel cut loose not just from sober society, but even from the society of recovering addicts, as exemplified by AA and its fellowship. They experience themselves as the addicts that even the other addicts don't want to have anything to do with.

In the next section of this chapter, I shall catalogue the different aspects of disconnection experienced by the men of the Pines. The men's destructive pattern of relapses often causes the non-addicted world to perceive the men as incomprehensible and frightening in their inscrutability. Those of us who have never struggled with an addiction find ourselves wondering how a man can give up a successful rehabilitation, his new apartment, and the friends he has made in AA to pick up a drug that will only bring him back to the street again. Both the chronically addicted and the non-addicted rely upon physical or quasi-mystical explanations that do nothing to close the gap between this alien behavior and the behavior of men pursuing sober lives.

Yet another level of disconnection felt by the chronically addicted is that they themselves cannot account for their relapses. Part of what makes them feel alien is the narrative incoherence of their lives. We, who structure our lives around the pursuit of agency and communion, may not fully achieve these twin goals, but we fashion narratives that offer accounts of why or why not. For example, someone may have chosen a life of accomplishment over close relationships; or another person has placed his family first over his work; or a man's obligation to a dying parent has blocked his freedom to marry a desired partner. Most "earthlings" have stories that, despite unhappiness or tragedy, make sense. Until the chronically addicted reach a sustained sobriety, they will continue to feel this otherness about the apparent illogic of their stories.

Another problem of being "aliens" is the knowledge that one has come from another place and that this place does not resemble the sober world. Though the chronically addicted men of this book come from diverse places, all have shared a common experience of feeling different long before their chronic addiction escalated this alienation. Because of social conditions of homophobia, racism, or poverty; or familial circumstances of incest, physical abuse, or abandonment; or psychological conditions of trauma, severe anxiety, or depression, each man early in his life felt that his place did not belong among the normal world. Paradoxically, even Billy Zeitel (see Chapter 7, "Who Was Inside Mickey Mantle?") through the quirk of his athletic gifts, lived a life, before his decline into addiction, that separated him from the normal path to agency and communion.

Choosing to Be Aliens

In attempting to articulate the varieties of disconnection felt by the men, I should also point out that some men who reach the same place of chronic addiction did not begin life with a sense of stigmatization or rejection by family or society. A subset of the chronically addicted are self-styled aliens; their initial separation from the conventional path of identity was a conscious choice. This preference for drugs over sober life can be traced all the way back to the cults of Dionysus, who saw their drunken revels as a path to the divine.[5] Certain men who embrace substance use have simply found themselves unwilling to accept the story of identity that our society offers to them. In many cases, they discovered that alcohol or drugs could free them from what Baumeister has called the "burden of the self."[6] What exactly is this burden? Recall the words of the "Black Irishman" from our discussion of destructive agency in Chapter 2.

People always tell me I'm a quitter, that I ran away from responsibility and relationships. And I'd agree, but I always told myself, bullshit. I'm not running away. I'm running to something—to feeling free the way most stiffs couldn't. . . .

The life of alcohol or drugs can be seen initially as a way of detaching the self from a life burdened by responsibilities and relationships. The men's refusal to participate in the work world or in conventional families or marriages might be seen as what Seymour Fiddle has called an urge to "unmask" the hypocrisy of the sober world.[7] Men suffering from chronic addiction may feel that they are engaged in the pursuit of a purer or truer story. The ecstasy[8] that they have discovered through alcohol or drugs represents a superior existence to the daily and inhibiting routine required by conventional society. Applying existential terms to this perspective, the men might argue that if the pursuit of agency or communion is simply one way of creating meaning in an otherwise meaningless world, then why not see the release and pleasure offered by drugs as an alternate path with its own advantages and disadvantages?

Though this vision of alcohol or drugs as a source of liberation or creative energy may sustain the men for a long while, they ultimately acknowledge the toll that physical addiction takes upon their lives. That same Black Irishman from Chapter 2 went on to say to me:

The fuck of it is that your body isn't built for that much liberty. I've been taking liberties with my body and it's finally saying no. Pancreatitis, sugar in the blood, legs going numb. I feel like a tree in October. Things turning brown and yellow, and falling off me right and left.

Jim Carroll, the poet and musician, who had found moments of intense excitement and pleasure in his heroin use, described the end of his addiction in this way:

> I wind up in the last scene: strung out and nothing to do but spend
> all day chasing dope. Any way counts, folks. No way to any Riviera
> and no rich momma to run to. Like you just know when you're in
> the real junkie thing when you wake up in the morning and say to
> yourself and know it and go through with it, "Today I either get my
> fix or get my ass busted into the Tombs, fuck it all.[9]

Fiddle cites the words of Dante's description of "The Gluttons" in purgatory.

The sockets of their eyes were caves agape; their faces death-pale, and their skin so wasted that nothing but the gnarled bones gave it shape.[10]

When I first read these words, I realized I had seen a living face like this. In the early 1980s, I went on a trek to visit hill tribes in Thailand. In one of the small villages we passed through, we entered a hut and came upon an old man lying on a wooden bed, smoking opium. The long stem of his pipe extended to the floor so that he did not have to rise from his bed; his skin was barely stretched across his skull and his eyes had the hollowness that Dante described.

Choosing Death over Recovery

In the end then, regardless of the route the men have taken to their experience of disconnection, their chronic addiction brings them all to the same place. As one resident of Lebanon Pines expressed it in Chapter 1, the wax at the bottom of the candlesticks eventually all looks the same. What they find at the bottom of the candlestick is a simple existential choice—a descent toward death or the prospect of rejoining the world from which they have been separated. In light of this choice, the various types of chronically addicted men must either accept the gathering momentum toward death or figure out a way of aligning their sense of identity with the "story of recovery" that seems the only route to reentry into mainstream society. This juncture of decision is a familiar place for men who have arrived at Lebanon Pines or who repeatedly return to its grounds.

If the men choose to begin the process of coordinating their sense of identity with a story based in the pursuit of agency and communion, both they and their treatment providers face the daunting task of converting them from aliens to earthlings—this is in essence the set of challenges I described at the end of Chapter 10, "Invisible Men," in discussing the recoveries of Clark Grady and Seymour Harter. As we shall examine later on in this chapter, an additional challenge involved in this conversion the recognition of how society itself contributes to these categories of alien and earthling, and therefore creates a major resistance to bringing the chronically addicted back into sober life.

For the present, however, let us consider the other option, the possibility that some men confronted with the prospect of death through their addiction actually embrace this alternative. I have come to see two important ways to understand men who select this option. First, for those men who have found in drugs and alcohol an alternate story to the conventional one of agency and communion, the demand to give up their story results in a despairing alienation. Unable to sustain their alternate story, they are unwilling to invest effort in a new search for meaning. These men are most likely to say "Fuck it," and slowly drift back into their substance use with occasional half-hearted efforts at rehabilitation to placate the legal system or avoid the discomfort of the street. I fear that Danny Doyle, the poker player with the winning hands from Chapter 4, fits this type quite closely.

Less obviously, there are some men who have never sought a story in the first place. The attraction of the altered consciousness that substances could provide to them was not a mystical arrival at ecstasy, or a romantic statement about the freedom of a tramp's life, or the camaraderie of a drinking circle, but the simple fact that alcohol and drugs could free them from the burden of having to make a story at all, of having to establish a defined self among other selves. Through drugs, they could be closer to a kind of death, a non-knowing life that could not be parsed into a narrative. For these men, their chronic addiction confronts them only with a deep sadness. The breakdown of their bodies and their dependence on social services limits their use of substances, and somehow death does not come with the swiftness they desire. All sobriety does is demand a story they have no interest in writing.

This kind of man is quite common in the world of chronic addiction, but his life is only minimally represented in this book. For the most part, by their very willingness to speak with me, the men I interviewed had not succumbed to this full-scale embrace of death. John Brown (Chapter 3) had felt this way at points in his life, but certainly ended his life with a commitment to the value of the world. Thomas Turner (Chapter 5) and Michael Cochran (Chapter 9) had engaged in very bitter periods in their lives, but still had returned repeatedly to a hope of recovery. In fact, these men's willingness to narrate their stories to me was a statement about the possibility of good and value coming out of their lives. For this reason, we should consider some of the men who refused to be interviewed. One man in particular sticks in my mind.

Men Without Stories

When I first heard about him in a staff meeting, I thought he would be ideal for my study. He had long ago abandoned his family and drifted for decades up and down the east coast of this country, living on the streets or in one-room motels. He had had plenty of treatments and none had taken effect. It seemed to me that he could provide a deep insight into the world of the chronic street alcoholic. Unfortunately, when one of the counselors at the Pines approached him to tell his story to me, he declined. When asked why, he told the counselor to tell me he wasn't interested in anybody knowing his story; he wanted to be left alone. There are many men like him who pass through the detoxes, the shelters, and Lebanon Pines with barely a word or notice. They seem to be claiming a right to silence and oblivion.

These men, and their insistence on being story-less, remind me of what the psychologist Karl Scheibe has called nature's fundamental moral indifference to our lives.[11] When we make stories of our lives, we are constructing narratives that define protagonists with goals and concerns. We are turning the indifferent world into a world that matters and holds significance to us. Outside our effort to fashion meaningful narratives, a world of physical matter carries on, oblivious to our interests or commitments. Scheibe quotes Annie Dillard's depiction of this material world, "Nature's silence is its one remark."[12] He goes on to point out that individuals who refuse to invest their lives with any kind of narrative meaning are akin to Melville's famous Bartleby the Scrivener who, when asked to account for his virtual paralysis at work, can only say, "I would prefer not to."[13]

As the men who elect to be story-less know full well, their lack of narrative keeps them from participating in any form of living community; without a story, there exists no means to locate their identity in a shared narrative of common experience. Advocates for support groups to aid recovery from addiction or trauma emphasize repeatedly how the sharing of stories allows a sense of connection and fellowship to develop. Denzin has written about the experience of the recovering individual in AA.

> In order to find himself he has to learn to speak a language that others before him have produced. He can only learn that language by listening to others who are also learning how to talk and think with the same set of meanings.[14]

In the same vein, Judith Herman has described the connection the survivor of trauma feels to the other members of a therapy group once she has shared her story and allowed herself to identify with the stories of others.

> Only at this point can she contemplate her story as one among many and envision her particular tragedy within the embrace of the human condition.[15]

One's story told aloud and linked to the group gives one a membership in a band of storytellers, a home in which to rest. The men of the Pines who deny themselves this home deny themselves a sense of identity. In a literal sense, they cannot be identified and pass through our streets as perpetual aliens, separate and unknown.

If these are men rejecting what, as McAdams would suggest, is the essential enterprise of being human, what are they electing in its stead? My best answer is a form of "death-in-life." The head-nodding semi-awake state induced by heroin or the blacked-out alcoholic state on the verge of unconsciousness represent retreats into an autistic universe that block out any kind of meaning or engagement with life. In such states, one is not really "here" and therefore expectations of accountability and responsiveness to others are undermined. The story-less man has found a way to evade the moral responsibility that is inherent in being a part of storied community.

In Malcolm Lowry's novel *Under the Volcano,* the drunken Consul, having destroyed his marriage through his alcoholism, wanders into a church and pauses before a statue of the Virgin. For a moment, he prays for reconciliation with his wife, but then gives in to a deeper impulse to reject the life he feels incapable of having.

> "Please let me make her happy, deliver me from this dreadful tyranny of self. I have sunk low. Let me sink lower still, that I may know the truth. Teach me to love again, to love life." That wouldn't do either . . . "Where is love? Let me truly suffer. Give me back my purity, the knowledge of the Mysteries, that I have betrayed and lost. Let me be truly lonely, that I may honestly pray. Let us be happy again somewhere, if it's only together, if it's only out of this terrible world. Destroy the world!" he cried in his heart.[16]

The literature of modernity is filled with this kind of alienated stance toward life, and often alcohol or drugs are the companions of this alienation. We can trace this attitude all the way back to Dostoevsky's depiction of the underground man who declares in his polemic:

> Does not man, perhaps, love something besides well-being? Perhaps he is just as fond of suffering? Perhaps suffering is just as great a benefit to him as well-being? Man is sometimes extraordinarily, passionately, in love with suffering, and that is a fact. . . . Whether it's good or bad, it is sometimes very pleasant, too, to smash things.[17]

Or more recently, we can find this world-rejecting sentiment in the poetry of John Berryman, who suffered from alcoholism and took his own life. In his "dream song" poems, he used the alter ego of "Henry" to express his own struggles and grievances with life.

> Henry hates the world. What the world to Henry
> did will not bear thought.
> Feeling no pain,
> Henry stabbed his arm and wrote a letter
> explaining how bad it had been
> in this world.[18]

Implicit in all of these views is more than a rejection of life; these men are also voicing a fascination with or affirmation of destruction and death. In discussing Tyler Casey's inability to move on with life after the trauma of war, I mentioned Freud's concept of Thanatos, a death instinct that urges us toward destruction and the negation of life. Without subscribing to the notion of Thanatos as a basic biological motive of human beings, I have witnessed this impulse toward death in many of the men I have known from the Pines. Some lines of verse by Malcolm Lowry, who was himself an alcoholic, captures this very point.

> His soul had never been empty of fear,
> And he would sell it thrice now
> For a tankard of beer
> He seemed to have known no
> love, to have valued dread
> Above all human feelings. He
> liked the dead;
> The grass was not green, not even
> grass to him;
> Nor was sun, sun; rose, rose;
> smoke, smoke; limb, limb.[19]

Of the all the men I interviewed, Tommy Reilly, the angry poker player from Chapter 4, "The Boys of Skipper's Deck," most clearly conveyed to me his dissatisfaction with life on life's terms. At the end of interview, he made it clear to me that he was not likely to stop drinking, despite his efforts at rehabilitation and alcohol's destructive effects on his body.

Approximately a year after I interviewed him, he killed himself through an overdose of heroin. He had called his former counselor at the Pines shortly before his death to tell her his intentions. He was deaf to any pleas for further treatment or words of encouragement or hope. In thinking about Tommy since his death, I have come to believe that his decision to tell me his story was, in part, an acknowledgment that his death was near. Having fought against being part of a community all his life, and sensing that this struggle was ending, he allowed himself to take a step toward reclaiming an identity. He could take this step, knowing it would be unlikely to be followed by many more in the time he had remaining.

To summarize my analysis thus far, I have suggested that the unifying theme of chronically addicted men is more than just frustrated agency and communion, but a pervasive sense of disconnection from the world of both non-addicted and recovering individuals. I have tried to characterize a variety of forms of disconnection that men in chronic addiction experience, including their pariah-like status as chronic addicts, their lifelong sense of separation born out of negative life circumstances and psychological conditions, and the incomprehensibility of their addictive behaviors. In addition, I have identified a subset of chronically addicted men who have chosen their disconnected status, either in favor of an alternate identity based in drug and alcohol use, or in an effort to reject a storied identity of any kind.

Having articulated these various forms of disconnection, I would like to turn to the question of how these men and we, the non-addicted and the recovering, might reach across this divide that separates us—by what means can we help the chronically addicted rejoin our community, assuming they have indicated a desire to become part of the agentic and communal world? To answer this question, we will need to turn to an examination of the other side of divide—the world of earthlings that the rest of us inhabit. As most of us well know, this world is hardly a safe haven where the pursuit of agency and communion is over a smooth and untreacherous path.

Why Earthlings Fear Aliens

In breaking down the barriers that exist between the chronically addicted and the sober world, I would start by raising the question of why we do not want to look at the homeless man sleeping on the street. Most of us find him frightening for a variety of reasons. His unkempt appearance raises the aura of illness, infection, and the hovering presence of death. His desperate circumstances suggest that he might ask us for money, or even more ominously, try to rob us. His homelessness and poverty also frighten us because they convey a palpable message of failure and loss, of what can happen to a life that is bereft of love and work.

In sum, we fear this sleeping man for the message he conveys about the consequences of a loss of identity in our contemporary society. Without a job, without people who love us, any one of us could end up on the street like him. This nagging fear is what drives us to avert our eyes and quicken our step. It may also contribute to our willingness to accept a disease model explanation of his condition. If he has a bad genetic makeup, he is qualitatively different from us. Without his bad genes, the chances of our reaching his state seem very slight. We can sympathize with his plight, but simultaneously experience a sense of relief at his essential otherness.

On the other hand, if we allow ourselves to grant his sameness to us, his essential earthling status, we are forced to ask how an earthling can travel from the comfort of our storied lives, grounded in agency and communion, to the empty page of homelessness and the street. Asking this question, we open ourselves up to the examination of the conditions that lead a son, a father, a brother, a husband to transform himself to a state of alien otherness. This book has asked us to consider several factors in our society that combine with addiction to push these men away from the rest of us. If we are to reclaim these men as part of our world, we need continually to acknowledge the destructive role that negative social conditions like homophobia, racism, violence, and materialism can play in thwarting the development of meaningful identity.

Even more fundamentally and subtly, we must also ask if there is a problem with the very tenets that define our sense of identity. This question would provoke our greatest fear in confronting the disconnection of the chronically addicted. Suppose their despair is also telling us that even if we do everything right, pursue lives of accomplishment and relationship, there might still be something wrong with who we are. Suppose composing a life story is not enough to offset the existential threats of isolation, freedom, death, and meaninglessness.

The Nihilistic Challenge to the Life Story of Identity

The sleeping man can be a symbol of the victory of nihilism over our efforts at constructing a story that gives meaning to our lives. As the representative of individuals who have rejected the banality or drudgery of "Love and Work" or, even worse, who have rejected the concept of identity altogether, chronically addicted men pose a challenge to the rest of us to who value our earthling existence. In McAdams's language of identity, we earthlings are individuals with the capacity to author a life story that gives unity and purpose to our lives. We have found a way, as McAdams puts it, to "engage in the heroic battle for meaning, waged on a precipice above the void"[21] and emerge victorious. McAdams believes that the key to this victory is the ability to believe in something larger than ourselves.

> The stories we live by are enhanced by our faith and our fidelity to something larger and nobler than the self—be that something God, the human spirit, progress through technology, or some other transcendent end.[22]

And in these words, we detect what contemporary psychologists like Baumeister or Cushman find to be the key reason behind why so many earthlings feel secretly a private sense of being alien, a feeling that is not markedly different from the chronically addicted. If our stories need to be attached to a transcendent end, and these ends seem equally acceptable, how can we legitimately value one over another? On what basis to we form our criteria? Can we turn our faces toward a God who, during the horror of the holocaust, seemed to turn His face from us? Can we trust progress through technology in the light of Hiroshima? Should we believe in the "human spirit' when we devastate our environment and destroy our fellow living species? In even more immediate terms, should I celebrate the transcendent value of my own story from my wooded country home when the next generations of Thomas Turners are being raised in the violence of New Haven's projects?

Both Doug Richards and Billy Zeitel saw the story of their lives as serving the transcendent ends of the American Dream in which the self serves as an agentic hero who wins love and admiration through power. Both men found this vision inadequate to sustain them in their lives, especially after their addictions progressed and caused them personal and financial setbacks. If they had not become injured or had maintained control over their substance use, and their stories concluded happily, would we then have declared their efforts at identity formation a success?

Perhaps the alienation we experience is not simply that the contents of our stories are not attached to the right transcendent end, but that we have chosen to rely on stories generated by the self as our primary means of knowing the world. As Greenberg (drawing on Heidegger) suggests, rather than accept our complicated and ultimately unknowable relationship with the world, humans attempt to name the world, to become its author. The attaching of our story to a transcendent value does nothing to change our desire to remove the world's otherness. Greenberg writes:

> These . . . values are discovered by the person living the good life in which he or she occupies that authoritative place. Determined in this fashion, such "values" cannot but fill the emptiness with more emptiness. The horizon was wiped away in the first place by attempting to bring things to a standstill (of which Heidegger also understands the "Christian god" to be an example). And "values" are simply another manifestation of that attempt.[23]

The horizon to which Greenberg refers is our location within a world rather than our stance apart from it. The problem of seeing identity as a story about how the individual creates meaning in the world is that this formulation loses sight of the individual's already existing place within the world. To be in the world is to be part of a story that our own story can never fully represent or capture. When we substitute our representations of the world for the world itself, we blind ourselves to the full range of connections and relationships that actually exist between ourselves and the world. We must be open to letting the world tell us, as opposed to always telling what the world is.

So another potential reason we fear the chronically addicted and maintain our disconnection from them is that they challenge us to consider the inadequacy of our stories—our representations—to account for the world we inhabit. The inexplicability of their addictive behavior and the ineffectiveness of our conventional stories to help them in their lives parallels the unknowability of the world that neither religion nor science has conquered. And this parallel increases our fear of their world and our own.

Paradoxically, in this same parallel, we may also find a bridge between our worlds. By accepting the limits of our stories, our ultimate failure to author the world, we are acknowledging our commonality with the man sleeping on the sidewalk. We are no longer separated by competing stories, or by our acceptance of story and his rejection of narrative. We become fellow characters in a common story, and our goal is no longer to replace one story with another, but to enter into a dialogue and exchange of shared experience.

Expanding Identity to Include
Embeddedness in the World

The guiding principle of this effort to forge a better relationship between the chronically addicted men and the sober world is what I call *embeddedness*. The dominant story of identity defines two relational positions of the self to others. We are either differentiated or connected. In either case, these two ways of being are conceived of as motives; we strive toward a sense of agency and we strive toward a sense of relationship with others. By embeddedness, I mean the pre-existing state in which we find ourselves in the world. We do not strive to achieve embeddedness; it consists of the aspects of ourselves that already are and we simply uncover (or recover) them. In our ardent pursuit of a life story, we may often neglect these non-narrative aspects our identity. Many individuals in modern society plunge forward writing a story of love and power that severs ties to their families of origin, their geographical roots, their religious background, their natural environment, even the demands of their bodies.

A wonderful metaphor for individuals who create a life story with little sensitivity to their embeddedness in the world is the proliferation of voice mail. We call out to each other, only to reach a disembodied voice that replies, "I am not here right now, leave a message." In contemporary society, we seem to be perpetually in some other place, presumably in pursuit of some even more important message than the one that is being left for us. Later from some other place, we can call in to check our messages and find out what other disembodied voices have communicated to our own. The Internet has only taken this level of contextless communication one iteration further. What is lost is all context, a sense of relational connection that extends beyond the individual's personal motives.

Embeddedness is not won or lost, pursued or relinquished; it is simply there to be noticed or ignored. There is a subtle, but important, difference between embeddedness and communion. In McAdams's understanding of communion, individuals may seek, as one aspect of communion, to merge with an entity greater than themselves. They might strive to feel affiliation with an organization, a sense of connection to nature, or a spiritual communion with God. In contrast, embeddedness does not denote the movement of an "I" toward a greater "We" or toward a "Oneness" with an entity beyond the self. It refers to the inherent state of connectedness—the particular is already embedded in the whole; it does not choose to merge with or seek out the other; boundaries between otherness and self are not identifiable. Embeddedness is difficult for the contemporary western mind to fathom; all of our societal influences direct us toward differentiation and efforts at self-definition. As Greenberg has pointed out, we often fear any force that has the potential to remove our strong sense of an autonomous self. We have become so forcefully invested in our "sole authorship" that the recognition of the prominent influence of an "other" in our lives poses a threat to our very integrity.

> Concrete social relations in our society are mediated by an under-standing of ourselves that does not tell us how to be in relation to others, and particularly how to maintain a sense of self when an Other arises in front of us in such a way as to rupture our self-con-structed narratives.[24]

In contrast, I am arguing that knowing who we are means awareness of our embeddedness, our "thrownness" into a world that we did nothing to create nor choose. To develop greater knowledge of our identity would then mean to develop an awareness that relies on receptivity, as well as striving. It means a slowing down to observe what others from the past have written, what the natural world writes daily, what our bodies take in and give out.[25]

Perhaps one might think of the experience of embeddedness as looking peripherally rather than ahead. All the time we reach outward to build a tes-tament to the self or reach toward another person to build a relational con-nection, we are reaching from a place, and this place is as much who we are as what we are reaching toward. Knowledge of our embeddedness is know-ing this place, the place where we find ourselves, not the one we are striving to reach.

Embeddedness de-emphasizes the heroic aspect of our story-making, but in doing so allows us to become part of a larger supporting cast that shares a mutual responsibility to each other. Rather than seeing the project of life as focused on the fashioning of a tale, embeddedness encourages us to listen. By modeling a healthier way of giving up the self than is offered by addiction to drugs, treatment providers with an awareness of embeddedness are offer-ing hope to the chronically addicted. Embeddedness suggests a way of being in the world that is neither all story nor story-less. It suggests a way of receiv-ing stories that are both about and not about the self. Inherent in this experi-ence of embeddedness is the awakening of empathy for all others who are mutually embedded in our world.

If embeddedness were a more central part of contemporary identity, I do not think that the marginalization that John Brown, Thomas Turner, Carl

Sobilesky, Clark Grady, and Seymour Harter experienced would have been as likely to occur. I also do not think the various kinds of passivity and self-centered pursuit of pleasure exhibited by many of the men would have flourished. An awareness of embeddedness would lead to obligation, not just on the part of sober world, but in the moral commitments of the chronically addicted as well.

Once individuals become alert to their mutual connectedness, the choice to say "Fuck it" acquires a different meaning. If the very nature of one's sense of identity is grounded in connectedness, the nihilistic surrender of the self to death or addiction violates others and attacks the obligations inherent in those connections. If one's existence is embedded in a larger story, the possibility of choosing to enter or exit that story does not exist. Bahr pointed out that one of the most damaging aspects of disaffiliation on Skid Row is the loss of expectations and obligations. The recognition of one's inherent embeddedness in spheres of nature, family, community, religion, ethnicity, nation, and common humanity raises a parallel awareness of obligation to these spheres.

Too often individuals in contemporary society experience this obligation in reverse. Nature, religion, community, ethnic heritage, love, work are understood as vehicles to be employed in the pursuit of happiness. Their worth is judged by how they enhance the self.[26] Embeddedness begins from a different framework and asks us to uncover our responsibilities to each of these worlds that encircle us.[27]

Embeddedness and Generativity

The concept of our contribution to the world and to generations that follow us certainly has a place in the life story theory of identity. As we defined in Chapter 2, *generativity* is a concern with the outcome of one's story, with the enduring legacy of one's life. McAdams and de St. Aubin have suggested that the emergence of generativity in an individual's life story is a psychosocial process that draws upon both *cultural demand* and *inner desire*.[28] Cultural demand consists of society's developmental expectations that individuals who have reached a certain level of maturity will contribute to the society through generative activities such as parenting, teaching, supervising, coaching, donating money, time, resources, and so forth. Cultural demand also consists of the opportunities society provides to individuals to allow this generative contribution to take place (e.g., schools, social service agencies, health facilities, cultural and social organizations, charities, etc.).

Inner desire translates strivings for agency and communion into generative motives. Our desire to differentiate the self (agency) becomes a concern with *symbolic immortality*—how our children, or our accomplishments, or our good works—will perpetuate our legacy beyond our own lives. On the other hand, our desire to connect the self with others (communion) grows into a desire to give away what wisdom and value we have accumulated in order to enhance the lives of others in the world. We find our generative satisfaction in knowing that our lives were useful and even needed by others. As in all aspects of the life story, individuals may experience a balance of agentic or communal generativity, or lean more heavily toward one over the other.

Interestingly, in American society with its emphasis on individualism and personal happiness, the relationship between generativity as a cultural demand and an inner desire seems to have become particularly skewed. Culturally based demands for generativity such as voting, paying taxes, and universal health coverage are viewed with great distrust by many in the population. As the recent trial of Timothy McVeigh, the bomber of the Oklahoma City Federal Office Building, made clear, the actions of the federal government can even become the object of paranoid hatred.

When generativity is felt more as an inner desire than a cultural demand, its ability to move the self outside of its own dominion becomes clouded. Acts of generosity can take on a self-serving air (as when donors name buildings after themselves) and acts of self-surrender seem too closely tied to the self being surrendered (as when a guilt-inducing mother calls attention to her every sacrifice). Even worse, chronically addicted men, who have little sense of any cultural demands upon them to contribute, are likely to feel a particular cynicism about generativity. They are all too familiar with the self-serving and present-focused nature of their addiction that blocks out efforts to construct a legacy that will survive their death. Similarly, they have often exploited the need of co-dependent others who sacrifice themselves in efforts to protect or enable the addict.

A greater recognition of embeddedness would go a long way to righting the current imbalance between the psychosocial relationship of cultural demands and inner desire for generativity. One clear shift that awareness of our embeddedness might achieve is a modification in the location of generativity in the psychosocial model of identity. At present, Erikson's stages place generativity as the second to last of the stages in the human life cycle, perceiving it to flourish as adults raise offspring, rise to positions of authority in their work, and gain influence in their communities. In contrast, the recognition of embeddedness as a central component of identity would mean that mutual obligation, service to others, and environmental sensitivity would be part of individuals' consciousness from the earliest ages. Rather than understanding generativity as an aspect of identity that develops over time, we would recognize our connection to others and our obligations to those others, both in the present and the future, as an inherent part of our existence.

In working with the chronically addicted, we would no longer focus on their "past selfishness" and their consequent need to develop a new more generative self. Instead, we would encourage them to see the connections and obligations that already exist in their lives. To illustrate this point in concrete terms, one has only to witness what happens to many of the men after only a few weeks at Lebanon Pines. They find their way to the vegetable gardens and the woodshop, the kitchen and the dog kennel. They line up for the chapel service and are up early for work. Like bulbs dormant until a spring thaw, this group of men has begun to release tendrils that seek to take hold in the world around them. These fragile shoots are expressions of embedded identity that has remained suspended over their addictive years. How these manifestations of a renewed sense of identity are received by treatment providers and other individuals in their lives, and how this delicate beginning is cultivated after the men leave the Pines, will make a critical difference in their resistance to despair and relapse.

One goal of treatment providers might be to help the men to see that meeting these generative obligations is not simply the trading of the satisfaction of one inner desire (their addiction) for another (the desire for a legacy of self). Their meeting of these obligations is an expression of the men's presence in the world; it actively repudiates their alien status and acknowledges their membership in the same world to which the rest of us belong. Once this fundamental alienation is addressed, the men's ability to benefit from generative fellowships like AA should be greatly enhanced. When the men are able to experience their generativity as inherent (rather than another test of the self at which they are likely to fail), they will be more likely to set aside feelings of inferiority and anxiety evoked by their attendance at meetings. They will also be more likely to see the meetings not solely in terms of what they can gain for themselves personally, but as a commitment and obligation to others. They will also be more likely to extend that sense of obligation to others beyond the world of AA.

As evidence of this idea, Shannon Jackson and I conducted a study of individuals who had managed to achieve long-term sobriety. We found that individuals with five or more years of sobriety were more involved in more generative actions (helping others, volunteering, teaching, etc.) than individuals with less time in sobriety. Interestingly, these long-term sober individuals were more generative in their lives, despite attending fewer AA meetings than individuals with less accumulated sobriety. This finding suggests that the lessons of AA service may solidify and then become transferred to wider domains of the individuals' non–alcohol-related lives.[29]

In concluding this section on the disconnection of the chronically addicted men from the sober and recovering world, I am reminded once more of the question asked by the doubting editor, "Why would anyone want to read about a bunch of drunks who don't get better?" Four years of writing this book later, my answer is simply this: If we don't allow the men to enter our awareness, they will certainly not get better. Their recovery depends upon a mutual awareness of our embeddedness in each others' lives. An awareness of our relationship to the chronically addicted need not be manifested in a way that coddles or indulges them; connection does not mean enabling. An awareness of our mutual embeddedness in the world means a willingness to be present in their lives, a receptivity to their efforts, and an ongoing expectation that they have the capacity (if not yet the ability) to accept the obligations and responsibilities of being part of sober society. How they come to accept and act upon those obligations, once they are awakened to their existence, remains an essential part of treatment.

How Treatment Can Enhance the Recovery of Identity and Meaning

Assuming that a developing sense of embeddedness is established in both chronically addicted men and their treatment providers, how might the men build upon their decision to choose life over death and sobriety over addiction? Despite being in the throes of a horrible disease, despite the overwhelming compulsion to use, all of the men have had enough sober time and rehabilitation to know that a method of recovery exists. There is an AA group to join, an antidepressant to take, a helpful counselor waiting to listen. Yet preceding all the steps of recovery, chronically addicted men will need to translate their hope for sobriety into a conviction that the steps they are about to take will not lead them back to their alien world and their state of disconnection.

In the face of the terrible suffering and guilt that they have endured, the men must be able to find a way to embrace what Victor Frankl has called a tragic optimism.[30] Tragic optimism is a fundamental belief that suffering can be redemptive, that we endure pain to reach greater understanding and to achieve our life's purpose in an even more profound manner. Accordingly, the beginning stages of treatment will need to focus on the specific question of hope overcoming despair.[31] Men who cannot find this sense of optimism will see themselves as simply going through the motions of recovery yet another time.

One concrete way in which treatment providers and the chronically addicted are mutually embedded is that they are engaged together in a relationship whose purpose is recovery. The nature of recovery includes hope, and to the extent that both parties, the provider and the client, are participating in this relationship, they are obligated to feel hope. Both individuals need to be alert to moments when hope is tangible, and moments when it appears to be absent. Identifying what conditions are associated with the waxing and waning of hope will strongly enhance the connection felt between each participant in the recovery relationship.

To facilitate the rediscovery of hope, society must offer comprehensive services to the men attempting to recover—residential facilities like Lebanon Pines, AA meetings, intensive case management, effective medication, group treatment, and work rehabilitation. In addition, as already indicated, individual psychotherapy will need to address the men's fragile reentry into the sober world and their optimism about remaining in this world. Psychotherapy that does not repeatedly return to the themes of connection and hope may be overlooking vital elements in the trajectory of recovery.

One danger in the abstinence model endorsed by AA-oriented treatment centers is that relapses are inadvertently given too much weight. Repetitive relapsers are sometimes banned from further treatment because of their "revolving door" behavior. Individuals who relapse even briefly often feel an explosion of shame and self-hatred that leads only to increased substance use. A recovery relationship committed to the detection of hope might approach relapses in a different manner, evaluating the meaning and actual circumstances of each relapse in its own right. For example, though a number of the men at Lebanon Pines continue to relapse, one can find much cause for hope in the ratio of sober days to days of active use, or in the ratio of days lived in sober supported housing versus shelters, jails, and psychiatric hospitals. A model approach that takes this more optimistic and less either/or approach to recovery can be found in Alan Marlatt's relapse prevention approach (see Chapter 1, Battling Sobriety).

Embeddedness and Relapse Prevention

What makes Marlatt's approach so promising is its sensitivity to the embeddedness of a recovering person's life in a full range of biological, emotional,
cognitive, behavioral, vocational, and interpersonal dimensions. Interestingly, one of the negative emotional states Marlatt highlights as a trigger for
relapse is emptiness (along with others that are also relevant to the men of
the Pines—anxiety, depression, anger, guilt).[32] In fact, the only modification
I would hope to make to his excellent and carefully researched efforts at
relapse prevention is to change the emphasis on emptiness with regard to
treating men suffering from patterns of chronic relapse. In Marlatt's current
model, emptiness, or what I would call their sense of disconnection, is listed
among several negative emotional states that are grouped as one component
of an eight-pronged relapse-prevention program. Given my experience with
the men of the Pines, I would feel compelled to place their sense of disconnection as the foremost challenge to their choice to sustain sobriety. My suggestion would be that relapse-prevention treatment needs to address this
disconnection openly and repeatedly, while exploring how it is linked to their
defenses against despair—surrender, blind habit, and destructive agency.

In acknowledging their struggle to overcome this emptiness, I would also
change the emphasis that current recovery programs tend to place on the
individual. For example, seven of Marlatt's eight components deal specifically with ways in which the individual can modify personal emotions, cogni-
tions, and behaviors. No components address the social or political
circumstances in which recovering individuals find themselves. Similarly,
therapeutic communities address the maladaptive and antisocial beliefs and
behaviors of addicts, but do not tend to place the addict's behavior in a
sociopolitical context.

In all of AA's literature and the research literature on relapse prevention and
the psychiatric treatment for addiction, I have found little or no mention of
how relapses could be prevented by investing the recovering persons in efforts
to change the social and economic circumstances that promote addiction. One
consequence of a heightened sense of embeddedness in the world would be
the awakening of an obligation to ameliorate conditions that have caused both
one's personal suffering and the suffering of others.

As we have seen throughout this book, an unfortunate consequence of the
categorization of addiction as a disease is that it locates the problem within the
individual rather than encouraging us to think about the social context of addiction. Relapse-prevention programs might become even more successful and

more relevant to chronic relapsers if social influences upon addicted individuals such as homophobia, racism, poverty, materialism, and stigma were discussed explicitly in the treatment. Addicted individuals who choose to engage with life by taking an active stance against these life-thwarting influences might be considerably less likely to succumb to feelings of emptiness and lack of meaning in their lives. The study I cited on the relationship of generativity to sustained recovery certainly supports this position.[33]

One of the positives repeatedly noted about the disease concept perspective on addiction is that it frees addicted individuals from some of the burden of guilt they feel about their addicted state; they are able to see their addiction as a disease rather than a moral failing. It seems to me that the same reduction in self-loathing might also be achieved if individuals could identify a connection between their addictive behavior and forces in society that reinforce their surrender to despair and sense of emptiness. Making this connection does not free individuals from the need to make responsible choices in recovery any more than does an acceptance that one suffers from the "disease" of addiction.

Disease concept proponents use the analogy that just as acceptance of one's lifelong condition of diabetes does not give an individual license to eat sweets and skip insulin treatments, acceptance of one's alcoholic or drug-addicted condition does not mean one has a freedom to behave as one chooses. My goal in suggesting that we help chronically addicted men make more explicit links between addictive behavior and social conditions is that such connections reinforce the removal of their alien status and encourage them to participate actively in the world. Just as individuals with diabetes attend to their diet, recovering individuals would recognize the need to attend to the ways their lives are connected to the world; they would become active questioners of the values and meanings that underlie the actions of the communities or societies in which they reside.

They Continuing Need for Residential Facilities like Lebanon Pines

As the men's stories recounted here reflect, the experience of connection that will contribute meaning to their lives cannot be adequately achieved through short-term involvement with counseling, group therapy, or medication trials. In the development of their addictions and through the years of suffering from them, the men have lost the most basic opportunities to experience connection in their lives. The foundations of most individuals' lives in this society—love, work, communal responsibility—are not easily regained for the men of the Pines. With these elements missing, rehabilitation requires a great deal of case management support and structured guidance until the men can regain (or gain for the first time) the skills to recover meaningful relationships, accomplishments, and responsibilities.

Having made a plea to give embeddedness a prominent role in recovery from chronic addiction, I want to conclude by stating emphatically that we should not lose sight of the "blind habit" aspect of addiction. The use of substances may be a response to meaninglessness and despair, but the repeated use over time creates both behavioral and physiological patterns and an accompanying lifestyle that take on an independent momentum. In fact, addiction can seal off the men into a world that locks them in and others out.

Prior to any concerted effort at counseling or exploration of identity and meaning, these men need to step away from the addicted routine of their lives and break the physical, behavioral, and psychological patterns of their habit. Lebanon Pines and other facilities like it offer the men a way of stepping off the merry-go-round of street life, detoxes, and shelters. Once housed at the Pines, the men have a chance to regain a physical and psychological equilibrium. Through work therapy and AA attendance at the Pines, they can begin to create the external structure that will counteract the daily habit of drinking or drugging. After some months at the Pines, they are then sufficiently clear-headed and receptive to begin the process of questioning what a life free of substances might mean to them.

Unfortunately, it is exactly at this point that our current social services system falls short. Every man who makes it to the Pines should ideally have the option of a case manager and weekly psychotherapy (in addition to daily AA) to begin to undo the damage that both addiction and destructive social forces have done to their lives. The Pines can offer only four counselors (trained in addiction treatment and not psychological services) for one hundred men. Outside referrals result in long waiting lists at clinics that may not have therapists who are adequately trained in dual diagnosis problems or who are ready for the sweeping existential crises many of these chronically addicted men are likely to bring to their sessions. Under the new managed care pressure in the health care industry and the budget-slashing state and federal welfare reforms, the situation has even worsened. The men are forced to stay for shorter periods of time at Lebanon Pines and their eligibility for halfway house coverage or psychotherapy treatment has been significantly curtailed. Since I began to write this book, I have seen the closing of a twenty-eight-day rehabilitation program run by the state and the phasing out of several ten-to-fourteen-day evaluation programs (SCADD has tried to compensate for some of these changes by running a twenty-one-day program on the grounds of the Pines).

One of the most dangerous misconceptions that one might draw from this book is that a program like Lebanon Pines is not worth the effort, since such a high percentage of the men who stay there do not achieve sustained sobriety when they leave. Anyone who has seen the difference between a man who has been living on the streets when he comes into the New London detox and after he has spent a few months at Lebanon Pines knows that the Pines can play a vital and nearly miraculous role in building up a man's health, self-respect, and sense of hope. I challenge anyone to see the beautiful grounds and facilities of the Pines, all maintained by the men, and come away feeling that there is not positive growth and increased self-respect occurring there. Similarly, when one sees the compassion and wisdom that Bill Sugden and his staff offer to the men on a daily basis, the value added to the residents' lives hardly seems a matter of dispute.

The problem, as so often is the case with social services, is that we do not go far enough in funding and supporting Lebanon Pines and, even more, the treatment needs of the men when they leave the Pines. Men ready for discharge from the Pines face waiting lists to enter halfway houses that are located within blocks of their familiar bars and drug haunts. They leave with uncertain work prospects and only tentative arrangements for continued counseling or psychotherapy. They return to the very same social conditions that have exacerbated their addictions.

Envisioning Men's Centers

Interestingly, in my work with addicted women over the years, I have seen the extraordinary benefits produced by the Women's Centers located in New London and Groton, Connecticut. Women's Centers all over the nation offer women crisis intervention services, shelter from battering, legal advocacy, twenty-four-hour hot lines, education about women's issues, housing and childcare support, and counseling. Survivors of rape, domestic violence, childhood abuse and incest, women with problems of self-esteem, eating disorders, divorce, or widowhood can find support groups to give them strength and a sense of connectedness to each other. The New London Women's Center provides supported apartments for a year or more to help women who have left abusive partners begin new lives, either alone or with their children. All of these services carry a message of inclusion and commitment.

Men could benefit from these lessons. A Men's Center might do active outreach to kinds of men who feel disconnected—the chronically addicted, the psychiatrically ill, ex-offenders, men who have suffered from abuse or become abusers, but also men who are unemployed, divorced, or widowed; single men who feel isolated or elderly men living on their own; men with questions about their sexuality; men who suffer from disabilities, men who are immigrants and new to this society and culture. A Men's Center would offer referrals, crisis intervention, short-term counseling, support groups, similar to a Women's Center, but it might also reach out to men in ways that are tailored to their initial difficulties with communicating feelings. It might sponsor a softball or bowling team, offer employment and skills workshops, and courses in management of finances. Of great importance, and again patterned after the Women's Centers' work with mothers, it would offer training and support for fathers.

What differentiates a Women's Center or a Men's Center from other support services in the community is that they avoid the labeling and categorizing that occurs when a woman or man seeks help through a particular social service agency. When a woman enters the door of the Women's Center, she may have a particular past and may be seeking a particular service, but she enters as first and foremost a woman, connected by her gender to all the other women who participate in the Center. For many men who have lost a sense of connection and embeddedness in the lives of others in society, this sense of unity, based in an affirmation rather than a negative label or deviant status, could have a very positive and transforming influence.

With the relapse history of the men who come to Lebanon Pines, we should never expect a "cure" or a near-perfect rate of recovery. As the AA slogan puts it, addiction is a "baffling and cunning" condition that defeats many men who try to overcome it. Yet for each painful story like Tommy Reilly's, there are other men like Seymour Harter (see Chapter 10) or Carl Sobilesky (see Chapter 4) who with AA involvement, proper case management, counseling services, and access to the resources of a Men's Center might be able to live meaningful sober lives in the community.

Lebanon Pines is the kind of place that practices Frankl's tragic optimism. In spite of the long odds, in spite of the suffering and defeats, each time the van turns down its long tree-lined road to head for the main circle and the admissions building, a man sitting inside has allowed hope to enter his mind again. As the van comes to rest, and he steps out into the pine air, he is stepping toward the challenge of sobriety. His step forward sets in motion a set of questions—will we see him coming toward us or will we look away? Will we sustain him when the despair he has evaded hits him with full force? Will we make it possible for him to see that his life is part of our lives, and that the choices that he makes have meaning? His process of recovery entails a recovery of each domain of identity—embeddedness, agency, and communion. Our process of recovering him is based in our willingness to be connected to his emerging sense of self. In this mutual acknowledgment of our embeddedness in each others' lives, a deeper and more optimistic humanity is located. In the expression of this humanity, we both finally come to know who each of us is, and who we are together.

Update

An Update on the Men's Lives

1.   John Brown died of complications of AIDS in 1993.
2.   Danny Doyle is at one of SCADD's halfway houses.
3.   Arthur Drum is wanted for a variety of criminal acts and is currently a fugitive at large.
4.   Carl Sobilesky is at a long-term facility for alcoholism in northwest Connecticut, similar to Lebanon Pines.
5.   Tommy Reilly died in 1995 from an overdose of heroin. His counselors and family members believe his death was intentional.
6.   Thomas Turner relapsed and lost contact with SCADD. He is rumored to have died.
7.   Roland Diggs, while serving as a driver for Lebanon Pines, relapsed and stole a van. He was apprehended and discharged. He is still out on the street and actively using.
8.   Doug Richards is newly married and sober.

9. Billy Zeitel was caught using cocaine on the grounds of Lebanon Pines. He recently attempted to return, but was refused readmittance.

10. Tyler Casey relapsed and has continued to move in and out of treatment.

11. Michael Cochran relapsed, divorced his new wife and moved from Arizona to Seattle. After more sober time, he relapsed again and then moved back to Arizona. He is currently sober.

12. Clark Grady is back at Lebanon Pines.

13. Seymour Harter is back at Lebanon Pines.

Appendix—Interview Methods

I interviewed thirty-one men, thirty of whom were residing at Lebanon Pines and one who was an ex-resident and working as the manager of his own three-quarter house. The men were selected in consultation with the counseling staff of Lebanon Pines. My goal in choosing men to interview was to achieve a representative sample of major and recurring themes that the men presented as linked to their addiction. Although thirty-one men agreed to participate, six other men who were approached refused to participate or backed out by not showing up for the scheduled interview. All interviews with the men of the Pines were conducted in an office of the Counselor Building on the grounds of the facility. The one interview with the ex-resident was conducted in the kitchen of his three-quarter house. All of the interviews were tape recorded and lasted two to three hours.

The interview followed this procedure: The men read and signed a consent form that explained that their anonymity would be protected and that the interviews would be used for this book. They were also informed that they could withdraw from the project at any time. No man chose to do so.

We began the interview with my request for a self-defining memory. I explained what I was looking for in the following way:

> What I mean by a self-defining memory is a memory that helps you to understand who you are as a person and tells you what is important to you. You might imagine that you've met a friend or a woman you were trying to get to know and you went for a walk. You were having a nice time and really opening up to each other. At a certain moment, you decided to tell a memory that would reveal something important about who you are as a person. It should be a memory that you've thought a lot about in your life, that evokes strong feelings, and that you can see clearly in your mind, almost like a photograph or moving picture.

After the men provided the memory, we began the life story portion of the interview. I told the men to tell their story in any fashion that they desired and that I would interject questions only to clarify information or find out their reactions to a particular incident. The men needed very little prompting and talked quite extensively and openly about their lives. We would usually break for lunch or coffee and then they would resume the narrative. At the end of the life story, I asked each man the following questions:

> Now that you have told your story, what do think its major theme or moral might be? And now that you have told your story, what do you see the future holding for you?

In the final segment of the interview, I asked the men to tell stories about four cards from the Thematic Apperception Test (T.A.T.). The four cards I used were: Card #1 (a boy seated before a violin); Card #4 (a woman is reaching at a man who is turning away from her); Card #8BM (a boy is in the foreground and in the background what appears to be a surgical operation is taking place; there is also a rifle to the side of the foreground); and Card #7BM (the heads of an older man and younger man are pictured side by side). These cards were chosen to tap into themes of achievement (Card #1), relationship with women (Card #4), violence and illness (Card #8BM), and father/son relationships (Card #7BM).

Notes

CHAPTER 1

1. Cash, C. L. (1986). *Evaluation of Lebanon Pines: A long term care program for chronic alcoholics.* Document published by Southeastern Council on Alcoholism and Drug Dependence Inc., Gilman, CT. p. 20.

2. Cash (1986) documented in the first five years of Lebanon Pines' existence, the number of admissions for men with previous multiple admissions to detox dropped by almost 50 percent from the previous five-year period. Since the vast majority of these men did not stay at Lebanon Pines for anywhere near five years, this finding cannot simply be attributed to their extended stay at Lebanon Pines. Other data presented in this report suggest that the men were healthier and able to achieve greater periods of sobriety once discharged from Lebanon Pines. Looked at from a cost perspective, one resident with chronic alcoholism cost the state $312,865 in total resource consumption (admissions, arrests, days in care) in the five-year period before the opening of the Pines. In his five years of intermittent contact with Lebanon Pines, his total resource consumption costs to the state were reduced to $93, 297 (Cash, 1986, p. 44).

3. A detox is usually a forty-eight-hour or seventy-two-hour stay in a treatment center or hospital setting with the purpose of stabilizing the client medically as he or she with-

draws from the addictive substance. After the detox period is over, the client is usually referred to an inpatient or outpatient treatment program of a longer duration. These programs are referred to as rehabs (rehabilitation program). The traditional inpatient rehab would run for twenty-eight to thirty days and consist of several group meetings, educational material (films and readings with an AA focus), and individual counseling. There are also briefer ten- to fourteen-day evaluation programs. SCADD had its own detox and ten-day program. After clients went through the detox or the ten-day program, they could be assessed for going to one of SCADD's three "halfway houses" or going up to Lebanon Pines. The halfway houses are run by a manager and consist of residents recently in recovery. They require abstinence and AA attendance, as well as house meetings and shared chores. There is also a fair amount of freedom, given their location in the community. Lebanon Pines is one of a small number of longer-term residential programs for chronic addiction that encourage individuals to stay in structured treatment (work therapy, counseling, group meetings, AA) for more extended times before discharge. These extended stays used to mean nine months to a year or more, but with the changing structure of health insurance and welfare systems the stays tend to be shorter (two to three months would now be more common). See Wittman, F. D. and Madden, P. A. (1988). Alcohol recovery programs for homeless people: A survey of current programs in the U.S. Report prepared for National Institute on Alcohol Abuse and Alcoholism, Rockville, MD. This report provides an overview of twenty-one programs that serve the chronically addicted. Interestingly, only two or three of the programs offer a living situation and services comparable to Lebanon Pines.

4.   "Alcoholics appear to be as variable in personality as are non-alcoholics." Miller, W. R. (1995). Increasing motivation for change. In R. K. Hester and W. R. Miller (Eds.), *Handbook of alcoholism treatment approaches: Effective alternatives.* (2nd ed., pp. 89–104). Boston: Allyn & Bacon. p. 90.

5.   For a still relevant and comprehensive account of the debilitating effects of street and shelter life, see Bahr, H. M. (1973). *Skid row: An introduction to disaffiliation.* New York: Oxford University Press. This sociological study offers not only an in-depth portrayal of the men and women on "skid row," but also an analysis of stereotypes and societal attitudes toward these individuals.

6.   For a brilliant historical review of the development of this perspective toward addiction, see Levine, H.G. (1978). The discovery of addiction: Changing conceptions of habitual drunkenness in America. *Journal of Studies in Alcohol, 39,* 143–174.

7.   See Fingarette, H. (1988). *Heavy drinking: The myth of alcoholism as a disease.* Berkeley, CA: University of California Press. Fingarette offers a philosophical critique drawing on both logical argument and empirical studies to challenge the disease concept portrayal of the alcoholic as out of control due to a progressive illness. See also Peele, S. (1989). *Diseasing of America: Addiction treatment out of control.* Boston: Houghton Mifflin, and Thombs, D. L. (1994). *Introduction to addictive behaviors.* New York: Guilford Press, Chapter 2 "The Disease Concept, " (pp. 19–48) for a very good critical evaluation of the disease concept approach. For the original statement of the disease concept, see Jellinek, E.M. (1960). *The disease concept of alcoholism.* New Haven, CT: Hillhouse. For a contemporary proponent, see Wallace, J. (1982). Alcoholism from the inside out: A phenomenological analysis. In N. J. Estes, and M. E. Heinemann (Eds.), *Alcoholism: Development, consequences, and interventions* (pp. 1–23). St. Louis, MO: Mosby.

8.   See Jellinek, E. M. (1962). Phases of alcohol addiction. In D. J. Pittman and C. R. Snyder (Eds.), *Society, culture, and drinking patterns* (pp. 356–368). New York: John Wiley.

9.   Fingarette (1988), pp. 51–54. The Goodwin study discussed by Fingarette may be found in Goodwin, D. W., Schulsinger, F., Hermansen, L., Guze, S. B., and Winokur, G. (1973). Alcohol problems in adoptees raised apart from alcoholic biological parents. *Archives of General Psychiatry, 28,* 238–243.

10.   Fingarette (1988), p. 52.

11.   Marlatt, G. A., Deming, B., and Reid, J. B. (1973). Loss of control drinking in alcoholics: An experimental analogue. *Journal of Abnormal Psychology, 81,* 223–241. For other critiques of the loss-of-control hypothesis, see Mello, N. K. and Mendelson, J. H. (1972). Drinking patterns during work-contingent and non-contingent alcohol acquisition. *Psychosomatic Medicine, 34,* 139–164; Mello, N. K. and Mendelson, J. H. (1985). *Alcohol: Use and abuse in America.* Boston: Little, Brown.

12.   See Peele, S. (1989). Chapter 5 "The Addiction Treatment Industry" makes clear how the medical community became heavily involved in promoting Twelve Step based inpatient treatment programs and discusses the hospital chain of CompCare as one example (p. 126).

13.   See Svanum, S. and McAdoo, W. G. (1989). Predicting rapid relapse following treatment for chemical dependence. A matched samples design. *Journal of Consulting and Clinical Psychology, 57,* 222–726. In an even more recent study comparing two forms of treatment (AA focus versus cognitive-behavioral treatment) for alcoholics at a VA hospital program, the researchers found that no more than 25.5 percent of the men treated were abstinent one year after treatment. See Ouimette, P. C., Finney, J. W., and Moos, R. (1997). Twelve step and cognitive-behavioral treatment for substance abuse: A comparison of treatment effectiveness. *Journal of Consulting and Clinical Psychology, 65,* 230–240.

14.   See MacKay, P., Marlatt, G. A., and Donovan, D. M. (1991). Cognitive and behavioral approaches to alcohol abuse. In R. J. Frances and S. I. Miller (Eds.), *Clinical textbook of addictive disorders* (pp. 452–481). New York: Guilford Press.

15.   See Vaillant, G. E. (1983). *The natural history of alcoholism.* Cambridge, MA: Harvard University Press. pp. 283–284, for a discussion of how his AA-based treatment efforts did not improve outcome substantially over the results that might have been expected through the "natural" course of the disease.

16.   A notable and moving exception is the recent book by George McGovern about the failed struggle of his daughter with alcoholism and her eventual death of exposure after passing out and falling into a snow bank. McGovern, G. (1996). *Terry: My daughter's life-and-death struggle with alcoholism.* New York: Villard.

17.   In fact, some recovering individuals will make an explicit point of distinguishing themselves from this more negative type of addiction. In her memoir of addiction and recovery, the journalist Caroline Knapp makes a point of contrasting the "classic image of falling-down booze-hound: an older person, usually male, staggering down the street and clutching a brown paper bag" with the high-achieving members of her AA group (vice president of a financial institution, architect, Ph.D. in biology) (p. 13 for quote, p. 14 for list of people). Knapp, C. (1996). *Drinking: A love story.* New York: The Dial Press.

18.   See Alcoholics Anonymous (1976). New York: Alcoholics Anonymous World Services Inc.

19.   Alcoholics Anonymous (1980). *Dr. Bob and the good oldtimers: A biography, with recollections of early A.A. in the midwest.* New York: Alcoholics Anonymous World Services. See pp. 63–75 for Dr. Bob's account of how he met Bill Wilson.

20.   See Sarbin, T. (1995). Emotional life, rhetoric, and roles. *Journal of Narrative History, 5,* 213–220. Sarbin discusses the notion of how much of our emotional life is based in our adoption of existing cultural scripts that guide our conduct in morally ambiguous situations. Drawing on Sarbin's framework, I have derived a cultural script of

addiction/recovery, see Singer, J. A. (August, 1996). The internalization of a cultural script for addiction. Paper presented at the Annual Convention of the American Psychological Association, Toronto, Ontario. See also Delbanco, A. and Delbanco, T. (March 20, 1995). AA at the crossroads. *The New Yorker,* pp. 50–63.

21. Bill Sugden, Director of Lebanon Pines, personal communication.

22. See Coleman, E. (1982). Family intimacy and chemical abuse: The connection. *Journal of Psychoactive Drugs, 14,* 153–158.

23. AA members often call this kind of sobriety "a dry drunk." By this, they mean that the individual has managed not to drink, but has not incorporated into their life the tenets and values of AA. They feel that this kind of sobriety (also called white knuckling because it is based solely in willpower and not a spiritual or social support) is doomed to relapse.

24. Yalom, I. D. (1980). *Existential psychotherapy.* New York: Basic Books. These four criteria, death, freedom, isolation, meaninglessness, according to Yalom, form the existential structure of our modem lives.

25. Baumeister, R. F. (1991b). *Meanings of life.* New York: Guilford Press. pp. 25–26.

26. It is interesting to consider how many times I have heard people in the addiction treatment world compare alcoholism to a chronic health problem like diabetes or heart disease. What is often neglected in this analogy is that the etiology of many forms of these "physical diseases" are linked to personal behavior and social factors. The development of diabetes and heart disease in adulthood are linked to dietary factors and obesity in addition to one's genetic vulnerability. Heart disease has also long been linked to social stressors and personality factors like the hostility component of Type A behavior.

27. Some personality researchers might have approached the study of the men through the administration of an extensive battery of self-report questions such as the MMPI (Minnesota Multiphasic Personality Inventory) or the NEO-PI, a personality inventory that measures five major traits—neuroticism, openness, extraversion, conscientiousness, and agreeableness. My work in personality stems out of a different tradition called "personology." Pioneered by Henry Murray (see Murray, H. A. (1938). *Explorations in personality.* New York: Oxford University Press), this perspective places an intensive emphasis on the "whole person" and views the collection of extensive autobiographical material as a critical part of the research inquiry. For a review of this narrative approach to personality, see Singer, J. A. (1996). The story of your life: A process perspective on narrative and emotion in adult development. In C. Magai and S. McFadden (Eds.), *Handbook of emotion and adult development and aging* (pp. 443–478). New York: Academic Press.

28. Please see the Appendix for a description of the methodology used to collect the interviews with the residents of Lebanon Pines.

29. See in particular, McAdams, D. P. (1988). *Power, intimacy, and the life story: Personological inquiries into identity.* New York: Guilford Press; McAdams, D. P. (1993). *Stories we live by: Personal myths and the makings of the self.* New York: William Morrow and Co.

30. Singer, J. A. and Salovey, P. (1993). *The remembered self: Emotion and memory in personality.* New York: The Free Press.

31. Yalom (1980).

32. In his historical study of identity, Baumeister points out that he decided to approach his attempt to understand the meaning of identity by studying the points in history at which crises in identity began. He writes that this approach

> . . . conforms to a time-honored procedure in psychology—approaching the study of something by studying the phenomena that accompany its loss. The same logic underlies Freud's efforts to understand the nature of the psyche

by studying insane persons, the physiological psychology that learns about the function of some part of the brain by destroying it and seeing what functions deteriorate, and current efforts to learn about the nature of intelligence by studying the mentally retarded. (p. viii)

See Baumeister, R. F. (1986). *Identity: Cultural change and the struggle for the self.* New York: Oxford University Press. By studying the destruction of identity and meaning in men's lives of chronic addiction, we may indeed learn more clearly about the actual functions of these two organizing forces in our own lives.

CHAPTER 2

1.   Alighieri, D. (1954). *The inferno.* New York: New American Library. Translated by John Ciardi, p. 28.
2.   McAdams, D. P. (1994). *The person.* Fort Worth, TX: Harcourt Brace. p. 655.
3.   Baumeister (1986).
4.   Stendhal (Beyle, M.) (1830/1984). *The red and the black.* New York: Modem Library. Translated by C. K. Scott Moncrieff.
5.   For twentieth century existential discussions of meaning and identity, see Becker, E. (1973). *The denial of death.* New York: The Free Press. Camus, A. (1955). *The myth of Sisyphus and other essays.* New York: Alfred A. Knopf; Farber, L. H. (1978). *Lying, despair, jealousy, envy, sex, suicide, drugs and the good life.* New York: Harper & Row; Marcel, G. (1961). *The philosophy of existentialism.* New York: Citadel Press; Sartre, J. P. (1955). *No Exit and three other plays.* New York: Vintage Books; and Yalom, I. D. (1980).
6.   Erikson, E. H. (1963). *Childhood and society.* 2nd. Ed. New York: W. W. Norton.
7.   McAdams, D. P. (1988). Biography, narrative, and lives. *Journal of Personality, 56,* 1–18. See p. 5.
8.   McAdams (1994). p. 747.
9.   McAdams, D. P., Hoffman, B. J., Mansfield, E. D., and Day, R. (1996). Themes of agency and communion in significant autobiographical scenes. *Journal of Personality, 64,* 339–377.
10.   Bakan, D. (1966). *The duality of human existence: Isolation and communion in Western man.* Boston: Beacon.
11.   More formally, Freud proposed a distinction between Eros (a unifying and integrative force) and Thanatos (a force of separation and disintegration); see Freud, S. (1920/1973). Beyond the pleasure principle. In J. Strachey (Ed.), *The complete works of Sigmund Freud, standard edition* (vol. 18). London: Hogarth, pp. 1–64.
12.   Bakan (1966), p. 15.
13.   McAdams et al. (1996), p. 346.
14.   The four components of agency are drawn from McAdams et al. (1996), pp. 347–348.
15.   McAdams et al. (1996), p. 348.
16.   The four components of communion are drawn from McAdams et al. (1996), pp. 348–351.
17.   Singer and Salovey (1993). See also Moffitt, K. H. and Singer, J. A. (1993). Continuity in the life story: Self-defining memories, affect, and approach/avoidance personal strivings. *Journal of Personality, 62,* 21–43.
18.   See also Kotre, J. (1984). *Outliving the self: Generativity and the interpretation of lives.* Baltimore, MD: Johns Hopkins University, for an instructive and thoughtful monograph on the various forms that generativity can take in adult life.

19. Eighth Special Report to the U. S. Congress on *Alcohol and health* (September. 1993). From the Secretary of Health and Human Services. NIH Pub. # 94-3699. p. 233.

20. McAdams (1993), p. 34.

21. McAdams (1993), p. 30.

22. McAdams (1993), p. 83. McAdams is drawing on a distinction made by Baumeister (1986).

23. McAdams (1993), p. 83. This is also a distinction made by Baumeister (1986).

24. McAdams (1988), p. 18,

> A person's world establishes parameters for life stories. In this way identity is truly psychosocial: The life story is a joint product of person and environment. In a sense, the two write the story together. Jerome Brunet (1960) speaks of this story writing as the making of myths. He writes that the "mythologically instructed community provides its members with a library of scripts" against which the individual may judge his or her own "internal drama." (p. 281). He concludes, "Life, then, produces myth and finally imitates it." (p. 283)

See also Singer and Salovey (1993), p. 209.

25. McAdams (1988); McAdams et al. (1996); McAdams, D. P., de St. Aubin, E., and Logan, R. (1993). Generativity among young, mid-life, and older adults. *Psychology and Aging, 8,* 221–230.

26. Yalom, I. D. (1980). pp. 8–9.

27. Becker, E. (1973), p. 7.

28. Yalom (1980), p. 8.

29. Baumeister, R. F. (1991a). *Escaping the self: Alcoholism, spirituality, masochism, and other flights from the burden of selfhood.* Baumeister writes about the means individuals use to escape from the burden of the self, including taking responsibility for one's decisions,

> Taking control and exerting control form an important part of the self, and escape from the self, therefore, could be expected to involve being passive.
> . . . Passivity preserves one from risk, while responsibility extends the self and makes it vulnerable. If you are trying to escape yourself, added responsibility is the last thing you want. Hence escape will tend to promote passivity and avoidance of commitment, responsibility, and other possible implications of action. (p. 67)

30. See Steele, C. M. and Josephs, R. A. (1990). Alcohol myopia: Its prized and dangerous effects. *American Psychologist, 45,* 921–933 for a review on how alcohol use restricts individuals' focus to the most salient cues in a situation, often causing them to overlook less salient and longer-term implications of their behaviors.

31. Baumeister (1991a) points out that impulsivity is another alternative to responsible action associated with the self,

> One large category of meaningless or irresponsible action is impulsive action, that is, doing something without reflection, without planning, and to a substantial extent without responsibility. When people are criticized by others for something they have done, one defense is to say that it was merely an impulse. (p. 68)

32. Yalom (1980), p. 482.

33. See Kierkegaard, S. (1849/1941). *The sickness unto death.* Princeton: Princeton University Press, translated by Walter Lowrie. Kierkegaard defines his understanding of despair quite beautifully, "When death is the greatest danger, one hopes for life; but when one becomes acquainted with an even more dreadful danger, one hopes for death. So when the danger is so great that death has become one's hope, despair is the disconsolateness of not being able to die." p. 25. See also Camus, (1955); Marcel, (1961); Sartre, (1955).

34. Yalom (1980), p. 483. Another helpful analysis of how to supply meaning to life comes from Baumeister, R. F. (1991b). He argues that individuals need to feel a sense of self-worth and efficacy, as well as the notion that their life has a concrete purpose and moral value.

35. Baumeister, R. F. (1991a). Baumeister sees this reaction as an example of what happens when a calamity strikes an individual. The self is burdened with feelings of disappointment and failure, and alcohol (if used in combination with an effective distraction) serves to deflect thoughts of the calamity and ease the weight on the self. Similarly, in the face of major life stressors or when confronted with worry over one's competence or capacity to meet challenges, alcohol offers an escape from these self burdens (pp. 144–147).

36. "Freedom's just another word for nothing left to lose." From the song, "Me and Bobby McGee" by Kris Kristofferson.

37. Fingarette (1988), p. 100.

38. Fingarette (1988), p. 102.

39. Fingarette (1988), p. 103.

40. Fingarette (1988), p. 104.

41. Fingarette (1988), p. 105, In contemplating change of a central activity in our lives, we experience ". . . the deeply-rooted habit-bound self opposing the fragile reed of a new desire to be other than who or what we have been. And the more genuine our desire to change, the more tense and intense the conflict."

42. Baumeister (1991a), p. 156.

> Thus, alcohol intoxication produces a state of mind that conforms to the pattern we have seen for escape from the self: a narrow, immediate focus on events combined with a tendency to ignore broader meanings and implications.

43. O'Neill once wrote, "It was a great mistake, my being born a man, I would have been much more successful as a sea gull or fish . . . I will always be a stranger who never feels at home . . . who must always be a little in love with death!" Cited in Sheaffer, L. (1968). *O'Neill, son and playwright.* New York: Little, Brown, p. 165. O'Neill also has his disillusioned radical, Larry Slade, in *The iceman cometh,* voice similar sentiments, "I have no answer to give anyone, not even myself. Unless you can call what Heine wrote in his poem to morphine an answer . . .

> 'Lo sleep is good; better is death; in sooth,
> The best of all were never to be born.'" (p. 582)

O'Neill, E. (1988). *The complete plays—1932–1943.* New York: The Library of America. I see the "I'd rather drink" attitude as crucially linked to this type of death wish.

44. Yeats, W. B. (1974). Sailing to Byzantium. In *The collected poems of W. B. Yeats* (p. 191). New York: Macmillan.

45. Dwyer, M. (July 14, 1996). A grungy shocker on heroin comes ashore. *New York Times,* Section 2, p. 9. Another relevant movie that carries a similar theme of the rejection of conventional life by an alcoholic is *Leaving Las Vegas* (1995) in which Nicolas Cage

plays a screenwriter who goes to Las Vegas with the goal of drinking himself to death.

46. Baumeister (1991a), p. 34.

47. Baumeister (1991a), p. 35.

48. See Csikszentmihalyi, M. (1990). *Flow: The Psychology of Optimal Experience.* New York: Harper & Row, for a discussion of the pleasure of absorption in activities that allow one to set aside consciousness of the self.

49. Baumeister (1991a), p. 36.

50. Becker (1973), p. 84.

CHAPTER 3

1. Though this view is no longer taken seriously by contemporary researchers and clinicians, it used be believed that male homosexuality was *the* primary cause of alcoholism (see Abraham, K. (1908/1926). The psychological relationship between sexuality and alcoholism. *International Journal of Psychoanalysis,* 7, 1–10). For a scholarly and critical review of this line of thinking, see Israelstam, S. and Lambert, S. (1986). Homosexuality and alcohol: Observations and research after the psychoanalytic era. *The International Journal of Addictions, 21,* 509–537. My own clinical experience at SCADD has tended to confirm that gay men display a similar diversity in the etiology of their addictions to heterosexual men. Although I have certainly seen men for whom the acceptance of their sexuality is the central obstacle to their recovery, I have seen a greater number of gay men (particularly in their twenties and thirties) who see their sexual orientation as central to their identity and a source of strength. What is critical in the lives of these men, regardless of their own attitudes about their sexuality, is the attitude of our society toward homosexuality. Homophobia compounds their struggles to reach sobriety and often reinforces their addictive lifestyles. As Hellman wrote in a helpful and compassionate article, "The individual must begin a process of recovery not from homosexuality, but from the consequences of anti-homosexual prejudices." p. 113. See Hellman, R. E. (1992). Dual diagnosis issues with homosexual persons. *Journal of Chemical Dependency, 5,* 105–117.

2. Cory, D. W. (1951). *The Homosexual in America: A subjective approach.* New York: Greenberg.

3. Fifield, L.T., Decrescenzo, T. A., and Latham, J. D. (1975). Alcoholism and the gay community. Summary of "On my way to nowhere: Alienated, isolated, drunk; an analysis of gay alcohol abuse and an evaluation of alcoholism rehabilitation services for the Los Angeles County." Los Angeles, CA: Gay Community Services Center. See also Israelstam, S. and Lambert, S. (1984). Gay bars. *Journal of Drug Issues, 14,* 637–653.

4. Israelstam and Lambert (1984), p. 641.

5. Cabaj, R. P. (1989). AIDS and chemical dependency: Special issues and treatment barriers for gay and bisexual men. *Journal of Psychoactive Drugs, 21,* 387–393. p. 389. See also Israelstram and Lambert, (1984), p. 643.

6. Israelstam and Lambert, (1986), p. 515.

7. Fiddle, S. (1967). *Portraits from a shooting gallery.* New York: Harper & Row. See p. 36 for a discussion of the "nod."

CHAPTER 4

1. Caplow, T. Transcript of Homelessness Project staff meeting., Bureau of Applied Research, February, 25, 1965. Cited in Bahr, H. M. (1973), p. 163.

2. As Bahr (1973), pp. 154–160, points out these affiliations are functionally based and shift to a certain degree depending on the relative financial and physical health of the eligible members. The drinking circle I describe in this chapter is a more developed and

sustained version of what sociologists call skid row bottle gangs. A bottle gang is a group of street alcoholics who pool their money in order to purchase a collective supply of booze. Bahr describes the rules of membership, etiquette, and profit-sharing that define the relationships of the members.

3.   In *The Iceman Cometh* (1946/1988) by Eugene O'Neill, the salesman, Hickey, describes how drinking with his cronies at Harry Hope's saloon was destroying his relationship with his wife, yet how that same drinking offered him solace from the despair he felt over the destruction of this relationship,

> And she kept encouraging me and saying, "I can see you really mean it now, Teddy. I know you'll conquer it this time, and we'll be so happy, dear." When she'd say that and kiss me, I'd believe it too. Then she'd go to bed, and I'd stay up alone because I couldn't sleep and I didn't want to disturb her, tossing and rolling around. I'd get so damned lonely. I'd get to thinking how peaceful it was here, sitting around with the old gang, getting drunk and forgetting love, joking and laughing and singing, and swapping lies. And finally I knew I'd have to come. And I knew if I came this time, it was the finish." (p. 699)

4.   "Skipper's Deck" is a fictitious name, but the motel it represents, and others like it, still exist in New London.

5.   Danny's characterization of his first encounter with alcohol, and later on with marijuana and heroin, is similar to many of the men I interviewed. The use of a substance for the first time is associated with a transformation and release, an ecstatic stepping out of one's self, releasing the burden of insecurity and self-loathing (see Baumeister, 1991a, pp. 21–38).

6.   Squirrel was the nickname for another member of the circle who had also had numerous stays at Lebanon Pines. I had several sessions with him over the years. He died of a heart attack while in bed at a Hartford detox.

7.   A "skid bid" is a brief stay of one or two nights in a city or county jail.

8.   "L&M" is short for Lawrence & Memorial Hospital, the major hospital of New London County, only a few blocks away from Ocean Beach.

9.   De Leon, G. (1984). *The therapeutic community: Study of effectiveness. Social and psychological adjustment of 400 dropouts and 100 graduates from the Phoenix House therapeutic community.* United States Department of Health and Human Services Publication No. (ADM) 84–1286.

10.   See Bahr (1973).

CHAPTER 5

1.   See Wilson, W.J. (1987). *The truly disadvantaged: The inner city, the underclass and public policy.* Chicago: The University of Chicago Press, and Hacker, A. (1992). *Two Nations.* New York: Charles Scribner's Sons for comprehensive discussions of the increasing rather than decreasing problem of a black economic underclass. In choosing the title for his book about the disparities between blacks and whites in American society, Hacker was echoing Benjamin Disraeli's words about the rich and poor in Victorian England, "Two nations, between whom there is no intercourse and no sympathy; who are as ignorant of each other's habits, thoughts, and feelings, as if they were dwellers in different zones, or inhabitants of different planets" (Hacker, 1992, p. ix). This quotation could certainly apply to my experience of growing up in Woodbridge next to the projects of New Haven. Other valuable books that describe the social and cultural problems of racial segregation are Lukas, A. (1985). *Common ground.* New York: Alfred A. Knopf, and Kotlowitz, A. (1991). *There Are No Children Here.* New York: Doubleday.

2.   Kierkegaard (1849/1941), p. 115.

3.   See Richters, J. E., and Martinez, P. (1993). The NIMH community violence project: I. Children as victims and witnesses of violence. *Psychiatry, 56,* 7–21.

4.   Yalom (1980), p. 104.

5.   In existential terms, one's negative and destructive behavior is an argument against a God who has allowed one's life to suffer torment.

> It is (to describe it figuratively) as if an author were to make a slip of the pen, and that this clerical error conscious of being such . . . would revolt against the author, out of hatred for him were to forbid him to correct it, and were to say, "No, I will not be erased, I will stand as a witness against thee, that thou art a very poor writer. Kierkegaard (1849/1941), p. 119.

6.   See Finnegan, W. (Sept. 10, 1990, pp. 51–86 and Sept. 17, pp. 60–90). Out there. *The New Yorker* for a compelling portrait of a young black man caught up in the drug trade of New Haven. The names Thomas is mentioning are the names of street gangs that were associated with different color tops for the crack vials.

7.   McAdams (1993), p. 103.

8.   McAdams (1993), p. 107.

9.   See Lowinson, J. H., Ruiz, P., Millman, R. B., and Langrod, J. G. (Eds.) (1992). *Substance abuse: A comprehensive textbook.* Baltimore: Williams & Wilkins (p. 47).

10.   See Bandura, A. (1986). *Social foundations of thought and action: A social cognitive theory.* Englewood Cliffs, NJ: Prentice-Hall.

11.   Denzin, N.K. (1993). *The alcoholic society: Addiction and recovery of the self.* New Brunswick, NJ: Transaction. Denzin, drawing on the work of the ethical philosophers Scheler, describes the nature of this resentment, "Ressentiment [*sic,* drawing on spelling originally used by Nietzsche] is a backward-looking emotionality. It is a form of self-hatred that is located in the real and imagined actions that another has taken toward a person. It is a self-poisoning emotion that colors all of the interactions the subject has with others, particularly those in authority positions." (p. 350) Denzin also writes that Ressentiment is often created by structural inequities in the society and that the sense of powerlessness to change these structures attracts individuals experiencing these barriers to escape through alcohol. "When the economic, interactional, gender, moral, political, legal, and religious structures of a society produce large categories of persons who experience the emotions of Ressentiment, then such structures lay the foundation for higher rates of alcoholism among the members of these special populations who come to feel that Ressentiment is in fact their destiny." (p. 351)

12.   Denzin (1993) has talked about addiction creating a divided self. As the individuals sink deeper into their addictive behaviors, they feel their conduct separating more and more into contrasting emotional patterns. Sober behaviors are associated with diminishing feelings of pride or self-respect, while their dominant addictive behaviors are linked to negative emotions of shame, self-loathing, and resentment. Without intervention, the negative self associated with addiction most often wins out and the individual' only recourse is self-destruction. (p. 121)

13.   Beck, Thombs, & Summons (1993).

14.   Greenberg, G. (1994). *The self on the shelf.* Albany: State University of New York Press, p. 240.

15.   For a contrasting portrait of the difference a paternal role model can make, see the passage from *No day of triumph* by J. Saunders Redding excerpted in David, J. (Ed.), (1968). *Growing up black.* New York: William Morrow and Co. Redding, a sociologist and historian describes the impression his father left upon him, "He was up at dawn, painting

the trim, repairing the roof, putting out ashes, shoveling snow from the sidewalk. In fifteen years he was never late for his work, and only once did he allow an illness to keep him home. His endurance was a thing of spirit." (p. 227)

16. The theme of Wilson's (1987) book is that structural conditions in our society have led in great part to the creation of the black underclass. The relocation of jobs away from urban centers, the transformation of our industrial economy to a service and technology-oriented one, periodic recessions since the 1970s, the increasing polarization of high wage and low wage labor markets have all combined to create much higher black unemployment and inner city poverty. Though racism persists, these conditions are not primarily products of racism, and eradication of discrimination will not end them. Wilson argues that the society must take "universal" rather than "race-specific" measures to ameliorate these conditions. Federal initiatives to bring more jobs and economic prospects to areas that have lost their previous industrial base must be accompanied by more constructive social welfare policies that incorporate training and "workfare" opportunities, as well as greater access to affordable quality child care. In emphasizing economic structural arguments, Wilson also objects to conservative arguments that primarily blame the difficulties of the black underclass on their practice of socially deviant and irresponsible behaviors, which were putatively encouraged by liberal social policy (e.g., Murray, C. [1984]. *Losing ground: American social policy, 1950–1980.* New York: Basic Books).

17. Source: Percentage of minority student enrollment: 1995–96. Connecticut State Department of Education, published in *The Hartford Courant,* (July 10, 1996), p. A12.

18. Whitman, W. (1892/1958). *Leaves of grass.* New York: Signet (New American Library). This quotation comes from the poem entitled, "I Sing the Body Electric," p. 98.

19. Thomas Turner told me that his parents would warn him to stay away from the buildings and streets connected to Yale University; the reason they gave him was that the scientists would kidnap him and perform experiments on him. Though this may have been a story to scare a child from going into places where he might not be welcome, it conveys clearly the distrust and fear felt between the two communities.

20. Gospel According to St. Luke, Chapter 23, Verses 39–43. *The Holy bible.* New York: New York Bible Society (p. 91).

CHAPTER 6

1. Cushman, P. (1995). *Constructing the self, constructing America: A cultural history of psychotherapy.* Reading, MA: Addison-Wesley.

2. Cushman (1995), p. 22. See also Heidegger, M. (1962). *Being and time.* New York: Harper & Row, and Gadamer, H-G. (1975). *Truth and method.* New York: Continuum.

3. Cushman (1995), p. 23.

4. Cushman (1995), p. 23.

5. Cushman (1995). p. 60.

6. Cushman (1995), p. 118.

7. Cushman (1995), p. 65.

8. Cushman (1995), p. 85.

9. Cushman (1995), p. 86.

10. Greenberg (1994), pp. 211–212.

11. Becker (1973), pp. 6–7.

12. Cushman (1995), p. 64.

13. See Baumeister (1991a), p. 36 for a discussion of the often misguided connection between the use of alcohol and creativity. Also see Hyde, L. (1993). Alcohol and poetry: John Berryman and the booze talking. In R. J. Kelly and A. K. Lathrop (Eds.), *Recovering Berryman: Essays on a poet* (pp. 205–228). Ann Arbor: The University of Michigan Press.

14. Cushman (1995), p. 79.

15. Kohut, H. (1977). *The Restoration of the self.* New York: International Universities Press.

16. *Diagnostic and statistical manual of mental disorders (DSM) Fourth edition.* (1994). Washington, DC: American Psychiatric Association. The DSM-IV lists the major criteria for a Narcissistic Personality Disorder as the following: grandiose sense of self-importance; preoccupied with fantasies of unlimited success; believes that he or she is "special" and unique; requires excessive admiration; sense of entitlement to especially favorable treatment; interpersonally exploitative; lacks empathy; envious of others or believes others envy him or her; shows arrogant, haughty behaviors or attitudes (p. 661). Doug Richards easily meets the necessary limit of five or more to qualify for this diagnosis. From a different perspective, Doug's personality could also be linked to his drinking behavior as a function of his excessive need for power; see McClelland, D. C., Davis, W. N., Kalin, R., and Wanner, E. (1972). *The Drinking man.* New York: The Free Press. See also McClelland, D. C. (1975). *Power: The inner experience.* New York: Irvington Publishers. McClelland argues there are different developmental stages in power motivation; each stage roughly accords with Freudian psychosexual stages (oral, anal, phallic). The stage III power orientation, associated with the phallic stage, seems to correspond well with Doug Richards' personality. Here are characteristics McClelland found correlated with Stage III power orientation—freedom to love several women; lies to family and friends; collects valuable objects; reasons for drinking are problematic; dislikes child care (p. 64). All of these attributes are clearly present in Doug Richards' life.

17. See Warheit, G. J., Blafora, F. A., Zimmerman, R. S., Gil, A. G., Vega, W. A., and Apospori, E. (1995). Self-rejection/derogation, peer factors, and alcohol, drug, and cigarette use among a sample of Hispanic, African-American, and white non-Hispanic adolescents. *International Journal of Addictions, 30,* 97–116. This article demonstrates that over a longitudinal study of drug and alcohol use, peer acceptance and peer use were the most powerful predictors of subsequent substance use.

18. Miller, A. (1953). Death of a Salesman. In J. Gassner (Ed.), *Best American plays, 3rd Series, 1945–1951* (pp. 1–48). New York: Crown Publishers.

19. Cushman (1995), p. 350.

20. Cushman (1995), p. 342.

21. Cushman (1995), p. 342.

22. Cushman (1995), p. 340.

CHAPTER 7

1. Baumeister (1991a). *Escaping the self,* writes;

> Fan activities provide the sort of frequent moderate escape that relieves the stressful burden of vulnerability that accompanies the modern self, and the same may be said for other vicarious pleasures, such as watching movies or television. These activities restrict attention to a limited sphere, effectively removing the individual from the issues and concerns of his or her daily life. p. 207.

2. See Bellah, R. N., Madsen, R., Sullivan, W. M., Swidler, A., & Tipton, S. M. (1985). *Habits of the heart: Individualism and commitment in American life.* New York: Harper & Row; Cushman (1995), Baumeister (1991b.). Lasch, C. (1978). *The culture of narcissism: American life in an age of diminished expectations.* New York: W. W. Norton & Co.

3. Cushman (1995), also comments on this turn of events in military recruitment, p. 84.

4. Baumeister (1991b), p. 113.

5.   Baumeister (1991b), p. 110.

6.   Baumeister (1991b), p. 109.

7.   Martin, H., and Thrasher, D. (1989). Chemical dependency and the treatment of the professional athlete. In G. W. Lawson and A. W. Lawson (Eds.) *Alcoholism and substance abuse in special populations* (pp. 315–339). Rockville, MD: Aspen Publishers. See p. 333.

8.   Martin and Thrasher (1989), p. 330.

9.   It is not surprising that 85 percent of athletes surveyed in a study of elite athletes described the reduction of stress and anxiety as their primary reason for using drugs. See Anshel, M. H. (1991). A survey of elite athletes on the perceived causes of using banned drugs in sport. *Journal of Sport Behavior, 14,* 283–310. As Lawrence Taylor, the ex–New York Giants football star said in a *Sport* magazine article, "In my case, it wasn't hard to see that drugs were a way of escaping rather than dealing with my problem—the pressure of playing in a huge place like New York, having to please so many people." See Taylor, L., and Falkner, D. (1987). LT: Living on the Edge. *Sport, 78,* 68–77. Darryl Strawberry echoes this complaint, "Me and Doc were two young stars, black players, who came to New York, and the expectations were extremely high. . . . The pressure, it was so great." *Sports Illustrated,* (February 27th, 1995), *82,* 16–35. This information and a variety of other interesting perspectives on the relationship between addiction and sports can be found in an excellent literature review conducted as an independent study by Eric Stoddard, a former student of mine at Connecticut College. His paper, Stoddard, E. (1994). The causes of recreational drug use among professional athletes, is available through the Department of Psychology at Connecticut College.

10.   ". . . [I]t is not uncommon for the athlete to be rewarded and valued by others on the sole basis of his athletic ability. Unfortunately, the athlete may view this as the only thing he has to offer. If he fails, the rewards (social and monetary) may cease to exist, and if he succeeds, he is expected to do so always." Martins and Thrasher (1989), p. 331.

11.   Sports psychologists are increasingly studying how to help athletes redirect their lives productively after career-ending injuries. "You don't want [injured athletes] to suddenly jump into a new negative activity like drinking, smoking, or playing pool. . . . You want them to carefully examine their values and interests, and choose a replacement for sports that is appropriate and satisfying" [Albert Pettipas, Ed.D.], quoted in Murray, B. (July, 1996). Mending battered spirits along with broken bones. *The APA Monitor, 27,* 27.

12.   Baumeister (1991b). p. 110, "Thus, the modern emphasis is on being esteemed by others for who you are, not for what you have done."

13.   See Whitaker (1990), Myths and heroes: Visions of the future. *Journal of College Student Psychotherapy 4,* 13–33, p. 23, for a biting analysis of how sports heroes are linked through alcohol advertising to false messages about the success (with friends and lovers) alcohol consumption can bring.

14.   See *Midrash rabbah: Song of songs 1:4.*

CHAPTER 8

1.   Norman, M. (May 26, 1996). The hollow man. *The New Times Magazine,* p. 54.

2.   McAdams (1990), see Chapter 3 of this book.

3.   See Abueg, F. R., and Fairbank, J. A. (1992). Behavioral treatment of posttraumatic stress disorder and co-occurring substance abuse. In P. Saigh (Ed.), *Posttraumatic stress disorder: A behavioral approach to assessment and treatment* (pp. 111–146). Boston: Allyn & Bacon. Male Vietnam veterans with a current diagnosis of Posttraumatic Stress Disorder

were found to be twice as likely to meet criteria for current alcohol abuse or dependence as their counterparts without PTSD, p. 113,

4.   See Moffitt and Singer (1993).

5.   Denzin (1993), p. 98

6.   Dentin (1993), p. 101

7.   Denzin (1993), pp. 71–72.

8.   There is a vast literature at this point on the posttraumatic stress disorder symptoms suffered by Vietnam combat veterans. For two good overviews, see Laufer, R. S., Frey-Wouters, E., and Gallops, M. S. (1985). Traumatic stressors in the Vietnam war and post-traumatic stress disorder. In C. R. Figley, (Ed.), *Trauma and Its wake* (pp. 73–89). New York: Bruner/Mazel; also see Hendin, H., and Haas, A. P. (1984). *Wounds of war: The psychological aftermath of combat in Vietnam.* New York: Basic Books. For broader overviews of the diagnosis of posttraumatic stress disorder, see Herman J. L. (1992), *Trauma and recovery: The aftermath of violence-from domestic abuse to political terror.* New York Basic Books, and Saigh, P. A. (Ed.) (1992). *Post-traumatic stress disorder: A behavioral approach to assessment and treatment.* Boston: Allyn & Bacon. According to the DSM-IV, the diagnosis consists of exposure to an event or events that involved actual or threatened death or serious injury, or a threat to physical integrity of self or others; the person's response involved intense fear, helplessness, or horror. In response to this exposure, the individual shows persistent reexperiencing of any one or more of the following—memories, dreams, flashbacks, intense psychological distress at stimuli that recall the trauma, intense physiological reactions to stimuli that recall the trauma. In addition, the individual may show a persisting avoidance of stimuli associated with a trauma and a general numbing of emotion—this avoidance may include blocking memories or thoughts; the numbing may include a detachment from relationships and activities that formerly brought pleasure to the person. Finally, the person shows persisting symptoms of increased arousal including difficulty with sleep, irritability, difficulty concentrating, hypervigilance, and an exaggerated startle response. The combination of any subset of these symptoms also leads to significant impairment of social and occupational functioning (DSM-IV, pp. 428–429).

9.   See Corday, S. M., and Polk, K. R. (1992). Premilitary antecedents of post-traumatic stress disorder in an Oregon cohort. *Journal of Clinical Psychology, 48,* 271–280; also Bremner, J. D., Southwick, S. M., Johnson, D. R., Yehuda, R., and Charney, D. S. (1993). Childhood physical abuse and combat-related posttraumatic stress disorder in Vietnam veterans. *American Journal of Psychiatry, 15,* 235–239; also King, D. W., King, L. A., Foy, D. W., and Gudanowski, D. M. (1996). Prewar factors in combat-related posttraumatic stress disorder: Structural equation modeling with a national sample of female and male Vietnam veterans. *Journal of Consulting and Clinical Psychology, 64,* 520–531.

10. In fact as the Corday & Polk (1992) article demonstrated, Tyler's dropping out of school and lower-middle-class background made him more likely to enlist and be sent to Vietnam. On the other hand, these authors also point out that the fact that he showed promise and was successful in the beginning of his military career (e.g., being selected for the Seabees) made him more likely to be placed in high-risk and combat situations.

11. The black silk pajamas refer to the garb worn by the Viet Cong guerrillas.

12. See Herman (1992), p. 45, for a description of how traumatized veterans constrict their field of consciousness and block out memories.

13. "If we are not to be shaken in our belief in the wish-fulfilling tenor of dreams by the dreams of traumatic neurotics [Freud's term for men suffering from combat trauma], we still have one resource open to us: we may argue that the function of dreaming, like so much else, is upset in this condition and diverted from its purposes, or we may be driven

to reflect on the mysterious masochistic trends of the ego (pp. 13–14)." Freud, S. (1920/1962). Beyond the Pleasure Principle. In J. Strachey (Ed.), *The standard edition of the complete psychological works of Sigmund Freud,* vol. 18 (pp. 64). See also Herman's (1992) conception of the repetition compulsion, "[Most theorists] speculate that the repetitive reliving of traumatic experience must represent a spontaneous, unsuccessful attempt at healing. Janet spoke of the person's need to "assimilate" and "liquidate" traumatic experience, which, when accomplished, produces a feeling of "triumph." In his use of language, Janet implicitly recognized that helplessness constitutes the essential insult of trauma, and that restitution requires the restoration of a sense of efficacy and power" (p. 41). I presented a similar position on the repetition compulsion in *The Remembered Self,* p. 24 (Singer and Salovey, 1993).

14. Denzin, p. 362.

15. For a comprehensive review of the research literature on the relationship between alcohol abuse and trauma, see Stewart, S. H. (1996). Alcohol abuse in individuals exposed to trauma: A critical review. *Psychological Bulletin, 20,* 83–112. For a discussion of how to treat co-occurring PTSD and substance abuse, see Abueg, F. R., and Fairbank, J. A., (1992), pp. 111–146.

16. Baumeister (1991a) refers to this kind of escapist behavior in drink as a mental narrowing that breaks the linkage of the present from thoughts of the past and the future, "It is in the escapist phenomenon of shrinking the time span that the term *mental narrowing* is most obviously appropriate. Masochistic sexual activity, drunkenness, or preparations for suicide all focus the mind very strongly on the here and now, shrinking one's time span to the immediate present, shutting out past and future. Anything outside of one's immediate sensory environment seems far away. Past and future events recede from awareness." (p. 62)

17. See Keane, T. M., Fairbank, J. A., Caddell, J. M., Zimering, R. T., and Bender, M. E. (1985). A behavioral approach to assessing and treating post-traumatic stress disorder in Vietnam veterans. In Figley (1985), pp. 257–294.

18. Freud (1920/1962), p. 36.

19. Hemingway, E. (1942). Soldier's home. In *The short stories of Ernest Hemingway* (pp. 243–251). New York: Modern Library, pp. 250–251.

20. A similar relationship to time is displayed by holocaust survivors as captured in Langer, L. L. (1991). *Holocaust testimonies: The ruins of memory.* New Haven, CT: Yale University Press. Langer describes how survivors struggle to locate the horrors of their past into a continuous narrative of their lives. "Testimony is a form of remembering. The faculty of memory functions in the present to recall a personal history, vexed by traumas that thwart smooth-flowing chronicles. Simultaneously, however, straining against what we might call disruptive memory is an effort to reconstruct a semblance of continuity in a life that began as, and now resumes what we would consider, a normal existence. . . . [W]itnesses struggle with the impossible task of making their recollections of the camp experience coalesce with the rest of their lives. If one theme links their narratives more than any other, it is the unintended, unexpected, but invariably unavoidable failure of such efforts." (p. 3)

21. For an example of the fine cognitive-behavioral work that can be done with Vietnam war vets suffering from PTSD and substance abuse, see Abueg, F. R., and Fairbank, J. A. (1992). In particular, this treatment is sensitive to the so-called abstinence violation effect in which the men, after breaking a period of sobriety, see the first drink as a sign of complete failure. The treatment program works to shift attributions away from the depressive

triad of internal, stable, and global—"See, I am a drunk. I can't do anything right. I might as well go on drinking since there really is no hope" (p. 139)—to seeing slips as situationally and affectively determined. It helps the men build up alternative coping strategies to high-stress situations and uses the relapse as a "learning experience rather than a failure experience" (p. 139). In related research, it is demonstrated that combat survivors who show less PTSD symptoms and better postwar occupational achievement are men who use more problem-focused coping strategies as opposed to responding to stress with mental escapism or behavioral avoidance (e.g., substance abuse), see Wolfe, J., Keane, T. M., Kaloupek, D. G., Mora, C. A., and Wine, P. (1993). Patterns of positive readjustment in Vietnam combat veterans. *Journal of Traumatic Stress, 6,* 179–193.

CHAPTER 9

1. Baumeister (1986), p. 18–19.
2. McAdams, D. P. (1996). Personality, modernity, and the storied self: A contemporary framework for studying persons. *Psychological Inquiry, 7,* 295–321. The quotes that follow are found on pg. 315 of this article.
3. McAdams (1988), p. 3. See also Lifton, R. J. (1979). *The broken connection: On death and the continuity of life.* New York: Simon & Schuster.
4. Loftus, E. (1993). The reality of repressed memories. *American Psychologist, 48,* 518–537. See also Ofshe, R. and Watters, E. (1993). Making monsters. *Society, 30,* 4–16.
5. There is no doubt though that chemically dependent families are more prone to incidents of abuse and neglect. See Sheridan, M. (1995). A proposed intergenerational model of substance abuse, family functioning, and abuse/neglect. *Child Abuse and Neglect, 19,* 519–530, and also Barnard, C. P. (1989). Alcoholism and sex abuse in the family: Incest and marital rape. *Journal of Chemical Dependency, 3,* 131–144.
6. Deutsch, H. (1942). Some forms of emotional disturbance and their relationship to schizophrenia. *Psychoanalytic Quarterly, 11,* 301–321.
7. Around the time of these events, I happened to see a low budget horror film called *The Stepfather* in which a deranged man assumes fake identities and marries into existing families. He is seeking a perfect family and when his new family lets him down, he decompensates and violently disposes of them. In one scene of the film, he is sitting with a group of men who are reading naively about the murder of a previous family with whom he lived. One man says out loud, "How could any man do such a thing? Kill a whole family and grind them up like hamburger?" The stepfather looks up and says a little tensely, "Maybe they disappointed him."
8. See the last chapter of Singer and Salovey (1993) for a discussion of the honesty and credibility of narrative memories.
9. See the DSM-IV criteria for Antisocial Personality Disorder. They include failure to conform to social norms with respect to lawful behaviors; deceitfulness; impulsivity or failure to plan; irritability or aggressiveness (proneness to fights or assaults); reckless disregard for safety of self and others; consistent irresponsibility: lack of remorse for having hurt, mistreated, or stolen from another (pp. 649–650).
10. Buss, A. (1980). *Self-consciousness and social anxiety.* San Francisco: W. H. Freeman.
11. I have noticed that I am more and more prone to base physical descriptions of people on comparisons to film stars ("He has a little bit of an Al Pacino look about him" or "She has that slightly faded Southern-belle look of Jessica Lange").
12. The power motive was developed by Murray, H. A. (1938). *Explorations in personality.* New York: Oxford University Press, and examined extensively by McClelland, D. C.

(1985). *Human motivation.* Glenview, IL: Scott, Foresman, and Winter, D. G. (1973). *The power motive.* New York: The Free Press. The motivational theme of power can be scored by coding the content of stories generated to pictures used in the Thematic Apperception Test (T.A.T.). Stories that depict protagonists as seeking to attain greater strength, status, or influence will be scored positively for power. Winter's coding system may be found in Smith, C. P. (1992). *Motivation and Personality: Handbook of Thematic Content Analysis.* New York: Cambridge University Press.

13. The devastating psychological effects of abuse and torture are rendered compellingly in Judith Herman's book, *Trauma and recovery: The aftermath of violence—from domestic abuse to political terror* (1992). She writes about the survivor of abuse, "The formation of a malignant negative identity is generally disguised by the socially conforming "false self." (p. 110)

CHAPTER 10

1.   Cited in Bahr (1973) on the frontispiece.

2.   In an extraordinary chapter on the existential problem of isolation, Irvin Yalom cites passage after passage in which philosophers and writers attempt to depict the inevitable gulf that separates human beings from each other. For example, he draws upon the words of Thomas Wolfe's protagonist in *Look Homeward, Angel.*

> . . . He understood that men were forever strangers to one another, that no one ever comes really to know anyone, that imprisoned in the dark womb of our mother, we come to life without having seen her face, that we are given to her arms a stranger, and that, caught in that insoluble prison of being, we escape it never, no matter what arms may clasp us, what mouth may kiss us, what heart may warm us. Never, never, never, never, never, never. (Wolfe, T., cited in Yalom [1980], p. 356.)

Yalom emphasizes that the relationships we form cannot fully defeat this realization of our existential loneliness—it is "an isolation that persists despite the most gratifying engagement with other individuals and despite consummate self-knowledge and integration." (p. 355). Clearly though, as we make our efforts to carry on from day to day, our engagement in loving relationships makes this burden of isolation more tolerable. Yalom quotes Martin Buber, "A great relationship breaches the barriers of a lofty solitude, subdues its strict law, and throws a bridge from self-being to self-being across the abyss of dread of the universe" (Buber, M., *Between Man and Man,* cited in Yalom [1980], p. 363).

3.   A first step is to give them an opportunity to speak and tell their story to people who might otherwise pass them by. One of my strongest motives in writing this book was exactly this reason—to provide an outlet for men like Clark and Seymour to speak up and be noticed. I must also point out that there were a few men, very similar to Clark and Seymour, who declined to be interviewed. Their refusal is just another part of their commitment to invisibility. They do not want to be known in a wider way, to have their narrative shared with others. Their life histories in the nursing charts were brief; their answers in intakes and counseling sessions were monosyllabic. When their discharge date arrived, they gathered their belongings into a backpack or duffel bag and shook hands with averted eyes. They were gone without a trace and we seldom saw them again.

4.   Beck, K. H., Thombs, D. L., and Summons, T. G. (1993). The social context of drinking scales: Construct validation and relationship to indicants of abuse in adolescent populations. *Addictive Behaviors, 18,* 159–169. This article reports the linkage of drinking for social facilitation and stress control to greater likelihood of binge drinking and drunkenness.

5.   Dinwiddie, S. H. (1992). Patterns of alcoholism inheritance. *Journal of Substance Abuse, 4,* 155–163.

6.   Jellinek, E. M. (1960), p. 145.

7.   Camus, A., *L'Envers et l'endroit,* cited in Yalom (1980), p. 358.

8.   Ogden, T. H. (1979). On projective identification. *International Journal of Psycho-analysis. 60,* 357–373.

9.   Goffman, E. (1961). *Asylums.* New York: Doubleday. This work in sociology remains the classic text on the problem of institutionalization for individuals suffering from psychiatric illnesses.

10.   Nakamura, M., Overall, J. E., Hollister, L. E., and Radcliffe, E. (1983). Factors affecting outcome of depressive symptoms in alcoholics. *Alcoholism—Clinical and Experimental Research, 7,* 188–193. This article reports findings that individuals who have used alcohol for social facilitation are more prone to show residual symptoms of depression after a period of sobriety.

11.   The men's early substance abuse disrupted the critical stages of identity formation described by Erikson, E. H. (1964). *Childhood and society.* New York; W. W. Norton, and Marcia, J. E. (1980). Identity in adolescence. In J. Adelson (Ed.), *Handbook of adolescent psychology* (pp. 159–187). New York: Wiley.

12.   William B. Swann has performed extensive research on what he calls the need for self-verification, or confirmation of one's self-views or understandings. Swann has demonstrated that individuals may often prefer consistency in self-views over more positive potrayals of the self. See Swann, W. B. (1997). The trouble with change: Self-verification and allegiance to the self. *Psychological Science, 8,* 177–180. Swann's perspective is increasingly being considered in the treatment of the chronically addicted; see Linehan, M. M. (1997). Self-verification and drug abusers: Implications for treatment. *Psychological Science, 8,* 181–183.

13.   In a fairly typical narrative of an AA-based recovery, the journalist Caroline Knapp describes her newfound sobriety.

> Laughter is still new to me, or feels that way. Sometimes a pack of us women go out to dinner on Tuesday nights after a meeting, and we sit in a booth and howl. Sitting there, I sometimes realize how little laughing I did in those last few years of drinking, how the drink seems to drain my world of pleasure, slowly but surely, the way life drains out of a cut flower. If anybody had told me I'd laugh in sobriety as much as I do, I never would have believed it. But my life has acquired a quality of lightness, and a sense of possibilities I didn't know I'd lost. The days seem simple and clean, so much simpler and cleaner than they did before. (Knapp [1996], p. 247.)

14.   See Orwin, R. G.. Goldman, H. H., Sonnefeld, L. J., Smith, N. G., Ridgely, S. M., et al. (November, 1992). *Community demonstration projects for alcohol and drug abuse treatment of homeless individuals—final evaluation report.* Rockville, MD: National Institute on Alcohol Abuse and Alcoholism, NIH Publication No. 93-3541.

15.   See Orwin et al. (November, 1992), p. IV-25, for a discussion of the range of uses of the term *case management.*

16.   The intensive case management model can be traced to the work of Stein, L., and Test, M. A. (1980). Alternative to mental hospital treatment I: Conceptual model, treatment program, and clinical evaluation. *Archives of General Psychiatry, 37,* 392–397. They first applied this model of lower client ratios, more frequent client contact, and aggressive brokering of services to the deinstitutionalized mentally ill. In the community

demonstration projects, intensive case management for the chronically addicted typically followed the guidelines laid down in the Minneapolis demonstration project, which contrasted an intensive approach with an intermediate approach.

> The primary difference between the two case management groups was the caseload size, with the intensive group having a case manager to client caseload of 1:15–20, whereas the intermediate group ratio was 1:40–50. Their implementation designs were also different. The intensive case managers were to focus more on outreach and field work, maintaining closer and more frequent contact with clients and in a variety of settings. This would give the case managers more opportunities to monitor and assist clients on an ongoing basis and to develop a trusting and empathic relationship with clients." Orwin et al. (November, 1992), p. V-32.

17. Kirby, M. W., and Braucht, G. N. (1993). Intensive case management for homeless people with alcohol and other drug problems: Denver. In K. J. Conrad, C. I. Hultman, and J. S. Lyons, (Eds.), (1993). *Treatment of the chemically dependent homeless: Theory and implementation in fourteen American projects* (pp. 187–200). New York: The Haworth Press. See pp. 188–189.
18. Kirby and Braucht (1993), p. 189.
19. Braucht, G. N., Reichardt, C. S., Geissler, L. J., Bormann, C. A., Kwiatkowski, C. F., and Kirby, M. W. (1995). Effective services for homeless substance abusers. *Journal of Addictive Diseases, 14,* 87–109.
20. Conrad, K. J., Hultman, C. I., and Lyons, J. S. (1993). Treatment of the chemically dependent homeless: A synthesis. In Conrad, Hultman, & Lyons, (1993) (pp. 235–246).
21. For example, see Peter, J. (March 1st, 1997). Rowland's Rx for drug use: Get a job. *The Day, 116,* p. 1, p. 2. This article details the efforts of the governor of Connecticut, John Rowland, to move 7,000 substance abusers off of general assistance for a savings to the state of $20 million.

CHAPTER 11

1. Todorov, T. (1995). *The morals of history.* Minneapolis: University of Minnesota Press. (Trans. by A. Waters). p. 15.
2. Bahr (1973).
3. Bahr (1973), p. 286.
4. In the twenty-six self-defining memories that were codeable for agency and communion, only six showed any evidence of the successful attainment of either agency or communion.
5. Baumeister (1991a), p. 148.
6. Baumeister (1991a).
7. Fiddle (1967), p. 50.
8. Baumeister (1991a), p.148.
9. Carroll J. (1987). The basketball diaries. New York: Penguin Books, p. 191.
10. Fiddle (1967), p. 323.
11. See Scheibe, K. E. (1995). On a certain emotional blindness in human beings. *Journal of Narrative and Life History, 5,* 239–245.
12. Scheibe (1995), p. 241.
13. Scheibe (1995), p. 242.
14. Denzin (1993), p. 344.
15. Herman (1992), p. 235.

16. See Lowry, M. (1947/1971). *Under the Volcano*. New York: Penguin. p. 289

17. See Dostoevsky, F. (1864/1972). *Notes from the Underground*. In I. Howe (Ed.), *Classics of Modern Fiction 2nd ed.* (pp. 13–110). New York: Harcourt Brace Jovanovich, p. 37.

18. See Berryman, J. (1965). *77 Dream Songs*. New York: Farrar, Straus, & Giroux, from "Dream Song 74," p. 81. Berryman left an unfinished novel about his own mixed success with recovering from alcoholism, Berryman, J. (1973). *Recovery*. New York: Farrar, Straus, & Giroux. There is also a collection of essays about the relationship of Berryman's alcoholism to his writing, Kelly, R. J., and Lathrop, A. K. (1993). *Recovering Berryman: Essays on a poet*. Ann Arbor, MI: The University of Michigan Press.

19. See Scherf, K. (Ed.) (1995). *The collected poetry of Malcolm Lowry*. Vancouver: University of British Columbia Press. These lines come from the poem, "As the poor end . . ." Ted Hughes, another poet, also captured this same sentiment in a poem about a lamb that seemed to be dying from the moment of birth. The lamb was well-formed outwardly, but suffered an inner deformity of will. It found death more alluring: life was unable to attract its attention. Lines from this poem, "Sheep," are quoted in Malcolm, J. (1995). *The silent woman: Sylvia Plath & Ted Hughes*, pp. 56–57. New York: Alfred A. Knopf. The entire poem can be found in Hughes, T. (1982). *New selected poems*. New York: Harper & Row, pp. 194–196. Malcolm herself makes the point that death has a great hold all over us,

> It is only by a great effort that we rouse ourselves to act, to fight, to struggle, to be heard above the wind, to crush flowers as we walk. To behave like *live people*. (p. 57)

I originally came across the Hughes and the Malcolm quote in an excellent review of her book by Dinnage, R. (April 6th, 1995). Kicking the myth habit. *New York Review of Books*, p. 6–8

20. McAdams (1993), p. 165.

21. McAdams (1993), p. 174.

22. Greenberg (1993), p. 228.

23. Greenberg (1994), p. 244.

24. For a powerful example of the ability to take in the natural world and to feel its union with our bodies, one can read the poem, "The Bath" by the fine American poet, Gary Snyder. (See Snyder, G. (1974). *Turtle island*. New York: New Directions, pp. 12–14.

25. Baumeister (1991b), pp. 104–105.

26. "The primary good that we distribute to one another is membership in some human community. And what we do with regard to that membership structures all our other distributive choices: it determines with whom we make those choices, from whom we require obedience and collect taxes, to whom we allocate goods and services." Walzer, M. (1983). *Spheres of justice: A defense of pluralism and equality*. New York: Basic Books, p. 31.

27. See McAdams, D. P., and de St. Aubin, E. (1992). A theory of generativity and its assessment through self-report, behavioral acts, and narrative themes in autobiography. *Journal of Personality and Social Psychology, 62*, 1003–1015.

28. Jackson and Singer (1997). Generativity in recovering alcoholics. Unpublished manuscript, Department of Psychology, Connecticut College, New London, CT.

29. Frankl, V. E. (1984). *Man's search for meaning*. New York. Washington Square Press, p. 161.

30. Gorush (1993) writes, "Regardless of the pathway that a person has followed into alcohol abuse, there is one element necessary for a person to change the habits and patterns that involve alcohol abuse and to explore better ways of meeting their needs: hope." p. 311.

31. Daley, D. C., and Marlatt, G. A. (1992). Relapse prevention: Cognitive and behavioral interventions. In J. H. Lowinson, P. Ruiz, R. S. Millman, J.G. & Langrod, (Eds.), *Substance abuse: A comprehensive textbook, 2nd ed.* (pp. 533–542). Baltimore: Williams & Wilkins, p. 539.

32. Jackson and Singer (1997).

Index